FROM MOSES TO QUMRAN

Studies in the Old Testament

FROM MOSES TO QUMRAN

Studies in the Old Testament

by

HAROLD H. ROWLEY

Essay Index Reprint Series

BOOKS FOR LIBRARIES PRESS
FREEPORT, NEW YORK

INTERNATIONAL STANDARD BOOK NUMBER:
0-8369-2130-5

LIBRARY OF CONGRESS CATALOG CARD NUMBER:
74-128307

PRINTED IN THE UNITED STATES OF AMERICA

CONTENTS

This volume is inscribed to

OTTO EISSFELDT

whose learning has been an inspiration
matched only by the friendship
which he has given me over many years

PREFACE

FOR SOME YEARS I have been requested by many friends to publish a volume of collected essays, and have only delayed to respond to the request because I lacked the time to prepare them for re-issue. Even now it has been impossible to give them the sort of revision I should have liked. The text is only slightly modified here and there, but I have made a number of additions to the footnotes, taking some account of publications which have been issued since these studies first appeared. It has been impossible to do this as thoroughly as I could have wished, and I express in advance my regret for any important omission. To make reference to everything that has appeared with any bearing on the many subjects here touched on would have given to these essays an encyclopaedic character that I cannot hope to achieve.

Most of the essays will introduce the reader to the very varied views which have been expressed, especially by contemporary scholars, on all the subjects I have dealt with. Many of the authors of these views are my friends, with whom I am reluctant to differ. Yet as it would be impossible to agree with them all, even with a mental equipment comparable to the physical endowment of a chameleon, I could find nothing better than to offer my own contribution to the discussions through a critical examination of the issues.

I would express my gratitude to those who have given me permission to re-issue these essays: to the authorities of Overdale College for 1; to the Editors of the *Zeitschrift für die alttestamentliche Wissenschaft* and of the *Expository Times* for 2; to the Director of the John Rylands Library, Professor Edward Robertson, for 3, 5, and 8; to the Delegates of the Clarendon Press and the Editors of the *Journal of Semitic Studies* for 4; to Messrs T. & T. Clark for 6; and to the Editor of the *Hebrew Union College Annual* for 7.

H. H. ROWLEY

ABBREVIATIONS

'Ab. Zar.   'Abodah Zarah
A.f.O.   Archiv für Orientforschung
A.J.S.L.   American Journal of Semitic Languages
A.J.Th.   American Journal of Theology
A.N.E.T.   Ancient Near Eastern Texts relating to the Old Testament, ed. by J. B. Pritchard
A.R.I.   Archaeology and the Religion of Israel, by W. F. Albright
A.R.W.   Archiv für Religionswissenschaft
A.Th.R.   Anglican Theological Review
B.A.   The Biblical Archaeologist
B.A.S.O.R.   Bulletin of the American Schools of Oriental Research
Bi.Or.   Bibliotheca Orientalis
B.J.   Josephus's *Bellum Judaicum*
B.J.R.L.   Bulletin of the John Rylands Library
B.O.T.   De Boeken van het Oude Testament
B.W.   The Biblical World
B.Z.A.W.   Beihefte zur *Zeitschrift für die alttestamentliche Wissenschaft*
B.Z.N.W.   Beihefte zur *Zeitschrift für die neutestamentliche Wissenschaft*
C.A.H.   Cambridge Ancient History
Camb. B.   Cambridge Bible
C.B.Q.   Catholic Biblical Quarterly
Cent.B.   Century Bible
C.Q.R.   Church Quarterly Review
C.R.A.I.   Comptes rendus de l'Académie des Inscriptions et Belles Lettres
D.B.   Dictionary of the Bible, ed. by J. Hastings
D.C.A.   Dictionary of Christian Antiquities, ed. by W. Smith and S. Cheetham
D.C.G.   Dictionary of Christ and the Gospels, ed. by J. Hastings
D.L.Z.   Deutsche Literaturzeitung
D.T.T.   Dansk Teologisk Tidsskrift
E.B.   Études Bibliques
E.Bib.   Encyclopaedia Biblica, ed. by T. K. Cheyne and J. S. Black

'Eduy.   'Eduyoth
E.H.A.T.   Exegetisches Handbuch zum Alten Testament
E.R.E.   *Encyclopaedia of Religion and Ethics,* ed. by J. Hastings
'Erub.   'Erubin
E.T.   *Expository Times*
E.Th.L.   *Ephemerides Theologicae Lovanienses*
F.S.A.C.   *From the Stone Age to Christianity,* by W. F. Albright
F.u.F.   *Forschungen und Fortschritte*
Gen.Rab.   Midrash Genesis Rabba
G.J.V.   *Geschichte des jüdischen Volkes,* by E. Schürer
G.V.I.   *Geschichte des Volkes Israel*
H.A.T.   Handbuch zum Alten Testament
H.J.P.   *History of the Jewish People,* by E. Schürer, Eng. trans. by S. Taylor and P. Christie
H.K.   Handkommentar zum Alten Testament
H.S.A.T.   *Die Heilige Schrift des Alten Testaments,* ed. by E. Kautzsch; 4th edn., ed. by A. Bertholet
H.S.A.Tes   Die Heilige Schrift des Alten Testamentes (Bonner Bibel)
H.T.R.   *Harvard Theological Review*
H.U.C.A.   *Hebrew Union College Annual*
I.B.   *Interpreter's Bible*
I.C.C.   International Critical Commentary
I.L.N.   *Illustrated London News*
J.A.O.S.   *Journal of the American Oriental Society*
J.B.L.   *Journal of Biblical Literature*
J.B.R.   *Journal of Bible and Religion*
J.C.S.   *Journal of Cuneiform Studies*
J.E.   *Jewish Encyclopedia*
J.E.O.L.   *Jaarbericht Ex oriente lux*
Jer. Pes.   Jerusalem Talmud, Pesaḥim
Jer. Yeb.   Jerusalem Talmud, Yebamoth
J.J.S.   *Journal of Jewish Studies*
J.N.E.S.   *Journal of Near Eastern Studies*
J.P.O.S.   *Journal of the Palestine Oriental Society*
J.Q.R.   *Jewish Quarterly Review*
J.R.   *Journal of Religion*
J.R.A.S.   *Journal of the Royal Asiatic Society*
J.S.O.R.   *Journal of the Society for Oriental Research*
J.S.S.   *Journal of Semitic Studies*
J.T.S.   *Journal of Theological Studies*
K.A.R.   *Keilschrifttexte aus Assur religiösen Inhalts,* by E. Ebeling
K.A.T.   Kommentar zum Alten Testament

K.A.T.   *Die Keilschriften und das Alte Testament,* by E. Schrader; 3rd edn., ed. by H. Zimmern and H. Winckler

Ker.   Kerithoth

Ket.   Ketuboth

K.H.C.   Kurzer Hand-Commentar zum Alten Testament

Ḳid.   Ḳiddushin

L.O.T.   *Introduction to the Literature of the Old Testament,* by S. R. Driver

M.G.W.J.   *Monatsschrift für Geschichte und Wissenschaft des Judenthums*

Meg.   Megillah

Miḳ.   Miḳwaoth

M.V.A.G.   *Mitteilungen der vorderasiatische Gesellschaft*

N.K.Z.   *Neue kirchliche Zeitschrift*

N.R.Th.   *Nouvelle Revue théologique*

N.T.   *Novum Testamentum*

N.T.S.   *New Testament Studies*

Num.Rab.   Midrash Numbers Rabba

O.E.D.   *Oxford English Dictionary*

O.L.Z.   *Orientalistische Literaturzeitung*

O.T.M.S.   *The Old Testament and Modern Study,* ed. by H. H. Rowley

O.T.S.   *Oudtestamentische Studiën*

P.E.F.Q.S.   *Palestine Exploration Fund Quarterly Statement*

P.E.Q.   *Palestine Exploration Quarterly*

Pes.   Pesaḥim

P.G.   *Patrologia Graeca,* ed. by J. P. Migne

P.L.   *Patrologia Latina,* ed. by J. P. Migne

P.R.E.   *Real-encyclopädie für protestantische Theologie und Kirche* ed. by J. J. Herzog; 3rd edn., ed. by A. Hauck

R.B.   *Revue biblique*

R.E.J.   *Revue des Études juives*

R.E.S.   *Revue des Études sémitiques*

R.G.G.   *Die Religion in Geschichte und Gegenwart*

R.H.P.R.   *Revue d'Histoire et de Philosophie religieuses*

R.H.R.   *Revue de l'Histoire des Religions*

R.Q.   *Revue de Qumran*

S.A.T.   *Die Schriften des Alten Testaments in Auswahl*

S.B.U.   *Svenskt Bibliskt Uppslagsverk*

S.D.B.   *Supplément au Dictionnaire de la Bible,* ed. by L. Pirot, A. Robert, H. Cazelles, and A. Feuillet

S.E.Å.   *Svensk exegetisk Årsbok*

S.J.Th.   *Scottish Journal of Theology*

I

The Authority of The Bible

I

THE AUTHORITY OF THE BIBLE[1]

ONE of the dominant demands of the present age is for the re-establishment of authority in religion, and in Protestant circles this leads to the re-examination of the authority of the Bible. At the time of the Reformation Protestants based themselves on the supreme authority of the Scriptures, and there is a widespread feeling that unless they can somehow cling to that they are without a foundation. Yet the modern study of the Bible has greatly transformed the appeal to the Scriptures. No longer are they thought of as completely inerrant and wholly supernatural.[2] Textual criticism has demonstrated that we do not possess the *ipsissima verba* of the original books of the Bible, and that often we cannot with confidence restore them. Moreover, historical and literary criticism has emphasized the human processes out of which the Bible came, and has made it impossible to appeal in quite the old way to proof texts culled indiscriminately from its pages.

Roman Catholic writers feel themselves to be on stronger grounds. An American Catholic writer has observed: "The *early Protestants* acknowledged the inspiration of the Bible, but did not properly understand its nature. The Bible was taken to be the sole rule of faith, and inspiration and revelation were held to be one and the same thing. As the Bible, in their opinion, was dictated by the Holy Spirit, its human element became gradually neglected, and finally totally denied . . . At the present day very few Protestant theologians acknowledge the true inspiration of the Bible. Those who do not follow the principles of rationalism emphasize the divine revelation in the Bible, that is, the divine message to man".[3] Against this the same writer offers

[1] First published as the Joseph Smith Memorial Lecture by Overdale College, Selly Oak, Birmingham, 1949.

[2] Cf. P. Benoit, in *Initiation Biblique*, ed. by A. Robert and A. Tricot, 3rd edn., 1954, p. 12.

[3] J. E. Steinmueller, *A Companion to Scripture Studies*, i, 2nd edn., 1943, pp. 11 f.

what he calls "proofs" of the inspiration of the Bible. Of these he presents two, the first being based on Scripture itself and the second on the Tradition of the Church.[1] Neither can be said to be a "proof". He cites, as so many Protestant writers have cited, 2 Tim. 3: 16, "All Scripture is given by inspiration",[2] and 2 Pet. 1: 20 f., "No prophecy of Scripture is of private interpretation". At the most these could only be regarded as claims to inspiration, and not proofs of the validity of the claim, and it is a mere misuse of language to call them proofs. Similarly, when the "proof" from Tradition is set out, it turns out to be merely the statement that throughout her entire history the Church has taught the inspiration of the Scriptures.[3]

It is not seldom said that while the Reformers accepted the final authority of the Bible, Roman Catholics acknowledged the final authority of the Church. Yet Catholics have always acknowledged the authority of the Bible, and have recognized the Bible to be the final authority for doctrine. Nevertheless, for them the authority of the Bible has always rested on the authority of the Church,[4] and the Bible has been allowed to be

[1] *Ibid.* pp. 6 ff. Cf. J. E. Steinmueller and K. Sullivan, *A Companion to the Old Testament*, 1946, pp. 4 f.

[2] R.V. renders "Every Scripture inspired of God is also profitable", and so the Catholic commentators C. Spicq (*Les Épîtres Pastorales* [E.B.], 1947, p. 377) and G. Bardy (*La Sainte Bible,* ed. by L. Pirot and A. Clamer, xii, 1946, p. 244). The latter observes that the verse deals with the usefulness of Scripture rather than with its inspiration. Nevertheless, as both observe, the doctrine of the inspiration of Scripture was so generally accepted by the Jews as to stand in no need of affirmation. R.S.V. returns to the rendering of A.V. ("All scripture is inspired by God"), and relegates the R.V. rendering to the margin, while N.E.B. has "Every inspired scripture has its use for teaching the truth."

[3] Cf. Steinmueller, *A Companion to Scripture Studies,* i, p. 8. Cf. also B. C. Butler, *The Church and the Bible,* 1960, p. 36: "The question between traditional Protestantism and Catholicism is whether this foundation is 'the Bible and the Bible only', or whether it is the Church, out of whose life, so history tells us, the Bible sprang, and from whose judgment it derives its authority for us." Since the Old Testament is part of the Bible of all branches of the Church, this remarkable statement claims that the Old Testament sprang out of the life of the Church!

[4] Cf. C. Lattey, *Inspiration,* 1946, p. 7: "The Church alone, however, can determine, not merely what is inspiration in itself, but what is actually inspired". Cf. *ibid.* p. 9: "It is only through revelation preserved in the traditional teaching of the Church, that we know what is inspired"; also

4

authoritative for doctrine only as it is interpreted by the Church.[1] But this means that it is the authority of the Church which is primary and final.[2] If the Bible is only to be accepted on the authority of the Church and interpreted by the Church,

Lattey, *The Interpretation of Scripture*, 1944, p. 6: "Only the infallible Church can tell us (1) what books are inspired Scripture, or (2) in what the inspiration of Scripture precisely consists." Cf., however, L. Pirot (in *Initiation Biblique*, ed. by A. Robert and A. Tricot, 2nd edn., 1948, p. 19): "Il n'est pas non plus nécessaire, pour qu'un livre soit inspiré, qu'il soit officiellement reconnu comme tel. L'inspiration vient de Dieu; la canonicité, c'est à dire l'inscription au catalogue des Saintes Écritures, résulte d'une décision de l'Église." The last sentence would seem to imply that a decision of the Church was not from God. It is improbable that the author really intended this, however.

[1] Cf. T. E. Bird, *A Study of the Gospels*, 1945, p. 2: "It goes beyond saying that they (i.e. the Sacred Scriptures) are to be understood only in the sense in which the Church interprets them"; and Steinmueller, *op. cit.* 1, p. 241: "The authentic interpretation is that which is given by the infallible authority of the Church." Steinmueller cites the decree of the Council of Trent: "No one . . . shall presume to interpret Sacred Scripture contrary to the sense which Holy Mother the Church held and holds, to whom it belongs to judge the true sense and interpretation of Holy Scripture." Cf. too the Encyclical *Providentissimus Deus* (cited *ibid.* p. 406), where it is laid down that men should "understand that God has delivered the Holy Scriptures to the Church, and that in reading and making use of His word they must follow the Church as their guide and their teacher." Cf. also B. C. Butler, *op. cit.* p. 75: "The criterion of truth in Christianity . . . is found in the supreme teaching authority of the Church, whose function is to discriminate between genuine and corrupt tradition."
Actually the number of texts on which the Roman Church claims to have given infallible interpretations is very small. Cf. R. C. Fuller, in *A Catholic Commentary on Holy Scripture*, 1953, p. 59, where it is stated that the total of such texts is under twenty, though many others are indirectly determined. In addition, the number of texts determined by the consent of the Fathers is even smaller (p. 60). Further, the replies of the Biblical Commission give authoritative direction on a number of Biblical questions, but as is emphasized by E. F. Sutcliffe, who gives a list of them (*ibid.* pp. 67 ff.), these are juridical documents, and are intended to be interpreted as such. On a great many passages of Scripture there is no authoritative interpretation, and scholars are aware that very diverse views are often expressed by Catholic writers.
[2] Cf. J. Calvin, *Institutes of the Christian Religion*, Eng. trans. by H. Beveridge, 1, 1869, pp. 68 f.: "A most pernicious error has very generally prevailed—viz. that Scripture is of importance only in so far as conceded to it by the suffrage of the Church; as if the eternal and inviolable truth of

5

then its authority is secondary, and is dogmatically grounded.[1] Views which profess to offer "proofs" do not need to fall back on such authority for their defence, for proof is submitted to the reason. It is my hope to offer in this lecture evidence which is valid at the bar of reason.

Lest I be misunderstood, let me say before I proceed further that I do not propose to fall into the error of supposing that man is only reason. He is guided by instinct and emotion as well as by reason, and many of the beliefs by which he lives are by no means wholly based on reason. Yet within its own sphere reason is supreme, and where there is an appeal to reason, the judgment of reason must be free and final. To say "I accept the tradition of the Church and ask for no proof of its teachings" is open to all who eschew the use of reason in this sphere, and who are willing to hand their souls into the care of others; but to offer to reason a "proof" which turns out to be but the bludgeon of authority is contempt of court. There is almost

God could depend on the will of men. With great insult to the Holy Spirit, it is asked, Who can assure us that the Scriptures proceeded from God; who guarantee that they have come down safe and unimpaired to our times; who persuade us that *this* book is to be received with reverence, and *that one* expunged from the list, did not the Church regulate all these things with certainty? On the determination of the Church, therefore, it is said, depend both the reverence which is due to Scripture, and the books which are to be admitted into the canon. Thus profane men, seeking, under the pretext of the Church, to introduce unbridled tyranny, care not in what absurdities they entangle themselves and others, provided they extort from the simple this one acknowledgment—viz. that there is nothing which the Church cannot do."

That this is not quite fair to the Catholic position is clear, even if not surprising in the age when it was written. For no Catholic claims that it is as a collection of men that the Church speaks with authority, but as the mouthpiece of the Spirit of God. No human interpretation, whether of Church or individual, can claim authority, save in so far as it is the expression of the Spirit of God. Where I would agree with Calvin is in resisting the claim that the voice of the Church is invariably the voice of God. With equal emphasis I would observe that no individual interpreter can be any more supposed to offer a guaranteed interpretation, to which any authority attaches in virtue of its being given by him.

[1] Cf. Steinmueller and Sullivan, *op. cit.* p. 4: "It is a dogma of the Church that the Scriptures are inspired." On the Roman view cf. J. K. S. Reid, *The Authority of Scripture*, 1957, pp. 103 ff.

certainly a non-rational (by which I do not mean irrational) factor in any man's belief in the authority of the Bible, but if it is wholly non-rational it cannot approve itself to reason. What is first of all in question is whether a belief in the authority of the Bible can approve itself to reason, when reason is free and unfettered.

We must first distinguish more clearly some of the terms that have been confused, according to the Romanist writer I have already quoted, and that have been implicitly confused in what has been already said. The authority of the Bible is no more to be equated with its inspiration than inspiration is to be equated with revelation. Yet all are related to one another, since all go back to God. No one supposes that the Bible has an authority of its own independent of God, but only that in so far as it has authority it is because it is the Word of God.[1] Its authority rests therefore on its inspiration.[2] If its writers derived their word wholly from themselves, while God was at most an interested spectator, it is idle to talk of inspiration or of the Word of God; but if God was active in their activity, and speaking to men through their word, it mediates the Word of God. It has then an authority derived not from its authors or its interpreters, and certainly not from the Church—since it belonged to it before there was a Church, and even before it belonged to the Canon of Scripture[3]—but from God.[4] As to revelation, it is hard to see how anyone could confuse it with

[1] Cf. H. Cunliffe-Jones, *The Authority of the Biblical Revelation,* 1945, p. 24: "The Bible itself is not the primary authority. It is authoritative because of that to which it witnesses, not by the mere fact of being itself . . . The Bible derives its authority from the Gospel."

[2] Cf. my *Relevance of the Bible,* 1942, pp. 21 ff.

[3] Cf. H. Wheeler Robinson, *Record and Revelation,* 1938, p. 306: "The authority of the Old Testament Canon has rested from the very beginning on value-judgements made by the Synagogue and accepted by the Church. No Tridentine decree can eliminate that historic fact and its theological significance." Cf. also A. M. Ramsey, in *Peake's Commentary on the Bible,* ed. by M. Black and H. H. Rowley, 1962, p. 5a: "Though the Church made the Canon of the New Testament, it was not thereby conferring authority on the Books. Rather it was acknowledging the Books to possess authority in virtue of what they were, and it was an authority supreme and divine."

[4] Cf. Ramsey, *ibid.* p. 7a: "The authority of the Bible is the authority of God who speaks through it to mankind."

7

inspiration, as our Catholic writer alleges that Protestants have confused it. For revelation is God's unfolding of His own nature and will, and it has many channels outside the Bible. The media of divine revelation are numerous and varied—Nature, history, experience, personality, and combinations of these[1]—and in so far as we find a revelation of Him in the pages of the Bible it is because through the inspired personality of the writers He delivered His word to men. Yet surely all Protestants would say that the supreme revelation of God was in the Person of Christ, and while the *story* of that revelation is given in the Bible, the revelation itself lay outside the Bible, and to confuse God's revelation of Himself in Christ with His inspiration of the writers of the Gospels is out of the question. Revelation is therefore much wider than inspiration. Nevertheless, in so far as the Bible is concerned, its inspiration is to be recognized only in so far as it embodies the revelation of God's character and will, and its authority rests on its divine origin, as evidenced by its inspiration. While, therefore, revelation, inspiration, and authority are distinguishable from one another, we can only discuss the authority of the Bible in relation to these other questions.

The problem is not seldom avoided by the simple assertion that the Bible is its own authority.[2] Men today can hear the living accents of God's voice speaking in it. While this is true, it is far from sufficient as an answer to our problem. For it is only its own authority to those who recognize that authority. There are many who do not hear the accents of God's voice speaking in it, and while we may say that He speaks to those who have ears to hear, and those who do not hear fail to do so because they are deaf, they may retort that there is such a thing as hallucination in the world of the spirit as well as in the physical world. Unless we can find some objective tests, we cannot pretend to establish the authority of the Bible.

The delusion of a mere subjectivism is sometimes covered by the appeal to the inner witness of the Spirit of God within a man. Millar Burrows says: "What is ultimately authoritative

---

[1] Cf. my *Faith of Israel*, 1956, pp. 23 ff.

[2] Cf. Luther: "Scripture is its own light" (cited with approval by E. E. Flack in H. C. Alleman and E. E. Flack, *Old Testament Commentary*, 1948, p. 9).

for us is that which commands the assent of our own best judgment, accepted as the witness of the Spirit within us. The only ultimate basis of assurance is the witness of the Spirit with the believer's own spirit."[1] That this is unsatisfying seems to me self-evident. For it puts the final authority for every man within himself, and gives equal validity to the varying judgments of men. Either God did inspire the authors of the Bible or He did not. That is something quite independent of my belief or of my neighbour's about it. If I believe He did and my neighbour does not, we cannot both be right, and if there is no external test that we can apply we are left to the stalemate of subjectivism. The question whether the authority of God is behind the Bible is quite independent of my recognition of that authority. It is perfectly true that belief cannot be compelled. It is also true that just as belief may sometimes be the result of an easy credulity, so may unbelief sometimes be the result of stubbornness of will. There is not seldom an interplay between will and belief that calls for examination. *Loyalty* cannot be compelled; yet lack of loyalty may be a revolt against authority and duty. And if *belief* cannot be compelled, unbelief may equally be a revolt against the authority of truth.

On the other hand, belief may not always be right. To quote Millar Burrows again, and this time with approval: "To follow blindly every strong impulse or inhibition on the assumption that it is the voice of God is decidedly dangerous, of course. That is the way fanatics and bigots are made. The danger in movements that emphasize direct divine guidance is that people of sensitive conscience may be led into unwise acts by the assumption that any suggestion that seems hard and unpleasant must come from above."[2] Yet Burrows rightly says that there are times when we may act on "an inner conviction so intuitive and unreasoned . . . and yet so compelling that we can only regard it as a witness of God's Spirit in our hearts."[3] Manifestly, therefore, we need some way of testing our beliefs

---

[1] *An Outline of Biblical Theology,* 1946, p. 50. Cf. Calvin, *op. cit.* I, p. 72: "Scripture . . . deigns not to submit to proofs and arguments, but owes the full conviction with which we ought to receive it to the testimony of the Spirit."

[2] *Op. cit.* p. 42.

[3] *Ibid.*

9

and our intuitions, to know when we ought to follow them and when we ought not.

That there is a real witness of the Spirit in our spirit, and that there is an authority of the Spirit within, I firmly agree,[1] just as I also firmly agree that there is an authority of the Church. But the authority of the Bible is not to be equated with either of these, and calls for quite separate examination.

The false objectivism of bibliolatry has happily been destroyed by modern critical study. Moreover, it stands condemned within the pages of the Bible itself. Jeremiah in his greatest word—which I see no reason to deny to him[2]—looked forward to the day when God's law should be inscribed on the living tables of men's hearts, and not on tables of stone.[3] And if tables of stone could not satisfy, no more can the pages of a book. On the other hand, I have said that a mere subjectivism is inadequate. Nor did Jeremiah contemplate a mere subjectivism. What he thought of was *the law of God* inscribed on men's hearts, so that a man in living out the law of his own

[1] Cf. H. Wheeler Robinson, *Record and Revelation*, p. 306: "As the unwritten word of the prophet became revelation only when it found intelligent and obedient response from his hearers, so the objective fact of the Old Testament as literary record still awaits the response of the reader through what theology has called the *testimonium Spiritus Sancti internum*."

[2] Many scholars attribute this passage to another author, but no compelling reasons are advanced, and the thought fits well into the general thought of Jeremiah. Cf. A. S. Peake, *Jeremiah and Lamentations* (Cent. B.), II, 1912, pp. 68 ff., 101 ff. Peake's own judgment is an "unshaken conviction that though in its present form we may owe it to Baruch, the prophecy itself comes from Jeremiah and from no other, and is the worthy crown of his teaching" (p. 70). Amongst others who maintain its authenticity are F. Giesebrecht, *Jeremia* (H.K.), 1894, p. 165; C. H. Cornill, *Das Buch Jeremia*, 1905, pp. 348 ff.; A. W. Streane, *Jeremiah and Lamentations* (Camb. B.), 1913, p. 195; L. E. Binns, *Jeremiah* (W.C.), 1919, pp. 241 ff.; J. Skinner, *Prophecy and Religion*, 1922, pp. 320 ff.; G. A. Smith, *Jeremiah*, 3rd edn., 1924, pp. 374 ff.; P. Volz, *Jeremia* (K.A.T.), 2nd edn., 1928, p. 284; F. Nötscher, *Jeremia* (H.S.A.Tes), 1934, p. 236; G. Vittonatto, *Il libro di Geremia*, 1955, p. 388; B. N. Wambacq, *Jeremias* (B.O.T.), 1957, pp. 206 ff.; W. Rudolph, *Jeremia* (H.A.T.), 2nd edn., 1958, pp. 184 ff.; A. Gelin, *Jérémie* (Bible de Jérusalem), 2nd edn., 1959, p. 153. On the other hand the following reject it: B. Stade, *G.V.I.* 2nd edn., I, 1889, pp. 646 f.n.; R. Smend, *Lehrbuch des alttestamentlichen Religionsgeschichte*, 2nd edn., 1899, pp. 249 ff.; B. Duhm, *Jeremia* (K.H.C.), 1901, pp. 254 f.

[3] Jer. 31: 31 ff.

heart would be living out the law of God. He did not suppose that in his day that law was inscribed on all hearts so that men had only to look within for final guidance. Nor is that law yet inscribed on all hearts. It is not therefore enough to point men within for the final authority. That final authority is not in a Book; it is not in our hearts; it is not in the Church. It is in God, and in God alone. That God's Spirit may be in our hearts or His law written on them may be readily allowed, and in so far as we are then guided by that Spirit to obey that law we submit to His authority. But in both cases there should be tests which we can apply. Nor can we rest content with the appeal to the Church as the custodian of tradition as the simple test to which all else is to be subordinated.

Here, indeed, we have some guidance within the Bible itself. In Israel there were the priests, who were the guardians and the interpreters of tradition, and the prophets, who were the vehicle of the divine Spirit. There was also the written word of the Old Testament. Yet how often we find in the Old Testament warnings against both priests and prophets, and even against reliance upon the written word to which men appealed! There were false prophets as well as genuine prophets, and no easy tests could distinguish the ones from the others. There were priests who were unworthy of their calling, who stand under the sharpest condemnation again and again. And Jeremiah could say that the written word to which men appealed was inscribed by the false pen of the scribes.[1] None of the media of revelation is infallible, and hence the authority of the media is never absolute.

Does not this bring us back once more to the subjective test? Are we not bound to oscillate between the subjective and the objective, finding no abiding satisfaction in either? Or at most, finding each his own satisfaction in his own judgment, and so reaching a fundamentally subjective authority in the end? I do not think so. I think there must be a combination of subjective and objective factors in any solution that is finally satisfying. There must be objective and rational factors which can commend themselves at the bar of reason in all rational men; but there must also be other factors which are subjective.

[1] Jer. 8: 8.

This is not confined to the question we are discussing, however. The man who makes great scientific discoveries is not the man who works with pure reason and logical argument alone. He is the man with trained powers of observation, who uses those powers. Often he follows some intuition, and then tests his intuition against all the battery of reason and experiment before he commits himself to it. If he declares his belief in some scientific hypothesis, and I in my ignorance declare my unbelief, no one blandly observes that it is true for him but not for me. Instead, they laugh at my folly for expressing a judgment on what I am not trained to judge. Where it is a question of recognizing the voice of God, sensitiveness of spirit takes the place of the scientist's trained observation to operate alongside the exercise of reason. This is not merely a matter of intelligence or sincerity. The false prophets were not all insincere, any more than I might be in my rejection of a scientific hypothesis. They were false in so far as they were insensitive to the Spirit of God. The true prophets were men who knew consecration of spirit and trembling awe in the presence of God; and it is men who know a like spirit who are sensitive to the voice of God, whether it reaches them through the Bible or through the commerce with God in the intangible realm of the spirit. Nevertheless, that sensitiveness of spirit needs to be reinforced by reason before it can demonstrate the authority of the Bible, just as the scientist needs the intellectual grasp of scientific principles as well as trained observation and intuition before he can convince others of the soundness of his hypothesis.[1]

Let it be recognized at once that it is impossible to demonstrate the inspiration and authority of every verse of the Bible. The Roman Catholic author whom I cited earlier protested against the ignoring of the human element in the composition of the Bible by the early Protestants, and once we recognize a human element we recognize a fallible element.[2] There is no

[1] Cf. what I have written in *The Servant of the Lord*, 1952, p. 128.

[2] M. F. Unger, who does me the honour of devoting a whole chapter to the critical examination of my views (*Inspiration and Interpretation*, ed. by J. W. Walvoord, 1959, pp. 189 ff.) complains (p. 194) because I say (*The Relevance of the Bible*, 1942, p. 32) that the non-critical approach to the Bible "is spiritually unsatisfying, since it involves dishonouring God", and

evidence that inspiration worked through the complete suspension of human personality.[1] The mark of the spokesman or

urges against me the "high moral and spiritual value" of the Old Testament. My recognition of the high moral and spiritual value of the Old Testament as a whole is not in doubt, as every reader of my book *The Faith of Israel*, 1956, is well aware. But on Unger's view of the Old Testament, God's law, as laid down through Moses, directed that children were not to be put to death for the sins of their fathers (Dt. 24: 16); yet when David violated this law to please the Gibeonites (2 Sam. 21: 2 ff.), God's anger against Israel was appeased (v. 15). It would seem that the attribution of fickleness to God is not regarded by Unger as dishonouring Him, and Unger would seem to hold that God's law is something that man is entitled to set aside when it is inconvenient.

To me such a view is still spiritually unsatisfying and dishonouring to God. To my observation (*The Relevance of the Bible*, p. 24) that "if there once existed an inerrant text as the direct handiwork of God, its Divine Author did not think it of importance to preserve it; and once it is admitted that the Bible now in our hands cannot be relied on to give the authentic word of God, the whole basis of the older appeal has gone", Unger replies that (1) copyists' errors may be responsible for such discrepancies as those between Kings and Chronicles (p. 197), and (2) the Massoretic text is today more highly regarded than it was formerly (p. 199). As to (2) I am in full agreement; cf. *O.T.M.S.* p. xxv: "In the field of Lower, or Textual, Criticism, the most significant tendency of our period has been seen in the greater respect paid to the Massoretic text." But the greater insistence on the reliability of the Massoretic text, the less can textual corruption be appealed to against the kind of difficulty to which I referred, and in particular textual corruption could never be appealed to as a means of resolving the contradictions between Kings and Chronicles as a whole. Unger is apparently aware of this, for he adds as a further variety of cause "differences in the compiler's or redactor's viewpoint". In so doing he concedes the human element in the composition of the Scriptures for which I contended, and if that human element led to contradictions, its fallibility is beyond question. Moreover, despite the greater respect for the Massoretic text, the fact that there are corruptions, as Unger himself agrees, means that a verbally inspired Bible has not survived to our day, and unless Unger's faith in the power of God is much less than mine, he would seem bound to agree that God did not regard this as important. W. Broomall (*Biblical Criticism*, 1957, p. 73) says: "It is now possible to reconstruct the original text of Scripture on the basis of the available data which we possess in such abundance today . . . It is possible to ascertain what was in the autograph copies themselves." No one who has seriously worked at textual criticism and considered the available data could make so absurd a statement.

[1] Cf. J. W. C. Wand, *The Authority of the Scriptures*, 1949, p. 62: "Inspiration does not put man's common faculties to sleep while God is left alone to speak, but it quickens these faculties beyond the point of genius."

13

author is on every passage he has given us[1]. The prophets had each his own style, and their interests and outlook are impressed upon their work. If they were inspired, God was using their personality to express His message, and while it is a divine message it is coloured by their personality and thought.[2] Moreover, they were not all equally *en rapport* with the Spirit of God, and hence there are varieties of level in the revelation that came through them. Every workman is limited by the material in which he works, and there are things which cannot be done with some materials which could be done with others. A carpenter cannot get the same results with any piece of wood that lies to his hand, and depends for his achievements not only on his own skill but on the hardness and the grain of the material he uses. Even God Himself is limited by the spiritual maturity and sensitiveness of those He uses, and that was why the Incarnation was necessary for the supreme revelation. It is not to be surprised at, therefore, that there are different levels of grandeur and loftiness within the Bible, and few would put Esther or Ecclesiastes on the same level as Isa. 53 or Rom. 8. Moreover, the books of the Bible were not consciously written by their authors to take their place in a Canon of Scripture. The books were collected, and into that collection human processes went. The seal of canonicity was the end of a long process, and when it was given men did not cast around to see what were the most suitable books they could find for the purpose. They but confirmed a selection which had been made gradually, and in some of its stages perhaps unconsciously, over a long period. Hence the general recognition of the Bible as inspired and authoritative does not mean the claim that these books and only these books were inspired and authoritative, or that every passage in every book was equally the vehicle of the Word of

---

[1] Cf. B. C. Butler, *The Church and the Bible*, 1960, pp. 50 f.: "The Holy Ghost does not just use the penmanship of the human author . . . ; he uses the human author as an author, to be the living, thinking, freely willing instrument by which he, the Holy Ghost, utters his mind to us."

[2] J. Stafford Wright, in his excellent pamphlet on *The Authority of the Bible*, p. 12, says: "The revelation is made through human agents, who show differences of style and outlook. This is what might naturally be expected of men living in different ages and under differing circumstances. But God chose His men."

God. It is well known that Luther had no high opinion of the Epistle of James, and it is probable that if he had been on the selection committee for the definition of a Canon he would have put up a fight against it.[1] On the other hand, there are not a few today who hold that some parts of the Apocrypha are as worthy of inclusion in the Canon as some parts of the Old Testament, and for the Roman Church these rank as Deutero-canonical.[2]

This is not to say that some parts of the Bible are inspired and the rest are not. What I have said is that because inspiration works through fallible men, there are different levels of inspiration even where all are inspired. I have more than once used the illustration of glass of various colours and degrees of opaqueness through which light passes. None of the light derives from the glass, but all is modified by the glass through which it passes, and even though the light comes from a common source it will emerge very differently from the various pieces of glass. In the same way divine revelation given through the inspiration of men of varied quality of personality will be given with varied richness, and if authority is in the measure of

[1] Cf. H. Bornkamm, *Luther und das Alte Testament*, 1948, pp. 158 ff., particularly for Luther's declamation against the book of Esther.

[2] The Church of England in its Sixth Article declares these books worthy to be read "for example of life and instruction of manners." So Luther had earlier said: "These are books not to be held in equal esteem with those of Holy Scripture, but yet good and useful for reading" (cf. F. Buhl, *Canon and Text of the Old Testament*, Eng. trans. by J. MacPherson, 1892, p. 67). The Westminster Confession, however, says: "The books commonly called Apocryphal, not being of divine inspiration, are no part of the Canon of the Scripture, and therefore are of no authority in the Church of God, nor to be otherwise approved or made use of than other writings" (cf. B. M. Metzger, *An Introduction to the Apocrypha,* 1957, p. 192). It is sometimes said that these books belonged to the Alexandrian Canon of Scripture, but the only evidence for this is that some of them were included in the great Christian codices of the Bible which come from the fourth and fifth centuries. As no two of these codices contain the same selection of such books, and as some of them include other works which lie outside the Apocrypha, this is an unwarrantable assumption. Some of the early Fathers expressed doubts about their canonicity, and even after the Council of Trent had declared them to be canonical, doubts continued to be expressed. Cf. my *Unity of the Bible*, 1953, pp. 92 f. and the literature there cited. To the literature should now be added, Metzger, *op. cit.* pp. 175 ff.

the divine quality of the word it will not be equal in all its parts, even though a measure of authority may be found in all.[1] Yet having said this I must add that viewing the Bible as a whole I find a surprising measure of inspiration and therefore of authority marking it, and there is no other religious book in the world which can compare with it, as I hope to establish.

Two things are now required of him who would maintain the authority of the Bible. He must first establish some test whereby these levels may be judged; and he must produce evidence that can approve itself to reason that the Bible is the Word of God, even if not all in the same degree. He must point to some evidence of the hand of God in the Bible that can be objectively tested by reason. If he can produce such evidence he may hope that men who accept the arbitrament of reason will recognize the hand of God and will therefore approach the Bible with humility and reverence to receive the Word of God. Their spirit will be susceptible to the influence of the divine Spirit. For I have already agreed that the Word of God can only be heard by those who have ears to hear, and the function of reason is not to mediate the Word of God but to open the ear to hear His Word. If objective evidence that can stand at the bar of reason can be produced, then it may be known whether it is idle delusion which leads some to hear the voice of God in the Bible, or deafness which leads others to protest that they do not hear that voice.

For the Christian the test whereby the level of inspiration and authority is to be judged is Christ, who is the supreme medium of divine revelation and by whom all other revelation is to be tested.[2] The Old Testament covers the story of a long period,

---

[1] Cf. B. C. Butler, *op. cit.* p. 71: "This brings us to the radical truth about all revelation of God to man, namely, that it is a divine self-disclosure within human experience, and therefore subject to the limitations of the human recipient. Here the philosophical axiom holds good that 'whatever is received or known is received or known according to the measure of capacity of him who receives or knows it'."

[2] J. D. Smart (*The Interpretation of Scripture*, 1961, p. 220) says that I do not clearly say by what criterion I measure inspiration. I indicate it here. Cf. also my *Relevance of the Bible*, p. 33: "All that we learn of God in the Old Testament that is in harmony with the revelation given in Christ is truly of God . . . And all that we learn of God in the Old Testament that is not in harmony with the revelation given in Christ is not of God." M. F.

and we can trace development within its pages. Within its variety there is a dynamic unity,[1] and it constantly points to something beyond itself. To the Christian Christ is the answer to this expectation, and in Him revelation through personality rises to its climax. The New Testament is the record of the revelation in Christ, first as seen by those who companied with Him in the flesh, and then by those who, like ourselves, can know Him only in the spirit. By the touchstone of Christ must the Old Testament revelation be tested, therefore, and in so far as it accords with the revelation in Christ is it enduringly valid, while in so far as it falls short of that revelation it shows the mark of the imperfections and fallibility of the persons through whom it was given and is superseded.

The Old Testament is not itself superseded, however, as many suppose. The two Testaments belong to one another and neither is complete without the other. For if the Old Testament looks forward to something beyond itself, the New looks back to the Old, without which much of it would be unintelligible. If Christ, who is set before us in the New Testament, is the test of the Old Testament revelation, it is not less true that the New Testament is the guarantee of the inspiration and authority of the Old.

Here we are passing beyond the substance of the Christian

Unger (*Inspiration and Interpretation*, p. 193) says: "But Professor Rowley's position becomes inconsistent when he faces the fact that we are also dependent upon inspired men for our knowledge of God's perfect revelation in Christ . . . Is not the 'perfect revelation' itself imperfect?" Here my critic confuses his view of *the Bible* as the revelation with my view that it is *Christ* who is the perfect revelation. Cf. my *Relevance of the Bible*, p. 47: "It is He who is the effulgence of the divine glory, and not His words and deeds alone, and behind and through the record of His words and deeds, however incomplete, we may find Him"; pp. 49 f.: "The final revelation is not the New Testament, therefore, but the Christ who is the theme of the New Testament"; p. 51: "The authority of both the Scriptures and the Church goes back to the authority of Christ. Neither Bible nor Church can take His place, though both may lead to Him." Cf. A. M. Ramsey, *Peake's Commentary on the Bible*, 1962, p. 1a: "The central fact of Christianity is not a Book but a Person—Jesus Christ, himself described as the Word of God."

[1] Cf. my paper on "The Unity of the Old Testament" in *B.J.R.L.* xxix, 1945–46, pp. 326–358, and *The Unity of the Bible*, 1953. See also *The Relevance of the Bible*, 1942, pp. 77–95.

faith to its rational justification. The acceptance of Christ as the standard whereby all is to be tested is precisely what requires some objective justification. And I do not think it is lacking. But just as Christ Himself stands outside the Bible, though our knowledge of Him is mediated through the Bible, so the hand of God is to be found not merely in the written record of the Bible, but in the persons and events of which we have knowledge through the Bible, and the whole complex of person, event, and record must be considered together to be fully comprehended. The hand of God is to be found not so much in the Bible as in the revelation of which the Bible contains the record.

It was the faith of Israel that God had chosen and saved her in the time of Moses, through whom He spoke to her. How far can that faith be demonstrated to have a basis of fact? There can be no reason whatever to doubt that the Israelites were once in Egypt under taskwork, and that Moses came to them from the wilderness in the name of Yahweh promising them deliverance—a deliverance to which they were required to contribute nothing save faith in his word and obedience to his call. There can be no reason to doubt that he led them out and that they experienced a deliverance of which they were merely spectators—i.e. a deliverance effected not by their own skill and valour, but by forces that were subject to no human control. The memory of that deliverance was deeply stamped on the nation for all time. No people would invent the story that they had been slaves in Egypt if they had not; no people would invent the story that they had been spectators of their deliverance if they had not; no people would invent the story that a God whom they had not hitherto worshipped had delivered them, unless they had strong reason to believe this.

But if all this is true, much more follows from it. If Moses believed that he was sent by Yahweh, might he not have been deluded? Here we have to face the fact that his delusion could not have effected the deliverance; yet the deliverance was effected. It was effected not by his action, or by the action of the people, but by wind and tide over which neither he nor they could exercise control. Could not this have been fortuitous? If it were, that would not account for his prior confidence and summons to the people to follow him in faith—a summons which was made not in his own name but in that of the God in whom his confidence rested. Here we have a complex of human and non-human factors, and neither could determine the other, and *the only possible common source of both was God.*[1] Deliverance was achieved by the timely act of Nature. But that timely act fulfilled the prior promise of Moses, who had no means of knowing how deliverance would be effected. When he went singlehanded from the desert in the name of Yahweh he did a surprising thing. If the enterprise had no deeper source than his own heart, he might have been expected to use the divine name that was familiar to the Israelites. What he actually did was something unique in the history of religion, and he must have been profoundly convinced that Yahweh really commissioned him to it. His conviction was justified and his faith vindicated, and the confidence that *God* would not let him down led to the experience that *Nature* came to his aid. Nature could not have given him his commission; his confidence in God could not of itself have stirred the forces of Nature. He therefore found the hand of God in the whole complex, and there is no other hypothesis which is both scientific and adequate.[2]

I have already observed that the Old Testament looks beyond itself into the future. Throughout its course ideas and principles which were incipient in the work of Moses were taken up and developed—and developed by men who were as

[1] Such a case as that of the confidence of Abū Bakr that God was on his side and the vindication of his confidence in the victory he achieved has been brought against me as a parallel here. In truth, it is in no sense parallel. Men have commonly believed that their gods would help them in battle, and whichever side has been victorious has claimed the vindication of its confidence. But Abū Bakr did not stand still and see the salvation of God, but believed that the power of God was exercised through him and his followers. It was otherwise in the case of the Exodus, where the deliverance came through non-human powers which could not be controlled by man. It is the interplay between human and non-human factors which gives its unique quality to the experience of the Exodus. In the case of the deliverance at Taanach in the time of Deborah and Barak, the Israelites did play a part in the victory; yet they themselves recognized that it was insignificant compared with that played by the storm, which immobilized the Canaanite chariots and turned them into a liability.

[2] On the interplay of personality and event as the unique medium of revelation, cf. my *Unity of the Bible*, pp. 16 f., 66 f.

conscious as he that they acted under divine constraint. Many of them were prophets, who primarily predicted the future as it should arise out of the present, the inevitable issue of the events and policies of their day. But they also looked into the more distant future and spoke of things unconnected by direct causal process with their own day. They spoke of the things that should happen on the horizons of time, and gave utterance to what we call "messianic" prophecy. There is great variety of conception as to the details of the prophecies, and it would be quite impossible to imagine any fulfilment which would at the same time fulfil every detail of them all. There is the thought of universal peace and righteousness, resting on a universal obedience to the law of Israel's God and universal worship of Him; there is the thought of a Davidic king who should exercise rule in that kingdom; there is the thought of a Suffering Servant through the organ of whose suffering the nations should be converted and saved; there is the thought of the kingship of the saints, personified in the figure of the Son of Man, whose rule would be the perfect expression of the will of God.

The Church claimed that all this was gathered up in Christ,[1] and that while not every detail was fulfilled in Him,[2] or will be, He inaugurated the realization of its hopes. There is no claim that without the New Testament one could deduce it from the Old, or that a process of natural evolution would carry us from the Old to the New.[3] There is the claim that God was speaking

---

[1] On the gathering of various elements of the predictions into the fulfilment, cf. what I have written in *The Unity of the Bible,* pp. 90 ff., and *The Faith of Israel,* 1956, p. 46; also *The Re-discovery of the Old Testament,* 1946, pp. 202 ff.

[2] Cf. A. M. Ramsey, *Peake's Commentary on the Bible,* 1962, p. 2a: "It was not so much in the foreseeing of the details of events that this predictive element lay as in the proclaiming of the divine rule over future history."

[3] J. D. Smart (*The Interpretation of Scripture,* p. 90) says I do not take with sufficient seriousness the discontinuity between the Testaments. In fact I recognize both continuity and discontinuity as elements to be given the fullest recognition. I say (*The Unity of the Bible,* p. 98): "The new pattern is never a mere repetition of the old. It is on a new level, or in terms of new conditions, and it brings a new message and a new power. It brings the evidence of the personality of the same God, whose initiative is never limited by His past revelation. The community of pattern does not mean

through the Israelite voices that announced these hopes and that He was active in the fulfilment, which gave a fullness to the meaning of the Old that it could not otherwise have had, and provided firm ground for the belief that the Old Testament not alone did lead to Christ in fact, but was intended by the God whose partial revelation it contained to lead to Christ.[1] That is a claim which can be objectively tested, and again it will be found that we have something of the same pattern as we have found in the case of what I may call the "Exodus complex"—by which I mean the historical and spiritual experiences associated with the Exodus, both those out of which it arose and those to which it led. The hopes of the Old Testament could not of themselves effect their fulfilment in the New; on the

that all could have been predicted beforehand, but that when the new pattern appears its community with the old can be perceived . . . For the divine signature is not given merely through some human voice that claims to be prophetic; it is given in the texture of the revelation." Cf. also the chapter on "Unity in Diversity", *ibid.* pp. 1 ff.

[1] M. Burrows (*An Outline of Biblical Theology*, p. 18) says: "The argument from prophecy will not convince any intelligent and informed person who does not already believe the Bible is inspired." This is surely going too far. It may be agreed that many unjustified arguments from prophecy have been employed, but this does not mean that every appeal to prophecy is lacking in validity. A. G. Hebert (*The Authority of the Old Testament*, 1947, p. 69) is more balanced here when he says: "In the predictions of the Messiah, as in the narratives of the Exodus, there is no such thing as 'inerrancy'; but there is a core of truth lying behind both, to which the writers in either case bear witness with a knowledge and an insight which are real but limited." Cf. also J. Coppens, *Les Harmonies des deux Testaments*, 1949, where the argument from prophecy is soberly presented, with a wealth of bibliographical references to contemporary literature. Coppens says (p. 12): "Nous restons fermement convaincu des liens multiples, non seulement théologiques, au sens fort du mot, mais aussi critiques et historiques, qui unissent les deux Alliances. La méthode historique réussit selon nous à démontrer que l'Ancien Testament fut la voie frayée par la Providence à l'avènement du Christ, qu'il constitue vraiment la préparation et une anticipation partielle de la révélation chrétienne, qu'il est à ce titre un phénomène historique tellement extraordinaire et unique qu'il mérite d'être qualifié de merveilleux et de surnaturel." Cf. T. W. Manson (*J.T.S.* xlvi, 1945, p. 128): "It must be emphasized that this Jewish and Christian attitude to Scripture . . . means rather that they saw world history and God's purpose side by side and were convinced that the two were connected."

other hand, it is certain that the fulfilment in the New did not create the hopes which antedated it.

It can scarcely be gainsaid that either these hopes were fulfilled in Christ or they have not been fulfilled at all and are now not likely to be. There have been false Messiahs, but the event has proved their claim to be ludicrous. The claim that Christ fulfilled these hopes is certainly not ludicrous. No precise and literal fulfilment can now be expected, since it is unlikely that any living Jew could produce convincing evidence of Davidic descent. And if an imprecise fulfilment were to happen—as the fulfilment in Christ was admittedly imprecise in some particulars—it is very improbable that it would show as remarkable an area of correspondence as that in Him.

The fulfilment in Christ was not literal, but it was indeed substantial.[1] The variety of figure under which the hopes were expressed in the Old Testament was taken up into Christ, and the fulfilment in Him was rather of an amalgam of these hopes.[2] His Messiahship was modified by His fulfilment of the role of Suffering Servant, and hence He founded no kingdom by conquest but by suffering. It was therefore a spiritual kingdom.

[1] J. K. S. Reid (*The Authority of Scripture*, 1957, p. 244) finds some value in this part of my argument. J. D. Smart (*op. cit.* pp. 220 f.) finds less value in it, and says that I am presenting the old argument from prophecy in a new form. On the other hand, M. F. Unger (*op. cit.* pp. 208 f.) finds my attitude to Old Testament prophecy disappointingly inadequate. It is hard to please everybody! I am persuaded that there is an evidential value in prophecy, but I am equally persuaded that it is weakened when we try to press it too far. In sound scholarship caution achieves more than confidence. W. F. Albright (*The Archaeology of Palestine*, revised edn., 1960, p. 255) well says that archaeology "can show the absurdity of extreme sectarian positions, from the once reputable doctrine of verbal inspiration of Scripture to the weird vagaries of believers in the divinatory properties of numbers, measurements, and alleged biblical ciphers."

[2] Cf. J. Coppens, *Les Harmonies des deux Testaments*, 1949, p. 105: "À côté de l'attente d'un messie royale, il y eut celle d'un messie-prophète, celle d'un messie pauvre, juste et souffrant. L'inspiration divine qui a fait sourdre ces diverses aspirations, les a progressivement rapprochées et unies. On peut croire que dans le Serviteur souffrant du deutéro-Isaïe, l'ébauche la plus parfaite écrite sous l'Ancien Testament, tous les traits ont déjà été juxtaposées par l'Esprit, au point que le Christ n'a eu qu'à enlever la patine du temps pour faire resplendir à nouveau l'image originale tracée par le prophète."

Yet this was in perfect accord with hopes found outside the Servant Songs of Deutero-Isaiah.[1] The well-known passage which stands in Isaiah and in Micah puts the Golden Age of peace and happiness in the days when all men should go up to the house of the Lord.[2] It would therefore have a spiritual foundation and would await the completion of the spiritual change in men. That is why the Church did not claim that Christ did more than inaugurate the kingdom. It still put the consummation in the future, since a spiritual change in individual men throughout the world cannot be effected in a moment.

It is not idle to see in Christ the fulfilment of the hope of the Suffering Servant.[3] In the fourth Servant Song the Servant is represented as suffering death for no evil that he had done, and by his death, which is described as a sin-offering for others, saving and winning others.[4] That Jesus suffered death for no evil that He had done is beyond dispute; that His death has been the organ of redemption to men of all nations is equally beyond dispute. That is an objective fact, and not a matter of

---

[1] Cf. G. A. Smith, *The Book of Isaiah*, I, 10th edn., 1897, p. 143: "The Messianic prophecies of the Old Testament are tidal rivers. They not only run to their sea, which is Christ; they feel His reflex influence."

[2] Isa. 2: 2–4; Mic. 4: 1–4.

[3] J. K. S. Reid (*op. cit.* p. 264) cites my observation (*The Unity of the Bible*, pp. 104 f.), "It is quite clear that our Lord was much influenced by this passage, and thought of His death before it took place in terms of the death of the Servant", as a trivialization of our Lord's view of the Old Testament, and comments that the suggestion is that Jesus brought His life into external conformity with it. I made no such suggestion, but merely accepted the New Testament evidence that Jesus believed Himself to be the fulfilment of Old Testament prophecy. When Peter confessed Him to be the Christ, He began to teach them that the Son of Man must suffer and be killed (Mk. 8: 29 ff.), and after His resurrection He began from Moses and the prophets to show that it behoved the Christ to suffer (Lk. 24: 26 f.). The terms of Mk. 10: 45 are widely held by scholars (cf. my *Biblical Doctrine of Election*, 1950, pp. 155 ff.) to be reminiscent of the fourth Servant Song, and if Jesus believed that He was the fulfilment of prophecy—as the Early Church believed, and as I believe—I see nothing trivial about His saying so to His disciples. As I observe in *The Missionary Message of the Old Testament*, 1945, p. 77: "History proved that it was not only in our Lord's mind that He fulfilled the thought of Deutero-Isaiah."

[4] Isa. 53: 7–12.

belief. I am not concerned with any theory of the Cross, or with any theological or psychological explanation of the fact. I am only concerned with the severely objective fact that many lives have been so completely changed that anybody, friend or foe, Christian or non-Christian, could be aware of the change, and that the change was somehow to be connected with the Cross of Christ. I am not thinking of it from the point of view of the convert, but from the point of view of others, to whom the change has been visible and objective. To use the words of Isa. 53: 5 in relation to any other is out of the question; to use them in relation to Christ, and to find their expectation realized in Him, is to use them in a demonstrably relevant way. "He was wounded for our transgressions, he was bruised for our iniquities: the chastisement of our peace was upon him; and with his stripes we are healed." Whatever explanation of the fact be offered, fact it is that the effect of His Cross on men has corresponded precisely with the anticipated effect of the sufferings of the Servant.[1]

In two respects I find a singular repetition of the pattern we have found in the Exodus. In the first place, faith is the condition of the deliverance but not its organ, and man's pledge of

[1] J. D. Smart (*op. cit.* p. 90) complains that in *The Unity of the Bible* I base my assertion of the Bible's unity largely upon the demonstration of a continuity of theological themes. As Smart refers elsewhere in his book to the present essay, whose argument is also summarized in *The Unity of the Bible*, there is little excuse for this misunderstanding. For here I am not dealing with a continuity of theological themes, but with concrete experience. In *The Unity of the Bible*, p. 91, I say: "The New (Testament) is neither a merely natural development from the Old, nor the substitution of something unrelated." Six pages later I observe that in the New Testament "we find a new revelation from the same God who revealed Himself in the Old", and the subsequent pages should make it clear to every reader that in my view the new revelation was not of ideas or themes, but a revelation in the Person of Christ, who by His life, death, and resurrection has achieved, and still achieves, a saving transformation of men in living experience. At the same time there is a continuity of theological themes to which I quite properly direct attention. Cf. J. Coppens, *Les Harmonies des deux Testaments*, 1949, pp. 24 f.: "Concluons de tout cet exposé que la comparaison entre l'Ancien et le Nouveau Testament se fera moins sur des points particuliers que sur des ensembles plus ou moins vastes de thèmes religieux et moraux, presque toujours centrés autour des croyances, des obligations et des espérances de la foi monothéiste."

loyalty is his response to the achieved deliverance and there-fore in no sense conditional. Israel was required to follow Moses in faith before her deliverance could be effected, yet the power by which she was delivered lay outside herself. So a man must be prepared to die unto Christ ere he can live in Him; yet the organ of his redemption is not his faith but the Cross of Christ. Israel's covenant with God was her pledge of undeviating loyalty to the God who had already delivered her; and the redeeming death of Christ is something that is achieved and does not need to be repeated. Its power becomes effective in the moment of a man's surrender of himself in faith and conse-cration. Here again I would emphasize that I am not really concerned with theology, though I am using theological terms. For my present purpose I do not mind whether a theological interpretation is given to the terms or whether they are inter-preted psychologically. I am only concerned with the order and relation of the experiences, and they bear striking marks of similarity to those of the Exodus complex.

Here perhaps I should explain that I am not thinking in terms of allegory or typology. I am not pretending that the purpose of the Exodus was to prefigure the redemption in Christ. I have something quite other in mind. If both were acts of revelation of the same God, it would be expected that the unity of His character would give unity even to the diverse acts of revelation. And the unity of pattern which I have noted is but one objective pointer to the hand of the same God in them.

The other respect is even more significant. Jesus believed that His death would have unique power; in indisputable fact it has had unique power. Neither of these facts can be explained by the other. Jesus believed that His death would achieve that which the death of the Servant was represented as certain to achieve. Either His belief was justified or it was not. If it was justified, then He is the fulfilment of the hope of that Old Testa-ment prophecy, and we have an objective fact whose signifi-cance cannot be evaded. If it was not justified, then how comes it that His death did in practice achieve what the Servant's death was expected to achieve, and correspond so precisely to the Old Testament hope and to His own confident expecta-tion? If it was a mere hallucination on His part to suppose He was the Servant, His hallucination could not give this mysterious power to His death. On the other hand, no power which His death proved in experience to have—by whatever theory that power is interpreted—could account for His prior expectation. And still less could it account for the Old Testament expectation. Even if it be supposed that His expectation was inserted in the Gospels in the Apostolic Age, we are in no better case. In the first place, we are not entitled to dismiss the evidence because it is inconvenient; and in the second place, if it is supposed that already in the Apostolic Age it was a matter of observed experience that the death of Christ had the power which the death of the Servant had been expected to have, the response to the hope of the Old Testament is no less striking.

Nothing is therefore to be gained by doctoring the evidence, and there is no real reason to deny that Jesus believed that His death would be unique in its effect, with a uniqueness which could only be expressed in terms of the Suffering Servant, and that in objective, historical fact His belief has been justified. This once more bears a striking resemblance to the pattern of the Exodus complex. There the prior confidence of Moses could not effect the deliverance; nor could the deliverance account for the prior confidence. In both cases the source of the confidence was declared to be God, and here we have the added factor of the expressed hope of the Old Testament as well as the confidence of our Lord to take into account with the fulfilment of the hope. If God was active in all, then all would be explained. But there is no other explanation which is both scientific and adequate.

Again, the Old Testament declared that Israel was called to be the light of the nations and that her law was destined for all men and her God was to be worshipped of all. It also recognized that not all who were of the nation Israel were worthy of their election, but declared that a Remnant would inherit the privilege and the task that were hers, to be joined by proselytes from the Gentiles who would then share her election and her mission. Those remarkable prophecies have been fulfilled in the Christian Church to a degree that is surely impressive.[1] The

---

[1] For a fuller study of the questions raised here, cf. *The Biblical Doctrine of Election*.

Church was founded by a company of Jews, a Remnant of Israel, who accepted the mission of Israel to the world seriously. Never had Israel sought proselytes as this Remnant did, and never were Israelite attempts to proselytize carried out under such discouragement of persecution as their efforts were during the early centuries. Today the Hebrew Scriptures are translated into countless tongues and cherished by millions of people who would never have heard of them through the Jews alone, and Israel's God is worshipped in almost every land under heaven. If the men who uttered the hopes were moved by the Spirit of God and those who were instrumental in the surprising measure of their fulfilment were moved by the same Spirit, we should have a sufficient and relevant explanation. But every additional objective fact, such as those which I have mentioned, makes the difficulty of explaining away greater. Where we have a whole range of facts which can be explained by a single hypothesis, it is more scientific to adopt that hypothesis than to seek to explain away the facts by numerous unrelated hypotheses.

I am aware that I have not exhausted all the examples that could be gathered from the Bible, but these will suffice. The confidence of Moses that he was divinely moved to promise deliverance and the manner of his justification; the immense fruitfulness of his work in the religious development that emerged from it; the wide variety of hopes expressed by Old Testament prophets that converged to find their fulfilment in Christ and His Church; the confidence of Christ and the Early Church that in them their fulfilment was to be found, in days when the world thought that confidence ludicrous, and the vindication of that confidence in objective fact—all this provides solid evidence that can deliver the Christian from any sense of intellectual shame in finding the hand of God in the Bible and in the history it records and in the persons concerned in it all. And if the hand of God is in it, its authority is not the authority of the Church, but the authority of God.

In a small company to which I spoke along the lines of this lecture, I was accused of arguing in a circle since I made the authority of the Old Testament depend upon the New, and that of the New depend upon the Old. I hope it is clear that I am doing nothing of the sort. What I am saying is that in the Old Testament there is evidence of the hand of God in the events it records and in the persons who figure in its story, and especially in the combination of event and person in a single complex. Similarly, there is evidence that the hand of God was in Christ and in all the fulfilment of His promise in subsequent history. Each Testament when viewed alone can satisfy objective tests. Beyond that there is the response of the New Testament to the hopes of the Old, and the common pattern in the crucial complexes of the two Testaments, to bind them together in a profound unity. If you proceed along a line from either end you will reach the other, without turning the line into a circle. But the evidence for the hand of God is not to be found simply in the fact that the one Testament points forward to the other, and the other points backward to the first. It is to be found independently in many moments of the process, though they cannot be fully understood unless they are seen to be moments of a process and viewed in the light of the whole. Moreover, the cumulative weight of the evidence is of importance. Not once nor twice but repeatedly in the complex of person and event, of promise and fulfilment, there is evidence of the activity of God and the significance of the evidence is vastly increased.

To pass beyond the Bible to other religions lies beyond our present theme. Lest I be thought to burke issues which are inevitably raised, however, something must be said. It may be asked whether Gautama's belief in the significance of his work and the subsequent vindication of that belief in the wide influence he has exerted is not parallel to our Lord's confidence and its vindication, and as much an evidence of divine authority for Buddhism as anything I have claimed for the Bible. Of the greatness of Gautama I am fully persuaded. That God did not leave Himself without witness amongst heathen peoples Paul could acknowledge,[1] and we may rightly find in Gautama His witness. And in so far as God was behind the witness of Gautama it had authority. Yet this does not mean that Gautama must be acknowledged to be on a level with Christ, or even with the Old Testament prophets. For here too God was limited by His instrument. Still less does it mean that there

[1] Acts 14: 17.

is any parallel between the vindication of Gautama in the spread of his influence and the vindication of our Lord, to which I have drawn attention. In the case of Gautama there is no parallel to the complex of event and personality to which I have drawn attention. Gautama exercised the influence of a teacher, and his teaching has been perpetuated and his influence extended. In the case of our Lord we have something quite different. It was something done to Him by His enemies, an act which was not His act,[1] which was more significant than His teaching, and which has been central in the spread of His influence. Similarly in the case of Moses. It was not merely the influence of his teaching that was important. It was the deliverance which was achieved not by his act which was central. The spread of an influence may be a purely natural process, and the range of the influence is no guarantee in itself of its divine origin. What I have here called attention to is something which was not a natural process, and something which could neither be foreseen by human insight nor controlled by human power. Moreover, the life and work of Gautama did not respond to hopes and promises which long antedated his time in a way comparable with that which we have seen in the case of our Lord. It is here that the uniqueness of the Biblical revelation is to be found, and it is without parallel in any other religion.

Let it not be supposed that I am insensitive to the sublimity of the teaching of the Bible because I do not seek to establish its authority on that. That is insufficient because another may deny that sublimity, or claim a like sublimity for the teaching of some other teacher, and objective tests of sublimity are more debatable. What I am concerned to argue is that there is demonstrable ground to believe that behind the Bible and its record is God, and that therefore its sublimity is not of merely human origin, but charged with a higher authority.

Once more, however, I must guard myself against being misunderstood. I am not attempting to replace faith by a

---

[1] It is, of course, true that the Cross was taken into the purpose of Christ, and in a profound sense He was active in His passion. Yet it remains true that He was crucified by His enemies, who were not consciously furthering His purpose, but, as they thought, destroying it.

logical demonstration that will make it superfluous.[1] I have already said that man is more than mind, and I do not forget that religion touches every side of his being. I am only seeking to show that though man is more than mind he is also mind, and that he need not suspend that side of his being when he speaks of the authority of the Bible. When it is said, as it is often said, that the authority of the Bible rests on faith, it is implied that it is subjectively based. Similarly, when it is said that it rests on the *testimonium Spiritus Sancti internum*, it is implied that it is subjectively based, in that a man is held to find within himself the evidence for the acceptance of its authority. What I am concerned to say here is that the authority of the Bible rests on objective evidence that God was active in event and personality, and that both belonged together, and that the whole process culminated in the death and resurrection of Christ, which were charged with demonstrably unique power. Faith is not rendered

---

[1] Cf. what I have said in *The Unity of the Bible*, p. 120n.: "To show that faith is reasonable is not to destroy faith; nor is the establishment of its reasonableness to be confounded with 'proof'." It is therefore surprising to find that J. D. Smart, who is examining what I have said there and here, should criticize me on the ground that my argument "can hardly claim to be 'rational proof of the activity of God', and to rest the authority of Scripture on any such dubious basis could have the opposite effect to what is desired" (*op. cit.* p. 221). To misrepresent what I have said is not to refute me. But Professor Smart does not seem to have read the Gospels with care, either. He says (*ibid.*): "It is inconceivable that Jesus should have felt it necessary to provide any such external signs visible to reason in order to prepare men for the recognition of his authority and as a kind of stepping-stone from reason to faith." Let Professor Smart read Mk. 2: 10 f.: "But that ye may know that the Son of man hath power on earth to forgive sins (he saith to the sick of the palsy), I say unto thee, Arise, take up thy bed, and go unto thy house"; Mt. 11: 2 ff.: "When John heard in the prison the works of the Christ, he sent by his disciples, and said unto him, Art thou he that cometh, or look we for another? And Jesus answered and said unto them, Go your way and tell John the things which ye do hear and see: the blind receive their sight, and the lame walk, the lepers are cleansed, and the deaf hear, and the dead are raised up, and the poor have good tidings preached to them"; Lk. 11: 20: "If I by the finger of God cast out devils, then is the kingdom of God come upon you." The Jesus who is so inconceivable to Professor Smart is the Jesus who is depicted in all the Gospels. While I offer reasonable evidence and not "proof", Wick Broomall (*Biblical Criticism*, 1957, pp. 24 ff.) claims to offer "proof" of the verbal inspiration of the Bible.

superfluous. But faith is the subjective response to the authority of the Bible and of the God who is recognized to be speaking through it,[1] just as loyalty is the response of the good citizen to the authority of the state. And faith opens the heart to the entrance of the Spirit, by whose operation the riches of the Word of God are increasingly seen and appropriated.

[1] J. D. Smart (*op. cit.* p. 221) says: "Faith is not a precondition of hearing God's word but rather is the response of the whole man to God's call in His Word. That a historical scholar such as Rowley should fail to recognize this . . . indicates once more the vacuum that was left when historical criticism had done its work most thoroughly." As Smart is here dealing with what I say in the present paper, I can only suppose that he tired before reaching the end.

2

Moses and Monotheism

2

MOSES AND MONOTHEISM[1]

ONE of the current issues in Old Testament study is concerned with the antiquity of Israelite monotheism. The view has long been common that monotheism began with the eighth century prophets and became explicit with Deutero-Isaiah.[2] Causse attributed the beginnings of monotheism to Elijah,[3] but Hölscher rejects this view on the ground that in the religion of Elijah none of the theoretical consequences of monotheism are found.[4] There is no denial of the existence of other gods and no universalism. Pfeiffer goes so far as to deny any real monotheism before Deutero-Isaiah. He says: "We can only speak of monotheism in the Old Testament before Second Isaiah by using the word in some other sense than the belief that there is only one god."[5] More often, however, the beginnings of monotheism have been found in the teachings of the eighth century prophets, and I. G. Matthews says that it was the conception of the brotherhood of man

[1] First published in German in *Z.A.W.*, N.F. xxviii, 1957, pp. 1–21, where material previously published in *E.T.* lxi, 1949–50, pp. 333–38 was, with the permission of the editors, utilized. On the subject of this paper cf. V. Hamp, *Sacra Pagina*, i, 1959, pp. 516 ff.

[2] Cf. A. Lods, *Israel from its Beginnings to the Middle of the Eighth Century*, Eng. trans. by S. H. Hooke, 1932, p. 257: "Israel only attained to monotheism in the eighth century and to a clear and conscious monotheism only in the sixth, and that by a slow process of internal development whose stages we can trace." I. G. Matthews (*The Religious Pilgrimage of Israel*, 1947, p. 129) thinks the foundation of ethical monotheism was laid by Amos.

[3] Cf. A. Causse, *Les Prophètes d'Israël et les religions de l'Orient*, 1913, p. 62. Cf. also P. Volz, *Mose*, 1907, p. 36, and W. Eichrodt, *Theology of the Old Testament*, Eng. trans. by J. A. Baker, i, 1961, pp. 224 f. Eichrodt speaks of the "practical monotheism" of Elijah; O. Procksch (*Theologie des Alten Testaments*, 1950, p. 139) attributes to him full monotheism.

[4] Cf. *Geschichte der alttestamentlichen und jüdischen Religion*, 1922, pp. 96 f.

[5] *J.B.L.* xlvi, 1927, p. 194. Oesterley and Robinson (*Hebrew Religion*, 2nd edn., 1937, p. 299) recognize implicit monotheism in the teaching of the pre-exilic prophets.

which we find in the teaching of Amos which was the foundation of ethical monotheism.[1] This view is commonly associated with the name of Wellhausen,[2] whose evolutionary presuppositions in the field of the history of religion are widely discarded today, and who is held responsible for the idea that polytheism gradually evolved into monotheism through the influence of the prophets.[3] Actually this idea is older than Wellhausen,[4] but it was doubtless under his influence that it became widespread. Writing in the *Zeitschrift für die alttestamentliche Wissenschaft* in 1925 W. L. Wardle said: "It may still be regarded as the prevailing view that Israel's religion passed gradually from an elementary stage of animism, totemism, fetichism, through the stage of tribal deity, to the stage represented by the religion of the prophets, and that this stage was reached only under their influence."[5] Wardle added that there were signs of revolt from this view. Long before this, however, there were scholars who were more cautious, and who, while recognizing development in Israelite religion, did not ascribe it to natural evolution, but to the seed of monotheism which was implanted in Israel's religion by Moses, and which grew to its full flower under the influence of those men of God whom we know as the prophets.[6]

---

[1] Cf. *The Religious Pilgrimage of Israel*, p. 129. Cf. also L. Wallis, *The Bible is Human*, 1942, p. 166: "This evolutionary process . . . gradually carried the spiritual growth of the Hebrew people up to a point where the 'remnant of Israel' . . . finally passed out of polytheism into ethical monotheism." On p. 6 Wallis attributes the development to terror of the Babylonians, which is believed to have caused a mass conversion to the view of the prophets.

[2] Cf. J. Bright, in *The Bible and the Ancient Near East* (Albright Festschrift), 1961, pp. 15 ff. But cf. R. Smend, *Th.Z.* xiv, 1958, p. 114: "Die Befreiung des Vatkeschen Werkes vom Hegelianismus war das Verdienst von Julius Wellhausen. Es heisst oft, was Wellhausen von Vatke übernommen habe, sei die Geschichtsphilosophie gewesen. Das ist ebenso unrichtig wie die Behauptung, Wellhausen habe von Vatke überhaupt den Anstoss zu weitergehender Kritik erhalten."

[3] M.-J. Lagrange (*Études sur les religions sémitiques*, 1903, p. 24) observes that it is "impossible de retrouver dans l'histoire un seul cas de monothéisme issu du polythéisme."

[4] Cf. S. A. Cook, *The Modern Churchman*, xxiv, 1934–35, p. 471.

[5] Cf. *Z.A.W.*, N.F. ii, 1925, p. 195.

[6] Cf. E. König, *Geschichte der alttestamentlichen Religion*, 1912, p. 199, where the author refers to the uniqueness of the God of Moses, and adds: "Diese

Today there are many challenges to the evolutionary view, which is held in some quarters to be sufficiently discredited by being connected with the name of Wellhausen. That all of Wellhausen's views can no longer be maintained is true.[1] It is equally true that no living teacher can be sure that all of his views will be maintained unchanged for almost a century. That Wellhausen was wrong in some of his presuppositions may be agreed; but that all his views were false is a presupposition as illegitimate as any with which he started. Hence, while I disagree at many points with Wellhausen and his school, I do so with respect and remember my debt to the men with whom I disagree. To build the tombs of the prophets of old and to stone contemporary prophets is a practice which stands condemned in the Gospels; to throw stones at the tombs of the scholars of a former generation is no more worthy an occupation.

Einzigartigkeit Jahves schloss aber natürlich den principiellen oder potenziellen Monotheismus in sich." In 1907 P. Volz (*Mose*, p. 65) contented himself with saying: "Die allgemeine Jahwe-religion hat ihre Anfänge vor Mose. Die Quelle des intensiven Jahwestroms aber ist Mose." In his *Prophetengestalten des Alten Testaments*, 1938, p. 43, he goes farther and says: "Ein zweites grosses Geschenk Gottes, das durch Mose der Welt überbracht wurde, ist der Glaube an die Einzigkeit Gottes." A. B. Davidson (*Theology of the Old Testament*, 1904, pp. 60 ff.) attributes to Moses a "practical monotheism", and holds that David was certainly a monotheist (p. 64). Cf. also B. Baentsch, *Altorientalischer und israelitischer Monotheismus*, 1906, p. 87; E. Sellin, *Geschichte des israelitisch-jüdischen Volkes*, 1935, p. 82; R. de Vaux, in *Initiation Biblique*, ed. by A. Robert and A. Tricot, 3rd edn., 1954, pp. 888 f. Similarly P. van Imschoot (*Théologie de l'Ancien Testament*, I, 1954, p. 37) says: "De tous ces traits il ressort que la religion de Moïse est monothéiste, bien que la négation des 'dieux étrangers' ne soit pas explicitement formulée, ce qui en fait un monothéisme plutôt pratique que théorique"; also O. J. Baab (*Theology of the Old Testament*, 1949, p. 48): "The concept of the oneness of God was not reached primarily through logical analysis by Hebrew thinkers; their approach was pragmatically religious and experience centered." B. Balscheit (*Alter und Aufkommen des Monotheismus in der israelitischen Religion*, 1938) finds the seeds of monotheism to lie in Israelite Yahwism from its beginnings. Cf. also Wardle, *loc. cit.*, p. 198.

[1] S. A. Cook (*loc. cit.* p. 477) observes: "It is necessary to remember that the Wellhausen literary theory of J, E, D, P is not to be confused with the reconstructions of history and religion based thereon by Wellhausen himself or others. Some are conservative, others radical, and others again are by no means 'evolutionary'."

37

One of the views which has come into fashion in recent years maintains that monotheism goes back to the beginnings of the human race.[1] This view is not new, of course. It was advanced as a scientific hypothesis by Andrew Lang.[2] It was presented by that distinguished Biblical scholar, M.-J. Lagrange, who held that the original Semitic religion was a monotheism in which El was worshipped, but that El was later split up into a multiplicity of gods.[3] More particularly, however, this view is associated with the name of Wilhelm Schmidt, the author of the voluminous work *Der Ursprung der Gottesidee*.[4] Schmidt seeks to establish the thesis that the more primitive a people is, the more nearly it approaches monotheism, which must therefore have been the original faith of man.[5] Polytheism

[1] E. Jacob (*Theology of the Old Testament*, Eng. trans. by A. W. Heathcote and P. J. Allcock, 1958, pp. 44 f.) rejects this view.

[2] Cf. *The Making of Religion*, 2nd edn., 1900, pp. 173 ff.

[3] *Op. cit.* pp. 70 ff. (also p. 25). Cf. the view of S. Langdon, published in the *Evangelical Quarterly*, April 1937, and reprinted in Sir Charles Marston, *The Bible Comes Alive*, 1937, pp. 259 ff., where Sumerian religion is said to have been originally monotheistic. For a criticism of Lagrange cf. Wardle, *loc. cit.* pp. 200 ff., and A. Lods, *Israel*, Eng. trans., pp. 254 f.; and for a reply to Langdon cf. T. J. Meek, *University of Toronto Quarterly*, VIII, 1939, pp. 186 ff. (published also in *Review of Religion*, IV, 1940, pp. 298 ff., to which I have not had access). With Meek's criticisms Albright associates himself in *F.S.A.C.*, 2nd edn., 1946, p. 322.

[4] Schmidt's ideas were accepted by J. Battersby Harford, *E.T.* XLVIII, 1936–37, pp. 68 ff., and by Langdon in the article above referred to, and criticized by Meek, *loc. cit.*, pp. 181 ff. Of the value of much of the material assembled by Schmidt there can be no doubt. That he established the thesis that primitive monotheism prevailed among men is, however, a different matter. C. Clemen (*A.R.W.* XXVIII, 1929, pp. 290–333) criticizes his view as a fiction, and quotes (p. 333) N. Söderblom for the observation: "Weder 'Mono' noch 'Theismus' will passen." Schmidt's view is rejected and criticized also by R. Pettazzoni, *R.H.R.* LXXXVIII, 1923, pp. 211 f., 220 ff. (also in *Essays on the History of Religions*, Eng. trans. by H. J. Rose, 1954, pp. 4 ff.: cf. p. 9: "It is now evident that my own point of view is as far from the evolutionist theory as from that of 'primitive monotheism' "). Cf. also G. van der Leeuw, *Religion in Essence and Manifestation*, Eng. trans. by J. E. Turner, 1938, pp. 159 ff., and S. Mowinckel, *He that Cometh*, Eng. trans. by G. W. Anderson, 1956, p. 453. R. H. Pfeiffer (*Religion in the Old Testament*, 1961, p. 17) declares that Schmidt's theory taxes our credulity.

[5] Cf. *The Origin and Growth of Religion*, Eng. trans., 1931, p. 179: "It is just at the most primitive levels that we find the religious element still in greater purity and comparatively uncorrupted."

is held to be the fruit of the disintegration of monotheism, and to be associated with the advance of culture.[1]
Presuppositions as unwarranted as those of the evolutionary school appear to lie behind this view, which rests
on a pessimistic view of human culture. I once heard
Wheeler Robinson scornfully describe it as the view that
monotheism is the religion of people who cannot count
beyond three.[2] To suppose that peoples whom we call
"primitive" preserve the earliest outlook of mankind is an
assumption that is without foundation. Schmidt observes that
these peoples have never played any important part in the
world,[3] and his work would seem to be directed to the establishment of the remarkable thesis that primitive monotheism
was the religion of the insignificant, and that its retention en-
tailed permanent insignificance. Moreover, such monotheism
as can be ascribed to "primitive" man by these means
is an arid faith in a God whose characteristic is his
"onliness". Vague qualities are attributed to him, but at the
best he is a shadowy Providence. Religion is to be tested by
the character, and not merely by the number, of the gods,
and Biblical monotheism is more than the belief that God
is one and beside Him is no other. Such "primitive monotheism" as this theory sets out to prove is quite other than
Biblical monotheism.[4]

In an important study the Swedish scholar H. Ringgren has
shown that two opposite tendencies are found in religion, the
one moving from polytheism to monotheism and the other

---

[1] *Ibid.* p. 289: "As external civilization increased in splendour and
wealth, so religion came to be expressed in forms of ever-increasing
magnificence and opulence . . . Despite the glory and wealth of the outward form, the inner kernel of religion often disappeared."

[2] This was in the discussion on Battersby Harford's above-mentioned
paper, which was read to the British Society for Old Testament Study as a
Presidential address.

[3] *Op. cit.* p. 256.

[4] Cf. S. A. Cook, *The "Truth" of the Bible*, 1938, p. 21: "In the interests
of progressive religion we must insist that those monotheistic or monotheiz-
ing beliefs or tendencies of which we have information are not to be mentioned in the same breath with that lofty spiritual teaching which is Israel's
permanent contribution to mankind."

moving from monotheism to polytheism.[1] By the hypostatization of qualities and functions a single god can disintegrate into many, while by various processes many may give place to one, the character of the consequent monotheism varying according to the process whereby it is achieved. It may advance from polytheism through a monarchic theism to monotheism, or it may take a pantheistic form, or become the abstraction τò θεîον. While, then, the dogmatism that assumes a linear development of religion towards monotheism is wrong, it is equally impossible to assume a development away from primitive monotheism. The question is not to be determined either way on grounds of general principles, but on grounds of evidence, and it is doubtful whether adequate data exist to recover with security the original religion of man.

Our concern here, however, is not with primitive monotheism but with Biblical monotheism,[2] which is certainly not derived from the supposed primitive monotheism. A much more important challenge to the view with which we started is the claim that Moses established monotheism in Israel.[3] This challenge is important because it claims no less a scholar than W. F. Albright amongst its champions. In his brilliant work *From the Stone Age to Christianity* he presented this view,[4] after some preliminary indications of it,[5] and several other scholars

---

[1] Cf. *Word and Wisdom*, 1947. Cf. also A. Bertholet, *Götterspaltung und Göttervereinigung*, 1933.

[2] Cf. R. Pettazzoni, *R.H.R., loc. cit.* pp. 193–229, where, in an important article on "La formation du monothéisme", it is maintained that the only genuinely monotheistic religions are Judaism, Christianity, and Islam, all prophetic religions, and all deriving from Judaism, and that a true monotheism could only be achieved in opposition to polytheism. Cf. p. 200: "De même que *logiquement* le monothéisme est la négation du polythéisme, de même *historiquement* il présuppose un polythéisme dont il est sorti par négation, c'est-à-dire par révolution." Cf. also Pettazzoni, *Essays on the History of Religions*, pp. 6, 9.

[3] J. Prado (*Sefarad*, v, 1945, pp. 187–217) maintains that the patriarchs were monotheists.

[4] *Op. cit.*, pp. 196 ff.

[5] Cf. *Archaeology of Palestine and the Bible*, 1932, pp. 163 ff., and *The American Scholar*, Spring 1938, pp. 186 ff. To the latter I have had no access, save through the references in Meek's reply in *University of Toronto Quarterly, loc. cit.* pp. 192 ff.

have followed him.[1] Yet actually, as Meek has shown,[2] Albright only established Mosaic monotheism by giving a new connotation to the term monotheism. He says: "If the term 'monotheist' means one who teaches the existence of only one God, the creator of everything, the source of justice, who is equally powerful in Egypt, in the desert, and in Palestine, who has no sexuality and no mythology, who is human in form but cannot be seen by human eye and cannot be represented in any form—then the founder of Yahwism was certainly a mono-

[1] Cf. G. E. Wright, *Theology To-day*, III, 1946, pp. 185 ff, and *The Old Testament against its Environment*, 1950, pp. 29 ff.; J. Bright, *Interpretation*, I, 1947, p. 85, and *The Kingdom of God*, 1953, pp. 24 f. F. James (*A.Th.R.* XIV, 1932, pp. 130 ff.) also maintains that Moses was a monotheist. Cf. also I. Engnell, *Gamla Testamentet*, I, 1945, p. 133. E. Jacob (*Theology of the Old Testament*, Eng. trans. by A. W. Heathcote and P. J. Allcock, 1958, p. 66 n.) says: "One cannot speak of evolution within the faith of Israel towards monotheism, for from the moment when Israel becomes conscious of being the people chosen by *one* God it is in practice a monotheistic people; and so one can speak with Albright, to name only one of the most recent and illustrious historians, of the monotheism of Moses, on condition that by this term there is understood a conviction of faith and not a result of reflection." Cf. also O. Procksch, *Theologie des Alten Testaments*, pp. 82, 92, and p. 605, where he says: "Der Monotheismus ist das Urdatum des alttestamentlichen Gottesglaubens." J. Bright (*History of Israel*, 1960, p. 139) says: "If one intends monotheism in an ontological sense, and understands by it the explicit affirmation that only one God exists, one may question if early Israel's faith deserves the designation." But surely this is just what monotheism means. The *Shorter Oxford English Dictionary* defines monotheism as "the doctrine that there is only one God". Nevertheless, Bright continues by saying: "It is probably best to retain the word 'monotheism' for the faith of early Israel. Though not a monotheism in any philosophical sense, it was probably such in the only way in which the ancient world would have understood the term." The point at issue is not whether the ancient world would have understood the term "monotheism", but whether her faith is accurately described by us in our terminology as "monotheism".

[2] *Loc. cit.* pp. 192 ff., and *J.B.L.* LXI, 1942, pp. 21 ff. For a criticism of both Albright and Meek, cf. M. Burrows, *J.Q.R.*, N.S. XXXIII, 1942–43, pp. 475 ff. Cf. W. Eichrodt, *Theology of the Old Testament*, Eng. trans., p. 222 n., where it is said that if the crucial sentence of Albright is to be taken to imply in fact a denial of the existence of other gods, then this is precisely the point which cannot be established from the evidence concerning Moses and the early period of Israel. Eichrodt further observes (p. 227): "If monotheistic belief had secured a foothold in Israel prematurely, it would have made no progress, but would have become a pale abstraction devoid of inner force."

theist."[1] Most of the elements of this definition are irrelevant to the question of monotheism, and of the one vital element there is no evidence.[2] For nowhere in the Pentateuch is Moses credited with the formal denial that any other gods exist, such as we find in Deutero-Isaiah, save in passages such as Dt. 4: 35, 39; 32: 39, which quite certainly did not issue from Moses.

On the other hand, no evidence can be provided to show that polytheism developed into monotheism in Israel by natural evolution or by philosophic speculation. There is no evidence that Moses was a polytheist in the sense that he

---

[1] *F.S.A.C.* p. 207. So also F. James, *A.Th.R.* xiv, 1932, pp. 130 ff. Cf. the picture of the God of Moses given by P. Volz in *Old Testament Essays: Papers read before the Society for Old Testament Study*, 1927, pp. 29 ff. P. van Imschoot (*Dictionnaire encyclopédique de la Bible*, 1960, col. 1217) says: "En délivrant les Israélites de l'Égypte, Jahvé a prouvé qu'Il est le Dieu qui est réellement et qui agit; par son alliance avec Israël Il s'est révélé comme une personne libre, comme un Dieu essentiellement moral et comme le Seigneur de son peuple et des hommes, qui exige la soumission totale de ses sujets; par les événements impressionants qui accompagnèrent la conclusion de l'alliance du Sinaï, Il s'est révélé comme le Dieu saint et redoubtable. Une religion pareille peut être considérée comme du monothéisme, bien que les récits de l'Exode ne nient pas formellement l'existence d'autres dieux." From this definition of monotheism the one thing which alone could make it monotheism is missing. Y. Kaufmann, who makes excessive claims for Israelite religion in the pre-exilic period and who maintains that it was wholly monotheistic and free from paganism and idolatry, even on the popular level, rejects the theory of primitive monotheism (*The Religion of Israel*, Eng. trans. by M. Greenberg, 1960, p. 29), and defines monotheism (*ibid.*) as "the idea of a god who is the source of all being, not subject to cosmic order, and not emergent from a pre-existent realm; a god free of the limitation of magic and mythology."

[2] Cf. Meek's criticism, *loc. cit.* pp. 32 ff. Schmidt also gives a connotation to the term monotheism from which this vital element is altogether eliminated. For he is prepared to recognize a man who believes in many gods as a monotheist, so long as he holds that One is supreme and the rest are subordinate to him (cf. *The Origin and Growth of Religion*, Eng. trans., p. 264; also *Anthropos*, XVI–XVII, 1921–22, col. 1022). It is hard to discuss issues when the fundamental terms are given different meanings by the parties to the discussion. For the monotheism here described by Schmidt is no monotheism. M. Burrows (*An Outline of Biblical Theology*, 1946, p. 55) says we have insufficient evidence to be able to say when monotheism first emerged in Hebrew religion, but holds it improbable (p. 57) that Moses was a monotheist. R. H. Pfeiffer (*Religion in the Old Testament*, 1961, p. 55) says true monotheism is inconceivable in the time of Moses.

practised the worship of many gods; yet there is no evidence that he was a monotheist in the sense that he denied the existence of more than one God. Yahweh was to be the only God for Israel, and Him only were they to serve. This would seem to lead to the conclusion that he was a henotheist,[1] and it is undeniable that henotheism was found in Israel in the post-Mosaic period. Albright dismisses Jg. 11: 24, which he calls the "parade example",[2] on the ground that it stands in a speech addressed to an alien people and arguing with them on the ground of their ideas. It is less easy to dismiss 1 Sam. 26: 19 f., where David, in speaking to Saul, says that the driving of him away is the same as telling him to go and worship other gods.[3] Nor need we be surprised that henotheism was found in Israel. For we find ample evidence that many in Israel declined from the height of the religion of Moses and fell into polytheism.

It is scarcely sufficient, however, to say that Moses was a henotheist,[4] and in any case this would still leave us with the problem of the transition from henotheism to monotheism. Moab and Ammon are commonly said to have been henotheistic, the one holding Chemosh to be Moab's god and the other Milkom to be Ammon's. Actually we have no evidence that Chemosh alone was worshipped in Moab and Milkom alone in Ammon, and it may well have been that while these were worshipped as the national gods, others stood beside them, just as in Israel through long periods Yahweh was regarded as the national God, though other gods were popularly worshipped alongside Him. Even if Moab and Ammon were henotheistic, however, we should still have to ask how it was that Israel

[1] Cf. Meek, *J.B.L., loc. cit.* p. 37.

[2] *Op. cit.* p. 220.

[3] Cf. also 2 Kg. 5: 17.

[4] Cf. *The Faith of Israel*, 1956, pp. 71 f.: "It is hard to find any evidence that Moses either believed or taught that Yahweh was the only existing God, and that He was therefore not alone the God of Israel but of all men. On the other hand, it does not seem sufficient to note that at Sinai it was affirmed that Yahweh was alone the legitimate object of Israelite worship, and that there was no denial of the existence of other gods." S. R. Driver (*Exodus* [Camb. B.], 1911, p. 413) describes the religion of Moses as an ethical henotheism, and similarly R. Kittel, *G.V.I.* 1, 6th edn., 1923, p. 389.

became monotheistic and they did not.[1] No profound and enduring influence on the religion of mankind came through them, whereas it did through Israel.

It is on this account that it is necessary to go beneath labels in our study of Israelite monotheism, and to perceive that if Moses was less than a monotheist he was more than a henotheist.[2] I have already said that some older writers maintained that in the work of Moses lay the seed of monotheism. Similarly Meek says: "It may be said with considerable assurance that Moses sowed the seeds of monotheism."[3] It is this that I would emphasize more than many writers have done, and this that offers some justification for the over-emphasis of Albright.[4] Moses did much more than lift Israel to the religious level that is so often ascribed to Moab and Ammon. On the human side he is the creator of Israel's religion, giving it a character all its own. For Israelite monotheism developed less out of the "oniness" of Yahweh as the legitimate object of worship than out of His character. The outstanding work of Moses in this connec-

[1] Cf. J. Coppens, *Histoire critique des livres de l'Ancien Testament,* 3rd edn., 1942, p. 47.

[2] Here I am in agreement with Bright, *History of Israel,* p. 139: "Certainly Israel's faith was no polytheism. Nor will henotheism or monolatry do, for though the existence of other gods was not expressly denied, neither was their status as gods tolerantly granted." Cf. F. James, *loc. cit.* pp. 141 f.: "The actual evidence regarding him (i.e. Moses) points more towards his having been a monotheist than a henotheist." Th. C. Vriezen (*An Outline of Old Testament Theology,* Eng. trans. by S. Neuijen, 1958, pp. 23 f.), while denying that Moses taught monotheism, since from the outset he did not give a conception of God but something else, holds that Mosaic religion can be better described as Mono-Yahwism than as monotheism or henotheism.

[3] Cf. *J.B.L., loc. cit.* p. 37; cf. also *University of Toronto Quarterly, loc. cit.* p. 197. Cf. further E. Jacob (in *Vocabulary of the Bible,* ed. by J. J. von Allmen, Eng. trans., 1958, p. 142 a): "Monotheism is affirmed theoretically only at a comparatively late date, but . . . from the Mosaic period the faith of Israel is practically monotheist." S. Mowinckel (*He that Cometh,* p. 126) says: "Everything which came into existence within the Jewish religion is in some way rooted in the character and origin of the Mosaic religion itself," but goes on to add: "But there is no specific historical value in such vague general statements about 'origins'."

[4] Cf. my *Missionary Message of the Old Testament,* 1945, pp. 21 f., 27; *The Re-discovery of the Old Testament,* 1946, pp. 87 f.; *The Biblical Doctrine of Election,* 1950, pp. 60 f.; *The Unity of the Bible,* 1953, pp. 22 ff.; and *The Faith of Israel,* pp. 71 f.

tion is not so much the teaching that Yahweh was to be the only God for Israel as the proclamation that Yahweh was unique.

There is ample evidence that before the time of Moses Israel was polytheistic.[1] Her whole environment was polytheistic. Egypt and Babylon were both polytheistic,[2] and we now know much of the pantheon of the people of Ugarit, who have provided us with our fullest insight into the ancient Canaanite religion. The Ḥabiru, who were causing so much trouble in Palestine in the fourteenth century B.C., and who are identified by some with the Hebrews entering the land under Joshua,[3] were polytheistic. For we find references to "the gods of the Ḥabiru".[4] Many of the personal names which we find in Israel

[1] V. Hamp expresses some surprise that I should make this statement (*Sacra Pagina*, I, 1959, p. 518). As I say below, it is hardly to be denied that Shaddai, El, Elyon, and Yahweh were originally separate deities. Moreover, the patriarchs are represented as worshipping at the shrines of local deities, associated with stones, springs, and trees, and while I do not subscribe to the common view that the patriarchs are sufficiently to be described as animists, I cannot see how their worship at these shrines can be thought of as other than the recognition of the existence of more than one god. In Jos. 24 we are told that on completing the conquest of the land of Canaan the people buried their strange gods at Shechem. This would imply that their polytheism had persisted to this time. It is true that I associate this story with things recorded in the book of Genesis (cf. *From Joseph to Joshua*, 1950, pp. 126 ff.), and hold that the transfer of the burying of strange gods from the time of Jacob to the time of Joshua has taken place. But in either case the story testifies to pre-Mosaic polytheism in Israel, since it can hardly be supposed that a people who had hitherto always worshipped a single god began to be polytheistic during the wandering and conquest, when they had Moses and Joshua as their leaders, and when during this very period they had entered into covenant with Yahweh and had been given the Mosaic Decalogue.

[2] On monotheistic tendencies in Babylonian religion by the exaltation of a single god and the ascription of supreme power to him, cf. B. Baentsch, *op. cit.* pp. 33 ff.; J. Hehn, *Die Biblische und die babylonische Gottesidee*, 1913, pp. 16 ff.; P. Heinisch, *Theologie des Alten Testamentes*, 1940, pp. 27 f.

[3] For my reasons for rejecting this view, cf. *From Joseph to Joshua*, 1950, pp. 39 ff. On the complex problem of the relation of the Ḥabiru to the Hebrews, much of the literature will be found cited there. Cf. also now J. Bottéro, *Le Problème des Ḥabiru*, 1956, and M. Greenberg, *The Ḥab/piru*, 1955.

[4] Cf. A. Jirku, *O.L.Z.* XXIV, 1921, pp. 246 f.; A. Gustavs, *Z.A.W.* XL, 1922, pp. 313 f.; B. Landsberger, *Kleinasiatische Forschungen*, I, 1929, pp. 326 f.

testify to the polytheistic background out of which they emerged. Alt has argued that each of the patriarchs, Abraham, Isaac, and Jacob, had his own special God.[1] Moreover, while in the Old Testament Shaddai, El, Elyon, and Yahweh are all equated and identified, it is hardly to be denied that they were once regarded as separate deities.[2]

The Egyptian heretic king, Akhenaten, is often supposed to have been the source of Mosaic monotheism.[3] Even Albright has lent some countenance to this, saying: "A priori, we shall expect that Israelite monotheism would come into existence in an age when monotheistic tendencies were evident in other parts of the ancient world, and not at a time when no such movements can be traced. Now it is precisely between 1500 and 1200 B.C., i.e. in the Mosaic age, that we find the closest approach to monotheism in the Gentile world before the Persian period."[4] The evolutionary presuppositions of this statement will not escape notice. It is commonly said that Akhenaten was a monotheist, because he suppressed the worship of all gods save one in Egypt. It is not certain, however, that he was a genuine monotheist in the sense of believing that only one

[1] Cf. *Der Gott der Väter*, 1929 (reprinted in *Kleine Schriften zur Geschichte des Volkes Israel,* I, 1953, pp. 1 ff.). Abraham is held to have worshipped "the God of Abraham", Isaac "the Fear of Isaac", and Jacob "the Mighty One of Jacob". E. A. Leslie (*Old Testament Religion,* 1936, pp. 67 f.) suggests that the name of Abraham's God was "the Shield of Abraham" (Gen. 15:1), and W. F. Albright (*F.S.A.C.,* pp. 188 f., 327) renders the title of Isaac's God "the Kinsman of Isaac" (accepted by O. Eissfeldt, *J.S.S.* I, 1956, p. 32 n.). J. P. Hyatt (*V.T.* v, 1955, pp. 130 ff.), on the basis of Alt's theory, argues that Yahweh was originally the patron deity of one of Moses' ancestors (p. 135). R. de Vaux (in *Initiation Biblique,* ed. by A. Robert and A. Tricot, 3rd edn., 1954, pp. 888 f.) holds that the patriarchs were monotheists, while C. A. Simpson (*The Early Traditions of Israel,* 1948, p. 425) says: "Momentary monotheism was a characteristic of primitive Jahvism from the first, necessary because of the very nature of the religion."

[2] Cf. H. G. May, *J.B.L.* LX, 1941, pp. 113 ff.; also O. Eissfeldt, *J.S.S.* I, 1956, pp. 25 ff.

[3] Cf. J. N. Schofield, *The Religious Background of the Bible,* 1944, p. 78: "Even the claim that this man, 'learned in all the wisdom of the Egyptians', was the founder of a moral monotheism is easily intelligible when we remember the monotheism of Akhenaten." Against this view cf. A. Lods, *Israel,* Eng. trans., pp. 318 ff., and *R.H.P.R.* XIV, 1934, pp. 173 ff.

[4] Cf. *The Archaeology of Palestine and the Bible,* 1932, p. 163.

God existed, and that therefore He was the only legitimate object of worship for all men. Mercer, indeed, denies that he was a monotheist.[1] In all true monotheism universalism is involved,[2] and there is little evidence that Akhenaten was concerned with the world that lay beyond his empire. His religious reform is believed by some to have had a political, rather than a genuinely spiritual, basis.[3] Yet even though we allow that Akhenaten was a monotheist, it does not follow that Moses was influenced by his ideas.[4] For if Moses took an important step on the road to monotheism, he took it along an entirely different

[1] Cf. *J.S.O.R.* x, 1926, pp. 14 ff; cf. also Pettazzoni, *R.H.R.*, *loc. cit.* pp. 197 f. J. A. Wilson (*The Burden of Egypt*, 1951, p. 223) says: "The most important observation about Amarna religion is that there were two gods central to the faith, and not one. Akh-en-Aton and his family worshipped the Aton, and everybody else worshipped Akh-en-Aton *as a god.*" Cf. p. 224: "The fact that only the royal family had a trained and reasoned loyalty to the Aton and the fact that all of Pharaoh's adherents were forced to give their entire devotion to him as a god-king explain why the new religion collapsed after Akh-en-Aton's death." L. A. White (*J.A.O.S.* LVIII, 1948, pp. 91 ff.) maintains that Akhenaten originated virtually nothing. A. Lods (*loc. cit.* p. 319) says: "The speculations of the priestly colleges of Thebes or Memphis concerning the unity of the divine, and the attempted reform of Amenophis IV, spring either from pantheism or from monarchical polytheism, and hence are of an entirely different character from the *moral* monotheism of the Israelites." P. Heinisch (*op. cit.* p. 29) similarly says of Akhenaten's religion: "Doch ist diese Religion nicht Monotheismus, sondern Pantheismus." Cf. W. A. Irwin, in *The Intellectual Adventure of Ancient Man*, 1946, p. 225: "Whatever one is to say of the still unsolved problem of Akhnaton's alleged monotheism, it was at the best quite different from and inferior to Israel's." Cf. also P. van Imschoot, *Théologie de l'Ancien Testament*, I, p. 18 n.; W. W. von Baudissin, *D.L.Z.* xxxv, 1914, cols. 5 ff.; A. Jirku, *G.V.I.*, 1931, pp. 80 f.; and A. Loisy, *La Religion d'Israël*, 3rd edn., 1933, p. 98; Th. C. Vriezen, *An Outline of Old Testament Theology*, Eng. trans., p. 24; J. M. A. Janssen, in *Dictionnaire encyclopédique de la Bible*, 1960, col. 506.

[2] Cf. Meek, *J.B.L.*, *loc. cit.* pp. 36 f.: "Monotheism to be monotheism must transcend national limitations; it must be supernatural and universal." Cf. also H. G. May, *J.B.R.* xvi, 1948, pp. 100 ff.

[3] Cf. A. Causse, *Les Prophètes d'Israël et les religions de l'Orient*, 1913, pp. 280 f.; H. W. Fairman, in Hastings' one volume *D.B.*, revised edn., ed. by F. C. Grant and H. H. Rowley, 1963, p. 234 b.

[4] A. Lods (*R.H.P.R.* xiv, 1934, pp. 197 ff.) denies that Israelite monotheism was derived from any foreign source. Cf. J. A. Wilson, *op. cit.*, pp. 225 f.

road from that of Akhenaten, whose religion fell far short of the significant heights reached by Moses.[1]

The religious achievement of Moses was not something that grew naturally out of his environment or circumstances, and the ideas that he mediated to Israel were not derived from Egypt or from any other people. Certainly they were not ideas that were floating around in that age.[2] "The real source of Hebrew monotheism", says Wardle, "we should probably find in the religious experience of Moses which underlies the tradition of Exodus 3."[3] Here we read that Yahweh sent Moses into Egypt to a people that did not worship God by the name Yahweh, to announce that He had chosen Israel and would redeem them from their bondage. Later, when the people came out of Egypt, they repaired to the sacred mount, where the covenant bond was established between Israel and God. This covenant was the pledge of loyalty given by Israel in response to the deliverance already achieved. This was quite other than the bond between Chemosh and Moab, and it is this which distinguishes Mosaic religion from ordinary henotheism.

It is commonly believed that Yahweh was the God of the Kenites before He became the God of Israel.[4] In recent years it has been claimed that the divine name Yahweh is found at

[1] Cf. Wardle, *Z.A.W.*, *loc. cit.* p. 209: "Such 'latent monotheism' as we find in Egypt or Babylon is quite different from Old Testament monotheism." Cf. my *Missionary Message of the Old Testament*, p. 20. Cf. also J. A. Wilson (*op. cit.* p. 226), who notes the "marked lack of ethical content in the hymns directed to the Aton." The same point is noted by K. A. Kitchen (in *The New Bible Dictionary*, 1962, p. 351), who denies that the origin of Mosaic monotheism is to be sought here.

[2] W. Eichrodt (*Theology of the Old Testament*, Eng. trans., p. 220) well draws attention to the fact that Israelite monotheism did not begin as a speculation, saying: "There can be no question at the beginning of the nation's history of any absolute monotheism in the full sense of the word . . . The study of the history of religions shows quite clearly that the level of a religion is not determined by the question whether or not it is acquainted with monotheism. However precious this particular understanding of God may be, it cannot be described as decisive for the truth of a religion. To believe that it can is typical of the rationalistic treatment of religion, which assesses it solely by its quality as an intellectual construction."

[3] *Loc. cit.* p. 198.

[4] Cf. B. Stade, *G.V.I.* I, 1887, pp. 130 f., and *Biblische Theologie des Alten Testaments*, I, 1905, pp. 42 f.; T. K. Cheyne, *E. Bib.* III, 1902, col. 3208;

Ras Shamra, where Yw figures as the son of El.[1] This is very uncertain,[2] however, and for our purpose is of little importance, since it is unlikely that the Israelites took over their worship of K. Budde, *Religion of Israel to the Exile*, 1899, pp. 17 ff.; W. Vischer, *Jahwe der Gott Kains*, 1929; A. J. Wensinck, *Semietische Studiën uit de Nalatenschap von A.J.W.*, 1941, pp. 23–50. Amongst other scholars who adopt this view are G. A. Barton, *A Sketch of Semitic Origins*, 1902, pp. 272 ff.; H. Gressmann, *Mose und seine Zeit*, 1913, pp. 434 f., 447 ff.; H. P. Smith, *The Religion of Israel*, 1914, pp. 50 f.; J. Morgenstern, *H.U.C.A.* IV, 1927, pp. 44 ff.; A. Lods, *Israel*, Eng. trans., pp. 316 ff.; H. Schmökel, *J.B.L.* LIII, 1933, pp. 212 ff.; Oesterley and Robinson, *Hebrew Religion*, 2nd edn., pp. 147 ff.; G. Beer, *Exodus* [H.A.T.], 1939, p. 30; M. Noth, *Evangelische Theologie*, 1946, p. 309; B. D. Eerdmans, *The Religion of Israel*, 1947, pp. 14 ff.; I. G. Matthews, *The Religious Pilgrimage of Israel*, pp. 49 f.; E. A. Leslie, *Old Testament Religion*, 1947, pp. 80, 83 f.; L. Koehler, *Old Testament Theology*, Eng. trans. by A. S. Todd, 1957, pp. 45 f.; H. Cazelles, in *Moïse, l'homme de l'Alliance*, 1955, p. 18; G. von Rad, *Old Testament Theology*, Eng. trans. by D. M. G. Stalker, I, 1962, pp. 9 f.; J. Gray, in *Peake's Commentary on the Bible*, ed. by M. Black and H. H. Rowley, 1962, p. 113 a; G. W. Anderson, *ibid.* p. 161 b; D. M. G. Stalker, *ibid.* pp. 212 a, 226 a. I indicated my adherence to this view in *The Missionary Message of the Old Testament*, pp. 12 ff., and *From Joseph to Joshua*, 1950, pp. 149 ff. M. Burrows (*An Outline of Biblical Theology*, p. 56) thinks it is very probable, but uncertain. B. W. Anderson (*Understanding the Old Testament*, 1957, p. 36) finds it attractive, but says: "The honest truth is that we do not know for sure the source from which Moses received the name Yahweh," adding that "the important point is what the name stood for in the worship of Israel from the time of Moses on."

[1] Cf. R. Dussaud, *R.H.R.* cv, 1932, p. 247, *C.R.A.I.,* 1940, pp. 364 ff., and *Les Découvertes de Ras Shamra et l'Ancien Testament*, 2nd edn., 1941, pp. 171 f.; H. Bauer, *Z.A.W.,* N.F. x, 1933, pp. 92 ff.; O. Eissfeldt, *J.P.O.S.* XIV, 1934, pp. 298 f.; A. Vincent, *La Religion des Judéo-Araméens d'Eléphantine*, 1937, pp. 27 f.; Ch. Virolleaud, *La Déesse 'Anat*, 1938, p. 98; A. Murtonen, *A Philosophical and Literary Treatise on the Old Testament Divine Names*, 1952, pp. 49 f.; P. van Imschoot, *op. cit.* I, pp. 19 f. J. Lewy (*R.E.S.,* 1938, pp. 58, 71 f.) suggests that Yw was a Hurrian god.

[2] Cf. R. de Vaux, *R.B.* XLVI, 1937, pp. 552 f.; A. Bea, *Biblica*, xx, 1939, pp. 440 f.; W. F. Albright, *F.S.A.C.,* pp. 197, 328; C. H. Gordon, *Ugaritic Grammar*, 1940, p. 100; W. Baumgartner, *Th.R.,* N.F. xiii, 1941, pp. 159 f.; R. de Langhe, *Un Dieu Yahweh à Ras Shamra?* 1942; J. Gray, *J.N.E.S.* xii, 1953, pp. 278 ff. M. H. Pope (*Wörterbuch der Mythologie*, 1962, p. 291) says: "Einige Gelehrte wollen den Gott auch in einem ugar. Text finden, doch ist der Zusammenhang dunkel. Man kann für *jw* auch *jr* lesen und das Wort dann zu akkad. *ārum* 'Junges' stellen. Nach dem Kontext wird aber von Baals Feind Jamm gesprochen, und *jw* könnte mit einem Wechsel von *m* und *w* für *jm* stehen. Da aber sogar die Lesung unsicher ist, kann an einem Zusammenhang mit dem Gott Israels Jahwe nicht gedacht werden."

Yahweh from the people of Ugarit.[1] That the name Yahweh is older than the time of Moses, however, there is little reason to doubt.[2] It is easy to find a contradiction between Exod. 6: 2 f., which states that God was not known to the patriarchs by the name Yahweh, and passages in Genesis, which represent God as saying to the patriarchs "I am Yahweh". It is less easy to estimate the significance of this contradiction. Obviously both cannot be precisely true. It has long been held, however, that the Israelite incursion into Canaan was in two waves, widely separated in time. Only one of these waves could have been led by Moses, and it could well be that he introduced the worship of God under the name Yahweh to the group he led, while the group he did not lead reached its worship of Yahweh otherwise. There could thus be substance in both of the traditions preserved in the Bible, and it is only the attempt to impose a unity on them and to make them tell of a single stream of history that is responsible for the contradiction.

It is improbable that the Israelites had worshipped Yahweh from time immemorial. Had they done so, and had the tribes that came out of Egypt been connected with the tribes that were not in Egypt by both blood and faith, there would have been no room for any tradition that Moses mediated Yahwism to them. So far as the tribes that were led by Moses are concerned, it is scarcely to be doubted that he introduced them to the worship of Yahweh as their God. It is true that by syncretism he identified Yahweh with the God their fathers had worshipped, but in so doing he made it clear that Yahweh was a new name by which they were to worship their God. This does not mean that it was a completely new name for God, first heard on the lips of Moses. The name may not have been an unknown name even to the Israelites in Egypt, though it was not the name they had hitherto used for their own God.

I have already said that it has long been a common view that Yahweh was the God of the Kenites before He was the God of Israel. Jethro, the father-in-law of Moses, was the priest of a God whose name is not given. So far back as 1862 it was sug-

---

[1] Cf. A. Bea, *Biblica*, *loc. cit.* p. 441; G. von Rad, *op. cit.* I, p. 11.

[2] E. Littmann (*A.f.O.* XI, 1936, p. 162) hazards the improbable suggestion that it is derived from the Aryan *Dyāu-s, from which Zeus and Jupiter are derived.

gested that he was the priest of Yahweh[1]. While this view has been rejected by a number of scholars,[2] and cannot claim to be certain, it seems to me to have all probability on its side. And in the absence of conclusive evidence we can only be guided by probabilities. We are not told the name of Jethro's God; but we are told that when Moses came out of Egypt with the Israelites, Jethro came to meet him, and that he was highly elated at the demonstration of the power of Yahweh in the deliverance of Israel. "Now I know that Yahweh is greater than all gods", he cried.[3] Buber objects that he could hardly have said this if Yahweh were his own God, for no one would make such an implied confession about his own God.[4] But this is scarcely cogent. Whatever belief in the power of Yahweh he might have cherished in the past, this unique demonstration of His power was something that could only have lifted it to a higher degree of knowledge and certainty. Buber supposes that Jethro was so impressed by this demonstration of the power of Yahweh that he forthwith identified his own God with Yahweh,[5] but of this there is no hint in the story. Meek, on the other hand, thinks that Jethro was converted to the worship of Yahweh by this proof of His power.[6] Yet again, not only is there

[1] By F. W. Ghillany, under the pseudonym of von der Alm, according to H. Holzinger, *Exodus* [K.H.C.], 1900, p. 3, and J. Coppens, *Histoire Critique,* 3rd edn., p. 47 n.

[2] So by A. R. Gordon, *The Early Traditions of Genesis,* 1907, pp. 106 ff.; E. König, *Geschichte der alttestamentlichen Religion,* 1912, pp. 162 ff.; R. Kittel, *G.V.I.* 1, 6th edn., p. 392 n.; C. Toussaint, *Les Origines de la Religion d'Israël,* 1931, p. 225; P. Volz, *Mose und seine Werk,* 2nd edn., 1932, p. 59; W. J. Phythian-Adams, *The Call of Israel,* 1934, pp. 72 ff.; T. J. Meek, *Hebrew Origins,* 1936, pp. 86 ff., 2nd edn., 1950, pp. 94 ff.; M. Buber, *Moses,* 1947, pp. 94 ff.; F. V. Winnett, *The Mosaic Tradition,* 1949, p. 69; O. Procksch, *Theologie des Alten Testaments,* pp. 76 f.; A.-J. Baumgartner, in *Dictionnaire encyclopédique de la Bible,* ed. by A. Westphal, II, 1935, pp. 181 f. E. Kautzsch (*D.B.,* Extra Vol., 1904, pp. 626 f.) regards the Kenite hypothesis as possible, but improbable.

[3] Exod. 18: 11.

[4] *Op. cit.* p. 95.

[5] *Ibid.* p. 98.

[6] Cf. *Hebrew Origins,* p. 88, 2nd edn., pp. 94 f., and *A.J.S.L.* xxxvii, 1920–21, p. 104. J. Coppens (*op. cit.* p. 47 n.) says: "L'insuffisance de l'hypothèse qénite est reconnue par Theophile James Meek . . . , mais cet auteur ne réussit pas à nous donner une meilleure explication des origines du Jahvisme."

no hint of this in the story, but the sequel gives quite another impression. For Jethro offers sacrifice, and presides at the sacred meal which follows.[1] Buber here stresses the fact that the sacrifice is offered to Elohim and not to Yahweh,[2] but it can hardly be supposed that the demonstration of the power of Yahweh in the deliverance of the Israelites would lead forthwith to the sacrifice to some other god.[3] Nor is it clear why Jethro should officiate as priest and preside at the sacred feast unless his own God was being approached. If, however, it were his own God, it would be clear why he should preside. For none but he was a properly initiated priest of his God. In the sacred feast we should then have the first incorporation of the Israelite leaders into the worship of Yahweh. Certainly there is nothing in the story to suggest that Jethro was being initiated into the worship of Yahweh, as Meek supposes; for it is unusual for a novice to preside at his own initiation.

Further, Jethro gives to Moses instruction and advice as to the administration of justice,[4] which was regarded as a religious rather than a civil function. All of this suggests that Jethro was acting not merely as the father-in-law of Moses, but as the priest.[5] For Moses is not represented as a youth, needing riper experience to guide him in managing the people. The man who had stood before Pharaoh and who had led Israel out of Egypt was not lacking in personality or natural wisdom. On that side there was little that he needed from Jethro. But of technical knowledge pertaining to the priestly duties Jethro could speak.

A Dutch writer, C. H. W. Brekelmans, has offered some criticism of what I have published on this subject,[6] and has suggested that Jethro was a chief rather than a priest, and that he came to meet Moses to supplicate for a treaty with him.

[1] Exod. 18: 12.
[2] *Op. cit.* p. 95.
[3] H. Gressmann (*Mose und seine Zeit*, 1913, p. 163) says: "Wie kann Jethro, der ausdrücklich als Priester der Midianiter bezeichnet wird, Jahwe als den Höchsten aller Götter feiern? Das ist nur dann verständlich, wenn Jahwe auch der Gott der Midianiter ist." Cf. also Oesterley and Robinson, *Hebrew Religion*, 2nd edn., p. 148.
[4] Exod. 18: 13 ff.
[5] Cf. G. B. Gray, *Sacrifice in the Old Testament*, 1925, p. 208.
[6] Cf. *O.T.S.* x, 1954, pp. 215 ff.

The sacrifice is said to have been for the ratification of the treaty. Of this there is once more no suggestion whatever in the story. Brekelmans says it may have been the custom for the suppliant for the treaty to preside at the meal which marked its ratification.[1] But it can hardly be supposed that it was customary for the suppliant for a treaty to give instructions as to how justice should be administered. Brekelmans says that if Jethro had offered priestly instructions they should have been offered to Aaron and his sons rather than to Moses.[2] But this is to ignore the fact that up to this point there had been no suggestion that Aaron was to be appointed to the priestly office.[3] Jethro would have needed prophetic foresight, as well as priestly knowledge, for this.

That the Kenites were Yahweh worshippers is suggested by other passages. Cain is the eponymous ancestor of the Kenites,[4] and he is said to have borne the mark of Yahweh upon him.[5] Moreover, in the days of Jehu's revolution, Jonadab, the son of Rechab, is a devotee of Yahweh,[6] and we learn from the book of Chronicles—itself confessedly late—that the Rechabites were of Kenite stock.[7] The same passage associates the Calebites and the Kenites.[8] To this we shall return below.

It has been claimed that there is one item of extra-Biblical evidence supporting the Kenite hypothesis. This is in the form of an Egyptian text in which the place name Yhw is found, referring to a spot quite certainly in the neighbourhood of

[1] *Ibid.* p. 221.

[2] *Ibid.* p. 223.

[3] R. de Vaux (*Ancient Israel: its Life and Institutions*, Eng. trans. by J. McHugh, 1961, pp. 394 f.) notes that in the oldest traditions of the Pentateuch Aaron is a rather hazy figure, and that though he stands at the side of Moses during the battle against the Amalekites, at the meeting with Jethro, and at Sinai, he is not in any of these traditions referred to as a priest or an ancestor of priests.

[4] Cf. Jg. 4: 11, where the Kenites are called Cain in the Hebrew, just as the Israelites are often called Israel.

[5] Gen. 4: 15. Cf. Stade, *Z.A.W.* xiv, 1894, pp. 250 ff, and W. Vischer, *Jahwe, der Gott Kains,* 1929, pp. 40 ff.

[6] 2 Kg. 10: 15 ff. Cf. Jer. 35.

[7] 1 Chr. 2: 55. On the Kenites in the genealogical lists of the Chronicler cf. R. Eisler, *Le Monde oriental,* xxiii, 1929, pp. 99 ff.

[8] The verse cited stands at the end of the genealogy of the descendants of Caleb.

Kenite settlements, and dating from the time of Rameses II.[1] Amongst the other places mentioned in the context are Seir, Laban,[2] and Sham'ath,[3] all of which have Edomite or Midianite connections.[4] It is of particular interest to note that this text is dated *circa* 1300 B.C., in the age to which I assign the life and work of Moses,[5] and Grdseloff, who published the text, observed that it renders the Kenite origin of Yahwism more probable.[6]

I cannot here discuss how this illuminates the whole complex of Israelite tradition. The tribes which pressed into the land from the south in the pre-Mosaic age included Judah and some Kenite and Calebite elements, as we are told in the Bible.[7] If these were Yahweh-worshipping people, the worship of Yahweh might have spread from them throughout the group of associated tribes by infiltration. There was no moment of dramatic acceptance of the worship of Yahweh, any more than there was any moment of the dramatic acceptance of Baal after the settlement of Israel in Canaan. Hence, in the southern corpus of traditions which we know as J, the worship of Yahweh is represented as going back to the beginnings of time.[8]

---

[1] Cf. B. Grdseloff, *Bulletin des Études historiques juives*, i, 1946, pp. 81 f.

[2] Cf. Laban in Dt. 1: 1, with which Grdseloff would connect it.

[3] Cf. 1 Chr. 2: 55, where the Shimeathites are mentioned in association with the Kenites.

[4] On the connections between the Kenites and the Midianites, see below, p. 55, n. 1. On the connections between the Kenites and the Edomites, cf. N. Glueck, *P.E.Q.* 1940, pp. 22 f. Cf. also J. Morgenstern, *Amos Studies*, i, 1941, pp. 251 f.: "Of the Kenites themselves we know very little. They were a semi-nomadic tribe . . . whose normal abode . . . centred in the extreme south of Judah and in the border sections of Edom." It may also be noted that several passages seem to locate the sacred mountain to which Moses led the Israelites in the Edomite or Midianite territory. Cf. Jg. 5: 4; Dt. 33: 2; Hab. 3: 3,7. On this cf. H. S. Nyberg, *Z̧.D.M.G.*, N.F. xvii, 1938, pp. 337 f.

[5] See *From Joseph to Joshua* for my discussion of this question.

[6] *Loc. cit.* p. 82.

[7] Jg. 1: 3-20. For evidence of the association of the Kenites with Judah cf. also 1 Sam. 27: 10, 30: 26 ff.

[8] Cf. Gen. 4: 26, where it is said that in the days of Seth, the son of Adam, men began to call on the name of Yahweh, and Gen. 4: 1, where it is said that the name of Yahweh was on the lips of Eve when she bore her first child.

These tribes were not with Moses, and in their traditions the beginnings of Yahwism in Israel are not connected with him. On the other hand, the tribes that came out of Egypt with Moses were introduced to the worship of Yahweh by him and by the Kenite Jethro,[1] after a memorable experience of deliverance, followed by the covenant of Sinai. The tribes led by Moses consisted principally of the Joseph tribes, and it is not therefore surprising that in the northern corpus of traditions, which we know as E, the beginnings of Yahwism are associated with Moses. The divergence between the two traditions is not, therefore, a meaningless contradiction. There is substance behind both.

It is sometimes suggested that the name of Moses' mother is the Achilles' heel of the whole Kenite theory. For she was called Jochebed, and this name appears to be compounded with the divine name Yahweh.[2] If, then, Moses' mother bore a theophorous name compounded with Yahweh before he was born, it cannot be supposed that he introduced the name Yahweh to the Israelites who were in Egypt. To counter this argument it is sometimes noted that our evidence for the name Jochebed is found only in the late Priestly source,[3] or even that it is not certain that it is compounded with Yahweh.[4] It is unnecessary to resort to either shift. If there were Yahweh-worshipping Kenites associated with the Israelites who entered Canaan from the south in the pre-Mosaic age, it would not be surprising for there to be some intermarriage between the

[1] Jethro is said to have been a priest of Midian in Exod. 3: 1; 18: 1, as is Hobab in Num. 10: 29. But in Jg. 4: 11 Hobab is called a Kenite. D. Nielsen (*The Site of the Biblical Mount Sinai*, 1928, p. 9) says: "The relation between Midianites and Kenites is not quite clear . . . The Kenites must either be a subdivision, a clan of the Midianite tribe, or, on account of their living on the border of the Midianites, are reckoned among them by Israelite tradition."
[2] Cf. Meek, *Hebrew Origins*, p. 91, 2nd edn., p. 97; G. Vos, *Biblical Theology*, 1948, p. 130.
[3] Exod. 6: 20; Num. 26: 59. Hence J. M. Powis Smith (*A.J.S.L.* xxxv, 1918–19, p. 15) thinks it need not be taken seriously.
[4] G. B. Gray (*Hebrew Proper Names*, 1896, p. 156) does not think the author of P connected the name with the Tetragrammaton, and M. Noth (*Die israelitischen Personennamen*, 1928, p. 111) questions whether it should be so connected.

associated tribes. Amongst these tribes there were some Levites,[1] and such intermarriage could bring a Levite family into association with a Kenite family, and so bring a Kenite name into a Levite home.[2] It is probable that the Levites and the Simeonites in this early wave of immigration reached Shechem, where they were guilty of some act of treachery, now reflected in Gen. 34, as the result of which they were "scattered in Israel", as the Blessing of Jacob indicates.[3] Some of the Levites then appear to have gone into Egypt, and amongst them the ancestor of Moses' mother, who had married a Kenite woman. It is well known that names tend to recur in families, and this Kenite name might have been passed down to become the name of Moses' mother, without involving any worship of Yahweh. This means that there was probably some Kenite blood in Moses, though derived at a distance through his mother.

This in turn explains why Moses fled to Jethro when he was forced to flee from Egypt. When Jacob left home through fear of his brother's wrath, he fled to his mother's kindred.[4] For Moses to do the same would therefore be most natural.[5] If he

[1] Jg. 1: 3 f. indicates that Simeon and Judah were associated in their entry into the land. On the other hand, Gen. 34 indicates that Simeon and Levi were associated in some act of violence in the Shechem area, and Gen. 49: 5 ff. brings these two tribes under a common curse. This last passage must be very ancient, going back to a time before Levi had become a priestly tribe. On the other hand, the book of Judges comes from a time after the Levites had assumed the priesthood, and this may account for the omission of any mention of Levi in the account of the conquest of the land. Ostensibly Gen. 34 deals with a time prior to the descent into Egypt and Jg. 1 with a time after the Exodus from Egypt. On this cf. my *From Joseph to Joshua*, pp. 109 ff.

[2] So Egyptian names are found amongst Jews in Elephantine. Cf. G. B. Gray, *Wellhausen Festschrift*, 1914, pp. 174 f.

[3] Gen. 49: 7.

[4] Gen. 27: 43.

[5] J. P. Hyatt (*V.T.* v, 1955, pp. 135 f.) suggests that the ancestor of Moses, whose God Yahweh was (see above, p. 46, n. 1), may have been in his mother's line, and that the family of Moses may have been in Egypt but a short time before Moses was born, and have come from Midian, and that this would account for his flight to Midian. This is held to be preferable to the view that Yahweh was the God of Moses' father-in-law, and Hyatt states (p. 130) that this view is based directly on Biblical evidence, as

knew that his mother was of Kenite descent, he could repair to a Kenite settlement without fear, knowing that he had some claim on them.

It is often supposed that the Kenite theory of the source of the divine name Yahweh reduces the work of Moses to the mere mediation to the tribes he led of the religion of his father-in-law.[1] Nothing can be farther from the truth. If Yahwism was the worship of the Kenites from time immemorial and none knew how it had begun amongst them, then it was fundamentally different for the tribes Moses led by the mere fact of the unforgettable experience through which they were led to it.[2] It was always associated amongst them with the memory of the deliverance they had experienced. Moreover, it is not to be supposed that Moses simply transferred to Israel the Yahwism of his father-in-law without change, and that such development as took place in their religion in the course of time just happened by itself with the mere passing of the years. It is antece-

against the speculative character of the Kenite hypothesis (p. 130). It offers no explanation of the Biblical statement that Cain, the eponymous ancestor of the Kenites, is represented as bearing the mark of Yahweh, or of the part played by Jethro in the Biblical story mentioned above. It connects Moses through his mother with the tribe to which Jethro belonged no less than the Kenite hypothesis does, and traces the origin of the worship of Yahweh to that tribe just as much, but to an obscure element of the tribe instead of to the whole of the group to which Jethro belonged.

[1] Cf. Meek, *op. cit.* p. 92, 2nd edn., p. 98. Cf. A. Fridrichsen, in *S.B.U.* II, 1952, col. 320, where it is suggested that this view but explains "ignotus ab ignoto".

[2] Cf. J. Meinhold, *Einführung in das Alte Testament*, 3rd edn., 1932, p. 59: "Wichtiger als die Frage, woher der Kult stammte, ist die, was Moses aus ihm machte." Cf. *B.J.R.L.* XXXIV, 1951–52, p. 100: "More important than the name of the deity is the character of the religion, and there is every reason to think that Moses gave a new character to Yahwism as compared with Kenite Yahwism." Cf. also *The Re-discovery of the Old Testament*, pp. 84 f. H. Cazelles (*Moïse, l'homme de l'Alliance*, 1955, p. 18) observes: "Ceci ne veut pas dire que la religion de Moïse soit un emprunt à la religion des Madianites." Cf. also R. H. Pfeiffer, *Religion in the Old Testament*, 1961, p. 56: "The contribution of the Kenites or others could have been merely the name *Yahweh* . . . Whether Jehovah was the god of the Kenites, of a shrine, of a mountain, the fact remains that he saved Israel from annihilation . . . A peculiar experience colored the religion of Israel, a critical episode, a historic event never to be forgotten."

dently likely that under the influence of a great leader, and in the circumstances of Israel's adoption of Yahwism, some new quality would be given to their faith.[1]

Yahweh had first chosen Israel in her weakness and oppressed condition, and had sent Moses in His name to rescue her from her bondage, though she did not hitherto worship Him. Then Israel in her gratitude pledged herself to this God in undeviating loyalty. That her pledge was not always kept is clear from the record of the Old Testament itself, but the taking of the pledge was a new and highly significant thing in the history of religion. Meek here objects that there was nothing new in this, since many a people has adopted another religion.[2] It is perfectly true that there have been many cases of the adoption of a foreign religion. Sometimes it has been imposed upon a subject people, or even readily adopted because of the prestige of a powerful people; sometimes, as in the case of Kenite religion among the southern tribes, it has spread by gradual penetration among peoples closely associated with one another, and intermarrying with one another; sometimes by infiltration from a neighbouring people, as frequently in the story of Israel. But here there is nothing of such a character. Here Israel's adoption of Yahweh was the response to His adoption of Israel, and the sequel to His achieved deliverance of her. Israel's covenant with Yahweh in the time of Moses was based on what God had done, and on Israel's gratitude for His deliverance.

It is probable that Moses gave a new Decalogue to the tribes he led. It is well known that in Exod. 34 we have what was once most probably a more primitive Decalogue than that contained in Exod. 20 and Dt. 5. In its present form we have more than ten commands in Exod. 34, but probably there were originally ten.[3] This decalogue, the Ritual Decalogue as it is often called, is usually assigned to the J document, which is

---

[1] Cf. J. Bright, *The History of Israel*, 1960, p. 116: "We may be quite certain that through Moses Yahwism was given a new content and made into a new thing."

[2] *Op. cit.* pp. 89 f., 2nd edn., p. 96.

[3] For literature on this Decalogue and for a number of proposed reductions to ten commands, cf. *B.J.R.L.* xxxiv, 1951–52, pp. 90 f. n.

associated with those southern tribes that Moses did not lead.[1]
Morgenstern thinks this decalogue was a Kenite decalogue.[2]
I have argued that it was of Kenite origin,[3] though it has come
to us through Israelites whom Moses did not lead, and who
may have gradually modified some of the original provisions
after their entry into Canaan, and who may have added the
agricultural festivals, which would not figure in the old Kenite
Decalogue. On the other hand, Moses gave to the tribes he led
another Decalogue, which is now expanded into the two forms
it has in Exod. 20 and Dt. 5.[4] This is often called the Ethical
Decalogue, because it is more interested in conduct than in
ritual, and even penetrates to the spring of conduct in motive.
It does not seem unreasonable to me that a new Decalogue
with a higher quality should be given to Israel by Moses when
a Covenant based on gratitude, which is itself an ethical
emotion, as fear and anger are not, was being mediated. Hence
I do not take the view that the work of Moses is to be resolved
into the mere mediation to Israel of the religion of the Kenites.
The divine name Yahweh was probably taken over, and the
forms of the religion; but a new spirit was given to the religion
and a new level to its demands. The sense of Yahweh's election
of Israel, of His deliverance, of His claims upon her obedience,
were all new, and through the truly prophetic personality of
Moses it was established on a higher basis than Kenite religion
had reached. That difference of level may be realized by the
comparison of the two Decalogues.

In all this there are the seeds of monotheism.[5] The God, or
gods, hitherto worshipped by the Israelites were identified with

---

[1] A few scholars hold that it is late and secondary. Cf. B. D. Eerdmans,
Alttestamentliche Studien, III, 1910, pp. 85 ff.; R. H. Pfeiffer, *J.B.L.* XLIII, 1924,
pp. 294 ff.; P. Heinisch, *Das Buch Exodus* [H.S.A.Tes], 1934, p. 243; F. V.
Winnett, *The Mosaic Tradition*, 1949, p. 54. E. Robertson (*The Old Testament Problem*, 1950, p. 94) holds that it is not an original decalogue, but a
midrashic expansion of the basic Decalogue, or of its parts.

[2] Cf. *H.U.C.A.* IV, 1927, pp. 54 ff.

[3] Cf. *B.J.R.L.*, *loc. cit.* pp. 88 ff.

[4] Cf. *B.J.R.L.*, *ibid.* pp. 100 ff., where I have defended this view.

[5] Cf. N. K. Gottwald, *A Light to the Nations*, 1959, p. 141: "Moses was no
monotheist but the quality of his henotheism made Jewish and Christian
monotheism possible." Cf. also G. W. Anderson, in *Peake's Commentary on
the Bible*, ed. by M. Black and H. H. Rowley, 1962, p. 162 a.

Yahweh, and ceased to count as against Him. There was no conflict between Yahweh and them. He just gathered them into Himself, and in so far as they had characteristics different from His, they ceased to have meaning for Moses. The name of Israel's God was henceforth Yahweh; but His character was not derived from her own or from Kenite traditions so much as from the redeeming acts which had brought blessing to Israel.

Here it is important to distinguish the syncretism of this process from ordinary syncretism, and particularly from the syncretism that identified Yahweh with Baal. There was always an undercurrent of feeling that Yahweh was not Baal, and in any time of national revival this found expression. Yahweh never gathered Baal into Himself, and refused to be swallowed up by Baal. Yet we never find any conflict between Yahweh and the God, or gods, of the patriarchs. They were negligible, save in so far as they were identified with Yahweh. All other gods, worshipped by other peoples, were entirely negligible. The gods of Egypt figure in the story of the deliverance of Israel, but Yahweh's conflict is not with them, but with Pharaoh; and they could be dropped from the story without varying its course.[1] This is not monotheism, and there is no reason to attribute universalism to Moses. Yet here we have surely the seeds of both.[2] It is not that Yahweh is merely supreme amongst the gods, their monarch and lord, to whom they are all subordinate. It is that all other gods are negligible beside Him or against Him.[3]

Moreover, Yahweh's power was not limited to a single land.

---

[1] Cf. my *Missionary Message of the Old Testament*, pp. 21 f.: "The Egyptian magicians figure in the story, trying to match their skill against that of Moses and Aaron, but the gods are an irrelevance, and Jehovah does as He pleases in the land of Egypt. This is more than the demand that though other gods may be real, Israel must not worship them. It is rather the declaration that though other gods may be real they are unimportant."

[2] A. Fridrichsen (*loc. cit.*) denies any speculative monotheism to Moses, but speaks of an "Ur-monotheism".

[3] Cf. E. Jacob, *Theology of the Old Testament*, Eng. trans., p. 39: "Before it is expressed in a well formulated monotheism, the faith of Israel is confident of the feebleness of the gods of the nations and contrasts that weakness to the living God."

He could be active in Egypt or in Palestine as freely as in His chosen seat.[1] A God who could thus be active wherever He wished, who could claim for Himself whatever people He wished, and beside whom no other gods counted, was no tribal or national god, and certainly not merely one of a host of gods. His "onliness" might not be affirmed; but His uniqueness is manifest. If He is not the only God, He is certainly more than one example—even the most important example—of the category of gods. Among all the gods He alone mattered, and He could do with Israel or with any other people what He would.

This is not monotheism, and it is unwise to exaggerate it into monotheism.[2] Nevertheless, it was incipient monotheism and incipient universalism, so that when full monotheism was achieved in Israel it came not by natural evolution out of something fundamentally different, but by the development of its own particular character.[3] In substance, therefore, this view is much closer to the view of Albright[4] than to the evolutionary view with which I began, though it refrains from ascribing full

[1] For the difference between this and the thought of Assyrian kings, cf. *The Biblical Doctrine of Election*, p. 60: "It is true that Assyrian kings claimed that their gods alone counted . . . but this was merely the reflexion of the self-glorification of the Assyrian kings . . . And when the Rabshakeh came to Jerusalem in the days of Hezekiah, he boasted that none of the gods of the nations had been able to deliver their people out of *his master's hand*. But in the story of the Exodus there is no suggestion of the prestige of Yahweh being enhanced by the exploits of His people. Here it is uniquely the case that Yahweh alone counts."

[2] O. S. Rankin (in *A Theological Word Book of the Bible*, ed. by A. Richardson, 1950, p. 92) observes: "Long after the time of Moses the religion of Israel remained monolatrous . . . The stage of monotheist belief, i.e. the belief which affirms that *only one* God exists, was only reached conclusively, as Old Testament literature shows, in the time of Deutero-Isaiah." G. von Rad (*Old Testament Theology*, Eng. trans. by D. M. G. Stalker, i, 1962, p. 211) says: "Monotheism as such was not a thing in which Israel of herself would have taken any particular interest."

[3] Cf. F. James, *Personalities of the Old Testament*, 1939, p. 32: "What he (i.e. Moses) gave Israel was a practical monotheism, out of which the later theoretical monotheism of a Second Isaiah naturally grew." Cf. G. R. Berry, *A.J.Th.* v, 1901, p. 262.

[4] Also cf. J. Bright, *The Kingdom of God*, pp. 24 f., and G. E. Wright, *The Old Testament against its Environment*, pp. 37 ff.

monotheism to Moses.[1] The development that followed was a development of the seed which Moses had already planted, and which came into Mosaic religion through the experience of Moses and the people, and not from any *Zeitgeist* or upsurge of the human spirit.[2] Moreover, when development came, it came through the personalities of the prophets, who can hardly be regarded as the expression of the Israelite life of their day. With the eighth and seventh century prophets we find incipient monotheism giving place increasingly to a more specific belief,[3]

[1] G. W. Anderson (*O.T.M.S.*, 1951, p. 290) says: "There is some danger of lapsing into mere logomachy in the debate about Mosaic monotheism; and it is well to remember both that the label matters less than the content of the packet, and also that it is inconvenient to have the same label for different things." With this I am in full agreement. In my view none of the labels, monotheist, henotheist, or any other, can fit the case with any precision. This is indeed clear from the fact that the scholars who claim monotheism for Moses have to define monotheism in unusual terms for their purpose. Cf. H. F. Hahn, *Old Testament in Modern Research*, 1954, pp. 101 f.: "To be unclear in the use of the pertinent terminology did not serve the purposes of good scholarship. What Baentsch called monotheism was sometimes no more than monarchical polytheism and at other times the henotheistic worship of one deity in preference to others whose existence was not thereby denied. It was never the belief in a single, unique deity to the exclusion of all others."

[2] Cf. T. K. Cheyne, *Expositor*, 4th series, v, 1892, p. 109: "My own historical sense emphatically requires that from the very beginning there should have been the germ of the advanced 'ethical monotheism' of the prophets." Also E. Sjöberg, *S.E.Å* xiv, 1949, p. 11: "Jahve var redan från början av en typ, som möjliggjorde en utveckling i den profetiska monoteismens riktning."

[3] Cf. what I have said in *The Re-discovery of the Old Testament*, 1946, p. 91: "With the eighth century prophets implicit monotheism becomes increasingly explicit. They emphasize Yahweh's sole control of the natural universe (Am. 4: 13; 5: 8) ... There is no categorical denial of the existence of other gods, but there is the clear implication that there can be no other God such as He ... This is still further emphasized by the conception of Yahweh's control of history." B. D. Eerdmans (*The Religion of Israel*, 1947, p. 96) observes that the thought of Deuteronomy has a strong tendency to monotheism, and this harmonizes with the view of Eichrodt (*Theology of the Old Testament*, Eng. trans., p. 221) that "not until the seventh century does the monotheistic formula appear which described Yahweh as the true God over all the kingdoms of the earth, the only God" (cf. 1 Kg. 8: 60; 2 Kg. 19: 15, 19 [on the date of which cf. *Re-discovery of the Old Testament*, p. 92 n.]; Dt. 4: 35; Jer. 2: 11; 10: 7; 16: 20). Cf. Jacob's account of the development of monotheism in Israel, *Theology of the Old Testament*, Eng. trans., pp. 44 ff.

and in Deutero-Isaiah we find the explicit formulation of monotheism with undeniable clarity.[1] The antiquity of monotheism in Israel may therefore be dated from the time of Moses, provided it is recognized that it was but the germ of monotheism in his day,[2] when a new impulse of incalculable significance to the world came into religion.[3]

---

[1] Cf. Isa. 44: 6, 8; 45: 5 f., 18, 21, 22. Moreover, Deutero-Isaiah drew from monotheism its corollary of universalism; cf. Isa. 42: 6; 45: 22; 49: 6. R. H. Pfeiffer (*J.B.L.* XLVI, 1947, pp. 193 ff.) argues that it is improper to speak of monotheism before Deutero-Isaiah, and presents the view that the monotheism of Deutero-Isaiah was the result of the combination of two distinct conceptions of God, the one a God of history, derived from the Israelite world and particularly from the prophets, and the other of a God of the physical world, derived from Edomite sources through the book of Job, which is improbably held to be older than Deutero-Isaiah. But surely we do not need to do more than cite Am. 5: 8 for evidence of the conception of Yahweh as the God of the physical world in Israel in pre-exilic days.

[2] Cf. W. A. Irwin, *The Old Testament: Keystone of Human Culture*, 1952, p. 24: "This belief (i.e. Mosaic religion) could lend itself to monotheistic evolution, as it actually did if this premise is correct; but it was yet some distance short of the concept of a single God of all men everywhere."

[3] Cf. what I have said in *The Re-discovery of the Old Testament*, p. 93: "Israel's monotheism came therefore through the progressive perception of the character and being of the God she worshipped. Never was He a pale abstraction, but an intensely personal Being, with a will and a character. Of the profoundest importance has it been to us that Christian monotheism was reached along this path. For it could never be an arid monotheism. Neither Greek monotheism, as developed by her philosophers, nor Indian pantheism could have led to the worship of the God and Father of our Lord Jesus Christ. But Israelite monotheism was as truly personal as our own." Cf. also J. Lindblom, in *Werden und Wesen des Alten Testaments* (B.Z.A.W. LXVI), 1936, p. 135.

3

The Meaning of Sacrifice in the Old Testament

3

THE MEANING OF SACRIFICE IN THE OLD TESTAMENT[1]

THE religion of Israel, like many other religions, employed a ritual of sacrifice, and not a little of the Pentateuch is taken up with the regulations governing that ritual. To many readers of the Old Testament this has little meaning today, since animal sacrifice has long ceased for the Jews, while for the Christians it is superseded. Yet it clearly played an important part in the life of ancient Israel,[2] and it demands more study from those who would understand the Old Testament than is commonly given to it.[3] To examine in detail all the sacrifices of which we learn is manifestly impossible in a single lecture,[4] and all that I can attempt is a rapid survey in the effort to find the function of sacrifice in Israelite thought.

The fact that Israel shared a sacrificial cultus with other ancient religions suggests that it came out of a wider background, and was not something that had its origin within her

[1] First published in *B.J.R.L.* xxxiii, 1950–51, pp. 74–110.

[2] H. Gressmann (*R.G.G.*, 1st edn., iv, 1913, col. 959) says: "Das Opfern war mit der Religion so selbstverständlich verbunden wie das Atmen mit dem Leben und brauchte daher nicht besonders eingeschärft zu werden."

[3] Cf., for instance, the scanty space given to the question of sacrifice in M. Burrows, *An Outline of Biblical Theology*, 1946, and O. J. Baab, *The Theology of the Old Testament*, 1949. Burrows says (p. 5): "Large areas of Hebrew religion, such as animal sacrifice or the veneration of sacred places, require relatively little attention, because they ceased to be important for the religion of the New Testament." The importance of Old Testament sacrifice is not negligible for the understanding of the New Testament, and still less for the understanding of the Old.

[4] The reader is referred for a fuller study to W. Robertson Smith, *The Religion of the Semites: the Fundamental Institutions*, 1889, 3rd edn., edited by S. A. Cook, 1927; G. B. Gray, *Sacrifice in the Old Testament: its Theory and Practice*, 1925; A. Wendel, *Das Opfer in der israelitischen Religion*, 1927; and W. O. E. Oesterley, *Sacrifices in Ancient Israel: their Origin, Purposes and Development*, 1927. Two long articles on the subject, still of value, are those of W. P. Paterson, in *D.B.* iv, 1902, pp. 329 ff.; and of G. F. Moore, in *E. Bib.* iv, 1907, cols. 4183 ff. Cf. also G. Widengren, *Religionens värld*, 1945, pp. 204 ff.

own tradition. With every side of her religion, indeed, this was so. It has long been impossible to think of her as receiving divine commands for the establishment and organization of her religion at a given point of her history without relation to her own past, or to the background of culture and religion in the contemporary world in which she lived.[1] More than ever has this become the case in recent years, in which our knowledge of that background has become rapidly richer and fuller. This does not mean, however—and I wish to make this quite clear at the outset—that the sufficient explanation of the Old Testament is to be found in the study of the thought and culture and practice of the surrounding peoples. Israel took over much, whose *origin* is therefore to be sought further back. Its *meaning*, however, is not necessarily to be sought further back. Often it was re-adapted and made the vehicle of her own faith and her own thought, and we have no right to assume that it was taken over unaltered in form or meaning.[2] For there was an element in her religion which she did not derive from any other people, but which was mediated to her through her own religious leaders, and especially through Moses, and what she took over was integrated into her own religion and made to serve its ends.

Again, however, I must guard myself against misunderstanding. Many of her people, and often her kings and leaders, sank to the level of contemporary thought and practice that had no relation to the God of Israel. They stand condemned within the pages of the Old Testament. They were practices which could not be integrated into the worship of Yahweh or made to serve its ends. For the religion of Yahwism was not a Nature religion, as the religion of Canaan was. Moreover, even the practices which were taken over could be interpreted in a

[1] For two quite different studies of Israel's development in the setting of her contemporary world, cf. W. C. Graham and H. G. May, *Culture and Conscience: an Archaeological Study of the New Religious Past in Ancient Palestine*, 1936, and W. F. Albright, *F.S.A.C.*, 1940 (2nd edn., 1946; German edn., revised, *Von der Steinzeit zum Christentum*, 1949).

[2] Cf. J. Pedersen, *Israel: its Life and Culture, III-IV*, 1940, p. 299: "The Israelite sacrifice does not differ much from that in common use among other Canaanite peoples, but to a certain extent it has acquired a special Israelitish character"; p. 317: "They"—i.e. the Israelites—"could independently appropriate the entire sacrificial cult, but also create new forms and new viewpoints from it."

Canaanite way, and no longer serve the ends of Israel's true religion. We can no longer, therefore, think of Israel's religion and Canaanite religion as set over against one another in sharp and complete antithesis, and engaged in a life and death struggle with one another. There was much that bound the two religions together, and not a little of Canaanite origin has survived in Judaism, so that the struggle was rather between the religion of Israel, that could adapt and reinterpret some elements of Canaanite religion but that had no place for others and that had a distinctive character of its own, and the religion of Canaan that retained those other elements and differently understood them all.

It will be clear from this that I do not propose to speak on the origin of sacrifice among men, or on the first meaning which it may have had. For such a discussion our net would have to be cast much more widely than in the Old Testament.[1] Suffice it to say that those who have conducted such an inquiry are not agreed as to its results. Of the various theories of the primary meaning of sacrifice we may note three:[2] (1) that the sacrifice was a communion offering that sought to bind the worshipper and the god together by their sharing in the body of the sacrificed animal;[3] (2) that the sacrifice was a gift presented to

[1] Cf. E. O. James, "Sacrifice (Introductory and Primitive)", in *E.R.E.* XI, 1920, pp. 1 ff., and *Origins of Sacrifice: A Study in Comparative Religion*, 1933, 2nd edn., 1937. Cf. also A. Loisy, *Essai historique sur le sacrifice*, 1920; E. W. Hopkins, *Origins and Evolution of Religion*, 1923, pp. 151 ff.; G. van der Leeuw, *Religion, its Essence and Manifestation: a Study in Phenomenology*, Eng. trans. by J. E. Turner, 1938, pp. 350 ff.; R. A. S. Macalister, in *E.R.E.* XI, pp. 36 ff.

[2] Cf. Oesterley, *op. cit.* pp. 11 ff.; Hopkins, *loc. cit.*; van der Leeuw, *loc. cit.*

[3] This was the theory of W. Robertson Smith. Cf. *op. cit.*, 3rd edn., p. 245: "We can affirm that the idea of a sacrificial meal as an act of communion is older than sacrifice in the sense of tribute . . . the object of the sacrifice is to provide the material for an act of sacrificial communion with the god." This view was followed by F. B. Jevons, *An Introduction to the History of Religions*, 9th edn., 1927, pp. 144 ff.; cf. p. 285: "The sacrificial and sacramental meal, which from the beginning has been the centre of all religion, has from the beginning also always been a moment in which the consciousness has been present to man of communion with the god of his prayers— without that consciousness man had no motive to continue the practice of the rite"; also by C. F. Burney, *Outlines of Old Testament Theology*, 3rd edn., 1930, pp. 55 f.

the god to induce him to act on behalf of the offerer;[1] (3) that

[1] This was the theory of E. B. Tylor. Cf. *Primitive Culture: Researches into the Development of Mythology, Philosophy, Religion, Language, Art, and Custom*, 5th edn., reprinted 1929, II, pp. 375 ff., esp. p. 376: "The gift-theory, as standing on its own independent basis, properly takes the first place. That most childlike kind of offering, the giving of a gift with as yet no definite thought how the receiver can take and use it, may be the most primitive as it is the most rudimentary sacrifice." Cf. also S. I. Curtiss, *Primitive Semitic Religion Today*, 1902, pp. 218 ff., esp. p. 221: "Sacrifice may be regarded as a gift on the part of the suppliant, which is designed favourably to dispose the being, who is God to him, in some undertaking on which he is about to enter; or to remove his anger. It may be something like a bribe to blind the eyes of the deity, a *keffareh*, so that the divine being who is displeased may overlook the offence on account of which he is angry", and p. 222: "The necessity for shedding blood does not exclude the character of sacrifice as a gift." So, too, Baumgarten, in *R.G.G.* 1st edn., IV, 1913, col. 956: "Ursprünglich ist das Opfer sogar nichts anderes als ein mit Gaben dargebrachtes Gebet, ein die Bitte nach antikem Urteil notwendigerweise begleitendes Geschenk, dargebracht in der Absicht, die Wirkung jener zu verstärken durch den Tatbeweis dafür, dass man sich den Erwerb des göttlichen Wohlgefallens etwas kosten lasse."

W. Eichrodt favours the view that the sacrifice is given to the deity in order to maintain his strength. Cf. *Theology of the Old Testament*, Eng. trans. by J. A. Baker, I, 1961, pp. 141 f. (cf. German 5th edn., 1957, p. 84): "The comparative study of religions indicates as the most important fundamental ideas of the sacrificial cultus those of *feeding*, the offering of gifts, sacral communion and atonement. The most primitive attitude is certainly that which sees the sacrifice as the means by which the deity is provided with nourishment and renewed strength." This was the theory advanced earlier by E. Westermarck, *The Origin and Development of Moral Ideas*, II, 1908, p. 611: "The idea that supernatural beings have human appetites and human wants leads to the practice of sacrifice . . . If such offerings fail them they may even suffer want and become feeble and powerless." Cf. also R. H. Pfeiffer, *Religion in the Old Testament*, 1961, p. 35: "The most likely view is that sacrifice was originally the provision of the food which the gods require, so that they either eat it alone (holocausts) or in the company of the worshippers (sacred meals)." A. B. Davidson (*The Theology of the Old Testament*, 1904, p. 315) regarded the gift idea as the prevailing idea in Old Testament sacrifices, and H. Wheeler Robinson (*J.T.S.* XLIII, 1942, p. 129) says: "I should regard the gift theory as giving the widest explanation, and the manipulation of the blood as being one of the chief points of departure." On this general view of sacrifice, cf. G. van der Leeuw, "Die *do-ut-des*-Formel in der Opfertheorie", in *A.R.W.* XX, 1920–21, pp. 241 ff. Cf. also S. H. Hooke, *The Origins of Early Semitic Ritual*, 1938, pp. 63 ff., where it is argued that all specific types of offering belong to two main classes; (1) offerings which have their origin in the central rite of the slaying of the god

the sacrifice released vital power by the death of the animal.[1] It is probable that no simple theory can express even the first meaning of sacrifice,[2] and that it was already of complex

and the ideas connected therewith, viz. placation, the removal of guilt, and substitution; and (2) gifts, given in recognition of the claims of the god, or intended to secure his favour. L. Koehler (*Old Testament Theology*, Eng. trans. by A. S. Todd, 1957, p. 182) divides all sacrifices into the two classes, (1) communion sacrifices, and (2) gifts. Cf. V. Maag, *V.T.* vi, 1958, pp. 10 ff.; also *Schweizerische Theologische Umschau*, xxviii, 1958, pp. 16 ff. J. Herrmann (*in Calwer Bibellexikon*, 5th edn., 1959, col. 968) finds three fundamental ideas behind sacrifice, (1) Gift, (2) Communion, (3) Expiation.

[1] So E. O. James, *op. cit.* p. 256: "The fundamental principle throughout is the same; the giving of life to preserve life, death being merely a means of liberating vitality." Cf. also R. Dussaud who, in speaking of Israelite sacrifice, says (*Les origines cananéennes du sacrifice israélite*, 1921, p. 27): "Le sacrifice met en mouvement des énergies plus puissantes, surtout le sacrifice par excellence, c'est-à-dire le sacrifice sanglant: avec sang, l'immolation met en liberté l'âme de la victime que le rite de la *semikha*, ou imposition de la main, a préalablement identifiée au sacrifiant"; also A. Bertholet (*R.G.G.* 2nd edn., iv, 1930, col. 704) who, while regarding sacrifice as also communion and gift, says: "im Opfer ruht eine Kraft, und durch das Opfer wird eine Kraftwirkung ausgeübt". Of the importance of this element in Old Testament sacrifices there can be little doubt. G. F. Moore (*E. Bib.* iv, col. 4217) says: "From first to last the utmost importance attaches to the disposition of the victim's blood." On sacrifice as substitution cf. A. Metzinger, *Biblica*, xxi, 1940, pp. 159 ff., 247 ff., 353 ff. H. H. Gowen (*A History of Religion*, 1934, p. 64) defines sacrifice as "man's effort to sustain the course of Nature by providing the requisite replenishment of power. It has therefore affinity with Imitative Magic". It will be seen below that while I would agree that sacrifice has its roots in magical practice, I do not think the Old Testament presents a magical view of sacrifice. H. Hubert and M. Mauss (*L'Année sociologique*, ii, 1899, p. 41) define sacrifice as follows: "Le sacrifice est une acte religieux qui, par la consécration d'une victime, modifie l'état de la personne morale qui l'accomplit ou de certains objets auxquels elle s'intéresse." Its purpose is to establish communication between the sacred world and the profane by means of a victim destroyed in the ceremony (p. 133).

[2] Cf. Loisy, *op. cit.* p. 11: "Le sacrifice ne procède pas que d'une seule idée ni d'une seule pratique; il n'apparaît qu'à un certain degré de l'évolution religieuse, et comme une sorte de synthèse où sont entrés des éléments divers. Par son fond, il tient des opérations magiques . . . et d'autre part, il tient aussi du don alimentaire." Most writers recognize complexity in the idea of sacrifice from its earliest traceable origins. So Hopkins, *loc. cit.*; Oesterley, *op. cit.* pp. 11 ff.; van der Leeuw, *Religion, its*

significance so far back as it goes. Within the thought of the Old Testament, no one of these views can give us the clue to the interpretation of all sacrifice.[1] Some sacrifices were clearly propitiatory; yet equally clearly all were not. The thankoffering, for instance, was clearly not propitiatory. Some sacrifices were thought of as having an effect upon the offerer and not merely on his behalf, or even upon others for whom the offerer made them. Job's sacrifice at the end of the round of his sons' banquets was partly to avert the anger of God at any thoughtless word or act on the part of his sons, and partly to cleanse his sons.[2] In a particular sacrifice one element might be to the fore, but it is probable that other elements were also often present.[3]

I have already indicated that Israel's sacrifices had a large element in common with the pre-Israelite sacrifices of Canaan. The view has been propounded, indeed, that Israel's sacrificial ritual was essentially of Canaanite origin.[4] This would well

Essence and Manifestation, pp. 350 ff. M.-J. Lagrange, whose study is limited to Semitic religions, also finds more than one element, and in particular combines the elements of gift and communion. Cf. *Études sur les religions sémitiques*, 1903, pp. 244 ff. Cf. also A. Bertholet, "Zum Verständnis des alttestamentlichen Opfergedankens", *J.B.L.* XLIX, 1930, pp. 218 ff.

[1] Cf. Gray, *op. cit.* p. 3. Gray stresses the gift element as against Robertson Smith's stress on the communion element, but expressly guards himself against being supposed to see only this element. J. Pedersen (*Israel III-IV*, pp. 299 ff.) also well emphasizes the variety of purposes sacrifice was designed to serve and the impossibility of interpreting Israelite sacrifice in terms of one idea. Cf., too, F. F. Hvidberg, *Den israelitiske Religions Historie*, 1943, pp. 91 f. O. Eissfeldt (*R.G.G.*, 2nd edn., IV, 1930, col. 712) observes that after the entry into Canaan the conception of sacrifice as communion tended to give place to the conception of it as gift. For a study of the variety of motives that lay behind Israelite sacrifice, cf. A. Wendel, *Das Opfer in der israelitischen Religion*, 1927, pp. 32 ff.

[2] Job 1: 5.

[3] Cf. R. de Vaux, *Ancient Israel: its life and institutions*, Eng. trans. by J. McHugh, 1961, p. 451: "Sacrifice is one act with many aspects, and we must beware of simple explanations."

[4] Cf. Dussaud, *op. cit.* 1921, and 2nd edn., 1941, with an appendix in which additional support for his view is drawn from the Ras Shamra texts, which were undiscovered when the first edition was issued. Cf. also Pedersen, *Israel III-IV*, p. 317: "Our knowledge of the Phoenician-Canaanite cult is now quite sufficient to warrant the conclusion that the greater part of the

accord with the common view of the meaning of Am. 5: 25 and Jer. 7: 22. In the former passage Amos asks: "Did ye bring unto me sacrifices and offerings in the wilderness forty years, O house of Israel?"; while in the latter Jeremiah says: "For I spake not unto your fathers, nor commanded them in the day that I brought them out of the land of Egypt, concerning burnt offerings or sacrifices." It is hard to subscribe to this common, literalistic view of these passages, however.[1] For in passages

Israelitish sacrificial practices had been learnt from the Canaanites." Similarly, J. P. Hyatt, *Prophetic Religion*, 1947, p. 128: "Modern discoveries and research have confirmed the belief that the Hebrew sacrificial system was largely of Canaanite origin. This has long been suspected on the basis of fragmentary evidence, and has been further proved by the discovery of cuneiform texts . . . at modern Ras Shamra." G. von Rad (*Old Testament Theology*, Eng. trans. by D. M. G. Stalker, I, 1962, p. 252) says: "It was only in Canaan that Israel entered into an old and widespread sacral practice, into which she later poured her own ideas." Cf. also Th. C. Vriezen, *An Outline of Old Testament Theology*, Eng. trans. by S. Neuijen, 1958, pp. 27 ff.

[1] I have discussed these and related texts in *B.J.R.L.* XXIX, 1946, pp. 340 ff. My argument was criticized by C. J. Cadoux, in *E.T.* LVIII, 1946–47, pp. 43 ff., to whom I replied, *ibid.* pp. 69 ff. Cf. also N. H. Snaith, *ibid.* pp. 152 f., and my reply, *ibid.* pp. 305 ff. So far as Am. 5: 25 is concerned, D. B. Macdonald noted the significance of the unusual order of the Hebrew words, and the unusual word for *bring*, more than half a century ago, and rendered: "Was it only flesh-sacrifices and meal-offerings that ye brought me in the wilderness?" where the expected answer is "We brought more than this; we brought true worship of heart and righteousness." Cf. *J.B.L.* XVIII, 1899, pp. 214 f. E. Würthwein (*Th.L.Z.* LXXII, 1947, col. 150) with less probability suggests that "the offerings which ye brought to me in the wilderness" was a gloss (but cf. *Z.A.W.* LXII, 1950, p. 48 n.). H. W. Hertzberg (*Th.L.Z.* LXXV, 1950, col. 223) thinks the emphasis should be put on "to me", and finds the meaning to be "Schon in der Wüste habt ihr mit euren Opfern und Gaben nicht mir gedient, sondern—euch selbst." So far as Jer. 7: 22 is concerned, I find the passage to indicate the relative importance of sacrifice and obedience, in accordance with the well-known Biblical idiom, whereby "not this but that" means "not that is more important than this". See *B.J.R.L., loc. cit.* p. 340, where several illustrations are given. Moreover, in Jer. 6: 19 f. Jeremiah again condemns sacrifices, but couples with his condemnation a complaint that the people had not hearkened unto the voice of God. If he really meant that the condemnation would have stood unchanged even if they had hearkened to the voice of God, he might have been expected to avoid mentioning irrelevances. Further, though in Jer. 7: 1–15 he announces the coming destruction of the

which stand in documents almost certainly older than the time of Amos, there are references to sacrifice in the Mosaic period, and the sacrifice of the Passover is integral to the story of the Exodus, which lay at the heart of the national consciousness. It is hard to believe that Amos or Jeremiah denied that this sacrifice was offered, or was ordained by God.[1] The prophetic

Temple, he makes it quite clear that if the people would amend their ways this might be averted. Clearly, therefore, he does not regard the Temple ritual as something that is unacceptable to God in itself, but only as something that is unacceptable when it is observed by people whose spirit is an offence to Him. R. de Vaux (*Ancient Israel: its life and institutions*, Eng. trans. by J. McHugh, 1961, p. 428) notes that Amos and Jeremiah must have known of the traditions of sacrifices in the wilderness, and holds that they did not repudiate them. He shares my view that the denunciations of these prophets were directed against the external and material cult, as practised by their contemporaries, and (p. 454) explains Jer. 7: 22 and Hos. 6: 6 as "dialectical negation", as I have argued. On Hos. 6: 6 cf. P. R. Ackroyd, in *Peake's Commentary on the Bible*, ed. by M. Black and H. H. Rowley, 1962, p. 609 a: "6b indicates that 6a is to be taken as a statement of what God requires as first essential, namely loyalty to the covenant, rather than as a negation of all sacrificial observance." R. Hentschke (*Die Stellung der vorexilischen Schriftpropheten zum Kultus*, 1957, p. 83) follows the view that Amos denies that sacrifices were offered in the wilderness and thinks he rejected the cultus *per se* (p. 87), while he renders Hos. 6: 6b "without sacrifices" (p. 88). On this rendering see below, p. 89.

[1] The oldest sources of the Pentateuch, that were almost certainly in existence in Jeremiah's time, ascribe sacrifice to Moses and say that he ordained it. Similarly, traditions which must antedate the time of Jeremiah say that Samuel sacrificed. There is no evidence that Jeremiah denied the accuracy of these traditions, but there is evidence that he held Moses and Samuel in high esteem. Cf. Jer. 15: 1. Similarly, the sacrifice of the Passover is inextricably woven into the tradition of the Exodus, which Jeremiah regarded as achieved by the power of God. There is no evidence that he denied that the Passover was sacrificed at that time, or denied that this was done in accordance with the divine will, and it is hard to see how Jer. 7: 22 can be understood as a challenge to all the traditions of the past, when it can be understood less drastically, and when there is independent evidence that Jeremiah valued other elements of the traditions that are inseparable from the ones he is supposed to be challenging. Th. C. Vriezen holds that Amos and Jeremiah rejected the sacrificial cult (*op. cit.* p. 63), though he recognizes that "the idea of the *expiatory* sacrifice was originally bound up with the Passover offering even in pre-Mosaic times" (p. 27). L. Koehler (*Old Testament Theology*, Eng. trans. p. 181) says that Amos was historically wrong in thinking sacrifices were not offered in the wilderness period, but was correct to the extent that the cult was installed by men and not God.

attitude to sacrifice cannot be determined by taking odd texts out of their context in this way, and interpreting them in a rigid and literalistic way. They must be studied in relation to their context and in relation to the totality of each prophet's teaching. It is also important to ask how their contemporaries understood them. Here we must remember that almost all modern scholarship is agreed that the book of Deuteronomy is the deposit of the teaching of the eighth century prophets;[1] yet it found nothing fundamentally repugnant to true religion in sacrifice in itself. I am therefore unwilling to set the religion of Israel, as represented by Moses and the prophets, over against sacrificial religion, and to suppose that sacrifice was wholly a Canaanite borrowing into her practice after the Settlement in the land.[2]

V. Maag (*Text, Wortschatz und Begriffswelt des Buches Amos,* 1951, pp. 221 f.) suggests that Amos relied on a lost historical source, differing from J and E, and without foundation in fact.

[1] While there are some who dispute this, they cannot be identified with those who regard the eighth century prophets as inflexibly opposed to all sacrifices. Indeed, the latter theory developed amongst scholars who regarded the teaching of those prophets as the background of Deuteronomy. G. von Rad (*Studies in Deuteronomy,* Eng. trans. by D. Stalker, 1948, p. 69) rejects the view that Deuteronomy rests on prophetic teaching. On the other hand A. Lods (*Histoire de la littérature hébraïque et juive,* 1950, p. 369) emphatically affirms it.
[2] A. Lods says: "The Israelite system of sacrifice, in its essentials, does not seem to have been either a Jahwistic innovation . . . nor a borrowing from the Canaanites, as Dussaud has recently maintained, nor a creation of the Jewish priests at the time of the exile. In the main it comes from the old pre-Mosaic Semitic stock of religious practices." See *Israel from its Beginnings to the Middle of the Eighth Century,* Eng. trans. by S. H. Hooke, 1932, p. 281 (original French edn., *Israël des Origines au milieu du viiie siècle,* 1930, p. 324; cf. also *R.H.P.R.* viii, 1928, p. 410). I am inclined to go farther than Lods, though not so far as Dussaud, and to hold that while Israelite sacrifice came from a background of ancient Semitic sacrifice, the institution would naturally be differently developed in different branches of the Semitic peoples, and that while Israel doubtless brought some sacrificial ritual with her when she entered Canaan, she borrowed much from the Canaanites for its development in the post-Settlement period. Cf. J. Pedersen, *Israel III-IV,* p. 317: "It is difficult to draw the line between what is Canaanite and what is strictly Israelite. The Israelites did not adopt the Canaanite custom as a dead system." H. Wheeler Robinson (*Redemption and Revelation in the Actuality of History,* 1942, p. 249) conjectures

It is nevertheless probable that not a little in Israel's ritual was of Canaanite origin.[1] This has been more generally recognized since the Ras Shamra texts became available for study, though it was already recognized before their discovery that Canaanite religion had exercised a powerful influence on Israel's religion. It is sometimes pointed out that technical names for sacrifices that stand in the Old Testament are found in the Ras Shamra texts,[2] and the antiquity of these sacrifices can no longer be questioned.[3] This does not carry with it, of

that the peace-offering is older in Israel than the Settlement in Canaan, while the burnt-offering was derived from the Canaanites. A. Lods (*R.H.P.R. loc. cit.* pp. 405 ff.) thinks that all the three main types of sacrifice, communion offering, whole offering and piacular offering rest on older pre-Settlement forms of sacrifice.

[1] Cf. R. Dussaud, *R.H.R.* cv, 1932, pp. 285 ff., and *Les Découvertes de Ras Shamra (Ugarit) et l'Ancien Testament*, 1937, pp. 109 ff., 2nd edn., 1941, pp. 178 ff.; S. H. Hooke, *The Origins of Early Semitic Ritual* (Schweich Lectures), 1938, pp. 63 ff.; R. de Langhe, *Les Textes de Ras Shamra-Ugarit et leurs apports à l'histoire des origines israélites*, 1939, p. 42. R. de Vaux (*Ancient Israel*, Eng. trans., p. 440) holds that the evidence "does not justify the conclusion that Israel took all its ritual for sacrifices from Canaan, but it does indicate that Israelite ritual is far closer to the ritual of Canaan than to that of Mesopotamia or Arabia". Cf. P. van Imschoot, *Dictionnaire encyclopédique de la Bible*, 1960, col. 1640: "On admet trop facilement l'influence exclusive de la civilisation cananéenne sur le développement du culte israélite. Même après la découverte des textes cultuels d'Ugarit, le rituel cananéen est encore trop peu connu pour qu'on puisse en tirer des conclusions certaines."

[2] Cf. J. W. Jack, *The Ras Shamra Texts: their Bearing on the Old Testament*, 1935, pp. 27 ff. See, however, the note of caution in W. F. Albright, *A.R.I.* 1942, 2nd edn., 1946, p. 61, and R. de Vaux, *Ancient Israel*, Eng. trans. p. 440.

[3] It should not be forgotten that the antiquity of much of the usage that is codified in the Priestly Code has long been recognized. Cf. A. Kuenen, *The Religion of Israel to the Fall of the Jewish State*, Eng. trans. by A. H. May, II, 1875, p. 252: "The priestly lawgiver neither could nor would create a new state of affairs, but closely annexed himself to what he found in existence . . . The sacrifices and feasts to Jahweh were of much older date"; A. Lods, *loc. cit.* p. 401: "les représentants les plus autorisés de l'école de Graf-Wellhausen, à commencer par Wellhausen lui-même, ont souligné expressément que ses institutions sont, pour une large part, très anciennes"; also H. Schulz, *A.J.Th.* IV, 1900, p. 282: "The sacrificial laws in the priestly Torah undoubtedly contain very early material. The sacrificial regulations for the priests of the old Jerusalem may lie at the bottom

course, as is sometimes concluded, the antiquity of the Biblical sources that refer to them. On the other hand, it does carry with it—though this is less often noted—the evidence that these forms of sacrifice did not originate in a divine revelation to Moses on the mount. Their antiquity goes back behind Moses.

On the other hand, it is impossible that all of Israel's ritual was derived from Canaanite sources.[1] In particular, it is unlikely that the Passover, which was offered before the entry into Canaan, was derived from Canaanite sources.[2] The origin of this rite is highly obscure, though it is probable that it long antedated the time of Moses.[3] What is more important than its origin is the meaning Israel attached to it, and from the time of the Exodus she seems to have made it the vehicle of her remembrance of that deliverance, so that whatever significance it may have had before is no longer relevant for her. Here is a notable

everywhere. Without the assumption of such a given basis the presence of the conception of guilt-offering ('āshām) alongside of that of sin-offering (ḥaṭṭā'th) . . . is wholly inexplicable"; S. H. Hooke, *The Origins of Early Semitic Ritual*, 1938, p. 45: "It is now generally recognized that even the late parts of the Pentateuch preserve much early material, and it is legitimate to use evidence from the Deuteronomic and Priestly legislation relating to the ritual, with due precautions, as some indication of the forms of ritual which existed in the pre-prophetic period."

[1] Cf. R. de Langhe, *op. cit.* p. 42, and also above, p. 88, n. 2.

[2] Cf. J. Pedersen, *Israel III-IV*, p. 317: "paschal sacrifice is probably pre-Canaanite"; p. 382: "It is clear that the Passover was such a popular festival before the immigration"; pp. 400 f.: "The events of the spring festival warrant the presumption that it is a combination of two originally independent festivals, a pre-Canaanite pastoral feast which sanctified the firstborn, and a Canaanite peasant feast which sanctified the barley crops." The originally separate character of these two feasts has, of course, long been recognized. Cf. E. Dhorme, *L'Évolution religieuse d'Israël: i. La religion des Hébreux nomades*, 1937, p. 210. It may be noted that Dussaud agrees with this view. He says: "On admet généralement que la pâque est constituée par la combinaison de deux fêtes, primitivement distinctes: l'Offrande des premiers-nés des troupeaux, pratiquée jadis par les Israélites nomades, et la fête des pains azymes, fête agricole cananéenne ouvrant la période de la moisson que clôturait la pentecôte." For a study of this spring festival and its ritual, cf. G. B. Gray, "Passover and Unleavened Bread: the Laws of J, E, and D", in *J.T.S.* xxxvii, 1936, pp. 241 ff. See also N. H. Snaith, *The Jewish New Year Festival: its Origins and Development*, 1947, pp. 13 ff.; H. Haag, *Luzerner Theologische Studien*, 1954, pp. 17 ff.

[3] Cf. T. H. Gaster, *Passover: its History and Traditions*, 1949.

example of the process to which I have referred, whereby practices that were once of a different significance were integrated into Israel's religion and made the vehicle of Yahwism. It is the significance attached to all the sacrificial and other rites that is more deeply important than antiquarian research into their origin. All the light that can be shed on their origin is to be welcomed, provided we do not delude ourselves into thinking that when we have found the origin we have explained and understood all.

Whatever the source of Israel's sacrificial ritual, whether she derived it from her own distant past or from Canaanite or other sources, or whether it came into being in the course of her own history, no simple idea will suffice to explain the meaning of it all. Some sacrifices were thought of as gifts; others as means of effecting communion with God; others as having propitiatory significance. Some were wholly consumed on the altar; some were partly consumed on the altar and partly given to the priests; in some the worshipper himself had a share.

Not all sacrifices were animal sacrifices. There were the first-fruits,[1] which were held to be sacred to God and His by right. These were not thought of as man's gift to God, but as His own property, so that it would be an act of sacrilege for a man to use them for himself.[2] God was recognized to be the source of all fruitfulness, and therefore entitled to a share of what His bounty provided. The same was true of the offerings of the first-born of animals. These, too, belonged to God,[3] and their purpose was not primarily to propitiate God, to effect communion with Him, or to bring Him a gift. They were the recognition of what was His own.

Of non-animal sacrifices in addition to firstfruits[4] we may recall the meal offerings and the freewill offerings of substance.

---

[1] On these cf. O. Eissfeldt, *Erstlinge und Zehnten im Alten Testament*, 1917.

[2] Cf. J. Pedersen, *Israel III-IV*, p. 304: "He acquires the full right to use the crops when he has given Yahweh his share."

[3] Cf. Exod. 13: 2.

[4] The tithes belong to the same category as the firstfruits, though they are, of course, distinct, and more defined in amount. Cf. Pedersen, *op. cit.* pp. 307 ff.; also Eissfeldt, *op. cit.* On incense and the place it acquired in the ritual, cf. M. Löhr, *Das Räucheropfer im Alten Testament: eine archäologische Untersuchung*, 1927.

It will be remembered that in the time of Joash there was a dispute between the king and Jehoiada the High Priest as to the source of the funds for the repair of the Temple, and the dispute was finally settled by devoting to this purpose freewill offerings of substance which might be placed by the people in a chest in the Temple, which could only be opened jointly by the priest and the king's officers.[1] At the time of Josiah this arrangement was still in force, and it was after the opening of the chest that Hilkiah announced the finding of the book of the Law.[2] Probably the *minḥāh* was a gift,[3] though what it signified is less certain. It seems clear that originally it denoted an animal sacrifice, since the term is used of Abel's sacrifice,[4] but it became in later times a meal offering. Whether it was a gift expressing devotion to God, or seeking to induce Him to grant a boon, is hard to determine.[5]

There were thank-offerings, which were also gifts, though with a more defined purpose. These were not seeking boons, but the recognition that boons had been received and that God was their author. Similarly with vows,[6] though these might have been contracted as a means of securing blessing. Once contracted, the vow imposed its obligation on a man, so that its purely voluntary undertaking had become a moral obligation which it was sinful to repudiate.[7]

Other sacrifices included the peace-offerings, and sacrifices which were connected more definitely with sin. The peace-offerings may have been designed for the maintenance or restoration of proper relations with God. The offerer shared part of them in the sacred feast in pre-exilic times,[8] while in the

---

[1] 2 Kg. 12: 4 ff.

[2] *Ibid.* 22: 3 ff.

[3] Cf. G. B. Gray, *Sacrifice in the Old Testament*, pp. 14 ff.

[4] Gen. 4: 4.

[5] For a study of the ritual associated with the *'ōlāh*, or burnt offering, and the *zebhaḥ*, with which the peace-offering is equated, cf. W. B. Stevenson, "Hebrew 'Olah and Zebach Sacrifices", in *Festschrift für Alfred Bertholet*, 1950, pp. 488 ff.

[6] Cf. J. Pedersen, *op. cit.* pp. 324 ff.

[7] On the legal limitation of the validity of certain vows, cf. Pedersen, *ibid.* pp. 328 f.

[8] Cf. Pedersen, *ibid.* p. 335, where they are called "covenant offerings". Their name, *shᵉlāmîm*, is connected with the word *shālôm = peace*, but

post-exilic times the name peace-offering was made to include the thank-offerings, the vows and the free-will offerings.[1] Of the sacrifices more closely connected with sin there were the sin-offering and the guilt-offering in post-exilic times,[2] though these do not figure in the pre-exilic sources of the Old Testament that have come down to us.[3] This does not mean that they were post-exilic inventions, however, and the fact that in Lev. 5: 1–9 they appear to be identified, and that they cannot now be distinguished with precision, is against such a supposition.[4] For it is probable that they were once distinct. Both appear to have been offered for more specific offences than the peace-offering—if the peace-offerings involved any idea of offence.

In addition to these individual sacrifices there were the daily

their precise purpose is difficult to define. Cf. L. Koehler, *Theologie des Alten Testaments*, 1936, p. 177: "Was שְׁלָמִים bedeutet, wissen wir nicht." Later, however, Koehler felt able to define it; cf. 3rd edn., 1953, p. 178 and p. 245, n. 140, and *Old Testament Theology*, Eng. trans., p. 188: "שְׁלָמִים is a *Schlussopfer* (the idea of being quits)." A. Haldar (*Associations of Cult Prophets among the Ancient Semites*, 1945, p. 212) thinks they were divinatory.

[1] W. P. Paterson (in *D.B.* iv, p. 338b) says it is too much to say that the sacrificer of the peace-offering "always stood upon the ground of salvation", in contrast to the offerer of the sin-offering, who had fallen from a state of grace. While this appears to be true of the post-exilic period, it is less certain for the earlier period.

[2] C. F. Burney (*Outlines of Old Testament Theology*, 3rd edn., 1930, p. 62) says: "It is not unreasonable to regard the sin- and guilt-offerings as later specialised forms of the older burnt-offering." Cf. H. Wheeler Robinson, *Inspiration and Revelation in the Old Testament*, 1946, p. 226: "The well-known pre-exilic sacrifices of the so-called 'peace-offering' . . . and of the whole burnt-offering . . . were extended in the post-exilic period by the development of the sin-offering and the guilt-offering which marked a deepened sense of alienation or remoteness from God."

[3] The word *'āshām*, which is the technical term for a guilt-offering, is found in pre-exilic writings, but never with this meaning. In 1 Sam. 6: 3, 4, 8, 17 it stands for the golden symbols which the Philistines returned with the Ark, and in 2 Kg. 12: 18 for money given to the priests. In Gen. 26: 10, which is commonly assigned to J, it means *guiltiness*, and so in Jer. 51: 5, and in Ps. 68: 21 (Heb. 22), which may be pre-exilic.

[4] Cf. J. H. Kurtz, *Sacrificial Worship in the Old Testament*, Eng. trans. by J. Martin, 1863, pp. 189 ff.; Gray, *Sacrifice in the Old Testament*, pp. 57 ff.; Oesterley, *Sacrifices in Ancient Israel*, pp. 75 ff., 80 f.; Pedersen, *Israel III-IV*, p. 372.

offerings of the community for the maintenance of right relations between the community and God;[1] and there was the solemn offering of the Day of Atonement,[2] when sacrifice was made for the sin of the community, and the scapegoat that bore the sin of the community was not sacrificed on the altar, but driven into the wilderness.[3] There can be no doubt that the roots of this ritual lay far back in the past, and primitive practices have doubtless survived in it.

Our information about these sacrifices is not all of the same age, and it is certain that there was development of usage in connection with some part of them during the period covered by the Old Testament. We must beware of supposing, however, that a sacrifice which is only attested in a late document first came into existence at the time of that document's composition. To trace the history of these sacrifices lies outside my purpose, and even to trace the history of their significance is not my intention. I have little doubt that sacrifice did not mean the same to the patriarchs, to priests or people during the monarchy, to prophets, and to the founders of Judaism. Yet there were some elements of its significance which were constant within the stream of the true tradition of Israel. That there were many in all ages who were spiritually insensitive is freely declared in the Old Testament, and I am not concerned with them. So far as the Pentateuch is concerned, I recognize that there are various strata within it; yet all were gathered by the final redactors within its compass, to be understood in terms of that dynamic element which reached its full development in the Judaism which made the Pentateuch the expression of its spirit. My concern is primarily with the conception of sacrifice cherished by the final framers of the Law, and to a lesser extent with the compilers of the older documents which are embodied in the Law, and with the great prophetic figures of the pre-exilic period.

---

[1] On the history of these cf. Pedersen, *ibid.* pp. 249 ff. G. F. Moore, in *E. Bib.* iv, col. 4209, surmises that the custom of offering a daily burnt offering and oblation probably originated in the royal temples of Judah and Israel.

[2] Cf. Lev. 16.

[3] On the ritual of this day and its significance, cf. Gray, *op. cit.* pp. 306 ff.; Oesterley, *op. cit.* pp. 226 ff.

It is important to recognize that not all sacrifice was related to the expiation of sin. Moreover, no sacrifice is represented as achieving anything by the mere act of offering it. In popular thought, so often challenged by the prophets, sacrifices were believed to have automatic power, as they were widely thought to have amongst non-Israelite people. But that is not the real teaching of the Old Testament, where it is clearly taught that sacrifices must be the organ of the spirit of the offerer, if they were to be effective. Where the sacrifice was offered for sin, the Law no less than the prophets asked for something more than the outward act. The Law required the confession of sin and humble penitence of spirit, without which the sacrifice could achieve nothing. It also required restitution, where the sin was against another and where restitution could be made. It is in Leviticus that we read:[1] "It shall be, when he shall be guilty in one of these things, that he shall confess that wherein he hath sinned; and he shall bring his forfeit unto the Lord for his sin which he hath sinned . . . and the priest shall make atonement for him as concerning his sin." It is in Numbers that we read:[2] "When a man or woman shall commit any sin that men commit . . . then they shall confess their sin which they have done; and he shall make restitution for his guilt in full, and add unto it the fifth part thereof, and give it unto him in respect of whom he hath been guilty." Moreover, there is a passage at which we shall look later, which makes it clear that it is the intention, rather than the act, which validates sacrifice, since there are cases where no sacrifice can avail since the spirit is wrong.

With all this it must be remembered that sacrifice was thought of as potent.[3] It was not merely an expression of the spirit of the offerer, and certainly not an empty form that neither added nor subtracted anything. It required the spirit to validate it, but once validated it was thought to be charged

[1] Lev. 5: 5 f.
[2] Num. 5: 6 f.
[3] Cf. H. Wheeler Robinson (*J.T.S.* XLIII, 1942, p. 131): "That the personal act of sacrifice was generally regarded as doing something, i.e. as efficacious, hardly needs demonstration. This is implied, on the one hand, in the detailed attention given to sacrifice in the Old Testament. This would be meaningless unless sacrifice were meaningful, to a degree far beyond a figurative and merely declaratory symbolism."

with power. It was never merely a plea, whether for aid or for forgiveness or for communion. It was potent to effect something, either within or on behalf of the offerer or of another. The sacrificed animal was not merely a substitute for the offerer. He laid his hands upon it,[1] and was conceived of as in some way identified with it,[2] so that in its death he was conceived of as dying—not physically, but spiritually. The death of the victim symbolized his death to his sin, or to whatever stood between him and God, or his surrender of himself to God in thankfulness and humility. And then it was thought of as the medium of his cleansing, or his fellowship with God, or as the assurance of blessing. Hence sacrifice both expressed the spirit of the worshipper and did something for him.[3] Sometimes, as in the thankoffering, the first of these was to the fore and the second was little in evidence.[4] But wherever the second was thought to be present, it could not operate without the first.

It is important to remember this in connection with the common view that the pre-exilic canonical prophets were against the institution of sacrifice as such, and that they declared it was wholly unacceptable to God. It is improbable that their words should be so interpreted, and far more probable that they opposed the sacrifices of their day because they were hollow and unrelated to the spirit of the offerer.[5] To

[1] Lev. 1: 4; 3: 2, 8, 13, etc.
[2] Cf. the remark above quoted (p. 71 n. 1) from Dussaud: "que le rite de la *semikha*, ou imposition de la main, a préalablement identifiée au sacrifiant". Also H. Wheeler Robinson (*J.T.S.* XLIII, 1942, p. 130): "The natural meaning of the laying of hands on the sacrifice is the closer identification of the offerer with his offering."
[3] Cf. E. Jacob, *Theology of the Old Testament*, Eng. trans., p. 269: "We envisage the sacrifice as the act through which God reveals and communicates his life-force, in which man receives infinitely more than he brings, and in which it follows that the sacramental element takes precedence of the truly sacrificial element."
[4] Cf. Pedersen, *Israel III-IV*, p. 300: "In every offering there is something of all the effects produced by the offering; but one or other element may become more or less prominent."
[5] Cf. H. Wheeler Robinson, *Redemption and Revelation*, p. 250: "The prophet's criticism of contemporary sacrifices was not necessarily intended to do away with them altogether, but was more probably intended to check the abuse of them, by which they became the substitutes, instead of the accompaniments, expressions and encouragements, of true piety and right

discuss this question here would involve too long a digression, and it is the less necessary since I essayed this a few years ago in a lecture in the same series as the present one.[1] The over-sharpening of antitheses, that was in vogue some years ago,[2] is less common today, and there is a greater readiness to recognize an affinity between priest and prophet,[3] or between the Law

conduct"; *Inspiration and Revelation in the Old Testament*, 1946, p. 226: "It is difficult to conceive how these prophets would have devised a worship wholly without sacrifices. They were attacking a false and non-moral reliance upon them, rather than the expression of true worship through a eucharistic gift"; E. Jacob, *R.H.P.R.* xxxix, 1959, p. 294: "Nous pensons que la distinction entre prophètes et prêtres se situait sur le plan de la coexistence et non sur celui de l'opposition"; R. de Vaux, *Ancient Israel: its life and institutions*, Eng. trans. by J. McHugh, 1961, p. 384: "There is an inaccurate but widespread theory which asserts, without nuances, that the priests were the ministers of public worship, and the prophets its enemies." Cf. also N. W. Porteous, "Prophet and Priest in Israel", *E.T.* LXII, 1950–51, pp. 4 ff.

[1] "The Unity of the Old Testament", in *B.J.R.L.* xxix, 1945–46, pp. 326–58. Cf. also *The Unity of the Bible*, 1953, pp. 30 ff., and "Ritual and the Hebrew Prophets", in *Myth, Ritual and Kingship*, ed. by S. H. Hooke, 1958, pp. 236 ff. (reprinted below, pp. 111 ff.).

[2] For survivals of the older view, cf. T. H. Robinson (in Oesterley and Robinson, *Hebrew Religion: its Origin and Development*, 1930, p. 202; 2nd edn., 1937, p. 232): "The God of Israel, alone among the deities worshipped by men, made no ritual demands; to Him sacrifice was always a weariness and, when substituted for morality, an abomination"; P. Volz (*Propheten-gestalten des Alten Testaments*, 1938, p. 19); "Die alttestamentliche Religion, die Propheten-Religion, ist Wort-Religion, und dadurch steht die alttesta-mentliche Propheten-Religion im schärfsten *Gegensatz zur Priester-Religion*, zur *Kult-Religion*. Priester-Religion ist Opfer-Religion; . . . Propheten-Religion ist Wort-Religion"; J. P. Hyatt (*Prophetic Religion*, 1947, p. 127): "The opposition of the prophets to the whole sacrificial and ritualistic system and practices of their day seems to have been absolute, and they thought it should be abolished as an offence against the God of Israel"; I. G. Matthews (*The Religious Pilgrimage of Israel*, 1947, p. 128): "These men had denounced ritual as of no avail, but now, if possible, they went farther, and made social ethics the essential, even the sole, requirement of Yahweh." Cf. L. Koehler, *Old Testament Theology*, Eng. trans., pp. 181 ff.; S. Herner, *Sühne und Vergebung in Israel*, 1942, pp. 30 f.; V. Maag, *Text, Wortschatz und Begriffswelt des Buches Amos*, 1951, pp. 225 f.

[3] Cf. N. W. Porteous, *Interpretation*, III, 1949, p. 414: "We must not allow the denunciations of Israel's prophets, justifiable as they undoubtedly were, to blind us to the service which Israel's cult must have rendered in main-taining through the centuries the faith and obedience of many a pious

and the Prophets, without ignoring the differences of emphasis and function that marked their work or their message.[1] This

Israelite." On the other hand, some scholars have overstressed the affinity between prophets and priests, and have turned some of the greater canonical prophets into cultic officials. Thus I. Engnell (*Studies in Divine Kingship in the Ancient Near East*, 1943, p. 87; *S.B.U.* I, 1948, cols. 59 f.) makes Amos a cultic official, while A. S. Kapelrud (*Central Ideas in Amos*, 1956, pp. 5 ff.) holds that he was responsible for Temple herds and an important person in what concerned the Temple cult, and M. Bič (*V.T.* I, 1951, pp. 293 ff.) makes him a hepatoscoper (against this cf. A. Murtonen, *V.T.* II, 1952, pp. 170 ff.). A. Haldar (*Associations of Cult Prophets among the Ancient Semites*, 1945) carries this tendency to its extreme and argues that all the prophets were members of guilds of diviners, and even holds that Jeremiah was a cultic prophet on the Temple staff (pp. 112 f.). For a criticism of this tendency cf. R. Hentschke, *Die Stellung der vorexilischen Schriftpropheten zum Kultus*, 1957, and K. Roubos, *Profetie en Cultus in Israël*, 1956. It is to be noted that Roubos links A. R. Johnson with Haldar and Engnell (pp. 112, 119), though he does not appear to have read Johnson's work and gives a very misleading idea of his views, which are marked by far greater caution (cf. *The Cultic Prophet in Ancient Israel*, 2nd edn., 1962).

[1] Cf. W. O. E. Oesterley, *Sacrifices in Ancient Israel*, p. 208: "Their"—i.e. the prophets'—"purpose was to purify, not to abolish, the offering of sacrifices"; p. 213: "If the prophets thought the ideas of sacrifice were wrong, they would assuredly have given some indications of this. But there is no hint to this effect; a fact which supports the contention that it was not sacrificial worship in itself that they condemned, but only its misuse in wrong directions"; J. M. Powis Smith, *The Prophets and their Times*, 2nd edn., revised by W. A. Irwin, 1941, p. 62: "It may hardly be supposed that Amos would have done away with sacrifice and ritual entirely if he could . . . It was not ritual as such to which he objected, but rather the practice of ritual by people who believed that thereby they set in motion magical forces and insured for themselves well-being and happiness" (cf. 1st edn., 1925, p. 50); H. Wheeler Robinson, *J.T.S.* XLIII, 1942, p. 137: "The prophets were virtually compelled to over-emphasize, or to emphasize too exclusively, one side of the ritual-righteousness antithesis, in order to make their meaning clear—to say, in effect, righteousness only, in order to say, not ritual only"; J. E. Coleran, *Theological Studies*, v, 1944, pp. 437 f.: "The prophetic condemnations of sacrifice, then, drive home a two-fold concept basic to true religion . . . If men will confess their dependence by external cult-acts, these acts must express their sincere disposition of soul. If the external cult does not express this, it is both hypocrisy, deceiving self, and irreligion, striving to deceive God"; P. S. Minear, *Eyes of Faith*, 1946, p. 22: "The prophets often protest against the emphasis on animal sacrifices and ceremonial ablutions, but rarely is such protest directed against all sacrifice as such . . . The prophets are fighting against a false separation of

means that the creators of the Law and the great prophets were emphasizing opposite sides of the same teaching. On the one side we have the detailed requirements of the ritual, with the recognition that the spirit must be brought to their observance.[1] On the other, we have the insistence on the spirit, without which the offerings are meaningless. On both sides it is perceived that the sacrifice must be in a genuine way the expression of the spirit of the offerer if it is to be effective.[2] No plea for

sacred from secular"; J. Paterson, *The Goodly Fellowship of the Prophets,* 1948, p. 27: "Many scholars assume that these prophets are advocating a system of religion without ritual or sacrifice. This seems quite impossible. The great prophets are united in their denial of the efficacy of mere ritual and in their demand for moral and spiritual relations between the people and God. . . . But neither Amos nor Isaiah nor Jeremiah would deny a place to sacrifice"; W. Eichrodt, *Theology of the Old Testament,* Eng. trans., I, 1961, pp. 364 f.: "*The prophetic attitude to the cultus* is not to be understood in terms of a simple either-or of morality and sacrifice, nor are the prophets to be characterised as champions of 'ethical religion'. To do so is once again to force these men into too narrow a frame, and to exaggerate the importance of the cultus in their sayings. The well-known passages, for all their pointed antithesis between cultic activity and righteous dealing, do not justify us in conceiving the prophetic ideal as a cultless, moralistic religion" (cf. German 5th edn., 1957, p. 244); P. van Imschoot, in *Bijbelsch Woordenboek,* 1941, col. 1148: "De leer der profeten wordt door vele niet-kath. critici uitgelegd alsof de profeten alle o.s. en allen uiterlijken cultus weroordeeld als Jahweh onwaardig, den zedelijken en transcendenten God, die niets anders van zijn vereerders eischte dan de volledige onderwerping aan zijn wil en het onderhouden van zijn zedelijke geboden . . . Deze interpretatie houdt niet voldoende rekening met den werkelijken toestand van den cultus, noch met de mentaliteit der tijdgenooten van de profeten, noch met den aard van hun taal, die het ideaal scherp tegenover de misbruiken van den cultus van hun tijd stelde en de schakeeringen verwaarloosde."

[1] Cf. what I have written elsewhere (*apud* H. Wheeler Robinson, *J.T.S.* XLIII, 1942, p. 136): "The final form of the sacrificial law of the Old Testament comes to us from men who valued the prophetic teaching, and the age of Judaism treasured alike the Law and the Prophets. It sought by the Law to guard the prophetic principles, and it conceived of the ritual as the organ of obedience, not the substitute for it. But it is clear that it conceived of the ritual as potent, and not alone as acceptable, and the power with which it was charged was divine power."

[2] In *B.J.R.L.* XXIX, 1945-46, pp. 351 ff., I noted the evidence of the Psalter for the understanding of the Law. N. W. Porteous (*Interpretation,* III, 1949, pp. 404 f.) draws attention to the same thing. He says: "It must never be forgotten that the clue to the meaning of what Israel did in her

forgiveness could be sincere, if there was no renunciation of the sin in the heart; no cry for cleansing could have any meaning, if there was still the purpose to renew the act that brought the stain; no prayer for communion could be genuinely expressed by a sacrifice, if there was no desire to walk in harmony with God's will. The offerings must bear the spirit of the worshipper to God, before they could mediate to him forgiveness, cleansing and communion. In Proverbs we read: "The sacrifice of the wicked is an abomination to the Lord."[1] It can bring him no blessing, but only increase his alienation from God. This is essentially the message of Amos and of other prophets. "I hate, I despise your feasts, and I will take no delight in your solemn assemblies. Yea, though ye offer me your burnt offerings, and meal offerings, I will not accept them: neither will I regard the peace offerings of your fed beasts . . . But let judgment roll down as waters, and righteousness as a mighty stream."[2]

It is for lack of the qualities of the spirit that the sacrifices stand condemned, and not because they are wrong in themselves, even though the spirit should be right.[3] The great eighth century prophets looked out on a society in which they saw the will of God being flouted on every side, and the fundamental qualities of God's character were conspicuously lacking in the people who brought Him their splendid sacrifices. None had the slightest desire to change his way, or to approach God in

religious practice is to be found reflected in the Psalter. It is quite unlikely that these ancient Hebrew hymns which have inspired so much that is best in Christian worship should have originally, many of them, been composed to accompany a ritual which did not represent a genuine synthesis of the religious and the ethical. To suppose anything else is to suppose that the Psalms were fundamentally irrelevant in the ritual setting to which they originally belonged. In other words, the evidence of the Psalter must be allowed to qualify the evidence of the prophets."

[1] Prov. 21: 27.
[2] Am. 5: 21–24.
[3] E. Jacob (*Theology of the Old Testament*, Eng. trans. by A. W. Heathcote and P. J. Allcock, 1958, p. 176) remarks on Hos. 6: 6, that the prophet's words do not underline the opposition between mercy and sacrifice, but imply that a sacrifice not inspired by *ḥesedh* lacks the spirit to make it effective. Cf. C. Hauret, in *Vocabulaire de Théologie biblique*, 1962, col. 961: "Sans les dispositions du cœur, le sacrifice se réduit à un geste vain et hypocrite; avec des sentiments pervers, il déplaît à Dieu."

genuine confession of sin and humble desire to be cleansed and renewed in spirit. They came in the hard and proud and impenitent spirit which the Law declared to invalidate sacrifice. But this cannot imply that had the prophets seen men coming to the altar with the genuine desire to submit themselves in spirit to God, they would have loosed against them the same denunciation.[1] The gravamen of their charge was not that men sacrificed, but that they offended God by lives that knew none of His spirit, and that they were inflexibly determined to continue in their way.[2] Such stand under the condemnation of the Law, as well as of the prophets. But where

[1] Cf. H. Wheeler Robinson, *J.T.S.* XLIII, 1942, p. 137: "Our parallelism suggests that for the prophets everything depended on the spirit in which an act was performed. Their own symbolic acts were, generally, the continuance in form of widespread symbolic magic which they themselves certainly condemned. Yet the psychology of symbolic magic was taken up into their faith in Yahweh and sublimated by the performance of similar acts, not to constrain Him, but as constrained by Him. Similarly, we may say that they condemned the *opus operatum* of sacrifice, so long as it was not lifted up into the spirit of true devotion to Yahweh, and true obedience to His moral requirements. Then the character of sacrifice would be changed, and it might become as acceptable to God as were their own symbolic acts."

[2] E. C. B. Maclaurin has published a study on *The Origin of the Hebrew Sacrificial System*, 1948, designed to prove that sacrifice was not original to Israelite religion, and that it was totally rejected by the pre-exilic prophets. The author frequently refers to passages useful for his purpose. Others are sometimes ignored, and sometimes explained away. Samuel and Elijah do not figure among the pre-exilic prophets. Maclaurin notes that there is no law of the priesthood in E, and asks "Could a cult exist in which blood-sacrifice was part of a definite ritual and which nevertheless did not possess any form of priesthood? It seems highly unlikely that this would be so" (p. 11). Clearly the compilers of the J and E documents saw no difficulty here, since they treated the patriarchs as their own priests. Similarly, Micah appointed his own son to be his priest (Jg. 17: 5) until a wandering Levite was made his professional priest (Jg. 17: 12). There is no suggestion that Elijah was a professional priest. Yet he could rebuild an altar and offer sacrifice (1 Kg. 18: 32 f.). Maclaurin asserts that the Passover sacrifice was originally a substitution for a human being, and then finds significance in the fact that E does not record the Passover sacrifice, while J does, and concludes that this proves the secondary character of the blood-sacrifice (p. 28). It is hard to follow the reasoning here, and it would be interesting to know (*a*) whether the sacrifice of human beings is held to have begun after the establishment of the priesthood, or to have been possible without

professional priests, and (*b*) whether it is supposed that there was a hiatus between the human sacrifice and the sacrifice of the Passover lambs, during which only the feast of Unleavened Bread was observed.

Maclaurin allows that at the Exodus the Passover was instituted, but suggests that it is unlikely that it was a blood-sacrifice (pp. 7 f.), disregarding the earlier source J, and drawing conclusions from silence in E. The inconvenient passage in Isa. 1: 11 f. is treated most unnaturally. Here every form of religious observance, including prayer, is condemned, since men's hands were full of blood. To suppose that the prophet imagines that prayer was in itself and of necessity an offence to God is out of the question for any who treat the prophets as the exponents of spiritual religion. But instead of accepting the plain meaning of the passage that it was because the life was evil in God's eyes that every form of religious observance was meaningless—a meaning which is obvious from the demand of vv. 16 f.—Maclaurin identifies the blood which was an offence to God and which invalidated prayer with the blood of the sacrificed animals (p. 13). Surely Isaiah had graver evils to protest against than the slaughter of animals; and if his meaning was that the fact that men did not seek judgment and relieve the oppressed, or judge the fatherless and plead for the widow, had nothing to do with the invalidating of their prayers, which was solely due to their animal sacrifices, it remains to be shown why he introduced an extraneous and irrelevant matter at so vital a point. For if Maclaurin's thesis means anything, it means that the Israelite who was full of good works and devotion to the will of God would be hounded from his Maker's presence, in Isaiah's view, if he dared to offer any sacrifice and thus fill his hands with blood. The virtue or vice of his life was quite immaterial to a God whose only vital interest was to protect animals from slaughter.

In the interest of this theory Maclaurin renders Hos. 6: 6 b "and the knowledge of God without burnt-offerings" (p. 29), and then denies to his opponents the right to render the preposition as comparative. That the preposition in itself could have either meaning is the fact, and that the comparative rendering is not only possible but more natural is evidenced by the fact that it is not theorists with an axe to grind who have so rendered it, but translators generally, both ancient and modern, whereas Maclaurin's rendering is one that would occur only to a writer whose theory was embarrassed by the verse. In order to maintain the view that "the religious aspect of sacrifice had been forgotten by those whom it is convenient, anachronistically, to call Bue Abraham"—presumably for Bne Abraham—"before they crossed the threshold of history", he argues that the altar does not necessarily imply sacrifice, and so concludes from silence that no animal sacrifices were offered on altars except where they are specified, and suggests that Gen. 15: 9 f. means that the Baal of Canaan—here called Yahweh—was instructing Abraham in a sacrificial rite with which he was quite unacquainted, and which was really Canaanite, and that the Canaanite Baal was here adopting the newcomers because he was dissatisfied with his old worshippers (pp. 3 f.). All of this will convince whom it may. But since this is acknowledged to have been a sacrifice, we might have been

the sacrifice was the organ of the spirit, it was believed to be potent to mediate blessing and renewal to men.

So, too, where the sacrifices made on behalf of the community were the organ of the common desire for harmony with God's will, they were believed to be potent. Yet there was nowhere any suggestion that such sacrifices were potent independently of the spirit of the community. In Exod. 19: 5, which is assigned by some scholars to the earliest document of the Pentateuch,[1] we read: "Now, therefore, if ye will obey my voice indeed, and keep my covenant, then ye shall be a peculiar treasure unto me from among all peoples." There is no promise that if due ritual is performed, the favour of God can be ensured, but instead the requirement of loyalty and obedience to the will of God. This is stressed even more in Dt. 28, where blessing is promised to the nation so long as it hearkens to the commandments of God, and disaster when it flouts His will. It is obedience in life, and not mere sacrifice that ensures blessing. When the prophets declared that a harvest of sorrow could be reaped because the

informed whether it is recognized to have been possible without a professional priest, or have been offered some evidence that Abraham employed such a priest. G. Nagel (in J. J. von Allmen, *Vocabulary of the Bible*, Eng. trans. by P. J. Allcock and others, 1958, p. 380 a) summarizes the thought of the Old Testament on sacrifice by saying: "No right conscience could be satisfied with sacrifices alone, for they always remain disproportionate to the gravity of the offence committed. In order to find peace one must obtain, over and above sacrifice, the grace of God, and one must bring to God true repentance and the fervent desire to make amendment of life. The external and internal action do not by any means exclude each other, and the second should always accompany the first, and bestow upon it its true value. The sacrifice was allowed to function normally but the soul committed itself entirely to the grace of God."

[1] So S. R. Driver, *L.O.T.* 9th edn., 1913, p. 31: Oesterley and Robinson, *Introduction to the Books of the Old Testament*, 1934, p. 37. Some scholars assign the verse to later hands, however. Thus O. Eissfeldt (*Hexateuch-Synopse*, 1922, p. 146*) assigns it to E, and G. Beer (*Exodus* [H.A.T.], 1939, p. 97) to E_1, while A. Weiser (*Introduction to the Old Testament*, Eng. trans. by D. M. Barton, 1961, p. 112) finds J and E elements to be mixed in Exod. 19, and does not specify which this verse is. W. H. Bennett ascribes it vaguely to a Redactor (*Exodus* [Cent. B.], p. 157), while others specify R^D. So Baentsch, *Exodus-Leviticus* [H.K.], 1903, p. 172; C. Steuernagel, *Lehrbuch der Einleitung in das Alte Testament*, 1912, p. 150; A. H. McNeile, *The Book of Exodus* [W. C.], 2nd edn., 1917, p. 110; *La Bible du Centenaire*, I, 1941, p. 94; C. A. Simpson, *The Early Traditions of Israel*, 1948, p. 199.

whole of society was rotten in the eyes of God, despite the splendour of the ritual, they were not saying anything that was alien in principle to what is said in the Law. In the ritual of the Day of Atonement, when atonement was made for the sins of the community, an essential element in the ritual was the priestly confession of the sins of the community.[1] That confession was made by the priest as the representative of the community, and in so far as it did not represent the spirit of the community it was meaningless. To treat this element of the ritual as a hollow formality, in which the sincerity of the priest, or the genuineness of its expression of the attitude of the community towards itself and towards God, is of no moment, is to do less than justice to the Law. Whether in individual sacrifice or in public sacrifice it was the attitude of heart of those for whom the offering was made that alone could validate the ritual. Yet where it was thus validated, it was in either case believed to be charged with power.

It is important here to realize that while sacrifice was thought to have potency, it was potent only when accompanied by genuine penitence and submission. On the other hand, penitence and submission alone were not sufficient for the cases where sacrifice was prescribed. They were primary as the condition of blessing, and it was always recognized in the true stream of Israel's religion that obedience was better than sacrifice;[2] but it was not supposed that man could save himself from his sin either by his penitence or by his sacrifice. It was divine power that reached down to save him in the moment when he offered himself with his sacrifice. The animal of itself could do nothing for him. But when its sacrifice was the organ of his approach in humble surrender and obedience to God, it became the organ of God's approach in power to bless him.

Wheeler Robinson has linked this fruitfully with the practice of prophetic symbolism.[3] Often the prophets performed

---

[1] Lev. 16: 21.

[2] 1 Sam. 15: 22. Cf. Ec. 5: 1: "Keep thy foot when thou goest to the house of God; for to draw nigh to hear is better than to give the sacrifice of fools."

[3] *Redemption and Revelation*, pp. 250 f.; *Inspiration and Revelation in the Old Testament*, pp. 227 f.; and "Hebrew Sacrifice and Prophetic Symbolism", in *J.T.S.* XLIII, 1942, pp. 129 ff.

symbolic acts, such as Jeremiah's wearing of a wooden yoke,[1] or Isaiah's appearance in Jerusalem unclothed.[2] These were not mere dramatizations of the word of the prophets, but were acted prophecies, as potent to release power for their own fulfilment as the spoken word of the prophets.[3] Yet they are to be differentiated from magic, in that they did not represent the desire of the prophet to control events by the exercise of a technique. Often the prophet hated the message with which he was charged. Yet he profoundly felt that he was under the divine control, and his word and act alike expressed God's will and not his own, so that the power with which they were charged was not human power to control God, but divine power released to fulfil the purpose of God.[4] In the same way, Wheeler Robinson suggests, the sacrifices were symbolic acts, "actualized approaches to God", not mere *opera operata* in the realm of magic, but expressions of the spirit of the offerer, which initiated a new relation to God. It cannot be denied that many in Israel had a merely magical view of sacrifice, as many of other nations have had, and thought that the correct performance of the ritual was all that mattered. But if they were "actualized approaches to God", they were meaningless without the approach in spirit which they were designed to actualize.

Much is said in the Law of unwitting sin in connection with the sin-offering and the guilt-offering, and it would seem that only unwitting sins were capable of being cleansed by sacrifice. Alongside unwitting sins we find mention of sins committed with a high hand, as though these were the only two classes of sins. It is as improbable that unwitting sins means sins committed in ignorance in every case as it is that sins committed with a high hand means sins knowingly committed. For the sin-offering and the guilt-offering were not valid for sins committed

[1] Jer. 27 f.

[2] Isa. 20.

[3] Cf. H. Wheeler Robinson, "Prophetic Symbolism" in *Old Testament Essays* (Papers read before the Society for Old Testament Study), 1927, pp. 1 ff.; also *Inspiration and Revelation in the Old Testament*, pp. 185 f.

[4] Cf. *Inspiration and Revelation in the Old Testament*, p. 227: "Genetically, they spring from the widespread practice of symbolic magic, but the prophets have transformed them into religion by assimilating them to the will of God"; *J.T.S. loc. cit.* p. 132: "Magic constrains the unseen; religion means surrender to it."

with a high hand. Yet they were valid for false dealing with a neighbour in the matter of a deposit, or of robbery or oppression, or of the wrongful retention of something that was lost. In none of these cases does it seem likely that the sinner would be ignorant of his sin at the time of his committing it. On the other hand, unwitting sin in many cases quite clearly means sins that were accidentally committed, violating some ritual taboo, of which the sinner became conscious only after his act. In this connection it is of interest to note that the leper who became cleansed of his leprosy had to offer a sin-offering and a burnt-offering.[1] Here either his leprosy was itself regarded as a ritual "sin", or it was believed to be the punishment for some undisclosed sin. It is more probable that the former was the case,[2] and that it was regarded as an unwitting sin because it came upon a man independently of his own volition.[3]

Clearly, however, the distinction between unwitting sins and high-handed sins is something different from sins committed in ignorance and sins knowingly committed, and if conscious sins could ever be atoned for by a sacrifice, then high-handed sins must be defined in some other way. It is probable that by these is meant deliberate sins, perpetrated of set purpose, rather than sins into which a man "fell" through human weakness, or involuntarily. Paul says: "For that which I do I know not; for not

[1] Lev. 14: 1–19.
[2] The sin for which leprosy could be regarded as a punishment would be some very heinous sin, for which no sacrifice could atone. The cure of the leper would be evidence that the sin was forgiven, and therefore not needing to be atoned for by his sacrifice. It is more likely that the sacrifice was for the ritual cleansing of the leper so that he could again take his place in society. (That the disease referred to in the Old Testament is not what we know as leprosy is immaterial to our purpose. On the nature of the disease cf. the important article by G. R. Driver, with the help of R. G. Cochrane and H. Gordon, in Hastings' one volume *D.B.*, revised edn., ed. by F. C. Grant and H. H. Rowley, 1963, pp. 575 ff.)
[3] It is to be noted that after childbirth a woman was required to offer a sin offering (Lev. 12). There could be nothing unwitting about the bearing of a child, and since the Hebrews valued the fruit of the womb as God's blessing to man, and even believed that God's first command to man was to be fruitful and multiply (Gen. 1: 28), it would not have been regarded as a sin in any moral sense. Hence, here again the purpose seems to have been to fit the woman ritually to take her place in society once more. (Cf. preceding note.)

what I would, that do I practise; but what I hate, that I do . . .
For the good which I would, I do not; but the evil which I would
not, that I practise."[1] It is probable that this passage gives the
clue to the Old Testament distinction, and that it is a distinction between sins which a man commits through ignorance or
through weakness, or willy-nilly, and those which he commits
because they are the expression of his real nature, arising out of
the essential purpose of his heart. For these no sacrifice could
atone.[2] Moreover, there are whole classes of sins for which no
ritual is provided. These are heinous sins, of too great a magnitude to be dealt with by ritual acts.[3] For murder and adultery
the Law provided no means of atonement, and only demanded
the execution of the murderer or adulterer. Yet sometimes we
find there is cleansing even for sins of this magnitude, and it is
clear that in the thought of the Old Testament sacrifice is not
the only organ of atonement. To remember this is of the first
importance in any study of sacrifice, or of the treatment of sin,
in the Old Testament.

One of the passages frequently associated with the prophetic
passages in which sacrifices are denounced, and held to reveal
an attitude of hostility to sacrifice in any circumstances,[4] is

---

[1] Rom 7: 15, 19.

[2] R. J. Thompson (in *The New Bible Dictionary*, 1962, p. 1121) observes:
"No sacrifices availed for breach of covenant—it is in this light that the
prophetic rejection of sacrifice is to be understood—or for sins of a 'high
hand' that put man outside the covenant."

[3] Cf. E. König, *Theologie des Alten Testaments*, 3rd and 4th edns., 1923,
pp. 294 ff.

[4] So C. J. Cadoux, *E.T.* LVIII, 1946–47, p. 45. Like many others Cadoux
rejects the last two verses of the psalm as a patent addition, because they
will not square with his interpretation of these two earlier verses. Some
modern editors have defended their originality, however. So, e.g. C. A.
Briggs, *The Book of Psalms* [I.C.C.], II, 1909, p. 10, where they are said to be
"essential to the completeness of the Strophe". G. Widengren (*The
Accadian and Hebrew Psalms of Lamentation as Religious Documents*, 1937, pp.
31 f.) also holds to the unity of the psalm, and maintains that the reason no
sacrifices were desired by God was simply that Jerusalem lay in ruins. If
these last two verses are original, the psalm could hardly have been written
before the exile. Without them, we have no means of determining its age.
I am inclined to agree with Cadoux that they are an addition, though not
on the ground of disagreement with the earlier verses on the question of
sacrifice, but because they have no relation to the individual penitence

Ps. 51: 16 f. (Heb. 18 f.): "For thou delightest not in sacrifice; else would I give it: Thou hast no pleasure in burnt offering. The sacrifices of God are a broken spirit; a broken and a which marks the rest of the psalm. It is usually supposed that they were added to counteract the previous verses which rejected sacrifices. I think C. Ryder Smith (*The Bible Doctrine of Salvation*, 1941, p. 85) is more penetrating here. He says: "Why did someone, after having read the psalm, add them, and why did others accept the addition? Not, surely, just because he and they wanted to push ritual in somehow, but because they felt that, when the experience so poignantly described in the psalm was theirs, they could go on to use the sacrifices of the Temple sacramentally. There were men who, having cried out for 'a clean heart' and 'a right spirit', knew that the right use of ritual would help them to find it." S. Daiches claimed that in the Psalms "sacrifices" frequently does not mean animal sacrifices (cf. "The Meaning of 'Sacrifices' in the Psalms", in *Essays Presented to J. H. Hertz*, 1944, pp. 97 ff.), and maintained that the last two verses of Ps. 51 had no reference to animal sacrifices, burnt offerings, whole offerings and bullocks being merely figures of speech for "sacrifices of righteousness", which he understood to mean sacrifices which consist in righteous living. This is forced and unnatural. Moreover, it is commonly recognized today that many of the Psalms accompanied ritual acts. This view of the Psalter is particularly associated with the name of S. Mowinckel, whose *Psalmenstudien*, 1921–24, will remain as one of the most creative studies on the Psalms, however much particular views may be criticized.

This view of the Psalms is older than the work of Mowinckel, however. In 1919 A. J. Wensinck wrote: "My thesis is that, for the greater part, the Psalms are spoken rhythmic illustrations of the acts of worship; just as the musical part of the Catholic Mass is an illustration and a rhythmisation of the ritual acts. In this connexion the description of the service in 2 Chr. 29: 27–30 is of importance: 'And Hezekiah commanded to offer the burnt offering upon the altar. And when the burnt offering began, the song of the Lord began also with the trumpets and with the instruments ordained by David king of Israel. And all the congregation worshipped, and the singers sang, and the trumpeters sounded: and all this continued until the burnt offering was finished" (reprinted in *Semietische Studiën uit de nalatenschap van A. J. Wensinck*, 1941, p. 57). If such a view is correct, it is improbable that such passages in the Psalms as Ps. 51: 16 f. (Heb. 18 f.) are rightly to be understood as the condemnation of all sacrifice. Indeed, I have elsewhere suggested that nothing could be more appropriate than this psalm to make the offerer of a sin offering realize that the spirit in which he came to the altar was of more importance than his offering, or to call forth from him the spirit of penitence which would make the offering the genuine organ of his approach to God (*B.J.R.L.* XXIX, 1945–46, pp. 352 f.). Originally written to express the feelings of a penitent who had sinned more deeply than the ritual law provided for, it could call forth from other sinners who used its ritual a profound sense of need and penitence in the presence of God.

contrite heart, O God, thou wilt not despise." These verses are taken right out of their context, as the prophetic passages are, and held to prove that the psalmist believed that sacrifices were futile in all circumstances.[1] It would seem wiser to examine it in relation to its context before such sweeping conclusions are drawn. By its heading this Psalm is associated with David's adultery with Bathsheba and the scandalous removal of Uriah that amounted to murder. The sins of adultery and murder were on David's head at that time, therefore. Most modern scholars ascribe the Psalm to a later date. But whatever its date, it can scarcely be denied that it would be appropriate to such a situation,[2] and the psalmist may have composed it with David in mind, to be used by others who were conscious of heinous sins. Certainly it represents the cry of one who was profoundly conscious of some very great sin. In such a situation as David's there would be nothing whatever inconsistent with the Law in this cry. No sacrifice was provided by the Law for murder and adultery, and it is therefore strictly in accordance with the Law to say that in such case sacrifice and offering are not desired by God.[3] It is gratuitous to assume that the psalmist meant to imply that sacrifice was equally useless in quite other circumstances where the Law did prescribe it. Whether David or another, the psalmist would seem to be one who had committed a sin that stood outside the categories dealt with in the ritual, but who was deeply penitent for his sin, or who wrote in the character of such a sinner.

That there could be pardon for such sins in the thought of the Old Testament is clear from the sequel to Nathan's rebuke of

[1] Other passages in the Psalms similarly held to be opposed to sacrifice in all circumstances are dealt with by C. Lattey, *J.T.S.* XLIII, 1941, pp. 161 f.

[2] B. D. Eerdmans (*The Hebrew Book of Psalms* [O.T.S.] IV, 1947, pp. 274 ff.) defends the ascription of the psalm to David.

[3] M. Burrows (*An Outline of Biblical Theology*, 1946, p. 244) says: "The fact that the Psalms were used in the temple makes it all the more remarkable that in them forgiveness and divine favour are often represented as dependent, not on sacrifice, but on confession and prayer." It is less remarkable if we remember the Law's insistence on confession, and the areas of sin for which no sacrifice was prescribed. H. Herkenne (*Das Buch der Psalmen* [H.S.A.Tes], 1936, p. 191) noted that the sins of David, with which the heading associates this psalm, lay beyond the field of prescribed sacrifices.

David. The conscience of the king was touched, and in genuine penitence he cried: "I have sinned against the Lord."[1] And Nathan said: "The Lord also hath put away thy sin; thou shalt not die."[2] Here, let it be observed, the cleansing was the response to penitence, and not achieved by the penitence. It was the act of God, as it must ever be, whether associated with sacrifice or not. Moreover, the divine forgiveness did not dispense with punishment. It is true that here the punishment took the form of the death of the child, but it was regarded as the punishment of David. Similarly, when Ahab humbled himself before the Lord following the rebuke of Elijah after the affair of Naboth, his repentance was accepted by God, though the penalty for his sin had still to be reaped. Here it was deferred to his son's days; but it was not to be avoided.[3] With our more individualistic outlook we find injustice here, though it would not occur to men of that time, with their stronger sense of the family and the race. Nor is it contrary to experience that children often pay the price of their father's sins, and that the effects of such a crime as that of Ahab and Jezebel against Naboth often take time to develop. Here, however, where the thought of the Old Testament is what concerns us, it is important to note two things. The first is the recognition that even the divine forgiveness does not cancel out all the effects of sin. While this is elementary, it is often forgotten. A man who has ruined his health by sinful excesses does not find himself restored to health by repentance. Moreover, others whom he has influenced may continue their excesses to his lasting reproach. David sinned and repented. But his son Amnon followed in the way of his father's lust,[4] and Absalom in that of his father's bloodguiltiness,[5] without repenting. The Bible does not conceal facts in the interest of an unreal theory, and Biblical theology is grounded in experience. The second thing to note is that in the thought of the Old Testament the cleansing of the sin was of more importance than the escaping of its

[1] 2 Sam. 12: 13.
[2] *Ibid.*
[3] 1 Kg. 21: 29.
[4] 2 Sam. 13: 11 ff.
[5] *Ibid.* 26 ff.

97

consequences.[1] The only penitence it valued was a genuine horror of the sin, and not a selfish desire to avoid the punishment.

While, therefore, we cannot think of salvation from sin in the thought of the Old Testament without thinking of sacrifice, we seriously err if we think only of sacrifice. There are many passages which tell of men's response in submission to the chastening discipline of God, or to His message of rebuke, where there is reference to restored relations with God without any mention of sacrifice. Penitence and submission on man's part are the invariable conditions of his salvation; but the organ of salvation, whether sacrifice is offered or not, is conceived to be the power of God.

Nevertheless, it must be recognized that there was peril in the Law's emphasis on unwitting sin and provision of sacrifices for its cleansing, since it is undeniable that unwitting sin could mean, and often did mean, sins committed in ignorance or involuntarily, and especially ritual rather than moral offences. The purpose of those who framed the Law was to stress the exceeding sinfulness of sin, but manifestly there could not be the same quality in the repentance when one was unconscious of the sin at the time it was committed, or not responsible for it, and such sacrifices tended to be regarded as mediating automatic cleansing. Hence, the evils against which the prophets had protested were not wholly guarded against, and while at its best Judaism was spiritually sensitive, at its worst it became a mere externalism.

But just as the prophets had declared to those of their contemporaries who supposed that the potency of the sacrifice lay in the due performance of the external ritual alone, and who knew no compunction for sins which exceeded any that sacrifice was prescribed for, that they were offering vain and meaningless sacrifices, which were an offence to God, and which but added to their sin, so there were voices in Judaism which renewed the same message and rebuked those who supposed that a formal act unrelated to the spirit could suffice to win God's

[1] I am not able, therefore, to agree with N. H. Snaith, when he renders Isa. 53: 11 b: "For it was their iniquities (i.e. punishments) he was bearing" (*The Distinctive Ideas of the Old Testament*, 1944, p. 92). It seems unnecessary to force the thought of this chapter below so much else in the Old Testament by imposing upon it the equation of punishment and iniquity.

favour. In the second century B.C. Ben Sira wrote: "The sacrifice of an unrighteous man is a mockery,[1] and the oblations of the wicked are not acceptable.[2] The Most High hath no pleasure in the offerings of the godless; nor is pacified for sins by the multitude of sacrifices."[3] In the Mishnah we read: "If a man say, I will sin and repent, I will sin again and repent, he will be given no chance to repent. If he say, I will sin and the Day of Atonement will clear me, the Day of Atonement will effect no atonement."[4] The writer of those words interpreted high-handed sin as has been done above. In the Tosephta we find: "Sin-offering and guilt-offering and death and the Day of Atonement all put together do not effect atonement without repentance."[5] Yet later, in the Talmud we read: "Be not like fools who sin and bring an offering without repenting."[6] These sayings were written by men who studied the Law and loved it, and who believed they were true to its spirit and principles in what they wrote; yet they were equally true to the principles of the great prophets. For there was no difference between them in these fundamental questions.[7] Where sacrifice was prescribed

[1] This rendering is preferable to that of R.V.: "He that sacrificeth of a thing wrongfully gotten, his offering is made in mockery." G. H. Box and W. O. E. Oesterley, in Charles's *Apocrypha and Pseudepigrapha of the Old Testament*, i, 1913, p. 435, render: "The sacrifice of the unrighteous man is a mocking offering." This is in part supported by the Syriac, which has "The sacrifices of the unrighteous are unrighteous." It agrees closely with the rendering of V. Ryssel (in Kautzsch's *Die Apokryphen und Pseudepigraphen des Alten Testaments*, i, 1900, reprinted 1921, p. 403): "Das Opfer des Ungerechten ist eine Gabe, die (Gottes) spottet."

[2] This rendering follows the Syriac. Box and Oesterley have: "And unacceptable are the oblations of the godless." Cf. Ryssel's "wie denn auch die Spöttereien der Gottlosen ihm nicht zum Wohlgefallen gereichen." R. V. following the Greek, has: "And the mockeries of wicked men are not well-pleasing."

[3] Sir. 34: 18 f. (31: 21–23).

[4] Yoma viii. 9. Cf. H. Danby, *The Mishnah*, 1933, p. 172.

[5] Tosephta Yoma v. 9 (ed. Zuckermandel, 1937, p. 190, line 23).

[6] T. B. Berachoth 23a. Cf. L. Goldschmidt, *Der babylonische Talmud mit Einschluss der vollständigen Mišnah*, i, 1892, p. 82.

[7] It is not, of course, to be supposed that I am obliterating the distinction between prophets and priests. There was a difference of function and of emphasis between them that is not to be overlooked. At the same time they are not to be thought of as exponents of two completely different religions. Cf. *The Unity of the Bible*, p. 46: "It is not our purpose to argue that there is

and was offered, it must be the organ of the spirit of the offerer before it could be the organ of the power of God unto him or on his behalf. Where sacrifice was not prescribed because the sin was so much more heinous, then penitence and humble submission were even more called for ere the divine power could operate in the heart of the sinner.

Before we leave the subject of sacrifice in the Old Testament, however, we must turn to the figure of the Suffering Servant in Deutero-Isaiah. It is well known that there are four passages here which are commonly linked together, Isa. 42: 1–4; 49: 1–6; 50: 4–9; and 52: 13–53: 12. If we bring together the thought of these four passages we see that it was the mission of the Servant to set justice in the earth, and to give his law to men. He is thus thought of as instrumental in bringing about the state of universal worship of the God of Israel and obedience to His will. Hence, his work is connected with the bringing in of the Golden Age that was elsewhere associated with the Davidic Messiah. There is no evidence that the Suffering Servant was equated with the Messiah in pre-Christian days,[1] and definite evidence no difference between the Law and the Prophets. Indeed, it has been insisted that the unity to be found in the Bible is a unity in diversity, and that differences must be recognized as well as an underlying unity. It is therefore unnecessary to minimize the difference between the Law and the Prophets in the interests of the unity which is maintained."

[1] Some recent writers contest this statement. Cf. J. Jeremias, in *Deutsche Theologie*, ii, 1929, pp. 106 ff.; N. Johansson, *Parakletoi*, 1940, pp. 113 ff.; W. D. Davies, *Paul and Rabbinic Judaism*, 1948, pp. 274 ff.; J. Jocz, *The Jewish People and Jesus Christ*, 1949, p. 162. No solid evidence coming from a pre-Christian date can be produced in support of their position, and the evidence of the New Testament is firmly against it. For the Gospels show that whenever our Lord spoke of His mission in terms of suffering, the disciples were completely bewildered and failed to understand what He meant. Hence, most scholars support the view which I have expressed in the text above. So Strack-Billerbeck, *Kommentar zum Neuen Testament aus Talmud und Midrasch*, ii, 1924, p. 274; G. F. Moore, *Judaism in the First Centuries of the Christian Era*, i, 1927, p. 551; M.-J. Lagrange, *Le Judaïsme avant Jésus-Christ*, 1931, p. 385; P. Volz, *Eschatologie der Jüdischen Gemeinde im neutestamentlichen Zeitalter*, 1934, p. 228; J. Héring, *R.H.P.R.* xviii, 1938, pp. 419 ff.; J. J. Brierre-Narbonne, *Le Messie souffrant dans la littérature rabbinique*, 1940, p. 133; H. Wheeler Robinson, *Redemption and Revelation*, 1942, pp. 199, 251 f.; M. Burrows, *An Outline of Biblical Theology*, 1946, p. 86. For a fuller discussion of this subject cf. my paper on "The Suffering Servant and the Davidic Messiah" in *The Servant of the Lord and other essays*, pp. 59 ff.

in the New Testament that the two figures were not equated, since the disciples were always bewildered when Jesus spoke in terms of suffering. Nevertheless, they are both related to the Golden Age of universal obedience to God's will, and have their roots in common ideas, even though they are different conceptions as to how their hopes should be realized.

The second song shows that the Servant has a mission to Israel as well as to the nations, while the third recognizes that his mission will involve him in grievous suffering, and the fourth declares this his suffering will be the organ of his mission, and not merely incidental to it. Men will say: "He was wounded for our transgressions, he was bruised for our iniquities: the chastisement of our peace was upon him; and with his stripes we are healed."[1] There is therefore potency in his sufferings, potency to effect something in, or on behalf of, others, and not himself. He himself is declared to be without sin, indeed: "although he had done no violence, neither was any deceit in his mouth".[2] His death was not the consequence of his own sin; it was potent on behalf of others. He is likened to a lamb that is led to the slaughter, and it is clear that his death is thought of in terms of sacrifice. Just as the sacrificed animal dies not for its own sins, but to be the bearer of man's spirit to God, and of God's blessing and cleansing to man, so the Servant is conceived. Moreover, the term 'āshām, which is the technical name for a guilt offering, is used of him.[3] The Servant is therefore said to be a sacrifice that is effective for those whose hearts are so moved by his sufferings that they humbly confess their own sin, and recognize that his death may be at once the organ of their approach in humble submission to God and of God's approach in cleansing power unto them. They therefore bring to the offering the spirit which we have seen to be essential to

[1] Isa. 53: 5.
[2] *Ibid.* 9.
[3] *Ibid.* 10. The text of this verse is almost certainly corrupt. R.V. has: "When thou shalt make his soul an offering for sin, he shall see his seed, he shall prolong his days." All editors find difficulties here, and many suggested changes have been put forward. One of the simplest is that of R. Levy, who differently divides the first two words (reading '*emeth śām* for '*im tāśîm*) and secures the sense: "Truly he gave himself an offering for sin; He shall see his offspring, he shall prolong his days." Cf. *Deutero-Isaiah*, 1925, pp. 266 f.

the validation of sacrifice, and acknowledge that the death he dies should rightly have been theirs, ere they find through his death their redemption from sin. "Surely he has borne our griefs, and carried our sorrows."[1] They then become aware that he has borne their iniquities, and that through him they are justified.[2]

The term *to justify* is commonly a forensic term, meaning *to declare in the right*. Here, however, it cannot have that meaning. For it could not be supposed that in virtue of the death of the Servant, God would give a verdict in favour of others, though He knew full well that they were not in the right. This would be to declare God to be an Unjust Judge, in contradiction to the uniform teaching of the Bible, and it is improbable that that was the thought of the writer. God's judgments are invariably declared to be in accord with strict justice, and no gift can corrupt Him to depart from righteousness. If men who are conscious of their sin are declared righteous, it is because they have become righteous. They have become separated from their sins and have been cleansed in their inner nature.[3] When Isaiah received his call he was conscious of his sin until the live coal from the altar touched his lips, when the voice said: "Lo, this hath touched thy lips; and thine iniquity is taken away, and thy sin purged."[4] It was not that there was pretence in the presence of God, but that he there became a new creature. So here, in relation to the Servant, when men are declared righteous, it is because through the sin-offering of his death they become righteous. There is potency in the sacrifice to cleanse them, when they bring to it the spirit that validates it for them by making it the organ of their approach to God.

Here, then, is something of outstanding importance in the

---

[1] Isa 53: 4.

[2] *Ibid.* 11.

[3] N. H. Snaith (*The Distinctive Ideas of the Old Testament*, 1944, p. 92) proposes to translate Isa. 53: 11: "The righteous one, my servant, will make many prosperous." This is highly improbable, and if, as is frequently supposed, Dan. 12: 2 is a reference to this verse, it could not have been understood by the writer of that passage as Snaith understands it. Moreover, this rendering takes too little account of the context in Isa. 53, where the Servant is referred to as a guilt-offering.

[4] Isa. 6: 7.

Old Testament teaching on sacrifice. It is the idea of a sacrifice that transcends animal sacrifice, in which instead of an animal without physical blemish,[1] one who is without moral blemish is put to death. Moreover the victim, while he is cruelly maltreated and slain by others, yields himself willingly unto them. "I gave my back to the smiters, and my cheeks to them that plucked off the hair: I hid not my face from shame and spitting."[2] Further, this sacrifice is conceived of as of far wider effectiveness than any of the sacrifices of the ritual. The ordinary sin-offering or guilt-offering could be effective for the individual offerer, and the sacrifice of the Day of Atonement for the whole Jewish community, when individual or people turned to God in the right spirit. But if the earlier Servant Songs declare that the Servant has a mission to all the world and that its execution will involve suffering, the fourth song both makes it clear that the suffering is the organ of the mission, and not merely incidental to it, and also shows that it is the organ of service to the Gentiles. It has been observed already that though the concept of the Davidic Messiah and the Suffering Servant might have common roots, they were different conceptions; also that they are related in that both have reference to the Golden Age. Both bring world-wide and beneficent consequences to men, and lead to the universal worship of God. In the pictures of the Davidic Messiah we see a state of society that far transcended the contemporary society known to the prophets,[3] and here we see a sacrifice that far transcends in quality and power any of the sacrifices of the Temple.

It lies beyond my immediate purpose to identify the figure of the Servant in the prophet's thought, since my concern is with the meaning of sacrifice, rather than with the definition of the victim. Nevertheless, it is necessary to say something on this point, and not to leave this profoundest of Old Testament words on sacrifice in the air. Jewish scholars have commonly held the Servant to be Israel, and in modern times that was the view of many nineteenth century scholars, and of not a few in

[1] This is constantly insisted on in the Law as a necessity in sacrificial victims.
[2] Isa. 50: 6.
[3] Cf. Isa. 2: 3 f.; Mic. 4: 2–4; Isa. 9: 6 f. (Heb. 5 f.), 11: 4–9, and other similar passages.

the twentieth century.[1] Others, especially during the last half
century, have claimed that the reference is to some unknown
individual, either contemporary with the prophet or belonging
to an earlier generation,[2] and several have proposed to identify
the Servant with the prophet himself.[3]

There is much to suggest a connection of the Servant with
Israel, though no simple identification will do here. There is
also much to suggest an individual, though again all the names

[1] So K. Budde, *Die sogenannten Ebed-Jahwe-Lieder*, 1900; F. Giesebrecht,
Der Knecht Jahwes des Deuterojesaia, 1902; A. S. Peake, *The Problem of Suffering
in the Old Testament*, 1904, pp. 34 ff., and *The Servant of Yahweh*, 1931, pp.
1 ff.; A. Lods, *Les Prophètes d'Israël*, 1935, pp. 275 ff. (Eng. trans. 1937,
pp. 244 ff.), and *Histoire de la littérature hébraïque et juive*, 1950, pp. 472 ff.
Some scholars have preferred to think of the Israel within Israel (so C. F.
Burney, *C.Q.R.* lxxv, 1912–13, pp. 99 ff.; O. C. Whitehouse, *Isaiah
xl-lxvi* [Cent. B.], pp. 18 ff.), or of the ideal Israel (so J. Skinner, *Isaiah,
Chapters 40–46* [Camb. B.], revised edn., 1917, pp. lvi ff.; G. H. Box, *The
Book of Isaiah*, 1916, pp. 194 ff., 265 ff.).

[2] Many suggestions have been made, e.g., an anonymous leprous Rabbi
(so B. Duhm, *Das Buch Jesaia* [H.K.], 1892, pp. xviii, 284 ff., 365 ff.; cf.
M. Schian, *Die Ebed-Jahwe-Lieder in Jesaias 40-66*, 1895; A. Marmorstein,
Z.A.W., N.F. iii, 1926, pp. 260 ff.; and M. Buber, *The Prophetic Faith*, 1949,
pp. 227 f.); Moses (so E. Sellin, *Mose und seine Bedeutung für die israelitisch-
jüdische Religions-geschichte*, 1922, pp. 81 ff.); Uzziah (so K. Dietze, *Ussia,
der Knecht Gottes, sein Leben und sein Leiden und seine Bedeutung für den
Propheten Jesaja*, in Abhandlungen und Vorträge der Bonner Wissen-
schaftlichen Gesellschaft, iv, Heft 1/2, 1929, and *Nachwort zu "Ussia"*,
1930); Jeremiah (so, in a modified form, F. A. Farley, *E.T.* xxxviii,
1926–27, pp. 521 ff.; S. H. Blank, *H.U.C.A.* xv, 1940, pp. 18 ff.);
Jehoiachin (so E. Sellin, *Das Rätsel deuterojesajanischen Buches*, 1908, pp. 131
ff.; cf. L. H. Bleeker, *Z.A.W.* xl, 1922, p. 156; E. Burrows, *The Gospel of the
Infancy*, 1940, pp. 59 ff.); Zerubbabel (so E. Sellin, *Serubbabel*, 1898, pp.
148 ff.); Meshullam, the son of Zerubbabel (so L. Palache, *The Ebed-
Jahweh Enigma in Pseudo-Isaiah*, 1934).

[3] So S. Mowinckel, *Der Knecht Jahwäs*, 1921; E. Balla, in *Eucharistērion*
(Gunkel Festschrift), i, 1923, pp. 245 ff.; J. Begrich, *Studien zu Deuterojesaja*,
1938, pp. 131 ff.; A. Weiser, *Einleitung in das Alte Testament*, 2nd edn., 1949,
pp. 153 ff. For modifications of the view of Mowinckel, cf. E. Sellin, *N.K.Z.*
xli, 1930, pp. 73 ff., 145 ff., and *Z.A.W.*, N.F. xiv, 1937, pp. 177 ff.;
P. Volz, *Jesaia II* [K.A.T.], 1932, pp. 149 ff., and *Prophetengestalten des Alten
Testaments*, 1938, pp. 316 ff.; K. Elliger, *Deuterojesaja in seinem Verhältnis zu
Trito-jesaja*, 1933, pp. 75 ff., 267 ff. For Mowinckel's modifications of his
own view, cf. *Z.A.W.*, N.F. viii, 1931, pp. 245 ff., *De senere profeter*, in
Michelet-Mowinckel-Messel, *Det Gamle Testamente*, iii, 1944, pp. 192 ff., and
He that Cometh, Eng. trans. by G. W. Anderson, 1956, pp. 187 ff.

suggested seem inadequate. It is hard to see how any writer in the exilic period could suppose that Moses, or Jeremiah, or Jehoiachin, or the prophet himself, could satisfy the conditions of this conception and serve as a sacrificial victim of such universal potency.[1] Hence, some have continued to advocate the traditional messianic interpretation.[2] Yet this is not without difficulties, and most of those who hold this view find themselves forced to delete the word *Israel* in Isa. 49: 3, on very inadequate grounds.[3] It seems wiser, therefore, to adopt no simple individual or collective view. It is probable that the Servant is in part the personification of the mission of Israel, and in part the delineation of one who should embody its mission in himself, and fulfil the mission with peculiar fullness, so that he should play a notable part in the achievement of the Golden Age.[4] Something of the fluidity of what has become

[1] For some views which find in the conception a variety of elements derived in part from the liturgy or from history, cf. H. S. Nyberg, *S.E.Å.* vii, 1942, pp. 5 ff.; I. Engnell, *ibid.* x, 1945, pp. 31 ff., and *B.J.R.L.* xxxi, 1948, pp. 54 ff.; A. Bentzen, *Indledning til det Gamle Testamente*, I i, 1941, pp. 98 ff., Eng. trans. *Introduction to the Old Testament*, ii, 1949, pp. 110 ff., and *Messias, Moses redivivus, Menschensohn*, 1948, Eng. trans. *King and Messiah*, 1955.

[2] So J. Fischer, *Wer ist der Ebed in den Perikopen Js 42, 1–7; 49, 1–9a; 50, 4–9; 52, 13–53, 12?* 1922, and *Das Buch Isaias* [H.S.A.Tes], ii, 1939, pp. 8 ff.; F. Feldmann, *Der Knecht Gottes in Isaias Kap. 40–45*, 1907, and *Das Buch Isaias* [E.H.A.T.], ii, 1926, pp. 16 ff.; J. van der Ploeg, *Les Chants du Serviteur de Jahvé*, 1936; O. Procksch, in *In piam memoriam A. von Bulmerincq*, 1938, pp. 146 ff.; P. Heinisch, *Theologie des Alten Testamentes*, 1940, pp, 316 ff.; A. H. Edelkoort, *De Christusverwachting in het Oude Testament*, 1941, pp. 372 ff.; R. T. Murphy, *C.B.Q.* ix, 1947, pp. 262 ff.; E. J. Young, *Westminster Theological Journal*, x, 1947–48, pp. 148 ff., esp. p. 151; L. Dennefeld, *Les Grands Prophètes* [Pirot and Clamer's *La Sainte Bible*], vii, 1947, pp. 156 f., 179, 184 f., 191 ff.

[3] A single unimportant MS omits the word. For a study of the value of the MS cf. J. A. Bewer, in *Studies in Memory of George A. Kohut*, 1935, pp. 86 ff. It is sometimes said that metrical reasons demand the excision, but actually the verse is metrically more regular with it than without it. Cf. F. Prätorius, *Z.A.W.* xxxvi, 1916, pp. 9 f.

[4] This is substantially the view of C. R. North, *The Suffering Servant in Deutero-Isaiah*, 1948, though with particular emphasis on the individual messianic element. His book provides an unrivalled review of the history of interpretation of the Servant. Cf. also the present writer's *The Servant of the Lord and other essays*, 1952, pp. 3 ff., and "Knecht Jahwes" in *R.G.G.*, 3rd edn., iii, 1959, cols. 1680 ff.

known as "corporate personality" is found here,[1] so that the Servant is both the community and an individual who represents it. While the mission will be peculiarly fulfilled in one, it is nevertheless the mission to which all are called, and all should enter in some measure into it. In either case, it seems to me certain that the prophet was looking into the future for the Servant. The Israel of his day did not fulfil his vision, and certainly no individual of that or an earlier day did. He could therefore only think of a future Israel that should fulfil this mission to the world through suffering, and of a future individual Israelite who should in himself and in his own sufferings carry that mission to a unique, and uniquely effective, point.[2]

Here, then, we must end our brief examination of the meaning of sacrifice in the thought of the Old Testament. We have not been able to study all the forms of sacrifice, or all the details of its varied ritual. Nor has our primary study been of such things as the originally apotropaic meaning of the Passover sacrifice, or of the terms of the message which later sacrifices were thought to present to God—a message of thankfulness, of plea, or of propitiation. Rather have we gone below that to the underlying thought of all sacrifice as the organ of the offerer's presentation of himself to God, the bearer of his spirit to the exalted Being he approached, and therefore meaningless unless he brought with it the appropriate spirit. It is not as an external act that it had meaning, but as an external act charged with his spirit. Yet neither can sacrifice be understood merely as man's approach to God. It is also God's approach to him, charged with power. It thus carries a two-way traffic, and

---

[1] Cf. H. Wheeler Robinson, "The Hebrew Conception of Corporate Personality", in *Werden und Wesen des Alten Testament* (B.Z.A.W. LXVI), ed. by J. Hempel, 1936, pp. 49 ff.; also in *The Psalmists*, ed. by D. C. Simpson, 1926, pp. 82 ff., and in *The People and the Book*, ed. by A. S. Peake, 1925, pp. 375 ff., and *The Cross of the Servant*, 1926. With the view of Wheeler Robinson, cf. that of O. Eissfeldt, *E.T.* XLIV, 1932–33, pp. 261 ff., and *Der Gottesknecht bei Deutero-jesaja*, 1933; also N. Johansson, *Parakletoi*, 1940, pp. 49 ff.

[2] Cf. what I have written on this subject in *Israel's Mission to the World*, 1939, pp. 10 ff.; *The Missionary Message of the Old Testament*, 1945, pp. 51 ff.; *The Biblical Doctrine of Election*, 1950, pp. 111 ff.

God's readiness to release power for the blessing of man through this avenue only waited for the opening of the two-way traffic by man's approach to Him in humility and submission. Yet all the animal sacrifices failed to meet man's need, since the sins that most needed cleansing were beyond the range of their power. A sacrifice greater than any the Law provided, and more far-ranging in its power, was therefore envisaged in the Old Testament, and its deepest word on sacrifice speaks of one never offered on the altar of the Temple or provided in the ritual of the Pentateuch, but one to which it looked forward beyond the Old Testament itself.

4

Ritual and the Hebrew Prophets

4

RITUAL AND THE HEBREW PROPHETS[1]

IT IS curious how labels get attached to men and to schools. In 1933 Professor Hooke edited a volume of essays published under the title *Myth and Ritual*, and since then he has been either praised or blamed as the leader of the "Myth and Ritual School". In reality those essays were largely a *mise au point* of studies which had been going on for some time, but mainly outside this country.[2] There had been a growing recognition of common elements in the culture and outlook of the peoples of the ancient Near East from the Nile to the Euphrates, and Professor Hooke and his colleagues underlined those common elements.[3] Little was then known of the Ras Shamra texts, which were only beginning to see the light, but from which a good deal of additional material can now be drawn for some aspects of the subject.

Some scholars, such as the late Henri Frankfort,[4] have since reacted strongly against the whole idea of a common pattern of culture, and have emphasized the diverse elements of Egyptian

[1] Previously published in *J.S.S.* I, 1956, pp. 338–60, and in *Myth, Ritual, and Kingship*, ed. by S. H. Hooke, 1958, pp. 236–60.

[2] While agreeing that studies in this field had been going on, especially in Scandinavia, prior to the publication of *Myth and Ritual*, Professor Hooke says it was not from these that the impulse which led to his volume of essays came (*Myth, Ritual, and Kingship*, p. 1), and that he did not know of Mowinckel's work until the project had been started (p. 2).

[3] O. Eissfeldt, in *O.T.M.S.*, 1951, p. 122, says that in this book and its sequel, *The Labyrinth*, ed. by S. H. Hooke, 1935, "the external analogies have been given precedence over the illustrative material to be found within the Old Testament itself." The measure of over-emphasis on what had hitherto been under-emphasized was less than in some more recent studies, and some, at any rate, of the writers had no desire to minimize the evidence of the Old Testament or to impose an alien pattern on the whole.

[4] Cf. the summary of his paper read to the 7th Congress for the History of Religions, held in Amsterdam in 1950, published in the *Proceedings* of the Congress, ed. by C. J. Bleeker, G. W. J. Drewes, and K. A. H. Hidding, 1951, pp. 99 f., and *The Problem of Similarity in Ancient Near Eastern Religions*, 1951.

and Babylonian civilization, and have dismissed "patternism" as something irrelevant to our studies. On the other hand, what has come to be known as the "Scandinavian School" has sometimes gone beyond Professor Hooke and his colleagues in emphasizing the common elements and in pressing "patternism" in ways which cannot be attributed to them. In truth, it is as misleading to speak of the "Scandinavian School" as to speak of the "Myth and Ritual School", since there are very real divergencies amongst the members of that supposed school. Professor Hooke and his colleagues were in some respects anticipated by Sigmund Mowinckel, in his very important *Psalmenstudien*,[1] and to him must be given a significant place in the history of "patternism". But since the headquarters of "patternism" moved to Sweden,[2] Mowinckel has sharply repudiated some of its developments and has been in turn severely criticized by Swedish colleagues. That there were common elements and diverse elements in the culture and practice of the peoples of the region with which we are concerned is hard to deny, and it is possible to repudiate the extremer views on either side without assuming a merely negative attitude to either.

Ivan Engnell, of Uppsala, has been a storm centre in recent Old Testament studies, partly by reason of his championship of Oral Tradition instead of Literary Criticism, and partly because of his development of one aspect of the "Myth and Ritual" views in his *Studies in Divine Kingship in the Ancient Near East*.[3] With the question of Divine Kingship I am not concerned in this paper. It may not be out of place to observe, however, that one of my predecessors in my chair in the University of Manchester, Professor M. A. Canney, in the very year in which *Myth and Ritual* was published, and quite independently of Professor Hooke's "school"—with which his name is never

[1] These *Psalmenstudien* were published in six parts in the *Skrifter* of the Norwegian Academy, 1921–24. For an estimate of their contribution to the study of the Psalter, cf. A. R. Johnson, in *O.T.M.S.*, pp. 189 ff.

[2] An important Danish contribution to "patternism", to which comparatively little attention has been given, is F. F. Hvidberg, *Graad og latter i det Gamle Testamente: en studie i Kanaanæisk-israelitisk religion*, 1938. This is now available in English as *Weeping and Laughter in the Old Testament*, 1962.

[3] Published in 1943.

associated—issued an article ten years before Engnell's book saw the light in which the self-same ideas were put forward in brief outline.[1] Canney argued that throughout our area and beyond kings were thought of as divine, and that in Israel the king was "virtually an incarnation of the deity".[2] In 1933 Manchester was as deeply involved in the ideas of the so-called "school" as any of its members, either then or later, whether in this country or in Scandinavia. Certainly not all of the members of Professor Hooke's team would have gone so far as Professor Canney, and I should stop a long way short of this.

The special aspect of the general subject which has been assigned to me for the present essay is one in which I think we owe the so-called "school" a debt of gratitude for the important contribution it has made to the study of the Old Testament—though again there are extremer expressions of that contribution which I do not endorse. The view that the Hebrew prophets were an entirely unique phenomenon in the religious history of the world—unique not only in the spiritual level they attained, but in the whole character of their work—is one that cannot be maintained. The recognition that there were prophets outside Israel very much like some of the early groups of prophets who come before us in the Old Testament has long been widespread, and nearly fifty years ago Hölscher's *Die Profeten*[3] emphasized what has come to be called the "ecstatic" character of Hebrew prophecy.[4] In the hands of some this

---

[1] Cf. *Oriental Studies in Honour of Cursetji Erachji Pavry*, 1933, pp. 63 ff. Professor Hooke (*Myth, Ritual and Kingship*, p. 1) says: "The truth of the matter is that Canney, Hocart, and myself are all members of the group who were working with Elliott Smith and Perry; and the kingship 'ideology', as our Scandinavian friends call it, developed by Canney and Hocart, was a product of the views put forward by Perry in his seminars and ultimately published in his book *The Children of the Sun*."

[2] *Ibid.* p. 74.

[3] Published in 1914.

[4] For the present writer's views on this subject cf. *The Servant of the Lord*, 1952, pp. 91 ff. There I say (p. 91 n.) that in my judgment the use of the term "ecstasy" has brought much confusion into the discussion of prophecy, and that there is commonly a looseness and want of definition in the use of the term (p. 93). This is underlined by A. R. Johnson (*The Cultic Prophet in Ancient Israel*, 2nd edn., 1962, p. 10 n.), who avoids the use of the term. Cf. E. Jacob (*Theology of the Old Testament*, Eng. trans. by A. W. Heathcote and P. J. Allcock, 1958, p. 242 n.), who says "if one understands by ecstasy

character has been ascribed to all Old Testament prophecy, and it has been maintained that every oracle arose out of some "ecstatic" experience.[1] This tendency to overpress evidence, and indeed to outrun it, is a constant danger to scholarship, and we shall find further instances of it as we proceed.

That the Egyptian story of Wen Amon[2] presents us with prophecy closely similar to that of the early Israelite prophets cannot be gainsaid. In that story we are told that a youth became possessed and continued in this state all the night, declaring that he was the mouthpiece of the god. More recently evidence of prophets at Mari at a much earlier date has come to light.[3] It is therefore quite impossible to treat Hebrew prophecy as an isolated phenomenon. It grew out of a background of ancient Near Eastern prophecy, going back very far and spreading widely.[4] In the Old Testament we read of prophets of Baal,[5] and evidence of similar prophets in neighbouring countries at a later time has long been familiar.[6]

the concentration of a subject on an object, to a point where that object alone impinges upon him to the exclusion of all others, the use of the term seems legitimate." J. Lindblom (*Festschrift Alfred Bertholet*, 1950, pp. 325 ff.) had earlier distinguished between *Verschmelzungsekstase*, or mystical absorption, and *Konzentrationsekstase*, or ecstatic concentration.

[1] Cf. W. Jacobi, *Die Ekstase der alttestamentlichen Propheten*, 1920, p. 4: "Ecstasy is of the essence of prophecy"; H. Gunkel, *The Expositor*, 9th series, I (1924), p. 358: "The fundamental experience of all types of prophecy is ecstasy"; also T. H. Robinson, *Prophecy and the Prophets in Ancient Israel*, 1923, p. 50. In *E.T.* XLVI, 1934–35, p. 43, T. H. Robinson maintains that an objective criterion, in the form of some kind of ecstatic experience, was demanded by both prophet and hearers for each oracle.

[2] A translation of this story, by J. A. Wilson, may be found in *A.N.E.T.*, 2nd edn., 1955, pp. 25 ff.

[3] Cf. A. Lods, in *Studies in Old Testament Prophecy*, ed. by H. H. Rowley, 1950, pp. 103 ff.; M. Noth, *B.J.R.L.* XXXII, 1949–50, pp. 194 ff., and *Geschichte und Gotteswort im Alten Testament*, 1950; F. M. Th. de Liagre Böhl, *Nederlands Theologisch Tijdschrift*, IV, 1949–50, pp. 82 ff.; W. von Soden, *Die Welt des Orients*, 1950, pp. 397 ff.; and H. Schmökel, *Th.L.Z.*, LXXVI, 1940, cols. 54 ff.

[4] Cf. A. Neher, *L'Essence du prophétisme*, 1955, pp. 17 ff.

[5] I Kg. 18: 19 ff. Their conduct as described in verse 28 was "ecstatic".

[6] Cf. Hölscher, *Die Profeten*, pp. 132 ff.; T. H. Robinson, *The Classical Quarterly*, XI, 1917, pp. 201 ff., and *Prophecy and the Prophets*, pp. 33 f. Cf. also J. Lindblom, "Zur Frage des kanaanäischen Ursprungs des altisraelitischen Prophetismus" in *Von Ugarit nach Qumran* (Eissfeldt Festschrift), 1958, pp. 89 ff.

Nevertheless, if Hebrew prophecy grew out of this background, we should not forget that it did grow. All should not be seen in terms of a particular manifestation, and that especially characteristic of an early period. That there was an abnormal element in even the greater prophets of the Old Testament may be allowed; but this does not mean that all prophecy was "ecstatic", or that every oracle was born in a special abnormal experience. Wheeler Robinson thought it unlikely that "a prophet of the classical period would have dared to prophesy without an inaugural vision such as Isaiah's in the temple, or an audition such as Jeremiah's, or such a characteristically peculiar experience as that of Ezekiel", and added: "Moreover, we may expect such experiences to recur from time to time, and our expectation is fulfilled."[1] Whether these experiences of vocation are rightly described as "ecstatic" need not detain us.[2] Quite apart from these experiences we find the prophets sometimes behaving in ways which would soon get them into trouble in the modern world. Isaiah on and off over a period of three years was liable to be seen walking through the streets of Jerusalem naked and barefoot;[3] and Jeremiah appeared in the Temple wearing a wooden yoke.[4] These were acted prophecies, usually described by the term "prophetic symbolism". They are not evidence of prophetic "ecstasy", to be put on the same level as Saul's stripping off his clothes and rolling about on the ground naked all night,[5] but they are evidence of abnormal behaviour. Nevertheless, no study of Hebrew prophecy can end with the outer behaviour of the prophet. The prophet claims to be the mouthpiece of God,[6] and it is by the message he delivers that his claim is to be judged.

[1] Cf. *Redemption and Revelation*, 1942, pp. 143 f. Cf. also J. P. Hyatt, *Prophetic Religion*, 1947, p. 17.

[2] J. Skinner admitted the use of the term. Cf. *Prophecy and Religion*, 1922, p. 4 n.: "The fact that the great prophets far surpassed their predecessors in their apprehension of religious truth is no reason for denying the reality of the ecstatic element in their experience, or for explaining it away as a mere rhetorical accommodation to traditional modes of expression."

[3] Isa. 20: 2 ff.

[4] Jer. 27: 2, 28: 10.

[5] 1 Sam. 19: 24.

[6] Cf. Exod. 7: 1 f., 4: 16; Jer. 1: 9; also the common prophetic formula, "Thus saith the Lord."

I 115

It is here that the development of Hebrew prophecy shows itself. Linked with prophecy elsewhere in its beginnings and in some of its forms of expression, it rises in the greater prophets whose oracles are preserved for us in the Bible to great spiritual heights. We must not close our eyes to the fact that all the prophets of Israel did not rise to these sublime heights. If one thing is clear to the student of the Old Testament, it is that there were many varieties of prophet in Israel, and the uniqueness that may be claimed for Hebrew prophecy is something that belonged to but a few of the prophetic figures that come before us, and something that lies in the content of their message rather than in the form of its delivery.[1]

A generation ago it was common amongst scholars to set the prophets and the priests over against one another in the sharpest way. The prophets were presented as men who had no use whatever for any of the practices of the cultus, and who thought it was wholly alien to the will of God.[2] Professor Volz wrote: "The Old Testament prophetic religion stands in the sharpest contrast to priestly religion, or Cult Religion. Priestly religion is the religion of sacrifice; the priest brings the gifts of men from below up to the Deity. Prophetic religion is the religion of the word; it brings the voice of God from above down to men."[3]

On such a view the prophets were limited for all practical purposes to the canonical prophets, and the familiar passages in which they denounce the ritual observances of their day were given an extreme interpretation and held to mean that they condemned the cultus root and branch. The passages on which this view was based were mainly Isa. 1: 10 ff., Am. 5: 21 ff., Hos. 6: 6, Mic. 6: 6 ff., Jer. 6: 20, 7: 21 ff., and together they were held to show that in the eyes of the prophets all sacrifice

[1] Cf. H. Birkeland, *The Evildoers in the Book of Psalms*, 1955, p. 18: "A text translated from Hebrew as opposed to Akkadian literature reveals such immense differences that everybody who can read discovers them at once. Common patterns existed, it is true. But in most cases they have to be detected by the scholarly work of specialists."

[2] Cf. J. A. Bewer, *The Literature of the Old Testament in its Historical Development*, 1922, p. 267: "Religion was a matter of the cult. The earlier prophets had violently protested against such a conception of religion and rejected the entire cultic apparatus as contrary to the will of God."

[3] Cf. *Prophetengestalten des Alten Testaments*, 1938, p. 56.

was an abomination to God, and the Temple itself was an offence in His eyes. Not all scholars took this extreme view, and I have more than once argued from the study of the prophetic books themselves that it cannot be maintained.[1] I agree with A. C. Welch that "the judgment that the prophets were unanimous in their attitude toward the cult, and that they agreed in condemning it *per se*, does not do justice to the facts",[2] and that the claim "that their common view was one which condemned the cult *in toto* can only be proved from isolated passages pressed beyond the terms of a just exegesis".[3] If the prophets had really meant that sacrifice under all circumstances was evil, they would not have needed to bring condemnation of the lives of men into association with their denunciation of the sacrifices. Isaiah condemns sacrifice, sacred festival and prayer, and says, "Your hands are full of blood."[4] If it was for this reason that their ritual observances were condemned, this would be understandable; but we should not then conclude that the condemnation of the observances was absolute. If the prophet meant that even if their hands were not full of blood, their sacrifices and their prayers would equally be an offence to God, he would have been wiser not to mention the irrelevance. Jeremiah spoke of the coming destruction of the Temple, but made it clear that if men would amend their ways, the Temple might be spared.[5] He could scarcely have thought that the Temple was in itself an offence to God. We ought therefore not to go beyond our text, but to be content to say that these prophets declared that the religious observances of

---

[1] Cf. *Melilah*, ed. by E. Robertson and M. Wallenstein, I, 1944, pp. 185 ff.; *B.J.R.L.* xxix, 1945–46, pp. 326 ff.; xxxiii, 1950–51, pp. 74 ff. (reprinted above, pp. 67 ff.); and *The Unity of the Bible*, 1953, pp. 30 ff.

[2] *Prophet and Priest in Old Israel*, 1936, p. 17.

[3] *Ibid.* pp. 17 f. Cf. also K. Roubos, *Profetie en Cultus in Israël*, 1956, pp. 68 ff., 113. Cf. E. Jacob, *Theology of the Old Testament*, Eng. trans. by A. W. Heathcote and P. J. Allcock, 1958, p. 246 n.: "The question of the 'anti-cultic' preaching of the prophets has often been examined within the course of recent years; it seems that opinion is taking a middle position, the prophets being neither cultic agents nor systematic opponents of the cult, but the heralds of God's sovereignty which the cult could express, but which it could also on occasion cause to be forgotten."

[4] Isa. 1: 15.

[5] Jer. 7: 5 ff.

their day were meaningless in the eyes of God because they were the observances of men whose lives were an offence to Him. They were not the expression of the devotion of their hearts, but rather the proud expression of the defiance of their spirit. That the prophets who spoke in this way say little in praise of the cultus is to be understood. For they were dealing with the situation of their own day, when for many the ritual was an end in itself.[1]

By the "Myth and Ritual School" this question has been approached from another side, and the simple antithesis between priests and prophets has now few defenders. So long ago as 1914 Hölscher had already suggested that there were prophets who stood beside the priests in the shrines, where they belonged to the cultic staff.[2] These prophets he differentiated from the canonical prophets, however. Since then, as we shall see, much water had flowed under the bridge. In the third part of his *Studies in the Psalms*, published in 1923,[3] Mowinckel took up the question of cultic prophets, and argued that there were such officials functioning in the shrines beside the priests,[4] and that not a few of the psalms were, at least in part, composed by them. Amongst the psalms he notes are some which he associates with the "great festivals",[5] some which he classes as prophetic

---

[1] Cf. B. W. Anderson, *Understanding of the Old Testament*, 1957, p. 460: "Many Protestants have tended to 'play down' the priestly emphasis of Judaism, even to the point of affirming that prophetic religion was fundamentally opposed to priestly religion . . . Israel's prophetic movement emerged out of the cultus. Many of the early prophets were 'cultic prophets', intimately associated with the sanctuary. And it is no exaggeration to say that all the great prophets were dependent upon the cultus, even those who criticized it most radically." W. Eichrodt (*Theology of the Old Testament*, Eng. trans. by J. A. Baker, I, 1961, p. 333) traces the formation of Temple prophecy to the degeneration of spirit-filled dynamism to a spiritual trade, whereby the prophetic proclamation of the divine will became the function of a cultic official, who gave his liturgically prescribed message at the point allotted to him in the service.

[2] Cf. *Die Profeten*, p. 143.

[3] *Psalmenstudien* III: *Kultprophetie und prophetische Psalmen*.

[4] In *Wisdom in Israel and in the Ancient Near East* (Rowley Festschrift), 1955, p. 206, Mowinckel says "the majority of prophets formed an official class of cult functionaries."

[5] Ps. 132; 89: 20–38 (E.V. 19–37); 81; and 95; 50; 82; 75; 87; 85; 14; and 12.

oracles,[1] some which he calls royal oracles,[2] and some which were for private cultic use.[3] His fundamental view of the psalms was that they were ritual texts, used to accompany the sacred acts of worship. It will be seen at once how closely this ties up with the ideas of the "Myth and Ritual School". For in the opening essay of *Myth and Ritual* Professor Hooke defined what was meant by "myth" in the words: "In general the spoken part of a ritual consists of a description of what is being done, it is the story which the ritual enacts. This is the sense in which the term 'myth' is used in our discussion. The original myth, inseparable in the first instance from its ritual, embodies in more or less symbolic fashion the original situation which is seasonally re-enacted in the ritual."[4] That has relevance to much more than the Psalter, of course, but Mowinckel's understanding of the use of the psalms was not dissimilar. In this he was followed by Welch,[5] who also rejected the view that prophets and priests were diametrically opposed to one another[6]—though Welch was not a member of the "Myth and Ritual School".

By older writers the Psalter had often been referred to as "The Hymn Book of the Second Temple", and the composition of most of the psalms had been assigned to the post-exilic period. Now, on the contrary, the antiquity of many of the psalms was maintained, and they were related to the pre-exilic ritual of the Temple in a more intimate way than the term "Hymn Book" suggests to us. The psalm was believed to express the meaning of the ritual it accompanied, and particular psalms were thought to belong to particular rites. Where all this concerns

[1] Ps. 60; 108; 20; and 21.
[2] Ps. 2; 110; 72; and 45.
[3] Ps. 91 and 62.
[4] p. 3.
[5] Cf. *The Psalter in Life, Worship, and History*, 1926, pp. 62 ff. On p. 59 Welch observed that "the psalter is remarkably acultic", but this did not mean unrelated to the cult; for on p. 63 he says: "It needs, then, to be emphasized at the beginning that the psalter was far more closely related to the cult-practice and its recurrent ritual than has been generally recognized in the ordinary English commentaries." While Welch makes no reference to Mowinckel in his chapter on "The Psalter and Worship", his footnote on p. 94 shows that he was familiar with the Norwegian scholar's work.
[6] Cf. *Prophet and Priest in Old Israel*, 1936.

STUDIES IN THE OLD TESTAMENT

our subject in the present essay is in that Mowinckel held that many of the psalms arose in the prophetic responses in the worship. The cultic prophets were believed to have been the representatives of the congregation, who were caught up into ecstasy in all the excitement of the religious festival, and who fulfilled the function which all the congregation should ideally have fulfilled, and made the response to which they were prompted by the divine power.[1] In later times, Mowinckel argued, their place was taken by the Temple singers.[2]

Some of these ideas of Mowinckel's were taken up and presented to English readers in a brief paper by A. R. Johnson nearly thirty years ago.[3] Following Mowinckel he developed the view that there were cultic prophets beside the priests, with a defined place in the ritual worship,[4] and that in post-exilic times they developed into the singers of the Second Temple. Following Mowinckel again he held that some of the psalms were composed by cultic prophets for use in the ritual of the Temple.[5] More recently he has published a monograph dealing with the first part of this thesis,[6] leaving the second part to be developed in a forthcoming monograph, of which only the title is yet available.[7]

That there is not a little evidence in the Old Testament to support this view is beyond question. It is impossible to cite all the evidence here, and unnecessary since it can be found in the works of Mowinckel and Johnson. Briefly it may be noted that it rests on the frequent association of priests and prophets with one another and with the Temple, and of prophets with cultic

[1] *Op. cit.* pp. 16 ff. Cf. the view of H. Junker (*Prophet und Seher in Israel,* 1927, pp. 22 f.), where the prophets are associated with the sacred dance at the shrines, and with the sacred poetry which was sung as its accompaniment.

[2] *Op. cit.* pp. 24 ff.

[3] Cf. *E.T.* xlvii, 1935–36, pp. 312 ff.

[4] Cf. also J. H. Eaton, *Obadiah, Nahum, Habakkuk and Zephaniah* (Torch Bible), 1961, pp. 24 f.

[5] Cf. *The Labyrinth,* pp. 80, 109, where Ps. 132: 11–18 and 110 are so interpreted. Cf. also H. Junker, *op. cit.,* pp. 38 ff.

[6] *The Cultic Prophet in Ancient Israel,* 1944, 2nd edn. 1962.

[7] *The Cultic Prophet and the Psalter* (cf. *The Cultic Prophet in Ancient Israel,* p. 5 n.). There is as yet no indication when this monograph may be expected (cf. 2nd edn., p. v.).

occasions. A few examples, all from the Book of Jeremiah, may suffice. In Jer. 26 we read that prophets and priests together heard Jeremiah's utterance in the Temple and together accused him to the authorities.[1] Elsewhere Jeremiah links prophet and priest together, and declares that their wickedness has been found in the Temple.[2] In yet another passage he speaks of prophets uttering false prophecies and the priests ruling at their direction.[3] Moreover, in the Book of Jeremiah we find a reference to a room in the Temple belonging to the sons of a prophet.[4] All of this and much more would seem to establish an association between prophets and priests, and in particular between prophets and the Temple.

Moreover, when the Shunammite woman wished to go to Elisha to tell him of the death of her child, her husband expressed surprise that she should go on a day which was neither new moon nor sabbath.[5] From this it is clear that it was customary to visit prophets on cultic occasions. An association between prophets and religious festivals, as well as between prophets and the Temple, seems therefore to be established.

This once more leaves open the question of the relation between the canonical prophets and such cultic prophets. Mowinckel distinguished between them, though, as will be seen, he blurred the distinction to some extent. One of the Swedish scholars has failed to find any distinction, and has claimed that all the Israelite prophets belonged to guilds of cultic prophets. Writing of him Eissfeldt says: "The question whether the writing prophets belonged to the cultic associations is answered with an emphatic affirmative, and it is plainly laid

[1] Jer. 26: 7, 11.
[2] Jer. 23: 11.
[3] Jer. 5: 31 (R.S.V.; R.V. has "by their means").
[4] Jer. 35: 4. The term "man of God" which stands in this verse is elsewhere frequently used for a prophet. Cf. 1 Sam. 9: 6 ff., 1 Kg. 13: 11, 18, 2 Kg. 5: 8. The phrase 'nš 'lm is found in Ugaritic (C. H. Gordon, *Ugaritic Handbook*, 1947, p. 129, Text I, line 22); and E. Dhorme (*R.B.* XL, 1931, p. 36) and H. L. Ginsberg (*The Ugarit Texts*, 1936, p. 112) connected this with the Hebrew 'ish 'elōhîm = "man of God". Whether this stands for "prophet" in Ugaritic is uncertain, however. Dhorme (*loc. cit.*) thought it meant "the servant of the gods", and Gordon (*Ugaritic Literature*, 1949, p. 112) renders "the servitors of the gods".
[5] 2 Kg. 4: 23.

down that no more difference is to be made between the writing prophets and their predecessors in this respect than in any other."[1] The Swedish scholar in question is A. Haldar, who has carried "patternism" to the length of equating all the Israelite prophets with guilds of diviners found in Babylonia.[2] There we find evidence of guilds of diviners who bear the names of *bārū* and *maḫḫū*. The *bārū* is defined as one whose divination depended on technical methods,[3] and the *maḫḫū* as one who received his oracle in a state of ecstasy,[4] but their functions are said to have overlapped, so that there was a "cumul des fonctions".[5] Haldar says it is "obvious" that the Hebrew "seer" and "prophet" are essentially different from one another—though it will be seen later that this is by no means obvious—and he equates the "seer" with the *bārū* and the "prophet" with the *maḫḫū*, and then proceeds to use the Babylonian material to interpret the function of the Hebrew seers and prophets.[6] Mowinckel had brought the cultic prophets into association with non-Israelite groups,[7] but had not involved the theory of cultic prophets in such embarrassment as this extreme view threatened to do. Engnell had earlier held that Amos was a cultic official,[8] and in this he was followed by Haldar.[9] More

[1] Cf. *O.T.M.S.*, pp. 123 ff.
[2] Cf. *Associations of Cult Prophets among the Ancient Semites*, 1945. On Haldar cf. J. Lindblom, *Festschrift Alfred Bertholet*, 1950, pp. 328 ff.
[3] *Op. cit.* pp. 6 ff.
[4] *Ibid.* pp. 21 ff.
[5] *Ibid.* p. 28.
[6] *Ibid.* p. 124.
[7] Cf. *Psalmenstudien* III, p. 5.
[8] In *Studies in Divine Kingship*, p. 87, Engnell argued that the term *nōḳēdh*, which is used of Amos in Am. 1: 1 and of Mesha of Moab in 2 Kg. 3: 4, denoted a cultic official, and in *S.B.U.* 1, 1948, cols. 59 f., he directly states that Amos was a cultic official. A. S. Kapelrud (*Central Ideas in Amos*, 1956, 2nd edn., 1961, pp. 5 ff.) follows this view and maintains that Amos "may have been a person of rather high rank who was responsible for a large part of the temple herds. Economically, as well as in what concerned the temple cult, he was therefore an important person". Both Engnell and Kapelrud cite the Ras Shamra text in which Atn-prln is described as *rb. khnm. rb., nqdm*. But it cannot be assumed that the area of meaning of Ugaritic *nqd* and Hebrew *nōḳēdh* was the same, and it is quite improbable that Mesha was a cultic official of any Israelite shrine.
[9] *Op. cit.* pp. 79 n., 112. Haldar says "Amos is said to be among the

recently it has been claimed that Amos was a hepatoscoper,[1] a mere technician in the art of reading liver omens on which to base his oracles. That there were diviners amongst the Israelite prophets is, indeed, quite certain from references found in the Old Testament. Micah says: "The priests give direction for payment, and the prophets divine for money."[2] It is almost certainly true that there were classes of diviners found in Israel, despite the condemnation of divination which we find in several passages.[3] Indeed, it is unlikely that we should have found such frequent condemnation if the practice had no footing amongst the people. But it is an abuse of "patternism" to read the Babylonian situation into the Hebrew, and to reduce all the Old Testament prophets to divining classes.[4] The

'shepherds' of Tekoa (Am. 1:1) and calls himself *bôḳēr* (7: 14), which shows him to have belonged to the cult staff" (p. 112), and assumes that "there was probably some sort of a filial of the Jerusalemitic priesthood". On this cf. N. W. Porteous, *E.T.* LXII, 1950–51, p. 8. Against the view of Engnell and Haldar, cf. K. Roubos, *op. cit.* pp. 4 ff. Roubos curiously links Johnson with Engnell and Haldar (pp. 112, 119) and gives his readers the completely erroneous impression that Johnson shares these views about Amos. It can only be supposed that he is unacquainted with the work of Johnson, whom he strangely describes as one whose inventiveness he cannot help admiring, and who draws conclusions with an ease at which he cannot but wonder. The facility with which Roubos has drawn his own conclusion is even more surprising, for in his monograph Johnson specifically states that he is not dealing with the canonical prophets, and that the question of how they are to be seen against the background of cultic prophecy is reserved for future consideration. In his Preface he observes (p. v.): "The whole subject of prophecy in ancient Israel is much more complex than is commonly recognized; and in this revised edition of my work I have felt it necessary to draw attention more than once to the disservice to Old Testament study which may be done by over-simplifying the issues and resorting to easy generalizations."

[1] Cf. M. Bič, *V.T.* I, 1951, pp. 293 ff. Against this cf. A. Murtonen, *ibid.* II, 1952, pp. 170 ff.

[2] Mic. 3: 11; cf. Ezek. 13: 6, 9; 22: 28.

[3] Cf. Lev. 19: 26; Dt. 18: 10; 1 Sam. 15: 23; 28: 3; 2 Kg. 17: 17; 21: 6; also Isa. 3: 2; Mic. 3: 11; Jer. 27: 9; 29: 8; Ezek. 13: 6, 9; 22: 28; Zech. 10: 2.

[4] H. J. Kraus (*Gottesdienst in Israel*, 1954, p. 110) says it is an undue simplification of the problems to dispose of the relations of the prophets to the cultus by the slogan "cult prophecy". It is curious that he shows no acquaintance with the work of Haldar, but justifies this comment by a

"Myth and Ritual School" did not begin in such doctrinaire rigidities.

It might seem, then, that we should draw as sharp a line between two sorts of prophet as was formerly drawn between prophet and priest, and that cultic prophets should be linked with the priests and set over against the canonical prophets as persons of a wholly different order, who should never have been designated by the same name.[1] We know beyond a peradventure that there were inner divisions between the prophets, and that each side accused the other of being false prophets. Jeremiah issued a sustained attack on the false prophets of his day,[2] and charged them with being poor technicians who stole one another's oracles to disguise their incompetence and lack of divine direction.[3] The Book of Deuteronomy bears witness to

reference to the works of Mowinckel and Johnson. Probably both authors would say that this comment is an over-simplification of their view, and would doubt whether Kraus had read their works with sufficient care to understand them. As the present essay may sufficiently show, their work arose out of a protest against the older simplification, and they are careful not to fall into a new simplification, but to recognize that in dealing with Old Testament religion no simple dichotomies are justified.

[1] A. Jepsen, *Nabi*, 1934, endeavours to establish this kind of sharp line between the greater prophetic figures of the Old Testament and the prophets of the *nābhî'* type, whose name has unfortunately become attached to them. His distinction is not between cultic prophets and non-cultic, but between professional prophets and non-ecstatic prophets. Its mistake lies, as so often, in the desire for something clear cut. N. W. Porteous (in *Record and Revelation*, ed. by H. W. Robinson, 1938, p. 233) says: "It is difficult to believe that Jepsen is right in making the cleavage between *nebi'im* and canonical prophets as absolute as he does. His theory has the weakness of every theory which depends on a thoroughgoing revision of the text that is not at all points convincing . . . It seems likely that they (i.e. the great prophets) had something in common with the *nebi'im* which made it natural for men to group them together with the latter." A. Neher (*L'Essence du Prophétisme*, 1955, pp. 207 ff.) identifies "nabism" with cultic prophecy, and holds that after the destruction of Shiloh the prophets substituted themselves for the priests and assumed priestly functions. R. Hentschke (*Die Stellung der vorexilischen Schriftpropheten zum Kultus*, 1957, p. 142) erroneously attributes to A. R. Johnson the view that the *nebhî'îm*, identified with the cultic prophets, exercised priestly functions (cf. *J.S.S.* v, 1960, p. 304).
[2] Jer. 23: 9 ff.
[3] Jer. 23: 30.

the prevalence and the danger of false prophets, when it twice offers guidance for their detection.[1] Unfortunately that guidance is not very clear. In one case it says that the prophet whose word does not come true is a false prophet; but in this case the guidance is too late to save people from being misled by his specious promises. In the other passage it says that even if the prediction comes true the prophet who draws people away from God is a false prophet; but since the prophets on both sides spoke in the name of God and claimed to be His mouthpiece, the bewildered hearers were not helped to distinguish between them. The fact that the compilers of Deuteronomy, who clearly wished to help men in this respect, could find no satisfactory way of doing so is sufficient to show that we cannot simply identify the false prophets with the cultic prophets and divorce the true prophets from the cultus.[2] Had there been so unmistakable a principle of discrimination, Deuteronomy might have been expected to indicate it.

The inner division between true and false prophets first comes before us in the story of Micaiah, in the time of Ahab and Jehoshaphat.[3] But Micaiah and the prophets who were opposed to him were as much, or as little, cultic prophets. They were clearly prophets of the same order, making claims to utter oracles which Yahweh gave them, and Micaiah can only offer the explanation that Yahweh had suffered a lying spirit to mislead Zedekiah the son of Chenaanah.[4] Similarly, when Jeremiah was ridiculed in the Temple by a prophet who spoke with

---

[1] Dt. 13: 1 ff. 18: 22.

[2] J. Jocz (*The Spiritual History of Israel*, 1961, p. 69 n.) says: "That there were cultic 'prophets' there can be little doubt. We venture the suggestion that these are somehow related to the 'false prophets' frequently mentioned in the Old Testament." This is one of those undue simplifications against which Johnson frequently warns. Cf. my *Servant of the Lord*, 1952, p. 128. J. H. Eaton (*op. cit.* p. 26) rejects such a view.

[3] 1 Kg. 22: 5 ff.

[4] 1 Kg. 22: 21 ff. Kraus (*op. cit.* pp. 114 f.) makes the astonishing assumption that this vision must have taken place at "the amphictyonic centre", and that it provides evidence for his theory that the call of the prophets was associated with the Ark. This is pure eisegesis. There is no reference whatsoever to the "call" of Micaiah, who was known to be a prophet long before this incident (cf. 1 Kg. 22: 8), and there is no suggestion whatever that when he was sent for he was in any shrine, or had to visit a shrine for this vision

a different voice from his,[1] it is apparent that both claimed a like status and a like inspiration, and once more the difference between true and false prophet is one which could not easily be discerned by the common people.

Clearly we cannot draw sharp lines to divide off the different classes of prophet from one another. That there were many varieties of them may be known with certainty. Apart from the term "man of God", which stands for a prophet, we find the terms *rō'eh* and *ḥōzeh,* both meaning "seer", and *nābhî',* whose precise etymological meaning is not agreed,[2] but which certainly stands for various kinds of prophet. In 1 Sam. 9: 9 we find the terms *rō'eh* and *nābhî'* equated, and though it is probable that originally they stood for identifiably different varieties of sacred person, it is impossible to carry any distinction through the passages where the various terms are used. The passage in 1 Sam. 9: 9 says "he that is now called a prophet (*nābhî'*) was formerly called a seer (*rō'eh*)". Both terms are applied to Samuel, and we find that Gad is called both a prophet and a seer in the same verse (the term for "seer" being there *ḥōzeh*).[3]

Of the varieties of the functioning of the persons described by these various terms a few examples must suffice. Samuel is found available for consultation at Ramah,[4] where he apparently presides at a sacred feast,[5] and he tells Saul to await him at the shrine of Gilgal.[6] Ahijah is available for consultation at Shiloh,[7] though it is improbable that there was a shrine there in his day.[8] Gad is the king's seer,[9] and there is no suggestion

before he could come into the King's presence. Moreover, since Micaiah was a northern prophet, it is not clear how the Ark, which was at Jerusalem, comes into the picture at all.

[1] Jer. 28: 1 ff.
[2] Cf. *The Servant of the Lord,* 1952, pp. 96 ff., where I discuss this question with reference to the views of other scholars.
[3] 2 Sam. 24: 11.
[4] 1 Sam. 9: 6 ff.
[5] 1 Sam. 9: 22 ff.
[6] 1 Sam. 10: 8.
[7] 1 Kg. 14: 1 ff.
[8] The Danish excavations at Shiloh have shown that the place was destroyed in the eleventh century B.C. and that its occupation thereafter was very slight for some centuries. Cf. Kjaer, *P.E.F.Q.S.,* 1927, pp. 202 ff., 1931, pp. 71 ff., and A. Mallon, *Biblica* x, 1929, pp. 369 ff.
[9] 2 Sam. 24: 11.

that he functioned in any shrine. Elisha is consulted in his own home by Naaman,[1] and is summoned to the presence of the kings of Israel and Judah on a campaign against Edom.[2] Nathan waylaid David on the roadside when he went to rebuke him for his conduct in relation to Bathsheba and Uriah,[3] and an unnamed prophet similarly waylaid Ahab after a battle,[4] and Elijah on another occasion waylaid the same king.[5] In all these cases the prophet appears to have functioned as an individual figure in various places, and certainly not always in relation to any religious observance in a shrine, though sometimes he is found there. The prophet Samuel even exercised the priestly function of sacrifice.[6] On the other hand we sometimes find prophets in companies. There were such companies living at Bethel,[7] at Jericho,[8] and at Gilgal,[9] or prophesying by the wayside under the hill of Gibeah,[10] or with Samuel at Ramah.[11] Large numbers of Baal prophets were maintained by Jezebel,[12] and at the end of Ahab's reign we find a similar group of Yahweh prophets at his court.[13] Evidence that some of the prophets found their oracles by divination has already been mentioned. Others were stirred to prophecy by music,[14] or found their messages through dreams.[15] It is quite impossible to reduce all these to a single category of prophet, or to define which were true and which were false in terms of the place where they functioned or whether they functioned alone or in groups. All

---

[1] 2 Kg. 5: 9.
[2] 2 Kg. 3: 11.
[3] 2 Sam. 12: 1.
[4] 1 Kg. 20: 38.
[5] 1 Kg. 21: 17 ff.
[6] 1 Sam. 10: 8.
[7] 2 Kg. 2: 3.

[8] 2 Kg. 2: 5.
[9] 2 Kg. 4: 38.
[10] 1 Sam. 10: 5, 10.
[11] 1 Sam. 19: 18 ff.
[12] 1 Kg. 18: 19.
[13] 1 Kg. 22: 6.

[14] 2 Kg. 3: 15; cf. 1 Sam. 10: 5. T. J. Meek (*Hebrew Origins*, 1936, p. 168; 2nd ed., 1950, p. 173) notes that in the latter of these passages there is no indication that the music was more than the accompaniment of the prophetic state, whereas in the former it was used to bring on that state. He therefore holds that this was a development of professionalism. "One mark of this growing professionalism," he says, "was the use of mechanical means to induce the prophetic ecstasy." H. Junker (*op. cit.* p. 32) thinks the prophets in 1 Sam. 10: 5 were returning from the shrine, and brings this passage into association with the procession psalms.

[15] Num. 12: 6; Jer. 23: 28.

we can say with confidence is that the prophet was a sacred person, who could exercise his prophetic ministry in a shrine or elsewhere, and that hard and fast lines could not be drawn between the various kinds of prophet, or the relation of a prophet to God be deduced from the circumstances in which he prophesied.

If there were cultic prophets who had a defined place in the ritual of the shrines, and who shared with the priests in the services which took place there as officials of the cultus,[1] it is impossible to suppose that the major canonical prophets exercised their ministry in this way. Here I am in the fullest agreement with T. J. Meek, who says: "It is questionable whether many of the canonical prophets were cult officials, despite the opinion of modern scholars to the contrary."[2] It is true that Amos prophesied in the shrine at Bethel,[3] but it is scarcely likely that it was as an official sharing in the sacred rite of the sanctuary that he functioned. Isaiah received his call in the Temple,[4] either when he was actually in the Temple or present in vision only, but there is no reason to suppose that he was on its staff.[5] Jeremiah prophesied in the Temple when he an-

---

[1] N. W. Porteous (*E.T.* LXII, 1950–51, p. 8) suggests that the cultic prophets were priests with an added gift. He says: "May the supposed cult prophets not merely be priests who, like Jeremiah and Ezekiel, were specially endowed to undertake the sacramental side of worship, but unlike them, did not feel forced into an attitude of criticism toward the cult? Haldar's principle of cumulation of functions might very well apply here."

[2] Cf. *Hebrew Origins*, 2nd edn., pp. 178 ff. Th. C. Vriezen (*An Outline of Old Testament Theology*, Eng. trans. by S. Neuijen, 1958, p. 56) finds four different kinds of prophets: "cultic prophets, attached to the temple, who were at the same time government officials, for temple and state are fundamentally one; there was a highly ecstatic prophetism, which reminds us of pre- and non-Israelite divinational phenomena; there were 'group-prophets', who belonged to mystical communities; and also independent prophets." Cf. p. 261: "We do not deny that in certain periods many prophets were connected with the temple, but we do deny that the prophets as such were official assistants at the cult."

[3] Am. 7: 10 ff.

[4] Engnell, in *The Call of Isaiah*, 1949, offers an interpretation of Isa. 6 in terms of the New Year festival and the royal rites that belonged to it as the background of the prophet's experience.

[5] Cf. T. J. Meek, *Hebrew Origins*, 2nd edn., p. 179: "It has sometimes been said that Isaiah was in the temple as a cult official when he had the vision

nounced its destruction,[1] but it could hardly have been as a participant in any official service. Haldar asserts that Jerimiah "obviously" belonged to the Temple staff,[2] but to other scholars this is anything but obvious. On another occasion we find him prophesying in the Temple,[3] but following that incident we find that the exiles in Babylon ask why ihe Temple authorities cannot keep him in order.[4] Within the Temple he is subject to the discipline of the Temple authorities, but there is no indication that the activities complained of were part of the organized worship of the Temple. Within the Temple precincts much went on besides the organized worship. In the New Testament we find Jesus teaching in the Temple,[5] thoug hHe cannot be supposed to have been a member of the Temple personnel. Just as He could gather a group around Him and speak to them, so, it may be presumed, Old Testament prophets could gather groups around them within the precincts of Temple or shrine, without necessarily being officially associated with the sanctuary.

Not all of Jeremiah's prophesying was done in the Temple. He could be sent for by Zedekiah to give him privately the word of the Lord;[6] he could go to the house of the potter,[7] there to find a message for men, or the sight of two baskets of figs could prompt an oracle.[8] Similarly Isaiah could go outside the city to meet the king and there deliver to him the word of

of his call, but because he had a vision of Yahweh in the temple it does not follow that he was a functionary there, or that he was in the temple; he could have had such a vision anywhere and in any capacity." Cf. also Roubos, *op. cit.* pp. 17 ff.

[1] Jer: 7: 2 ff., 26: 2 ff.
[2] *Op. cit.* p. 121. Haldar refers to Jer. 1: 1 *et passim.* Jer. 1: 1 states that he was "of the priests that were in Anathoth". This would not make him a member of the staff of the Jerusalem Temple, and if it did it would be *qua* priest and not *qua* cultic prophet. It is commonly supposed that Jeremiah may have been a descendant of the Abiathar who was priest in Jerusalem in the days of David, but who was dismissed to Anathoth in the reign of Solomon (1 Kg. 2: 26 f., 35). Cf. Roubos, *op. cit.* pp. 22 ff. On this question cf. what I have written in *B.J.R.L.*, XLV, 1962–63, pp. 203 ff.
[3] Jer. 28: 1 ff.   [6] Jer. 37: 17 ff.
[4] Jer. 29: 24 ff.   [7] Jer. 18: 2 ff.
[5] Mk. 11: 15 ff., 27 ff., 12: 1 ff., Jn. 7: 14 ff.   [8] Jer. 24: 1 ff.

the Lord.[1] Though Ezekiel was a priest,[2] his oracles are said to have been delivered in Babylonia, and there is no suggestion that any of them were given as part of a service of worship, or that he belonged to the personnel that conducted such a service. The theory of cultic prophets—and I would emphasize that it is a theory, though much seems to point to its soundness—does not mean that all the prophets of the Old Testament are turned into such prophets. On the other hand, it does not mean that all the cultic prophets are turned into false prophets. If the prophetic psalms were recited by cultic prophets in the ritual of the Temple, we must recognize that there were probably good and bad, true and false, amongst these prophets as there were amongst the others.

At the same time, if this view is correct, it would reinforce the conclusion that the antithesis between priests and prophets is not to be overstressed, and lend support to the belief that while the prophets of reform certainly denounced the hollowness of much of the religious observance of their day, they were not opposed to all religious observance and did not advocate a religion without any corporate expression in worship. It is improbable that men whose function is denoted by a common term were at such irreconcilable cross purposes as they would in that case have been with the cultic prophets. There were good and bad prophets, and there were probably good and bad priests, and the divergence between the reform prophets on the one hand and the good cultic prophets and good priests on the other was probably that the former saw no value in the ritual of the shrines of their day—since men did not validate the rites by the spirit they brought to them—and saw no hope of any real amendment of men's evil ways, while the latter sought to invest the forms of religion with their true meaning.[3] Besides

---

[1] Isa. 7: 3 ff.

[2] Ezek. 1: 3.

[3] Cf. H. F. Hahn, *Old Testament in Modern Research*, 1954, p. 141: "With this altered perspective on the prophetic function, it was possible to see the priest and prophet, each in his own sphere, working for the furtherance of religion without being continually at cross-purposes. The priest had the help of the cult-prophet in teaching the significance of ritual actions; the canonical prophet added yet more by infusing religious worship with an ethical content."

them were doubtless the mere formalists on the cultic side, who were unconcerned for the spirit so long as the ritual was duly carried out, and the popular prophets on the non-cultic side, who would provide the oracle that won them approval and profit, but who were insensitive to the Spirit of God. Are we then to conclude that the only remains of the compositions of the cultic prophets are to be found in the Psalter,[1] and that while the oracles of non-cultic prophets have been preserved in the prophetic canon, those of their cultic brethren have been anonymously preserved only in so far as they have secured a place in the Psalter? This would certainly be surprising. Most of the oracles in the prophetic books arose out of a given historical situation and were directed to people who lived in that situation. It is, of course, impossible to attach a precise date to the individual oracles, but the work of each prophet bears the marks of the period in which he lived. The psalms, on the other hand, do not appear to be addressed in general to a precise historical situation, and all attempts to date them with reference to such a situation have failed—with rare exceptions, such as Ps. 137. The failure here is quite different from the failure to give a precise date to the individual oracles in the prophets. It is impossible to date the psalms within centuries, and the widest differences have prevailed amongst the scholars who have sought to define their age. The psalms appear to be related to ritual situations, which were recurrent, and therefore to have been used repeatedly in the appropriate circumstances. On Mowinckel's view many of them were related to the royal festivals, and especially to the New Year festival, in which he believed the cultic prophets played an important part.[2]

It will be remembered that in Mowinckel's formulation of the theory of cultic prophets he suggests that they did not

---

[1] J. H. Eaton (*op. cit.* p. 25) holds that many psalms contain prophetic material, including oracles.

[2] Engnell says roundly that the only possible interpretation of the relevant psalms is that "*in their original situation* the psalms at issue are to be judged as rituals directly referring to the functioning in the cult of the sacral King" (*B.J.R.L.* xxxi, 1948, p. 56). On the function of the King in the cult cf. A. R. Johnson, *Sacral Kingship in Ancient Israel*, 1955, and "Hebrew Conceptions of Kingship", in *Myth, Ritual, and Kingship*, pp. 204 ff.

merely recite stereotyped formulae, but that they experienced a rush of the Spirit and formulated on the spot the response which they made in the name of the congregation. Such impromptu responses would not all be equally impressive, and it is antecedently likely that the more successful would be recorded and found to be a present help in trouble by the less original technicians in this service.[1] But if there were creative cultic prophets, it might be expected that on special occasions, and especially in moments of crisis for the nation, the responses of such prophets would have some relation to the situation, and would therefore be less suitable for inclusion in the Psalter, since they would not be the sort of responses that could be recurrently used. Moreover, apart from such responses, if many of the psalms were used to accompany ritual acts and were therefore liturgical texts, they may well be the composition of cultic prophets—not simply impromptu creations, but carefully and artistically prepared. For the special occasions special liturgical texts might have been prepared, and again these would be less suitable for inclusion in the Psalter.

It is not, therefore, surprising that some scholars have found traces of cultic liturgies preserved in the prophetic books,[2] and one of the features of recent study of the prophets—not merely amongst members of the "Myth and Ritual School" or the "Scandinavian School"—has been the detection of such liturgies within the prophetic canon. Mowinckel believed that

---

[1] Cf. *Psalmenstudien* III, p. 8. N. W. Porteous criticizes Mowinckel's theory that there were two sorts of cultic prophets. He says: "He (i.e. Mowinckel) suggests that, while the *nebhi'im* were undoubtedly associated with the sanctuary, it was only certain among them who were actually admitted to be cult functionaries, the great majority being representative of the congregation and performing the orgiastic exercises on its behalf. The prophets, therefore, are to be thought of as representatives of the lay element in the worship. Is it then really necessary to suppose that we have two classes of prophets associated with the sanctuaries, namely a majority of lay prophets and a minority of cult prophets?" (*E.T.* LXII, 1950–51, p. 8).

[2] J. H. Eaton (*op. cit.* pp. 25, 35, 52, 82, 108 f., 122) finds much liturgical material in the four prophets he studies. He regards Obadiah, Habakkuk, and Zephaniah as cultic prophets, and thinks the book of Nahum was recited in Temple services. R. Hentschke (*Die Stellung der vorexilischen Schriftpropheten zum Kultus*, 1957, p. 173) says that Nahum, Habakkuk, and Joel were probably cult prophets.

Joel and Habakkuk were liturgies to be attributed to cultic prophets,[1] on the ground that they contain a mixture of passages in the style of psalm and prophecy. Humbert propounded the view that the book of Nahum was a prophetic liturgy, composed for the celebration of the fall of Nineveh in 612 B.C.[2] Balla took the view that Habakkuk was a liturgy,[3] and this was adopted by Humbert in an extended study of this prophet.[4] Engnell followed the view that Joel was a cultic liturgy,[5] but Kapelrud has maintained that it was composed in the style of such a liturgy, rather than that it was ever used in the actual service of the Temple.[6] Once the suggestion of surviving cultic liturgies in the prophetic books had been made, there was a tendency to find ever more such passages.[7] Engnell

[1] *Ibid.* pp. 27 ff.

[2] Cf. *Z.A.W.* xliv (N.F. iii), 1926, pp. 266 ff., *A.f.O.* v, 1928–29, pp. 14 ff., *R.H.P.R.* xii, 1932, pp. 1 ff.; cf. O. Eissfeldt, *Einleitung in das Alte Testament*, 2nd edn., 1956, pp. 512 f.; A. Weiser, *Introduction to the Old Testament*, Eng. trans. by D. M. Barton, 1961, p. 258. A. Haldar (*Studies in the Book of Nahum*, 1947, pp. 3 ff.) rejects the view that the book is a liturgy (so also E. Osswald, *R.G.G.*, 3rd edn., iv, 1960, col. 1297), but thinks it arose in a cult-prophetic circle and had a propagandist aim. Cf. Haldar's view as expressed in *S.B.U.* ii, 1952, cols. 417 ff.

[3] Cf. *R.G.G.*, 2nd edn., ii, 1928, cols. 1556 f. Balla was followed by E. Sellin, *Einleitung in das Alte Testament*, 6th edn., 1933, p. 120. Cf. Weiser, *op. cit.* pp. 261 f.

[4] Cf. *Problèmes du livre d'Habacuc*, 1944, pp. 296 ff. (cf. *R.G.G.*, 3rd edn., iii, 1959, cols. 3 f.); also Engnell, in *S.B.U.* i, 1948, cols. 769 ff. J. P. Hyatt (*Peake's Commentary on the Bible*, ed. by M. Black and H. H. Rowley, 1962, p. 637 a) does not accept this view. On the other hand, Th. C. Vriezen (*An Outline of Old Testament Theology*, Eng. trans., 1958, p. 63; cf. p. 251) says Habakkuk "apparently contains a prophecy of a cultic prophet", while R. de Vaux (*Ancient Israel*, Eng. trans. by J. McHugh, 1961, p. 385) grants that Nahum and Habakkuk are imitations of liturgical works.

[5] Cf. *S.B.U.* i, 1948, cols. 1075 ff.

[6] Cf. *Joel Studies*, 1948; cf. also Weiser, *op. cit.* p. 179. T. H. Robinson (in Robinson-Horst, *Die zwölf Kleinen Propheten*, 1938, p. 63) had regarded Joel 2: 12–14 as a fragment of a penitential liturgy, and held 2: 19 to be taken from a liturgical text.

[7] H. Gunkel found Isa. 33 to be such a liturgy (cf. *Z.A.W.* xlii [N.F. i], 1924, pp. 177 ff.), and also the end of Micah (cf. *What Remains of the Old Testament*, Eng. trans. by A. K. Dallas, 1928, pp. 115 ff.; cf. also A. S. Kapelrud, in *S.B.U.* ii, 1952, cols. 278 f.); G. Gerleman found the book of Zephaniah to be such a liturgy (cf. *Zephanja textkritisch und literarisch untersucht*, 1942).

has gone so far as to divide the material found in the prophetic books into two main categories, the one being what he calls the "diwan type", which consists of direct oracle, and the other the liturgical type, which is modelled on the cultic usage.[1] He maintained that Isa. 24–27, the so-called "Isaiah Apocalypse", is of a liturgical character,[2] and further argues that the whole of Deutero-Isaiah is of this type. It is to be clearly emphasized, however, that he does not mean that the author was a cultic prophet attached to any sanctuary. Just as Kapelrud says that Joel was composed in the style of a cultic liturgy, so Engnell holds that Deutero-Isaiah was a prophetic imitation of a cultic liturgy. He therefore uses the word "liturgy" in "a strict form-literary sense, so that the question of its possible directly cultic connexion is left open".[3]

I am doubtful if cultic liturgies form any large part of the prophetic canon, though it may well be that some such passages have been preserved. Whatever can be read as oracle is more naturally to be read as oracle, and so far as the major figures are concerned—such as Amos, Isaiah, and Jeremiah—it is very hard to suppose that they were cultic prophets. Even if, as I believe, they did not hold the cult to be essentially and ineradicably evil, they regarded the worship of their day as hollow and vain, and it is more than doubtful if they took part as leaders and ministrants in ceremonies which they declared to be meaningless in their day. It is impossible, for instance, to think that Isaiah, who declared that it was idle for men to trample the courts of the Temple, and to keep sacred festival and offer sacrifice, since God could only see the blood that was upon their hands—it is impossible, I say, to think that he should have participated in the service as a spokesman of the people whose sacrifice God repudiated by his mouth. It is even

---

[1] Cf. *S.E.Å.* XII, 1947, pp. 128 f., *The Call of Isaiah*, 1949, pp. 59 f., and *S.B.U.* II, 1952, cols 763 ff.

[2] Cf. *S.B.U.* I, 1948, col. 1031.

[3] Cf. *B.J.R.L.* XXXI, 1948, p. 64. W. Caspari (*Lieder und Gottessprüche der Rückwanderer*, 1934, pp. 129 ff.) offers an elaborate examination of Deutero-Isaiah from the point of view of the cult, with which he associates it closely. The argument is often forced, however. K. Elliger (*Die Einheit des Trito-jesaia*, 1928, pp. 15 ff., 24 ff., 29 ff.) finds liturgical passages in Isa. 59: 1–4, 9–18; 61; 62; and 63: 7–64: 11.

more difficult to think of Jeremiah fitting into the service as an official ministrant. Many scholars have believed that he declared that God had never ordained sacrifice at all, and not merely that contemporary sacrifice was an offence to Him. Though I do not share this view,[1] I find it impossible to think that he had any use for the kind of services he witnessed in his day. In a city in which evil of all kinds was rampant, where men neighed after one another's wives and cheated and oppressed, where he felt that corruption had reached such a pitch that even if a single righteous person within it might guarantee its safety it yet could not be saved,[2] the thronging of the Temple courts was an idle mockery and an affront to God, which he could only view with impatience.

So far as Ezekiel and Deutero-Isaiah are concerned, their work fell in Babylonia, in the period of the exile, and throughout most of the ministry of both the Temple was no longer standing. We know too little of the organization of the synagogue for it to be reasonable to treat Ezekiel and Deutero-Isaiah as cultic prophets. Only within very modest limits does it seem to me to be reasonable to find cultic liturgies preserved in the prophetic canon. It is not easy to think of the major prophets in that role, or to suppose that cultic liturgies which were composed by others have been attributed to them. The book of Nahum, which is so unlike the other prophetic books in character that some have thought of Nahum as one of the false prophets against whom such men as Jeremiah stood, may have been such a liturgy. Its author was a brilliant poet, who described the fall of Nineveh, whether before or after that fall, with superb skill, and whether it was prophecy or liturgy, it is probable that it was recited with great satisfaction more than once after Nineveh had fallen.

Though I am not inclined to find any large collection of cultic liturgies in the prophetic canon, I think it possible that some of the oracles were based on such liturgies. It is probable that the haunting and effective Song of the Vine in Isa. 5 was modelled on some well-known vintage song. It was only as it

---

[1] Cf. *The Unity of the Bible*, 1953, pp. 31 ff., 40 f., *B.J.R.L.* xxix, 1945–46, pp. 22 ff., xxxiii, 1950–51, pp. 79 ff. (cf. above, pp. 72 ff).
[2] Jer. 5: 1 ff.

developed that the prophet's hearers began to realize that it was more than a vintage song. It is possible that occasionally the prophets may have modelled other passages on familiar liturgical compositions, in the way that Kapelrud supposes was done in the case of Joel, and Engnell in the case of other passages.

If, then, I may sum up the fruits of the discussions of recent years, as they appear to me, they are far less substantial than some scholars have supposed. My own attitude to all these studies is one of great caution, and the more extreme of the positions I have indicated I have no hesitation in rejecting. It is wrong in method to impose the pattern of one culture upon another, and especially in this case. For we know that while Israel dwelt in a cultural milieu from which she undoubtedly derived much that found a permanent place in her religion, her prophets fought hard against some elements of that cultural milieu. Clearly, therefore, Israel is not to be understood simply in terms of that milieu, and that which she did not share with others is never to be forgotten. On the other hand, it is dangerous to forget the heritage she drew from the distant past and the influences she was subject to from those around her. The tendency of the more extreme exponents of "patternism" to reduce all to a single character takes too little account of the evidence, and is much too simple to be probable. So far as the prophets are concerned, the imposition of a uniform type on them and the making of them all into cultic prophets seems to me to be another example of the same lack of penetration.

Happily not all of these studies have been of this Procrustean variety, and it is on this account that I find something of real value to have come out of them. The view that there were cultic prophets rests not on *a priori* ideas, and the forcing of foreign practices on the Old Testament, but on evidence that lies within the Old Testament. But that evidence tells of many varieties of prophet in Israel—varieties not alone of spiritual level, but of means of functioning. The prophet was always a sacred person because he was believed to be possessed by the spirit of God, but he was not necessarily, in virtue of being a prophet, appointed to a defined place in the worship of some shrine.[1] Hence I accept the view that there were cultic prophets without turning the major canonical prophets into members of such guilds.[2] On the other hand I do not divide the prophets into two sharply separated groups, but think they were divided as the colours of the rainbow are divided. The evidence that they were on the staff of any particular shrine is wanting, though there is no evidence against this; it seems to me to be more likely that any prophet was free to function in a shrine though not limited to such functioning, and the extent to which prophets exercised this freedom and the intimacy of their relationship to the ritual of the shrines varied greatly. The softening of the lines between the various groups of prophets, without their reduction to a common type, seems to me to be a great gain.[3]

Similarly the softening of the lines between priests and prophets is in my view a gain. But once more the abandonment of the older, hard antithesis between these classes does not mean that no difference of attitude towards the cultus is to be found amongst prophets and priests. To think of prophets only in terms of the best and priests only in terms of the worst is unwise. There were good prophets and good priests, and while there was undoubtedly a difference of emphasis between them, they were

[1] Cf. what the present writer has said in *The Servant of the Lord*, 1952, p. 105: "Since prophets were religious persons, devotees of their God, it is natural to find them in the shrines in which religion centred. But that does not make them members of the staff of the shrines."

[2] Cf. N. W. Porteous, *E.T.* LXII, 1950–51, p. 7: "It may be admitted that an impressive case has been made out for the existence in Israel of cult prophets forming a regular part of the personnel of the sanctuaries." Porteous earlier on the same page says: "Like the priests the prophets seem to have an official standing. Whether that inevitably points to their being actually cult officials is not so clear." E. Jacob (*Theology of the Old Testament*, Eng. trans. by A. W. Heathcote and P. J. Allcock, 1958, p. 240) recognizes the existence of cultic prophets, but adds: "We must not, of course, rush to the opposite extreme and make all the prophets into cultic agents." In a footnote he observes: "It is true to say that the prophets use cultic means, but they are not enslaved by them and for certain prophets the means of access to their ministry is not through the cult."

[3] R. de Vaux (*Ancient Israel: its life and institutions*, Eng. trans. by J. McHugh, 1961, pp. 384 ff.) rejects the view that there were cultic prophets on the Temple staff. Cf. Johnson, *The Cultic Prophet in Ancient Israel*, 2nd edn., 1962, p. 74 n.

all exponents of the same religion. The Bible contains the Law and the Prophets, and it would be curious if these were governed by irreconcilably opposed ideas as to the nature of religion and the will of God. The growing emphasis on the unity of the Old Testament reflected in the many books devoted to the theology of the Old Testament is not unrelated to the studies we have been reviewing.

So far as the preservation of prophetic liturgies in the prophetic books is concerned I am sceptical of the claims that are made to detect them. A few may have survived, and some passages may be based on such liturgies. But it is not here that I look for the solid fruits of these studies. Rather is it in the new light they have shed on the Psalter by bringing it into relation with both prophecy and the cultus. Here once more there has been a significant perception that beneath all its variety of form and of idea, the Old Testament has a deep unity, and that not alone the Law and the Prophets, but the Psalms have a real place in that unity, and that all belong essentially together.

5

The Book of Job and its Meaning

5

THE BOOK OF JOB AND ITS MEANING[1]

THAT the book of Job is the supreme literary masterpiece in the Old Testament and one of the greatest creations of the world's literature is generally agreed.[2] An American Jewish scholar says: "Of the masterpieces which time has handed down, of the Biblical books in especial, it is the one which in every age is felt to be modern."[3] Yet the most extraordinary variety of view continues to be held about this book, and its many problems have found no agreed solution.[4] In the present lecture I have no intention to add to their number, or to review all the opinions that have been held. It is my purpose rather to make clear the nature of the critical problems that arise and to indicate which of the many solutions seems to me most likely to be right, and then to state my view of the significance of the book.

Much ink has been wasted in discussing the precise literary category into which it falls, and whether it is epic or drama.[5] It has been compared with the work of Homer,[6] or with the

---

[1] First published in *B.J.R.L.* XLI, 1958–59, pp. 167–207.

[2] Carlyle's words are often quoted: "one of the grandest things ever written with pen . . . There is nothing written, I think, in the Bible or out of it, of equal literary merit" (*On Heroes*, Lecture 2, The New Universal Library edition, p. 67). Cf. also J. A. Froude, *The Book of Job*, 1854, p. 3: "Towering up alone, far away above all the poetry of the world." C. F. Kent (*The Growth and Contents of the O.T.*, 1926, p. 285) calls it "The Matterhorn of the Old Testament."

[3] Cf. M. Buttenwieser, *The Book of Job*, 1922, p. 3. Similarly T. H. Robinson, *Job and his Friends*, 1954, p. 124. Cf. also P. Humbert, *V.T. Supplements* III (Rowley Festschrift), 1955, pp. 150 ff.

[4] For a full review of recent literature on Job, cf. C. Kuhl, *Th.R.*, N.F. XXI, 1953, pp. 163 ff., 257 ff.

[5] Theodore Beza (*Job Expounded*, 1589 ?, Preface, pp. 3 ff.) regarded the book as a tragedy. Cf. also H. Gärtner, *Der dramatischen Charakter des Buches Hiob*, 1909.

[6] Cf. J. Neyrand, *Études*, CLXXIII, 1922, pp. 124 ff. W. M. L. de Wette cites some older writers who compared Job with the Homeric epics (*Introduction to the Old Testament*, Eng. trans. by T. Parker, II, 1843, p. 556 n.),

creations of the Greek dramatists,[1] Aeschylus,[2] Sophocles,[3] and Euripides,[4] or with the Dialogues of Plato.[5] In truth it is not to be classed with any of these. In the words of A. S. Peake "it is itself".[6] The genius of the author gave it its unique literary form as the means of expressing his profound message.

Before that message can be understood, however, it is necessary to examine the contents of the book, and to decide how far they derive from the author, or how far they existed before his time or have been added later. The general outline of the

but adds that this is altogether absurd. The works referred to are J. H. Stuss, *De Epopoeia Iobaea*, 1753; A. A. H. Lichtenstein, *Num liber Jobi cum Odyssea Homeri comparari possit?* 1773; C. D. Ilgen, *Iobi antiquissimi carminis hebraici natura atque virtutes*, 1789, and J. C. W. Augusti, *Grundriss einer historisch-kritischen Einleitung in's A.T.*, 1827, pp. 264, 266.

[1] Theodore of Mopsuestia held that it was modelled on the Greek dramas. Cf. the condemnation of his views by the Council of Constantinople, in *P.G.* LXVI, 1864, cols. 697 f.

[2] Cf. M. Jastrow, *The Book of Job*, 1920, pp. 185 ff.; J. J. Slotki, *E.T.* XXXIX, 1927–28, pp. 131 ff.; J. Lindblom, in *ΔΡΑΓΜΑ, Martino P. Nilsson dedicatum*, 1939, pp. 280 ff.; W. A. Irwin, *J.R.* xxx, 1950, pp. 90 ff.; H. G. May, *A.Th.R.* XXXIV, 1952, pp. 240 ff.

[3] Cf. R. Lowth, *Lectures on the Sacred Poetry of the Hebrews*, Eng. trans. by G. Gregory, 1847, pp. 372 ff., esp. p. 380 for the rejection of this view.

[4] Cf. H. M. Kallen, *The Book of Job as a Greek Tragedy Restored*, 1918. For the severe review of this book by C. G. Montefiore, cf. *H.T.R.* XII, 1919, pp. 219 ff.

[5] Cf. K. Fries, *Das philosophische Gespräch von Hiob bis Plato*, 1904; O. Holtzmann, in B. Stade, *G.V.I.* II, 1888, p. 351. G. B. Gray (in Driver-Gray, *The Book of Job*, 1921, p. xxiv) says: "Between the dialogue of Job, consisting exclusively of long set speeches in poetical form, and the prose dialogues of Plato, with their closely knit analytical argument carried on by means of much quickly responsive conversation, the difference is so great that the probability that the Hebrew writer was influenced by those Greek literary models is so slight as to be negligible."

[6] Cf. *Job* (Cent. B.), p. 45. R. H. Pfeiffer (*Introduction to the O.T.*, 1941, p. 684) well observes: "All general classifications fail to do justice to the overflowing abundance of its forms, moods, and thoughts: it is not exclusively lyric, nor epic, nor dramatic, nor didactic or reflective, unless the poem is cut down to fit a particular category. Even the more comprehensive characterizations, such as that of Friedr. Delitzsch (*Das Buch Hiob*, 1902, p. 15) 'a poem with dramatic movement and essential didactic tendency', or better still that of J. G. von Herder (*Von Geist der Ebräischen Poesie*, I, 148), 'an epopee of mankind, a theodicy of God', fail to do justice to the scope of the work."

book is familiar. There is first of all a prose Prologue, in which Job is presented as a man of piety and of utter integrity of character, as well as a man of great prosperity. His piety is maliciously represented by the Satan as mere self-interest, an investment that yields high dividends in his prosperity. Permission is given by God to put him to the test, and by a series of swift blows he is bereft of his family and his possessions, but without forfeiting his integrity of character. When God twits the Satan with his discomfiture, his cynicism rises to the occasion and he is given permission to carry the test further and smite the person of Job himself. With a zest which might have graced a better cause,[1] he struck Job with a phenomenal and painful disease, which medical men have tried to identify by the varied symptoms which are mentioned in the course of the book.[2] It is commonly, though not universally, identified as some form of elephantiasis.[3] In fact, it is as futile to try to give

[1] J. F. Genung, *The Hebrew Literature of Wisdom in the Light of To-day*, 1906, p. 174, says: "He does indeed handle Job with exceeding severity; not, however, so much in the spirit which delights in unmotived cruelty, as in the spirit of vivisection for scientific purposes."

[2] Cf. 2: 7 (inflamed eruptions), 2: 8 (violent itching), 2: 12 (shocking change of appearance), 7: 5 (maggots in the ulcers; on this verse cf. G. R. Driver, in *V.T. Supplements* III [Rowley Festschrift], 1955, p. 73), 7: 14 (terrifying dreams), 16: 16 (weeping eyes and loss of sight), 19: 17 (bad breath), 19: 20 (emaciation), 30: 17 (erosion of the bones), 30: 30 (blackening and falling off of the skin).

[3] Cf. the long dissertation on Job's disease which stands in the introduction to the commentary of A. Calmet (*Commentaire littéral sur tous les livres de l'A. et du N.T.*, III, 1724, pp. 608–13). Job's malady is usually identified with "black leprosy" or tubercular leprosy. But E. Robin (in Pirot-Clamer, *La Sainte Bible*, IV, 1949, p. 720) has some doubt about this, and Driver and Gray observe (*op. cit.* p. 24): "elephantiasis develops slowly . . . ; but the narrative almost certainly intends us to understand that Job was immediately smitten with intensely painful and loathsome symptoms, attacking every part of his body". As C. J. Ball (*The Book of Job*, 1922, p. 114) says: "There seems no reason why, if leprosy were meant, a popular story, which makes no pretence to poetical diction, should have preferred to describe this well-known scourge of the East by an ambiguous expression, instead of using the ordinary word." Dr. A. Macalister (in *D.B.* III, 1900, pp. 329 f.) identifies it with the oriental sore, or Biskra button, while E. W. G. Masterman (*P.E.F.Q.S.* L, 1918, p. 168) thinks this highly improbable, and suggests that it was most probably "a very extensive erythema". Amongst other suggestions we may note that of G. N. Münch

a scientific name to the disease as it is to linger over the theological problem of the presence of the Satan at the court of God. The author is merely setting the stage, and in his thought the disease of Job is the most terrible he can conceive.[1] Yet even this Job accepts with patience.

Then three friends arrive from afar to comfort him. Again it is useless to speculate how they had heard in their widely separated habitations of Job's affliction, or how they had contrived to arrive together. The artistry of the author was not concerned with such trivialities. For several days the friends sit beside Job, offering him no more than silent sympathy. Then Job breaks into a soliloquy, in which he bemoans his lot and laments that he was ever born. Each of the friends then speaks in turn, reproaching him with steadily increasing sharpness, and being answered one by one by Job. This is followed by a second cycle of speeches, and then by a third, which breaks down, however, before it reaches its end. All of these speeches are in superb poetry. Sometimes the friends reproach Job for the wild things he says in his distress, and Job bitingly replies that it is easy for the spectator to maintain his calm. But behind their speeches is the assumption that Job has brought his troubles on himself by some concealed wickedness, while Job repudiates such an idea with increasing passion. It is not that Job claims to have been perfect; what he maintains is that he has not been so heinous a sinner as to deserve such an unparalleled misfortune. The friends maintain the righteousness of God and recommend Job to repent of his sin and submit himself to God, when there may be hope of restoration for him. Stung by their reproaches he impugns the righteousness of God, but shares with the friends the thought that merit and fortune ought to be matched. At the same time he appeals to God to vindicate him before it is too late. He thus directs his appeal to God's better self, and turns from the God of his present experience to the

(*Die Zaraath* [*Lepra*] *der hebräischen Bibel* [Dermatologische Studien, No. 16], 1893, p. 143), that Job's complaint was chronic eczema. S. L. Terrien (*I.B.* III, 1954, p. 920) says a case might be made for the skin disorder known as *pemphicus foliaceus*.

[1] Cf. Driver and Gray, *op. cit.* pp. 24 f.: "the writer may or may not have had a single disease in mind throughout."

God he has hitherto known. For both Job and his friends are persuaded that his misfortunes come from God.

Next we have chapter 28, a magnificent poem on the elusiveness of wisdom, which man despite all his achievements can never find for himself, leading up to the declaration that God alone knows where it is to be found, and that in reverence towards Him and obedience to His will man may attain it.

Following this we have Job's final soliloquy, in which he appeals again to God to answer him. Before this cry finds its response, however, a new person appears abruptly on the scene. This is Elihu, of whose appearance we are given no explanation. He makes four speeches one after the other, to none of which Job offers an answer, and then he vanishes from the scene as suddenly as he appeared. Now, however, God appears and answers Job in a speech from the whirlwind. He offers no explanation of Job's misfortunes, but parades before him in swift succession some of the wonders of creation which are beyond Job's understanding. At the end Job bows in humble submission before God and says he will complain no more. Yet barely has he opened his mouth when God breaks in and opens up on him again, this time mainly with two long descriptions of the monsters Behemoth and Leviathan. After Job has bowed in submission this comes, as Peake observed, perilously near nagging.[1] Moreover, it must be confessed that this second divine speech does not equal in brilliance the first. When it is finished, Job resumes his speech of submission, and says: "I had heard of thee by the hearing of the ear; But now mine eye seeth thee, Wherefore I abhor myself, and repent in dust and ashes."[2] This is the close of the poetical part of the book.

Finally we have a prose Epilogue, in which God condemns the three friends of Job and declares Job in the right. The friends are bidden to offer a sacrifice and to ask Job to pray for them; and when he prays for his friends, he is accepted by God. His long trial is over, and his fortunes are restored and he lives happily ever after.

We need not spend time discussing whether the book can be

[1] Cf. *Job* (Cent. B.), p. 332.
[2] Job 42: 5 f.

read as literal history. Some older writers supposed that every speech was a true transcript of the words used in the debate.[1] Luther, while acknowledging its broad historicity, was not prepared to accept it in detail as exact history.[2] So early as the fourth century A.D., Theodore of Mopsuestia recognized the existence of Job, but regarded this book as a slanderous fiction which ought not to be in the sacred Canon.[3] Today the view is general that Job is the name of an ancient worthy, and that there was a historical person behind the book, but that the work as we have it is the artistic creation of the author, who used the ancient figure of Job as the vehicle for his message.[4]

The first of the critical problems which confront us is that of the Elihu speeches. What part do they play in the plan of the book? Elihu appears, and speaks, and vanishes. No notice is taken of him by Job or by God, and in the Epilogue God commends Job and condemns Eliphaz, Bildad, and Zophar, but

[1] Cf. F. Spanheim, *Opera*, II, 1703, pp. 1 ff.; A. Schultens, *Liber Jobi*, I, 1737, Preface, p. 33; J. H. Michaelis, *Adnotationes in Hagiog. V.T. Libros*, II, 1720, pp. 5 f.; B. Kennicott, *Remarks on Select Passages in the O.T.*, 1787, p. 153; S. Lee, *The Book of the Patriarch Job*, 1837, pp. 6 ff.

[2] Cf. the passage cited by E. W. Hengstenberg, *Commentary on Ecclesiastes with other Treatises*, Eng. trans. by D. W. Simon, 1860, p. 317. Hengstenberg goes beyond Luther and denies that Job ever existed. He says: "It was a great mistake when some, in order to do honour to the Scriptures, deemed themselves compelled to ascribe a purely historical character to this book" (pp. 316 f.). He adds: "If we regard him as an actual historical personage, we shift the boundary line separating the heathen world from the Church of God, and pronounce the redemptive means set up by God superfluous" (p. 317). C. F. Keil (*Lehrbuch der historisch-kritischen Einleitung in die Schriften des A.Ts.*, 1873, pp. 383 f.) describes the book of Job as "eine mit poetischer Freiheit durchgeführte Bearbeitung einer alten Sage".

[3] Theodore was condemned in A.D. 553 for holding these views. Cf. *P.G.* LXVI, 1864, cols. 697 f. Already in the Babylonian Talmud (Baba Bathra, 15a) we find the view recorded that Job never lived and was never created, but was merely a parable (*māshāl*), and this view was adopted by Maimonides (cf. *Guide of the Perplexed*, III, XXII, Eng. trans. by M. Friedländer, III, 1885, p. 93). Cf. also Genesis Rabba, 57 end, where amongst many Rabbinic speculations as to the period when Job lived, we find the view recorded that he never existed.

[4] Cf. H. Rongy, *Revue Ecclésiastique de Liége*, XXV, 1933, p. 171: "L'auteur génial de Job a pu emprunter son héros à la tradition; mais il n'a pas eu la naïveté de prendre pour réels ses beaux récits. Ils les a imaginés et arrangés pour introduire son autre fiction du dialogue poétique."

completely ignores Elihu. The Elihu speeches could therefore be dropped from the book without being missed, and without affecting its structure. On the other hand, the Elihu speeches pre-suppose the rest of the book, and indeed often pick up arguments from the speeches that precede. This strongly suggests that they do not belong to the original book and that they have been added afterwards, either by the original author[1] or by another.[2]

This conclusion is reinforced by considerations of style. S. R. Driver characterized the style of the Elihu speeches as "prolix, laboured, and sometimes tautologous", and noted that "the power and brilliancy which are so conspicuous in the poem generally are sensibly missing".[3] Similarly Buttenwieser says

---

[1] So A. Kamphausen, *T.S.K.* xxxvi, 1863, p. 810, and in Bunsen's *Bibelwerk*, I, III, 1865, p. 494; A. Merx, *Das Gedicht von Hiob*, 1871, pp. xvii, LXXXVI; E. Sellin, *Das Problem des Hiobbuches*, 1919, p. 28; G. H. Box, *Judaism in the Greek Period*, 1932, p. 123; R. Gordis, *Judaism*, iv, 1955, p. 206; H. Junker, *Das Buch Job* (Echter Bibel), 1951, p. 7. Cf. R. Cornely, *Introductionis Compendium*, I, 10th edn., rev. by A. Merk, 1929, pp. 467 f. J. Pedersen, *Israel I-II*, 1926, p. 531, says: "That the Elihu speeches do not form part of the original poem is probable for purely formal reasons; but as to their contents they fit so well into the general scheme that they are probably a rough draft made by the poet himself." On the other hand W. O. E. Oesterley and T. H. Robinson (*Introduction to the Books of the O.T.*, 1934, p. 174) feel these speeches would have been repudiated by the original poet. So also A. Lods, *Introduction à la littérature hébraïque et juive*, 1950, p. 677. E. König (*Das Buch Hiob*, 1929, p. 470) pronounces the view that these speeches were added by the author "eine unnatürliche Annahme".

[2] Some writers have analysed the Elihu speeches into the work of more than one hand. So Helen H. Nichols, *A.J.S.L.* xxvii, 1910–11, pp. 97 ff. (cf. G. A. Barton, *J.B.L.* xxx, 1911, p. 68), and M. Jastrow, *op. cit.* pp. 77 ff. W. A. Irwin (*J.R.* xvii, 1937, pp. 36 ff.) prefers Jastrow's analysis to that of Miss Nichols, and regards the Elihu speeches as a series of comments on the dialogue by a number of writers between 400 and 100 B.C. A. Lods, *Histoire de la littérature hébraïque et juive*, 1950, p. 683, sharply rejects such views, saying: "C'est, nous semble-t-il, discréditer les méthodes de la critique que de statuer ainsi, comme à plaisir, et contre toute vraisemblance, une multitude d'auteurs ayant même style et exprimant des idées toutes voisines, et cela pour rendre compte de quelques vétilles de rédaction qui peuvent s'expliquer autrement."

[3] Cf. *Introduction to the Literature of the Old Testament*, 9th edn., 1913, p. 429. With this compare the judgment of J. T. Marshall, *Job and his Comforters*, p. 6, where the Elihu speeches are said to be "on an immeasurably higher plane

the style here is "pompous and diffuse, with much empty repetition, in marked contrast to the Job dialogues, which are meaty, compact and concise. Of the seventy-two verses which make up the interpolation, thirty, or almost half, are taken up with a tiresome and vainglorious introduction."[1]

While it is the widely held view that these speeches are a later interpolation,[2] a few scholars of distinction have not adopted it. Budde[3] and Cornill[4] both defended the authenticity of the Elihu speeches and maintained that in them we have the

than the Dialogue". For a careful study of the language and style of the Elihu speeches, cf. Driver-Gray, *op. cit.* pp. XLI ff., and W. E. Staples, *The Speeches of Elihu* (University of Toronto Studies, Philological Series, No. 8), 1925, pp. 19 ff. J. Herz (*Wissenschaftliche Zeitschrift der Karl-Marx-Universität Leipzig*, III, 1953–54, pp. 107 ff.) finds the Elihu speeches to be distinct from the dialogue on stylistic grounds.

[1] *Op. cit.* p. 85.

[2] This view is found already in J. G. Eichhorn, *Einleitung in das A.T.*, 3rd edn., III, 1803, pp. 597 f., and W. M. L. de Wette, *op. cit.* pp. 558 ff. It is also found in L. C. F. W. Seinecke, *Der Grundgedanke des Buches Hiob*, 1863, p. 66; T. K. Cheyne, *Job and Solomon*, 1887, pp. 42, 90 ff.; H. Gärtner, *Der dramatische Charakter des Buches Hiob*, 1909, p. 47; R. H. Pfeiffer, *Le Problème du livre de Job*, 1915, pp. 12 ff.; W. Vischer, *Hiob*, 6th edn., 1947, p. 27; H. Richter, *Studien zu Hiob*, 1958, p. 119; and very many of the standard commentaries. Amongst recent Roman Catholic authors who have followed this view are to be found A. van Hoonacker (*R.B.* XII, 1903, pp. 161 ff.), P. Dhorme (*Le Livre de Job* [E.B.], 1926, pp. LXXVII ff.), J. Goettsberger (*Einleitung in das A.T.*, 1928, p. 227), E. J. Kissane (*The Book of Job*, 1939, p. XL), E. J. Sutcliffe (*A Catholic Commentary on Holy Scripture*, 1953, p. 418). It is also shared by so conservative a writer as E. König, *op. cit.* pp. 466 ff. N. H. Tur-Sinai (*The Book of Job*, 1957, pp. XXXVIII f.) expresses the view that whereas most of the book was composed in Aramaic and translated into Hebrew, the Elihu speeches were composed in Hebrew by a disciple of Ezekiel.

[3] Cf. *Beiträge zur Kritik des Buches Hiob*, 1876, pp. 65 ff., and *Das Buch Hiob*, 2nd edn., 1913, pp. XXIV ff. This view was quite common amongst older writers, after the rejection of the Elihu speeches had been advocated; cf. e.g. E. F. C. Rosenmüller, *Scholia in V.T.*, Pars. V, 1806, pp. 756 ff. (cf. p. 765, where Elihu is thought to be the author of the book), F. W. C. Umbreit, *Das Buch Hiob*, 1832, pp. XXV ff. n., J. G. Stickel, *Das Buch Hiob*, 1842, pp. 224 ff.; J. Hontheim, *Das Buch Job*, 1904, pp. 20 ff.; G. Wildeboer, *Die Litteratur des A:Ts.*, German trans. by F. Risch, 1905, pp. 380 f., 382 ff.

[4] Cf. *Introduction to the Canonical Books of the O.T.*, Eng. trans. by G. H. Box, 1907, pp. 426 ff.

climax of the book.[1] Here alone, they said, does the author offer a solution of the problem of suffering, with which the book deals; and surely he must have had some solution to offer.[2] But Elihu's solution is that suffering is disciplinary, to purge the heart of pride, which was Job's sin.[3] Unhappily for this view, the reason for Job's suffering was the cynical accusation of the Satan. Yahweh had already declared him to be a man of piety and of true wholeness of character. It is true that in the argument with his friends Job exposes himself to the charge of self-righteousness and spiritual pride by the vehemence of his maintenance of his innocence. But this can offer no explanation of his sufferings, since it was something to which he gave way after his misfortunes came upon him. He was afflicted, as the reader is told quite clearly in the Prologue, not for his chastening, but to vindicate God's trust in him. It has been suggested that God lightly abandoned Job to the tender mercies of the Satan.[4] It is improbable that this is what the author meant to convey, and more likely that in his thought Job was supremely honoured by God, in that God had staked Himself on his unfailing integrity. Nor did Job let God down. For despite all his complaint, Job never for one moment regrets his integrity of character.[5] Hence

[1] Other recent writers who retain the Elihu speeches for the original book are W. S. Bruce, *The Wisdom Literature of the O.T.*, 1928, pp. 22 f.; Kallen, *op. cit.* pp. 31 ff.; L. Dennefeld, *Introduction à l' A.T.*, 1935, p. 121, and *R.B.* XLVIII, 1939, pp. 163 ff.; P. Szczygiel, *Das Buch Job*, 1931, pp. 24 ff.; B. D. Eerdmans, *Studies in Job*, 1939, pp. 16 f.; J. H. Kroeze, *O.T.S.* II, 1943, pp. 156 ff.; A. M. Dubarle, *Les Sages d'Israël*, 1946, pp. 84 ff.; J. E. Steinmueller, *A Companion to Scripture Studies*, II (2nd edn.), 1944, p. 167; P. Humbert, *V.T. Supplements* III (Rowley Festschrift, 1955), p. 150; R. Gordis, *Judaism*, IV, 1955, p. 205.

[2] Cf. Cornill, *op. cit.* p. 426. Pedersen, *op. cit.* p. 531, observes: "It is strange that the interpreters should have taken these speeches as the valid expression of the views of the author, though the big words are clearly charged with irony; if so, the speeches of the friends would also have to be taken as the serious opinion of the author."

[3] This thought is already found in the first speech of Eliphaz, Job 5: 17 ff.

[4] Cf. B. Duhm, *Das Buch Hiob*, 1897, p. 8; "Mit einer Schnelligkeit und Kaltblütigkeit . . . geht Jahwe auf die Anregung des Satans ein."

[5] Cf. Gray, in Driver-Gray, *op. cit.* p. LV: "Job nowhere regrets his previous service of God, and never demands the restoration of the previous rewards; what he does seek is God Himself, God unchanged, still his friend —on his side, unestranged from him, and not, as the theory assures him He has now become, his enemy."

the solution of Elihu, whatever may be said of its spiritual value, is irrelevant to the book. If the author had a solution to offer, it must be presumed that it was relevant to the situation he had himself created. Moreover, if the Elihu speeches were the climax of the work, the author might have been expected to integrate Elihu into his plan, to introduce him to his readers, or even to let him be commended by God in the Epilogue. Yet, strangely enough, it is Job who is commended in the Epilogue, yet who is sharply rebuked by Elihu. It is surely incredible that the author of the Elihu speeches can have composed the Epilogue. We shall, however, have to consider below the view that the Prologue or the Epilogue or both come from a hand other than the author's.[1]

The view has been taken that the book once ended with the Elihu speeches, and the speeches of God and the consequent submission of Job, together with the Epilogue, were all additions.[2] This is hard to believe. For in that case the book lacks plan and finish, and the brilliant creator of the dialogue must have been an incompetent architect. The handing over of Job to the Satan is the last word of God, who is not remotely interested in the fate of the man to whose piety He had paid such tribute, and Job's appeal to God is without response. Job is left in the Satan's hand, and a solution irrelevant to the problem is all the reader is left with. Nor is it clear how it can be supposed that a later writer, with the Elihu speeches before him, added the Epilogue without referring to Elihu. It would seem

---

[1] This is not, however, the view of those who retain the Elihu speeches. Cornill says: "Without the Prologue the whole of the following speeches would remain suspended in the air, the reader would be entirely at a loss as to how he ought to take Job's constant asseverations of innocence, and might even at last feel tempted to side with the friends against Job" (*op. cit.* p. 432). He also regards the Epilogue as indispensable to the book (*ibid*).

[2] A. van Hoonacker, *R.B.* xii, 1903, p. 165, suggested that the book may have ended with chapter 31, thus rejecting the Elihu speeches, the divine speeches and the Epilogue. W. A. Irwin, *J.R.* xvii, 1937, pp. 45 f., argued that the divine speeches were added after the Elihu speeches, which were themselves a later addition to the original work. L. W. Batten, *A.Th.R.* xv, 1933, pp. 126 f., supposed that originally all that stood after chapter 31 was 42: 7–9, which he believed to be older than the Prologue, while 42: 12–17 he thought to be closely related to the Prologue.

wiser, with most scholars, to let Elihu go and to credit the author with more wholeness of purpose and plan.

The next serious problem is the relation of the prose Prologue and Epilogue to the poetic dialogue.[1] Here various views have been adopted. Some have supposed that the Prologue and Epilogue are older than the dialogue, and that the author took them over from some existing literary source, and composed the dialogue to wrestle with his problem.[2] Others have held that while there was an older popular story of an ancient worthy who was suddenly smitten with spectacular misfortune, the author of our book composed the Prologue and Epilogue as the setting for the dialogue.[3] Yet others have held that the Prologue and Epilogue are a later addition to the book, and that the dialogue preceded them.[4]

[1] On this question cf. G. Fohrer, *V.T.* vi, 1956, pp. 249 ff.

[2] So J. Wellhausen, *Jahrbücher für deutsche Theologie*, xvi, 1871, p. 555; K. Budde, *Das Buch Hiob*, pp. xiii f.; M. Vernes, *R.H.R.* i, 1880, p. 232; T. K. Cheyne, *Job and Solomon*, 1887, pp. 66 f., and *E. Bib.* ii, 1901, cols. 2467 f.; D. B. Macdonald, *J.B.L.* xiv, 1895, pp. 63 ff., and *A.J.S.L.* xiv, 1897–98, pp. 137 ff.; F. Delitzsch, *Das Buch Hiob*, 1902, p. 13; B. Duhm, *op. cit.* pp. vii f.; C. Siegfried, *J.E.* vii, 1907, p. 195; H. Gärtner, *Der dramatische Charakter des Buches Hiob*, 1909, pp. 29 ff.; P. Volz, *S.A.T.* III, ii, 1911, p. 2; C. Steuernagel, *Einleitung in das A.T.*, 1912, p. 694; L. Gautier, *Introduction à l'A.T.*, 2nd edn., ii, 1914, pp. 98 f.; R. H. Pfeiffer, *Le Problème du livre de Job*, 1915, p. 11; P. Bertie, *Le poème de Job*, 1929, p. 15; G. H. Box, *op. cit.* p. 120; Oesterley and Robinson, *Introduction*, p. 173; A. Lods, *La Bible du Centenaire*, iii, 1947, p. xi, and *Histoire de la littérature hébraïque et juive*, 1950, pp. 671 ff.; A. M. Dubarle, *Les Sages d'Israël*, 1946, p. 67; H. Richter, *Studien zu Hiob*, 1958, p. 59. H. Knight (*S.J.Th.* ix, 1956, p. 76) says: "The *Volksbuch* by its rationalising and dogmatic approach remains within the circle of those forensic notions from which Job's spiritual adventure and the transformation of his consciousness under the impact of the divine Spirit had successfully withdrawn him."

[3] So Gray, in Driver-Gray, *op. cit.* p. xxxviii; P. Dhorme, *Le Livre de Job* [E.B.], 1926, p. lxvii; H. Ranston, *The O.T. Wisdom Books and their Teaching*, 1930, pp. 114, 172; J. E. McFadyen, *Introduction to the O.T.*, 1932, p. 314; G. Hölscher, *Das Buch Hiob*, 1937, p. 4; H. Wheeler Robinson, *The O.T.; its Making and Meaning*, 1937, pp. 153 f.; F. James, *Personalities of the O.T.*, 1947, p. 194; A. Bentzen, *Introduction to the O.T.*, 2nd edn., ii, 1952, p. 175 ("the postulated differences between the narrative and the dialogue are not strong enough to account for a separation").

[4] So A. Schultens, *Liber Jobi*, i, 1737, Preface, p. 34; S. Lee, *op. cit.* pp. 36 f.; G. Studer, *Jahrbücher für protestantische Theologie*, i, 1875, pp. 706 ff.; K. Kautzsch, *Das sogenannte Volksbuch von Hiob*, 1900, pp. 69, 88. R. Simon,

It seems to me difficult to suppose that the Prologue and Epilogue are later than the dialogue.[1] For without the Prologue we have no setting for the dialogue.[2] We are not told who the three friends are, or what the dialogue is all about. That Job is suffering is clear from the dialogue, but that he has been a man of exemplary piety who was suddenly plunged into dire calamity and pain would not be clear to any reader. Indeed, W. B. Stevenson, who took this view of the origin of the book, denies that Job's sufferings were due to disease, and ascribes them to persecution.[3] Instead of finding Job to be the hero of the book, he thinks he was a rebel against God, who was given

Histoire critique du Vieux Testament, 2nd edn., 1685, p. 30, rejected the Prologue, as also does E. König, *op. cit.* pp. 462 ff. On the other hand Buttenwieser retained the Prologue and rejected the Epilogue (*op. cit.* pp. 65, 67), and so K. Fullerton (*Z.A.W.* xliii, 1924, pp. 116 ff.) and L. Finkelstein (*The Pharisees*, i, 1938, p. 235). W. B. Stevenson (*The Poem of Job*, 1947, pp, 21 ff.) holds that the poetic work once opened with Job 3: 2, and that the Prologue and Epilogue were later joined to it from an independent prose work, in which something else stood between the Prologue and Epilogue; cf. also Pedersen, *op. cit.* p. 531 ("there is no natural context between the poem and the prologue-epilogue, so it seems most probable that they are independent productions"). B. D. Eerdmans (*Studies in Job*, 1939, p. 5) declares the Prologue and Epilogue to be later than the dialogue.

[1] Cf. D. B. Macdonald, *J.B.L.* xiv, 1895, p. 63: "Without the Prologue, the poem itself would be as unintelligible as the second part of *Faust* without the first. Some introduction is absolutely necessary, and if this present prologue is a later addition, it must have been put in the place of something else that was cut away to make room for it. But of this there cannot be a fragment of proof, and it does not help in any way towards a solution of the problem of the poem." Similarly A. Lods (*La Bible du Centenaire*, iii, p. xii) says it is incredible that the Prologue was added later. Cf. S. Davidson, *Introduction to the O.T.* ii, 1863, p. 202; F. Bleek, *Introduction to the O.T.*, Eng. trans. by G. H. Venables, ii, 1894, p. 280; C. Steuernagel, *Einleitung in das A.T.*, 1912, p. 694; and S. L. Terrien, *I.B.* iii, 1954, p. 887.

[2] G. Studer, *Das Buch Hiob*, 1881, pp. 20 ff., thought chapters 29 f. were the original introduction to the poem. A. B. Davidson (*The Book of Job*, 1884, p. xxix n.) observed, with reference to Studer's view: "One of the latest writers on the book has found it necessary to amputate every limb from the poem, leaving it a mere trunk, consisting of ch. 3–31, and even this trunk is so misshapen that its shoulders are found in the region of its bowels."

[3] Cf. *op. cit.* pp. 31 ff.

wise counsel by the friends.[1] In that case the Prologue and Epilogue would be completely irrelevant to the dialogue. The dialogue surely requires some introduction,[2] and without it the book is a torso. On the other hand, there is no reason to suppose that it once had a different beginning and ending, but that the present Prologue and Epilogue have been substituted for them.[3] No trace of a different setting for the dialogue has survived, and it would be hard to invent anything more appropriate than what we now have. But even if our ingenuity could suggest something more appropriate, that would be no evidence that our invention was really a restoration of the original book.[4] We should need to explain why it was that our supposed introduction was replaced by something less appropriate, and how it was that the inferior so effectively ousted the

[1] *Ibid.* pp. 26, 45, 54.

[2] Cf. W. Baumgartner, in *O.T.M.S.*, p. 217: "How is one to conceive of the dialogue without the framework?"

[3] N. H. Tur Sinai (*The Book of Job*, 1957, p. 31) holds that the present Prologue and Epilogue are younger than the dialogue, but that they may have replaced a lost older framework.

[4] T. K. Cheyne (*Jewish Religious Life after the Exile*, 1898, p. 161) makes the contrary assumption, that the poetic part of the book, 3: 1–42: 7, has replaced a short prose section which he imaginatively reconstructs as follows: "And these three men, moved at the sight of Job's grief, broke out into lamentations, and withheld not passionate complaints of the injustice of God. They said 'Is there knowledge in the Most High? And does God judge righteous judgement?' But Job was sore displeased, and reproved them, saying, 'Bitter is the pain which racks me, but more bitter still are the words which ye speak' . . . And at the end of a season, God came to Eliphaz in a dream and said, 'My wrath is kindled against thee and thy two friends, because ye have not spoken of Me that which is right, as My servant Job has.' " This is approved by F. Buhl, in *Vom A.T.* (Marti Festschrift), 1925, p. 58. Cf. also D. B. Macdonald, *J.B.L.* xiv, 1895, pp. 63 ff.: "Job in the original story had taken God's part, while the friends had followed more or less implicitly the course of Job's wife in our prologue." Cf. also J. Lindblom, *La composition du livre de Job*, 1945, p. 11. This is mere modern fiction, for which no shred of evidence is, or can be, adduced. It is more profitable to seek to understand the masterpiece which has come down to us than to compose inferior words which we could devise, whose non-survival would have been so well merited. E. G. Kraeling (*Review of Religion*, x, 1946, p. 427) says: "It seems intrinsically unlikely and unthinkable that a folktale should have introduced three visitors with no other function than to accuse the God of Job in a few words." Cf. S. Spiegel, in *Louis Ginzberg Memorial Volume*, 1945, p. 325.

superior that no trace of it has survived. Or if we should suppose that the original introduction was inferior to the present Prologue, and on that account was replaced, we should need to explain why it was that the brilliant author of the dialogue was unsuccessful in composing a suitable setting for his story.[1] The position here is totally unlike that in relation to the Elihu speeches, which can be omitted without affecting in any way the structure of the book.

It is true that in the dialogue there is no reference to the explanation of Job's sufferings that has been given in the Prologue. But how could there be? Job and his friends would not need to be told of his former state or of his present misfortunes. Of the reason for his sufferings they could not, in the nature of the case, know, and as little could they guess. They had not been present in the heavenly court, and could not know that Job's sufferings were due to the Satan's cynical imputations against his single-minded piety. If there had been any reference to this in the dialogue, the author would have given himself away as a writer with little skill.

Not a few writers have charged him with contradicting in the dialogue what is said in the Prologue, and have found here an indication of a different hand.[2] In 19: 17 Job is thought to refer to his sons as still living, whereas in the Prologue they had all been killed.[3] Actually in the dialogue there are two passages which seem to recognize that Job's sons were dead (8: 4 and 29: 5), so that if there were a lapse in 19: 17, it would not show that the dialogue came from a different hand from the Prologue. In fact, however, the expression in 19: 17 is an unusual one if the reference is to Job's children. For the phrase used here is "the children of my womb". The reference could be to the

---

[1] B. Duhm (*Das Buch Hiob*, 1897, p. vii) and Oesterley and Robinson (*Introduction to the Books of the O.T.*, 1934, p. 173) think the friends already figure in the older book, while P. Volz (*S.A.T.* III, ii, 1911, pp. 2 f.n.) thinks the author of the poetic part of the work added them. P. Bertie (*op. cit.* pp. 15, 95) thinks they were imported by the author of the dialogue later than the introduction of Job's complaint, 3, 29–31.

[2] Cf. Oesterley-Robinson, *Introduction*, p. 172: "The whole conception of religion is different." On the other hand Hölscher (*op. cit.* p. 4) says the differences between the poem and its framework have been greatly exaggerated.

[3] Cf. Duhm, *op. cit.* p. 100; Cheyne, *E.Bib.* ii, col. 2467.

womb of Job's wife, which might be regarded as belonging to him; but it could equally be to the womb of his mother, regarded as his because from it he emerged.[1] Both R.V. and R.S.V. understand the verse in the latter sense.

There are certain differences between the dialogue and its setting, however, to which appeal has been made for the view that the Prologue and Epilogue were taken over from an existing source. Notable amongst these is the fact that whereas the divine name Yahweh stands frequently in the Prologue and Epilogue, it is studiously avoided in the dialogue, where we find El thirty-three times, Eloah thirty-three times, and Shaddai twenty-four times.[2] It is surprising that so much has been built on this. The dialogue consists of speeches put into the mouth of Job's three foreign friends and of Job in reply to them. It is not unnatural that the friends should use more general Semitic terms for God, and should not be represented as worshippers of the God of the Jews, or that Job in speaking to them should use these more general terms. Once in the dialogue we find the word Yahweh,[3] and it is often supposed that here the author slipped, or that a copyist has introduced the name in error.[4] It is to be noted, however, that even here it is on the lips of Job that we find the name, and in the Prologue Job is presented as a worshipper of Yahweh. He is said to be from the land of Uz, and though this cannot be identified, it is likely that it was a foreign land, and Job was not therefore a Jew.[5] Nevertheless,

---

[1] Cf. Buttenwieser, *op. cit.* pp. 24 ff. Cf. Job 3: 10, where Job says "my womb" when he means his mother's.

[2] For an analysis of the occurrences of the divine names, cf. Gray, in Driver-Gray, *op. cit.* p. xxxv.

[3] Job 12: 9.

[4] So, e.g. Peake, *op.cit.* p. 135; Strahan, *The Book of Job*, 1913, p. 118; Dhorme, *op. cit.* p. 157. J. Steinmann, *Le Livre de Job*, 1955, pp. 243 f., rejects 12: 7–10 as a gloss, and says that the presence of the name Yahweh would alone be sufficient to indicate a gloss. Ball, *op. cit.* p. 212, on the contrary, says: "It is surely significant that the poet . . . should here, and here only, introduce the special name of the God of Israel. In so doing he not only betrays his own nationality. He also reveals his purpose of comforting his people during a period of national calamity."

[5] Pfeiffer (*op. cit.* p. 682; cf. *Z.A.W.* XLIV [N.F. III], 1926, pp. 17 ff.) thinks the author's thought and language are Edomite. Similarly J. Lindblom (*La composition du livre de Job*, 1945, pp. 3 ff.) thinks the original work

he is declared to be one who reverenced Yahweh,[1] whereas the friends are nowhere so represented. It should be added that in the author's rubrics introducing the speeches of Yahweh and Job's answers, the divine name is again found; so that if we hold the Prologue and Epilogue to be older than the dialogue on this ground, we should need to suppose that these introductions to speeches stood also in the older book. We certainly cannot charge the author with inconsistency on this ground if he composed both setting and dialogue.

That there is an older tradition of a good man who suffered there is little reason to doubt, and our author probably took over this tradition to base his book on it. In the book of Ezekiel there are references to Job as a conspicuously righteous man,[2] and since these references almost certainly antedate the present book of Job they bear witness to an old tradition about a Job, who may well be the person around whom our author built his work.[3]

was Edomite. Cf. Gray in Driver-Gray, *op. cit.* pp. xxvii ff. Dhorme (*R.B.*, N.S. viii, 1911, pp. 102 ff.) connects rather with the Hauran, and so G. A. Barton, *J.B.L.* xxxi, 1912, pp. 63 ff. Cf. Gray, *loc. cit.* p. xxx. Eissfeldt (*Z.D.M.G.* civ, 1954, pp. 109, 116) connects Job with Ṣafā, though he does not exclude the possibility that the author of Job lived in Palestine (*Einleitung*, 2nd edn., p. 578). P. Humbert (*Recherches sur les sources égyptiennes de la littérature sapientale d'Israël*, 1929, pp. 75 ff.) thinks the home of the author was Egypt. Cf. R. Marcus, *Review of Religion*, xiii, 1949, pp. 9 ff., where, however, the author observes that Humbert is too confident about the Egyptian origin of some passages in Job (p. 9 n.). F. H. Foster, (*A.J.S.L.* xlix, 1932–33, pp. 21 ff.) argues that the work was a translation from Arabic, while J. P. Naish (*Expositor*, 9th series, iii, 1925, pp. 34 ff., 94 ff.) thinks Job was a Babylonian Jew early in the Persian period. H. Beveridge (*J.R.A.S.*, 1919, p. 234) thought the work could not be earlier than the sixth century B.C., since he found in 19: 24 an allusion to the Behistun inscription of Darius I, while V. L. Trumper (*ibid.* pp. 586 f.) thought it could not be later than shortly after the building of the pyramids. G. W. Hazelton (*Bibliotheca Sacra*, lxxi, 1914, pp. 573 ff.) sought to establish that it was written by Moses during his sojourn with Jethro in Midian.

[1] The divine name Yahweh is found on the lips of Job only in the expression of resignation in 1: 21. In the opening verse we are told that Job feared God, but that God is to be identified with Yahweh is apparent from 1: 8, where Yahweh declares that Job is one who served Him.

[2] Ezek. 14: 14, 20.

[3] Cf. G. Fohrer, "Überlieferung und Wandlung der Hioblegende", in *Festschrift F. Baumgärtel*, 1959, pp. 41 ff.

Moreover, the theme of a righteous sufferer need not be presumed to be an original one with the author of our book. That the righteous may suffer must have been observed by men from ancient times, and the theme has figured in the literature of many countries.[1] Many writers have cited certain Babylonian texts,[2] and especially one commonly referred to as the "Babylonian Job",[3] which in some respects offers a parallel to

[1] Cf. my *Submission in Suffering and other Essays*, 1951, where I survey thought on this subject in many religions. Cf. also E. F. Sutcliffe, *Providence and Suffering in O. and N.T.*, 1955, pp. 1 ff.; J. J. Stamm, *J.E.O.L.* No. 9, 1944, pp. 99 ff.; and *Das Leiden des Unschuldigen in Babylon und Israel*, 1946. On Egyptian texts that have been cited, cf. Buttenwieser, *op. cit.* pp. 11 f.; K. Fries, *op. cit.* pp. 12 ff.; P. Humbert, *Recherches sur les sources égyptiennes de la littérature sapientale d'Israël*, 1929, pp. 75 ff.; J. Steinmann, *Le Livre de Job*, 1955, pp. 25 ff. For the text containing the dialogue of a man with his own soul, cf. J. A. Wilson in J. B. Pritchard (ed. by), *A.N.E.T.*, 1950, pp. 405 ff.; H. Ranke, in Gressmann, *A.T.O.T.*, 2nd edn., 1926, pp. 25 ff.; B. van der Walle, *Chronique d'Égypte*, XIV, 1939, pp. 312 ff.; A. Hermann, *O.L.Z.* XLII, 1939, 345 ff.; A. de Buck, *Kernmomenten*, 1947, pp. 19 ff. Cf. also J. Paulus, "Le thème du Juste Souffrant dans la pensée grecque et hébraïque", in *R.H.R.* CXXI, 1940, pp. 18 ff.

[2] One text, called "A Pessimistic Dialogue between a Master and his Servant" is translated by Pfeiffer, in J. B. Pritchard (ed. by), *op. cit.* 1950, pp. 437 f. For the Akkadian text, cf. G. Reisner, *Sumerisch-babylonische Hymnen*, 1896, Anhang, No. VI, p. 143; E. Ebeling, *K.A.R.* I, no. 96, pp. 170 ff., and *M.V.A.G.* XXIII, no. 2, 1919, pp. 83 f. Translations, partial translations, and discussions (with or without Akkadian text in transcription) of this text may be found in G. B. Gray, *E.T.* XXXI, 1919–20, pp. 440 ff.; Ebeling, *M.V.A.G., loc. cit.* pp. 54 ff., and in H. Gressmann, *op. cit.* pp. 284 ff.; S. Langdon, *Babylonian Wisdom*, 1923, pp. 67 ff.; B. Meissner, *Babylonien und Assyrien*, II, 1925, pp. 432 ff.; T. Jacobsen, in *The Intellectual Adventure of Ancient Man*, 1946, pp. 216 ff.; J. J. Stamm, *Das Leiden des Unschuldigen in Babylon und Israel*, pp. 14 ff.; E. A. Speiser, *J.C.S.* VIII, 1954, pp. 98 ff.; E. F. Sutcliffe, *op. cit.* 1955, pp. 34 ff.; W. G. Lambert, *Babylonian Wisdom Literature*, 1960, pp. 139 ff. For the study of another Akkadian text, cf. P. Dhorme, *R.B.* XXXII, 1923, pp. 5 ff. (reprinted in *Recueil Edouard Dhorme*, 1951, pp. 655 ff.); B. Meissner, *op. cit.* pp. 431 f.; E. Ebeling, in Gressmann, *op. cit.* pp. 287 ff.; R. H. Pfeiffer, in Pritchard, *op. cit.* pp. 438 ff.; W. G. Lambert, *op. cit.* pp. 63 ff. Recently S. N. Kramer has published (*V.T. Supplements* III [Rowley Festschrift, 1955], pp. 170 ff.), a Sumerian text with some affinities with the Job story; cf. also H. Schmökel, *F.u.F.* XXX, 1956, pp. 74 ff.

[3] For a translation, cf. Pfeiffer, in Pritchard, pp. 434 ff. Several copies of fragments of this text have been found. For the Akkadian text, cf. H. C. Rawlinson, *The Cuneiform Inscriptions of Western Asia*, IV (2nd edn., 1891),

the book of Job.[1] Here the sufferer is a pious king, who is stricken by disease, mocked by his friends, and ultimately restored. So far there are elements parallel to the book of Job. More fundamental, however, are the differences.[2] The Babylonian sufferer cries to God for relief from his miseries, as many another in all ages has done. He is quite unaware what he can have done to deserve his troubles, but he is ready to believe that in some unremembered or unconscious way he must have offended against the deity and brought them on himself. This stands in contrast to Job, who consistently maintains that his misfortunes were not brought on him by himself. His innocence is proclaimed in the Prologue, and protested by Job throughout. Hence, as Buttenwieser says, the Babylonian story "lacks all those essential points that give the Job story its distinct

no. 60; V. Scheil, *Une saison de fouilles à Sippar*, 1902, p. 105, no. 37; R. Campbell Thompson, *P.S.B.A.* xxxii, 1910, pp. 18 ff.; S. Landersdorfer, *Eine babylonische Quelle für das Buch Job?* 1911, pp. 14 ff. (translation pp. 21 ff.); E. Ebeling, *K.A.R.* i, 1919, nos. 10, 11, 108, 175, pp. 14, 15, 187, 319, ii (Heft 8, 1923), no. 326, pp. 272 f.; W. G. Lambert, *Babylonian Wisdom Literature*, 1960, pp. 21 ff. Other translations, partial translations and discussions (some with Akkadian text in transcription) may be found in H. Zimmern, in Schrader-Zimmern-Winckler, *K.A.T.* (3rd edn., 1903), pp. 385 ff., and *Babylonische Hymnen und Gebete in Auswahl*, 1905 (Alte Orient vii, no 3), pp. 28 ff.; M. Jastrow, *J.B.L.* xxv, 1906, pp. 135 ff., and *Die Religion Babyloniens und Assyriens*, ii, 1912, pp. 120 ff.; P. Dhorme, *Choix de Textes Religieux Assyro-Babyloniens*, 1907, pp. 372 ff.; F. Martin, *Journal asiatique*, 10th series, xvi, 1910, pp. 75 ff.; R. W. Rogers, *Cuneiform Parallels to the O.T.*, 1912, pp. 164 ff.; C. J. Ball, *op. cit.* pp. 9 ff.; Gray, *E.T.* xxxi, 1919–20, p. 442, and in Driver-Gray, *op. cit.* pp. xxxi ff.; Langdon, *op. cit.* pp. 35 ff.; W. L. Wardle, *Israel and Babylon*, 1925, pp. 87 ff.; Ebeling in Gressmann, *op. cit.* pp. 273 ff.; J. Plessis in Pirot's *S.D.B.* i, 1928, cols. 824 ff.; T. Jacobsen, *loc. cit.* pp. 212 ff.; J. J. Stamm, *op. cit.* pp. 17 ff.; J. Nougayrol, *R.B.* lix, 1952, pp. 239 ff.; Sutcliffe, *op. cit.* pp. 27 ff. A part of this text was translated in A. H. Sayce, *The Religion of the Ancient Babylonians* (Hibbert Lectures), 1887, pp. 535 ff., but of this translation M. Jastrow, *J.B.L.* xxv, 1906, p. 141 n., says: "The translation is antiquated, and only a very few lines of it are correct."

[1] M. Jastrow, *The Book of Job*, p. 48, refers to a similar Indian tale. Cf. also A. and M. Hanson, *The Book of Job*, 1953, p. 9; also A. Lods, *R.H.P.R.* xiv, 1934, pp. 527 ff., and *Histoire de la littérature hébraïque et juive*, pp. 691 f.; S. L. Terrien, *I.B.* iii, 1954, p. 879.

[2] M. Jastrow, *J.B.L.* xxv, 1906, p. 188, suggests that the Babylonian text and the book of Job both derived from a common original.

character".[1] Further, the book of Job, as will be said later, is far more than a cry against God or an appeal to God. It carries a religious message which will be sought in vain in the Babylonian text.[2]

It seems most likely, therefore, that while the author of our book did not create the figure of Job as a righteous sufferer, he used this figure as the vehicle of his message, and wrote the Prologue as the introduction to his dialogue, setting the stage for the debate and introducing the three friends, and also explaining to the reader the reason for Job's suffering, since it was necessary to his purpose that he should do this, as will appear. As C. F. Aked perceived, the Prologue "is only the *machinery* of the drama, the author's way of getting his characters upon the stage and into action".[3] Oesterley and Robinson say that McFadyen and Kautzsch "stand almost alone in ascribing the framework to the poet himself".[4] Actually other names could also be cited,[5] and I would add mine to the list.

We must not ignore some objections which have been raised against the Epilogue, however. By some writers this is thought to mar the book, and to give away the whole case to the friends. For in the Epilogue Job's prosperity is restored. Here, then, we find that merit leads to prosperity, precisely as the friends had maintained it always does, and as Job had felt it should. We must remember that every writer is limited by the form he

---

[1] *Op. cit.* p. 10. Similarly Dhorme, *Le Livre de Job*, p. LXXXVI, says: "La comparaison entre le thème de ce poème et celui du livre de Job prouve jusqu' à l'évidence que le livre de Job est indépendant de la composition babylonienne." See also Landersdorfer, *op. cit.* p. 138. Cf. Ball, *op. cit.* p. 8: "We might as well expect to find Shakespeare as we know him in the pages of Holinshed or Plutarch, or in the plays of Plautus and Seneca, or in the dramas and romances of his Italian contemporaries, as to find the direct source of this extraordinary product of Israel's genius in Babylonian or any other older literature." R. Marcus, *Review of Religion*, XIII, 1949, pp. 12 f., observes that "the author of the Hebrew Wisdom book has touched depths of thought and feeling much more profound than those revealed in the Babylonian poem."
[2] For a comparison between the two texts, cf. J. Plessis, *loc. cit.* cols. 826 ff.
[3] Cf. *The Divine Drama of Job*, 1913, p. 18.
[4] Cf. *Introduction*, p. 173 n.
[5] Cf. above, p. 151, n. 3

adopts. The author of the book of Job had written the Prologue as the setting for his dialogue, and he was artist enough
not to forget it. To have ended the book without the Epilogue
would have been to leave it unfinished. In the Prologue Job
was delivered into the hands of the Satan to be tested. He had
stood the test and had not been found wanting. It is sometimes
pointed out that in the divine speech Job is severely condemned, and that this stands in contrast to the commendation
in the Epilogue and indicates diversity of authorship.[1] But the
condemnation and the commendation are not on the same
issue.[2] Job is condemned for presuming to pass judgment on
things beyond his understanding, and for the rash things he had
said after his misfortunes had come upon him. He is not condemned on the issue on which he is being tried. The wild
things he had uttered to his friends were not the cause of his
sufferings.[3] Nowhere does he express the slightest regret for his
integrity of character, or renounce the uprightness of his way.
The Satan had cast doubt on the disinterestedness of his piety,
and on this issue he had been proved wrong and Job had been
vindicated. It would have been intolerable to leave him still in
the hands of the Satan. No longer would this have been the
test of Job, but mere malice and vindictiveness. A human court
which left a defendant to languish in gaol after a verdict of
acquittal would be denounced as unjust. Job was acquitted,
and therefore he must be delivered from his misfortunes, since
they are the form his trial takes.[4] The Epilogue was not demanded by the message of the book; but it was demanded by
its form. The trial was over and the case against Job had been
proved to be empty. The Epilogue is merely the author's way
of indicating this and rounding off his book.[5]

[1] Cf. e.g. K. Fullerton, *Z.A.W.* xlii (N.F. i), 1924, p. 127.

[2] Cf. Gray in Driver-Gray, *op. cit.* p. lix.

[3] In the course of the debate Job says many things which were doubtless
thought blasphemous by the friends, as they have been by later readers.
But, as K. Fullerton (*Z.A.W.* xlii [N.F. i], p. 119) observes, the God whom
Job rejects is no real God, but the phantom God created by the dogma of
the friends.

[4] Cf. Davidson-Lanchester, *The Book of Job*, 1918, p. xli: "If the drama
be the trial of the righteous, the author must bring it to some conclusion."

[5] It is often remarked that the Satan finds no mention in the Epilogue,
and supposed that this indicates some lapse on the author's part, but the

There is no time here to examine some individual varieties of the view that rejects the Prologue and the Epilogue. E. G. Kraeling rejects as secondary most of the Prologue, viz. 1: 1–2: 10, but retains 2: 11–13, and believes that the Epilogue comes from the same hand as 2: 11–13, save that 42: 10–17 form a makeshift conclusion which probably came from the author of 1: 1–2: 10.[1] This at least recognizes that the restoration of the prosperity was demanded by the Prologue, but it fails to explain why the original introduction should have disappeared. The book cannot be supposed to have begun abruptly with 2: 11–13, and we are back at the point we have already considered. J. Lindblom published a stimulating work in Swedish[2] and a shorter one in French,[3] propounding highly original views. While finding the Prologue and Epilogue to be older than the dialogue, he postulates a somewhat complex history for the Prologue and Epilogue. He maintains that originally there was an Edomite form of these, in which neither Job's wife nor the Satan figured,[4] but that a later Israelite editor brought these in and substituted a new ending for the original one. Still later the Edomite ending came back in an amended form to stand beside the other.[5] I have already said

scene of the Epilogue is not in heaven, and if God had mentioned the Satan in His judgment He would have had to indicate to Job the cause of his sufferings. Yet this was precisely what could not be revealed if the book was to retain its value for men who must suffer in the dark. The author of the book was more clear-sighted than his critics.

[1] Cf. *The Book of the Ways of God*, pp. 167, 175. Kraeling also further substantially reduces the book by rejecting 29–31 (pp. 111 ff.), as well as the Elihu speeches (pp. 125 ff.) and one divine speech (pp. 143 ff.).

[2] Cf. *Boken om Job och hans lidande*, 1940.

[3] Cf. *La composition du livre de Job*, 1945. For Kraeling's critical review of this book see *Review of Religion*, x, 1946, pp. 425 ff.

[4] Other scholars who have thought the Satan passages to be secondary include Kautzsch, *op. cit.* p. 88; Jastrow, *The Book of Job*, pp. 52 ff.; L. W. Batten, *A.Th.R.* xv, 1933, p. 127; L. Finkelstein, *op. cit.* i, 1938, p. 235; Pfeiffer, *Introduction*, p. 669. On the other hand, Hölscher, *Das Buch Hiob*, pp. 2 f., says it is wrong to delete the Satan.

[5] *Op. cit.* pp. 3 ff. Jastrow (*loc. cit.*) finds four epilogues, 42: 10–17, 42: 7–9, 40: 1–14, 42: 1–6. McFadyen, *Introduction*, p. 314, rejects 42: 10–17. K. Fullerton, *Z.A.W.* xlii (N.F. i, 1924), pp. 126 ff., thinks 42: 7–9 a gloss by one who sympathized with the positions taken by the author in the dialogue, while 42: 1–6, 10–17 came from a single hand, who placed 42:

that I am not persuaded that the Prologue and Epilogue are from an earlier hand than the dialogue, and I find it difficult to believe that if they had been they could have had so complicated a history.

We may next look at the third cycle of speeches, which, as has been said, tails off. In chapter 22 Eliphaz opens this cycle, as he had opened the others. Job replies in chapters 23 f. Then Bildad speaks in chapter 25, and Job replies in chapter 26. Chapter 27 appears to be a further speech of Job's, introduced by the unusual formula "And Job again took up his parable and said". Zophar disappears altogether from this cycle. It has been suggested that this is deliberate on the part of the author, to suggest that the friends had run out of arguments.[1] It is to be observed, however, that there are some indications of disorder in the text in this cycle. In chapter 24 there is material which does not seem to fit the lips of Job, and which some scholars have held to be misplaced.[2] Again, in chapter 26, which contains Job's reply to Bildad, there is much that is inappropriate to Job, but which would accord better with the views of the friends, and the same is true of chapter 27. In this latter chapter

7–9 where it is. Dhorme (*op. cit.* p. LXXVI) speaks scornfully of the "fantaisies" of Fullerton, and observes that his "machiavélisme est plutôt le fait du critique que de l'auteur du livre de Job". Cf. also A. Alt, *Z.A.W.* LV (N.F. XIV, 1937), pp. 265 ff., for another analysis, according to which 42: 11–17 is the oldest part of the Epilogue. Alt thought these verses originally connected with 1: 14–17. Against such views W. E. Staples (*The Speeches of Elihu*, 1925, p. 7) maintains the unity of the epilogue.

[1] Cf. A. Schultens, *Le Livre de Job*, French trans. by E. de Joncourt, J. Sacrelaire and J. Allamand, 1748, Argument, p. 6: "À l'égard de Tsophar, il se tait quand son tour de parler revient, soit qu'il n'ait rien à ajouter à ce qui a été dit, ou qu'il soit convaincu de la justice de la cause de Job" (cf. *Liber Jobi*, II, 1737, p. 729: "Vel convictus itaque, vel conterritus Tsopharus, quem tertius nunc orbis certanimum tangebat, silet"). Cf. also H. Möller, *Sinn und Aufbau des Buches Hiob*, 1955, p. 63. K. Fullerton (*Z.A.W.* XLII [N.F. I, 1924], p. 121) says: "To explain this, as is usually done, as if it were intended to illustrate the gradual drying up of the Friends' powers of argumentation is most mechanical and quite unworthy of an author who shows the psychological insight displayed in the previous part of the Dialogue."

[2] C. Westermann (*Der Aufbau des Buches Hiob*, 1956, p. 103) rejects 24: 5–11 (except 9), 13–17 from the book of Job altogether.

it is common to find traces of a lost speech of Zophar's.[1] While the reconstructions of scholars differ considerably in detail,[2] there is a wide agreement that probably originally the third cycle of speeches was complete, but that part has been lost, and

[1] B. Kennicott, *V.T. Hebraicum cum variis lectionibus*, II, 1780, Dissertatio Generalis, p. 155, and *Remarks on Select Passages in the O.T.*, 1787, pp. 169 ff., held 27: 11–23 to be Zophar's, and McFadyen (*op. cit.* p. 316) attributed to Zophar 27: 7–23. Some authors reject as secondary 27: 7–23 (so Fohrer, *Das Buch Hiob*, 1948, p. 89, who also rejects 24: 1–8, 10–23; Volz, *S.A.T.* III, II, 1911, p. 27), or 27: 11–23 (so König, *op. cit.* pp. 271 f.), or 27: 13–23 (so H. Strack, *Einleitung in das A.T.*, 5th edn., 1898, p. 136). Marshall, on the other hand, retains 27: 7–23, and finds here Job's retraction (*op. cit.* p. 11). W. T. Davison (in *D.B.* II, 1899, p. 666) holds that 27: 7–23 are out of place, whether they are to be regarded as part of a speech of Bildad or Zophar or not, but otherwise he rejects only 28 and the Elihu speeches.

[2] The reconstructions that have been proposed are innumerable. A few examples must here suffice. B. Kennicott (*op. cit.* II, Dissertatio Generalis, p. 115) assigns 25 to Bildad, 26: 1–27: 12 to Job, 27: 13–23 to Zophar, and 28 ff. to Job; M. H. Stuhlmann (*Hiob: ein religiöses Gedicht*, 1804, pp. 148 ff.) assigns 25 and 28 to Bildad, 26: 1 – 27: 10 to Job, 27: 11–23 to Zophar, and 29 ff. to Job; E. Reuss (*Die Geschichte der Heiligen Schriften A.Ts.*, 2nd edn., 1890, p. 309) assigns 25 and 26: 5–14 to Bildad, 26: 1–4 and 27: 2–23 to Job, with 28 as unoriginal; G. Bickell (*Das Buch Job*, 1894, pp. 43 ff.) assigns 25: 1–3, 26: 12 f., 14c, 25: 4–6 to Bildad, 26: 2, 4, 27: 2, 4–6, 11 f., 28: 1–3, 9–11, 20–28 to Job, 27: 7–10, 14–20 to Zophar, 29 ff. to Job; Duhm (*op. cit.* pp. 120 f.) assigns 26: 1–4, 25: 2–6, 26: 5 f., 11–14 to Bildad, 27: 1–6, 12 to Job, 27: 7–11, 13–23 to Zophar, 29 ff. to Job, with 28 as unoriginal; C. Siegfried (*J.E.* VII, 1907, pp. 198 f.) assigns 25, 26: 5–14 to Bildad, 26: 1–4, 27: 2–6, 29 ff. to Job, with 27: 7–28: 28 as unoriginal; L. Laue (*Die Composition des Buches Hiob*, 1895, pp. 75, 90) assigns 27: 13–23 to Bildad, 26: 1–3, 9: 2–24 to Job, 28 to Zophar, 12 to Job, and deletes 25 as unoriginal; G. A. Barton (*J.B.L.* xxx, 1911, 70 ff.) assigns 24: 1–4, 9–16, 23, 25 to Job, 25: 1–6, 24: 17 f., 5–8, 30: 3–8, 24: 21 f., 19 f., 24 to Bildad, 26 to Job, 27: 7–11, 13–23 to Zophar, 27: 1–6, 12, 29: 2–25, 30: 1 f., 9–31 to Job, with 28 as unoriginal; Gray (in Driver-Gray, *op. cit.* p. 1) 23, 24 (except 23: 8 f. and 24: 13–17 and parts of 18–24) to Job, 25 (? and 26) to Bildad, 27: 2–6, 11 f., to Job, 27: 7–10, 13–23 to Zophar (?); P. Dhorme (*op. cit.* pp. 312 ff.; followed by H. Rongy, *Revue Ecclésiastique de Liége*, xxv, 1933, pp. 97 f.; cf. also Dhorme, *R.B.* xxxIII, 1924, pp. 343 ff., and S. L. Terrien, *I.B.* III, 1954, p. 888), assigns 23, 24: 1–17, 25 to Job, 25: 1–6, 26: 5–14 to Bildad, 26: 1–4, 27: 2–12 to Job, 27: 13, 24: 18–24, 27: 14–23 to Zophar, 29 ff. to Job; F. Buhl (in *Vom A.T.* [Marti Festschrift], 1925, p. 52) regards 24–28 as a conglomeration of fragments of varied origin (with this cf. F. Baumgärtel, *Der Hiobdialog*, 1933, p. 156, where the third cycle is described as "ein Trümmerfeld, in dem sich niemand mehr zurecht

what has survived is not in its original order.[1] It would be out of place here to discuss the reconstructions in detail, and in any case they do not substantially affect our understanding of the nature and purpose of the book.

We may turn next to the speeches of Yahweh. Some scholars have rejected these altogether,[2] and it has been argued that

findet"); E. J. Kissane (*The Book of Job*, pp. 163 ff.) assigns 26: 1–4, 27: 7–23 to Bildad, 29–30 to Job, 25, 26: 5–14 to Zophar, 27: 1–6, 31 to Job; Pfeiffer (*op. cit.* pp. 663 f., 671) assigns 23, 24: 1–12, 25, to Job, 25: 1, 27: 7–10, 16–23 to Bildad, 26: 1–4, 27: 11 f., 25: 2–6, 26: 5–14 to Job, 27: 13, 24: 21–24, 18–20, 27: 14 f. to Zophar, 27: 1–6, 29 ff. to Job; Lefèvre (in *S.D.B.* IV, cols. 1078 f.) assigns 23: 1–24: 17 to Job, 26: 5–14, 25: 2–6 to Bildad, 26: 2–4, 27: 2–12 to Job, 27: 13–23, 24: 18–23 to Zophar; R. Tournay (*R.B.* LXIV, 1957, pp. 321 ff.) holds that 24: 18–25 should be transferred to follow Zophar's speech 27: 13–23, and that 25: 2–26: 4 should follow 26: 5–14, which then belongs to Bildad's third speech; H. W. Hertzberg (in *Festschrift Alfred Bertholet*, 1950, pp. 238 ff.) assigns 23: 13–24 25: 2–6 to Bildad, 26: 1–4, 27: 11 f., 26: 5–14, 27: 2–6 to Job, and 27: 7–10, 13–23 to Zophar. While there is a substantial measure of agreement, amongst some of these the measure of disagreement is significant of the difficulty of any reconstruction. Marshall (*op. cit.* p. 72) attributes 25: 2–6, 26: 5–14 to Zophar. For further discussions of this cycle cf. C. Kuhl, *Th.R.*, N.F. xxi, 1953, pp. 277 ff.

[1] W. A. Irwin, *J.R.* xvii, 1937, pp. 40 ff., thinks the author of the Elihu speeches had the complete third cycle before him, and so suggests that we may use the Elihu speeches to reconstruct its contents. K. Fullerton, *Z.A.W.* xlii (N.F. 1, 1924), thinks chapters 29–31 have been tampered with in dogmatic interests.

[2] Gray was earlier inclined to reject both speeches; cf. *Critical Introduction to the O.T.*, 1913, p. 523. Later, however, he retained the first speech more decisively; cf. Driver-Gray, *op. cit.* p. lxiii. For a defence of the retention of the first speech, cf. M. Burrows, *J.B.L.* xlvii, 1928, pp. 117 ff. Marshall (*op. cit.* p. 6) rejected these speeches as on an immeasurably higher plane than the dialogue. They were rejected also by Staples, *op. cit.* pp. 11 f., O. S. Rankin, *Israel's Wisdom Literature*, 1936, p. 93, and earlier by M. Vernes, *R.H.R.* i, 1880, p. 232; while Hölscher (*op. cit.* p. 55) holds that it is wrong to delete them. For other writers who reject both divine speeches see p. 150 n. 2. C. Kuhl thinks the original work recorded a theophany, but without the divine speeches; cf. *Th.R.*, N.F. xxi, 1953, p. 271 (but cf. *Entstehung des A.Ts.*, p. 265, where the first speech is accepted and the second rejected). D. B. Macdonald, *J.B.L.* xiv, 1895, p. 69, held that the divine speeches were composed "at an earlier point in the poet's own development, before the problem had assumed for him the complexity and difficulty which it did later". On the other hand, Sellin (*Introduction to the*

the author of the Elihu speeches could not have known them, or he would not have inserted his solution of the problem. This does not seem cogent, since without some speech of Yahweh the structure of the book falls to pieces. As has been said, the Elihu speeches can be omitted without affecting the rest of the book. It is less easy to imagine that the book originally ended with chapter 31, or with chapter 37, after the Elihu speeches had been added. The speech of Yahweh is the appropriate answer to Job's closing soliloquy, leading to Job's submission, and so preparing for the dropping of the curtain in the Epilogue.

As the book now stands, however, there are two speeches by Yahweh. We have already noted that the second is inferior to the first in conception and in brilliance,[1] and after Job has bowed in submission to God a second speech is uncalled for, since it adds nothing essentially new, but merely continues in an inferior way what the first speech had said. Hence the

O.T., Eng. trans. by Montgomery, 1923, pp. 207 ff.) thinks they were added later by the author. More recently Macdonald (*The Hebrew Literary Genius*, 1933, pp. 28 ff.) assigns the divine speeches to another poet, whose attitude to life was quite different from the author's, and speaks of "the impudence of the argument" of these speeches (p. 29).

[1] On the first speech cf. Driver, *Introduction*, p. 427: "The first speech of Jehovah transcends all other descriptions of the wonders of creation or the greatness of the Creator, which are to be found either in the Bible or elsewhere." Similarly Peake, *op. cit.* p. 43: "The whole of Yahweh's speech is a sustained effort of the highest genius, unsurpassed in the world's literature." Lods, *Histoire de la littérature hébraïque et juive*, 1950, pp. 678 f. says: "Les discours de Yahvé, au point de vue littéraire, sont au moins égaux, en magnificence, en virtuosité verbale, en richesse d'images, aux plus belles pages du dialogue; ils ont, du reste, exactement le même style. Il est difficile de croire qu'il se soit trouvé un second poète d'une pareille envergure pour retoucher l'œuvre du premier." Cornill took a less appreciative view of the speech and in the second edition of his *Einleitung in das A.T.*, p. 232, described it as one of "unparalleled brutality, which is usually palliated and styled divine irony, but which, under such circumstances and conditions, should much rather be termed devilish scorn" (translation of R. H. Strahan, *The Book of Job*, 1913, p. 14; this edition of Cornill has not been accessible to the present writer). In the later editions (3rd edn., p. 237; 5th edn., 1905, p. 265=Eng. trans., 1907, p. 427) this language is toned down. H. Ewald (*The Book of Job*, Eng. trans. by J. F. Smith, 1882, p. 294) says: "The most suitable manner for these divine speeches is that of irony, which combines with concealed severity and calm superiority the effective and benevolent incisiveness of a higher insight."

second speech is widely rejected as secondary.[1] This, once more, does not affect our interpretation of the book as a whole.[2] It has the advantage that it brings together Job's words in 40: 4 f. and 42: 2–6, thus yielding a single speech of submission.

The poem on wisdom in chapter 28 is commonly held not to have belonged to this book originally.[3] As it stands it is apparently in the mouth of Job, but it does not fit into the speech he appears to be making, and it is not a reply to the arguments of the previous speaker. But if, as has already been said, part of the preceding chapter is really Zophar's missing speech, then chapter 28 would follow straight after this, without introduction. Yet it is no more appropriate to Zophar than to Job. The chapter is, indeed, complete in itself. It is a magnificent poem,

[1] The sections of the second speech dealing with Behemoth and Leviathan were rejected by Ewald, *op. cit.* pp. 319 ff.; Dillmann, *op. cit.* pp. 339 f.; Cheyne, *Job and Solomon*, 1887, pp. 56, 94, and *E.Bib.* II, 1901, col. 2483; and many others, including recently J. J. Weber, *Le livre de Job, l'Ecclésiastique*, 1947, p. 15; C. Kuhl, *Die Entstehung des A.Ts.*, 1953, p. 265; Eissfeldt, *Einleitung*, 2nd edn., p. 562. Budde (*Das Buch Hiob*, 1913, pp. 254 ff.) retains 40: 15–41: 3 (E.V. 11). Eissfeldt, *Einleitung in das A.T.*, 1934, p. 509, said: "Das eine spätere Hand, dem die beiden Gedichte hierher zu passen schienen, sie eingefügt hat, ist verständlich; dem ursprünglichen Dichter ist es aber schwerlich zuzutrauen, dass er sein Werk mit derartigen Gedichten, die mit seiner eigentlichen Absicht nichts zu tun haben, sondern nur verdunkeln, belastet hätte." This passage does not stand in the second edition. J. Herz, *Wissenschaftliche Zeitschrift der Karl-Marx-Universität Leipzig*, III, 1953–54, pp. 111 f., differentiates between the two speeches on stylistic grounds. Behemoth is usually identified with the hippopotamus and Leviathan with the crocodile, but B. D. Eerdmans, *Studies in Job*, 1939, pp. 27 ff., held that Behemoth is the dolphin, while G. R. Driver, in *Studi orientalistici* (Levi della Vida Festschrift), I, 1956, pp. 234 ff., identifies Behemoth with the crocodile and Leviathan with the whale. G. Haas, *B.A.S.O.R.* No. 132, December 1953, pp. 30 ff., draws attention to evidence that the hippopotamus was found in the Israelite coastal area in the Iron Age.
[2] There are many scholars who retain both the divine speeches. So A. Lefèvre, in *S.D.B.* iv, 1949, col. 1081; H. W. Hertzberg, in *Festschrift Alfred Bertholet*, 1950, pp. 253 ff.; Lods, *op. cit.* pp. 678 f.
[3] This chapter is almost universally rejected as secondary, but Junker (*op. cit.* p. 54) retains it and likens it to the chorus in a Greek tragedy. See also below, p. 168, n.1. It is rejected by Goettsberger, *op. cit.* pp. 226 f., as not integral to the original book; so also by E. J. Kissane, *The Book of Job*, 1939, p. xiii, and E. F. Sutcliffe, *A Catholic Commentary on Holy Scripture*, 1953, p. 418.

worthy of the genius of the author of Job, and possibly composed by him,[1] though scarcely for its present place.[2] Its burden is that in humble reverence towards God and obedience to His will man's truest wisdom is to be found. But this is the position Job reaches after the divine speech, and if he had reached it himself before the Lord spoke, there would have been little reason for the speech of God.[3] We may add that his final soliloquy, in which he cries out once more against God, seems also surprising after this chapter. We may therefore with high probability regard it as a secondary element of the book, even though it is greatly to be prized, and for its preservation we may be very thankful.[4]

While for most of these positions there is broad agreement amongst a number of scholars, with much divergence of detail,

[1] So Dhorme, *op. cit.* p. LXXVI; J. Chaine and A. Robert in Robert-Tricot, *Initiation Biblique*, 3rd edn., 1954, p. 181; Pfeiffer, *op. cit.* p. 671; Lods, *Histoire de la littérature héb. et juive*, p. 680. W. Baumgartner, however, will not allow that it is by the same author, though he recognizes a certain affinity of spirit (*O.T.M.S.*, p. 219). H. Duesberg, *Les scribes inspirés*, II, 1939, p. 156, calls this chapter "petit bloc erratique, situé probablement hors de sa place, mais qui donne le dernier mot du livre."

[2] A. Lefèvre, in Pirot's *S.D.B.* IV, 1949, col. 1079, defends the retention of this chapter, holding that it marks a pause, indicating that the dialogue is at an end. Cf. also C. Westermann, *Der Aufbau des Buches Hiob*, 1956, pp. 104 ff. Similarly E. Brennecke, in Alleman and Flack, *Old Testament Commentary*, 1948, p. 490, retains this chapter, though he rejects the Prologue and Epilogue as older and the Elihu speeches as later. J. E. Steinmueller, *A Companion to Scripture Studies*, II, 2nd edn., 1944, p. 168, holds that chapter 28 is original, and so W. Grossouw and C. Epping, in A. van den Born et al., *Bijbels Woordenboek*, 2nd edn., 1954–57, col. 847, and H. Haag's *Bibel-lexikon*, 1951, col. 825 (cf. C. Epping, in *Dictionnaire encyclopédique de la Bible*, 1960, col. 962). P. Szczygiel (*op. cit.* p. 253) retains the chapter but transfers it to follow 42: 6. S. Davidson (*Introduction to the O.T.* II, 1863, pp. 202 f.) retained 27: 7–28: 28 in their present form as integral to the book, though he rejected the Elihu speeches (pp. 204 ff.).

[3] Cf. Ball, *op. cit.* p. 12.

[4] H. A. Fine, *J.B.L.* LXXIV, 1955, pp. 28 ff., argues that chapters 27 f. form a unit, separable from the rest of the book, preserving the tradition of a patient Job who maintained his uprightness throughout. On this view chapter 27 is not to be redistributed and transferred in part to Zophar. Whether these chapters are by the author of the main part of the book, or were composed earlier or later than the dialogue, are questions left without answer.

it is only fair to say that there are scholars who would challenge them more radically. There are some conservative scholars who still maintain the unity of the whole book.[1] On the other hand there are some who peel off a great deal more than has yet been suggested. Baumgärtel thought that originally there was a single cycle of speeches, followed by a monologue by Job, fragments of which have survived scattered amongst his speeches in the present second and third cycles.[2] Snaith would go farther, and suggests that in the original form of the book the three friends did not figure at all, so that the verses relating to them in the Prologue and Epilogue, and all their speeches and Job's answers, are to be rejected.[3] The book is thus reduced to the Prologue, a single soliloquy by Job (contained in chapters 3 and 29–31), the first divine speech, Job's submission and the Epilogue. This seems to me quite arbitrary, and an unlikely theory of the origin of a masterpiece. All the serious wrestling in argument with the problem of innocent suffering is torn out of the book, and after the Prologue giving the setting for Job's trial we have but his bitter lament that he had been born and agonized cry to God, and then the divine response and his release. But

[1] So F. Prat in F. Vigouroux (ed. by), *Dictionnaire de la Bible*, III, 1903, cols. 1567 f.; L. Bigot, in A. Vacant (ed. by), *Dictionnaire de Théologie Catholique*, VIII, 1947, cols. 1479 ff.; H. Höpfl, *Introductio specialis in V.T.*, 5th edn., revised by A. Miller and A. Metzinger, 1946, pp. 280 f.; E. J. Young, *Introduction to the O.T.*, 1949, p. 313; H. Möller, *Sinn und Aufbau des Buches Hiob*, 1955. Such a view can be found in many older writers, e.g. C. F. Keil, *Einleitung in das A.T.*, 3rd edn., 1873, pp. 389 ff. Cf. also P. Humbert, *V.T. Supplements* III (Rowley Festschrift, 1955), p. 151 n.: "Nous tentons ici une voie nouvelle, essayant de montrer que les tensions, qui semblent manifester la non-unité du livre, révèlent au contraire une sorte de progression existentielle de l'œuvre conçue comme une unité."
[2] Cf. *Der Hiobdialog*, 1933. A. Weiser (*Einleitung in das A.T.*, 4th edn., 1957, p. 235; Eng. trans. by D. M. Barton, 1961, p. 291) rejects the views of Baumgärtel. Cf. also J. Hempel, *Die althebräische Literatur*, 1930, p. 179; Eissfeldt, *Einleitung*, 2nd edn., pp. 565 ff., 570 f., and Baumgartner, in *O.T.M.S.*, p. 219. Cheyne (*E.Bib.* II, col. 2476) omits 20–28.
[3] Cf. *The Book of Job*, 1945, p. 15. This view is closely similar to that of P. Bertie, *Le poème de Job*, 1929. A. Lods (*Histoire de la littérature héb. et juive*, p. 683) rejects it on the grounds (a) that it is *a priori* improbable that the author did not intend to discuss the problem of innocent suffering and (b) that the style of the rejected parts is precisely the same as that of the retained parts.

the nature of the divine speech is scarcely to be understood, save in the light of the things Job has said in his speeches to the friends. It is there that he has impugned the justice of God, and called forth the rebuke of the divine speech, that he has passed judgment on what lies beyond his understanding.

Lindblom, to whose view reference has already been made, also thinks that a simple dialogue originally stood in the book, but that for this a three cycle debate was later substituted.[1] He rejects the Elihu speeches, the wisdom chapter, and the second divine speech, and also, surprisingly, Job's submission in 42: 1–6.[2] He holds that these last mentioned verses were added after the second divine speech. These verses seem to me, as I shall say, as also to many other scholars, to be vital to the understanding of the book, and to yield an appropriate response of Job to the speech of Yahweh. Without them the only response of Job is found in 40: 4 f., and it amounts simply to the statement that he has nothing more to say. He has found no satisfaction of his tortured spirit. Hence I would align myself more closely with the normal critical view of the problems of the book.

We may therefore briefly review the form of the book as it emerges from our examination.[3] There is the Prologue, followed

[1] Cf. *Composition*, p. 91.

[2] *Ibid.* p. 90. C. Siegfried (*J.E.* vii, 1907, p. 199) deleted 42: 1–6 as secondary. Similarly K. Fullerton (*Z.A.W.* xlii [N.F. i, 1924], pp. 124 f.) says these verses are absolutely opposed to the Dialogue, and B. D. Eerdmans, *Studies in Job*, 1939, p. 18, rejects them. Jastrow thinks there were four epilogues (see above p. 161, n. 5), and also rejects the Elihu speeches and both divine speeches, all of which he thinks were appendices (*op. cit.* pp. 64 ff.). Further, he holds 29–31 to be supplementary (p. 70), 28 to be an addition (*ibid.*), and also the third cycle of speeches to be secondary (p. 71). Van Hoonacker (*R.B.* xii, 1903, p. 166) held that there were four editions of the book, the first ending with 31, the second adding the speeches of Elihu, the third adding the divine speeches and the Epilogue instead of the Elihu speeches, and the fourth combining the second and the third. G. Studer (*Das Buch Hiob*, 1881, p. 19) held that the book originally consisted of 3–31 only, and that the Elihu speeches, the divine speeches, the Prologue and Epilogue, and ch. 28 were successive additions.

[3] This examination of the structure of the book is a necessary preliminary to the study of its purpose and message. Cf. Buttenwieser, *op. cit.* p. 4: "A study of the religious significance of the book, if it is to be intelligent and thoroughgoing, must go hand in hand with a careful literary analysis."

by Job's opening soliloquy; then three cycles of speeches in which the friends speak in turn, being each answered by Job; then Job's closing soliloquy;[1] then the speech of God from the whirlwind, followed by Job's submission, the two parts of which, now separated, are brought together; and finally the Epilogue. It is complete in its artistry of form, and Job's submission, which closes the poetic part of the work, is, as we should expect it to be, the climax of the book.

Some writers have supposed that the purpose of the book was to solve the mystery of suffering.[2] If this was indeed its purpose it must be pronounced a conspicuous failure. The mystery of suffering is too great and complex to be solved in so short a study, even if any writer thought he could solve it at all. Some of the scholars who have believed this to be the purpose of our author have clung to the Elihu speeches because it is here alone that anything relevant to this subject can be found. I have already said, however, that Elihu's solution is not relevant to this book. That suffering is educative is doubtless sometimes true. "Whom the Lord loveth he chasteneth."[3] But he would be both bold and shallow who supposed that this was the explanation of all suffering. It was certainly not the explanation of Job's, for the reader is told this quite clearly in the Prologue. The dialogue nowhere penetrates the true reason for Job's suffering, and if the purpose of the debate was to solve this problem, it nowhere comes within sight of the solution. The Babylonian sufferer could not divine the explanation of his miseries, and as little could Job and his friends penetrate the reason for his. If this was what the author was interested in, he

---

[1] On the character of chapter 31, as the final speech of Job before the theophany, with its daring oaths as the evidence of Job's consciousness of innocence, cf. S. H. Blank, *J.J.S.* II, 1950-51, pp. 105 ff.

[2] This is implied in the observations of Cornill, *Introduction*, p. 426: "The poet . . . surely must have had a solution of the problem to offer; else he would have been attempting a task that exceeded his strength, and would not deserve to be described as an artist so much as a torturer of humanity, who delights in plunging the knife ever deeper and deeper into the mortal wound." C. Westermann, *Der Aufbau des Buches Hiob*, 1956, thinks the book is less concerned with the problem of innocent suffering than with man's complaint "Why must I suffer?"

[3] Heb. 12: 6.

was but beating the air, and his masterpiece was no more than a futility.

Others have thought the author was only concerned to overthrow the view that all suffering was self-entailed and that rigid justice was done in human affairs.[1] It has even been suggested that this was the orthodox view throughout the Old Testament until the book of Job came to set things right.[2] This rests on a very superficial reading of the Old Testament. The earliest document of the Pentateuch tells how Cain and Abel offered sacrifices to God, and records that Abel's was well-pleasing to God, while Cain's was not.[3] When we read thereafter that Cain murdered Abel, it is plain that the sacred writer did not wish the reader to infer that Abel got but what he deserved. When Uriah the Hittite was killed by the deliberate design of David, the prophet Nathan came to the king to rebuke him sternly in the name of God.[4] The prophet did not think Uriah deserved what came to him, and the reader of the Bible is not expected to draw that conclusion. This story stands in one of the oldest documents in the Bible, and does not teach the rigid equation of desert and experience. Later the prophet Elijah denounces Ahab for the judicial murder of Naboth, which Jezebel had staged in his name,[5] and again the reader is expected to draw the conclusion that Naboth died innocently. The eighth and seventh century prophets declaimed against the injustice that was rampant in Israel, instead of drying the springs of sympathy by any doctrine that whatever a man got he must have deserved. To suppose that the doctrine enunciated by Job's friends was in any period the accepted orthodox view of Yahwism is to ignore a great deal in the Old Testament.

That it was accepted in some circles is doubtless true. It is to be presumed that these were the circles of the prosperous—who

---

[1] Driver, *L.O.T.*, p. 409, declares this to be the principal aim of the book.
[2] Cf. Meinhold, *Einführung in das A.T.*, 3rd edn., 1932, p. 322; L. W. Batten, *A.Th.R.* xv, 1933, p. 126. Cf. also I. G. Matthews, *The Religious Pilgrimage of Israel*, 1947, pp. 171 f., where we are told that the friends of Job reiterated "the time-honoured assumption of the ancients", while Job "challenged the sacrosanct conclusions of the centuries."
[3] Gen. 4: 4.
[4] 2 Sam. 12: 1 ff.
[5] 1 Kg. 21: 17 ff.

frequently come under the lash of the sacred writers. Some writers have suggested that Jeremiah and Ezekiel were responsible for this doctrine.[1] But again this involves a strange reading of Jeremiah, whose sensitive spirit was more incapable of so perverse a view than the harder spirit of Ezekiel. Jeremiah, whose own mission involved him in acute suffering which caused him to cry out against God with something of the agony of Job,[2] is scarcely likely to have cherished so deluded a view. It was Jeremiah who asked "Wherefore doth the way of the wicked prosper?"[3] and who said of himself "I was like a gentle lamb that is led to the slaughter."[4] He can scarcely be supposed to have enunciated the doctrine expressed by Job's friends.

It is true that in days when men were excusing themselves from any share of responsibility for the misfortunes of their day by quoting the proverb "The fathers have eaten sour grapes and the children's teeth are set on edge", Jeremiah insisted on the measure of their individual responsibility and said "Every one shall die for his own iniquity."[5] But it is a far cry from this to the thought of Job's friends. In the New Testament we read "Whatsoever a man soweth, that shall he also reap";[6] but it would be a travesty of the New Testament to say that its teaching is that a man always gets what he deserves, and no intelligent reader of the New Testament could suppose that Jesus

---

[1] It is frequently maintained that before Jeremiah and Ezekiel the individual was regarded merely as a fragment of the community, and hence this problem could not arise. Cf. e.g. Peake, *Jeremiah*, II, p. 100: "The doctrine (*sc.* of the solidarity of the community) had affirmed the mutual responsibility of the members of the group which formed its social unit. The individual had but little independent significance"; C. H. Patterson, *The Philosophy of the O.T.*, 1953, p. 239, where it is said that before Jeremiah the idea "that Yahweh held individuals responsible for their own deeds" had not arisen.

[2] Cf. Jer. 20: 7 ff., and the passages commonly referred to as the "Confessions of Jeremiah" (on which cf. J. Skinner, *Prophecy and Religion*, 1922, pp. 201 f.; E. A. Leslie, *The intimate papers of Jeremiah*, 1953; J. Leclercq, in *Études sur les prophètes d'Israël* [Lectio Divina 14], 1954, pp. 111 ff.).

[3] Jer. 12: 1.

[4] Jer. 11: 19.

[5] Jer. 31: 30.

[6] Gal. 6: 7.

was crucified because He deserved to be. Nowhere does the Bible teach such a doctrine, for the Bible has no simple solution of the problem of suffering.[1] There are some whose sufferings are self-entailed; but there are some whose sufferings are not. Jeremiah insisted that some suffering is not innocent; the book of Job that some is. It is the way of the doctrinaire theologian to wish to reduce the complexity of experience to the simplicity of a single formula. Such were Job's friends; such was not Jeremiah, who could recognize now innocent suffering, and now suffering that was self-entailed.

It lies beyond our purpose to discuss the date of the book of Job, which has been most variously estimated. It must suffice here to say that it is by most held to be post-exilic,[2] and by many

[1] Cf. Driver, *L.O.T.*, pp. 409 f.

[2] Older writers thought of the patriarchical age or the time of Moses, but these are now universally dismissed. The age of Solomon is still accepted by E. J. Young, *Introduction to the O.T.*, 1949, p. 309. F. Prat, in Vigouroux, *Dictionnaire de la Bible*, III, 1903, col. 1567, dates the book between the time of Solomon and that of Hezekiah, and E. W. Hengstenberg (*Das Buch Hiob*, 1870, p. 62), before the time of Amos; A. Merx (*Das Gedicht von Hiob*, 1870, p. XLII; cf. D. Schenkel [ed. by], *Bibel-Lexikon*, III, 1871, p. 100) favoured a date *circa* 700 B.C.; O. Zöckler (in Lange's Commentary, O.T. VII, Eng. trans. by Ll. J. Evans, p. 252) suggested that Hezekiah was the author; de Wette (*op. cit.* II, p. 570), Ewald (*op. cit.* p. 82), J. G. Stickel (*Das Buch Hiob*, 1842, p. 261), F. Bleek (*Introduction to the O.T.*, Eng. trans. by G. H. Venables, II, 1894, p. 286), S. Davidson (*Introduction to the O. T.* II, 1863, pp. 195 ff.), early in the seventh century; E. König (*op. cit.* pp. 495 f.), H. Gunkel (*R.G.G.* III, 1912, pp. 47 f.), J. Goettsberger (*Einleitung in das A.T.*, 1928, p. 229), and J. E. Steinmueller (*A Companion to Scripture Studies*, II, 2nd edn., 1944, p. 165), the age of Jeremiah; Pfeiffer (*op. cit.* pp. 675 ff.) dates the Prologue and Epilogue not earlier than the sixth century, but the poetic parts of the book between 700 and 200 B.C., but probably in the time of Jeremiah; E. C. S. Gibson (*The Book of Job*, 1899, p. XXII), and N. H. Tur-Sinai (*The Book of Job*, 1957, pp. XXXVI f.), date the work in the period of the late monarchy or exile; Sellin (*Introduction*, 1923, p. 222; but cf. *Einleitung*, 7th edn., 1935, p. 145, where the range is given as 600–300 B.C.) between 600 and 450 B.C.; Dillmann (*op. cit.* pp. XXIX ff.), A. B. Davidson (*The Book of Job*, 1884, p. LXVII), and Cheyne (*Job and Solomon*, 1887, p. 74; but cf. *E.Bib.* II, 1903, cols. 2385 ff., where the date is brought down to the Persian period) in the time of the exile; Driver (*L.O.T.*, p. 431) during or shortly after the Babylonian captivity; J. P. Naish (*Expositor*, 9th ser., III, 1925, pp. 34 ff., 94 ff.) in the early post-exilic period, holding the author to be a disciple of Deutero-Isaiah; L. Gautier (*Introduction à l'A.T.* II, 1914, p. 120, and Ball (*op. cit.* pp. 31 ff.), in the Persian period;

to date from about 400 B.C.[1] It is probable that the perverse doctrine enunciated by Job's friends rested on the application of the individualism of one side of the teaching of Jeremiah and Ezekiel to the Deuteronomic doctrine of national merit and fortune. Deuteronomy had sought to inculcate national loyalty to Yahweh by promising abounding prosperity in days of loyalty and dire misfortune in days of disloyalty. With the greater emphasis on the individual which Jeremiah and Ezekiel brought—which can be recognized without forgetting that this was not the whole of their teaching—this may well have led in some circles to the wooden view held by Job's friends. They cherished the thought that a man's experience reflected his character, and we see as the argument proceeds how this steadily dries the springs of sympathy. When Eliphaz speaks at

A. Lefèvre (in Pirot's *S.D.B.* IV, 1949, col. 1075) in the first century of the Persian period; E. F. Sutcliffe (*Catholic Commentary on Holy Scripture*, p. 421) *circa* 500 B.C.; Duhm (*op. cit.* p. IX), Dhorme (*op. cit.* p. CXXXV), J. J. Weber (*op. cit.* p. 17), and Chaine and Robert (*op. cit.* p. 185) between 500 and 450 B.C.; R. H. Strahan (*The Book of Job*, 1913, pp. 18 f.) and C. F. Kent (*The Growth and Contents of the O.T.*, 1926, p. 291) about 450 B.C.; G. F. Moore (*The Literature of the O.T.*, 1913, p. 248), Gray (in Driver-Gray, *op. cit.* pp. LXV ff.), L. H. K. Bleeker (*Job*, 1926, p. 8), and Haag's *Bibel-Lexikon*, 1951, col. 825, in the fifth century; L. Bigot (in Vacant, *Dictionnaire de Théologie Catholique*, VIII, 1947, col. 1483) and H. Lusseau (in Robert-Feuillet, *Introduction à la Bible*, I, 1957, p. 652) in the latter part of the fifth century; A. Weiser (*Einleitung in das A.T.*, 4th edn., 1957, p. 236 [Eng. trans., p. 292], and *Das Buch Hiob*, 2nd edn., 1956, p. 13) between the fifth and the third century; J. E. McFadyen (*Introduction to the O.T.*, new edn., 1932, p. 319) between 450 and 350 B.C.; H. Creelman (*Introduction to the O.T.*, 1927, p. 239) *circa* 350 B.C.; T. K. Cheyne (*E.Bib.* II, 1901, col. 2489), C. Steuernagel (*Einleitung in das A.T.*, 1912, p. 710), O. Eissfeldt (*Einleitung in das A.T.*, 2nd edn., p. 578) L. Finkelstein (in *The Pharisees*, I, 1938, p. 231), in the fourth century; G. Hölscher (*op. cit.* p. 7) and A. Lods (*Histoire de la littérature héb. et juive*, p. 689), between 400 and 200 B.C.; Volz (*S.A.T.* III, II, 1911, p. 26) *circa* 300 B.C.; O. Holtzmann (in Stade, *G.V.I.* II, 1888, pp. 351 f.) in the third century; C. Siegfried (*J.E.* VII, 1907, p. 197), a date in the second century B.C., or even later (suggesting that Job 15: 20 ff. may possibly be an allusion to Alexander Jannaeus).

[1] So Budde (*Das Buch Hiob*, p. LIII), Peake (*op. cit.* p. 40), J. A. Bewer (*The Literature of the O.T.*, 1922, p. 317), Buttenwieser (*op. cit.* pp. 70 ff.), M. Jastrow (*op. cit.* p. 36), H. Junker (*Das Buch Hiob*, 1951, p. 7), A. Lods (*La Bible du Centenaire*, III, 1947, p. XIII, and *Histoire de la littérature héb. et juive*, p. 688).

first he has a measure of sympathy for Job.[1] Ranston describes him as one who had "something of the prophet about him, intense in religious conviction, a mystic recipient of heavenly visions".[2] He supposes that Job has somehow brought his troubles on himself, but he is sorry for him and tries to give him counsel that will bring him to fortune again. For Job all the pity is vitiated by the tacit condemnation which he feels to be undeserved. As the debate continues the friends rebuke Job in severer terms, and we increasingly feel how the thought that the unfortunate must be the wicked hardens the spirit of the man who entertains it. Bildad has been described as a traditionalist.[3] He knows all the clichés, and is as lacking in sympathy as he is in any originality of mind.[4] Zophar is said by Marshall to be the philosopher of the three,[5] and with this view Peake substantially agrees.[6] But he has the harshest spirit and the sharpest tongue of the three, and displays a dogmatism that perhaps proclaims his youth. One purpose of the book of Job is certainly to protest against the idea that misfortune is the evidence of sin, and to affirm that there is a problem of innocent suffering. But this is not where the author's originality is to be found. In this he is but reaffirming what is to be found in the Law and the Prophets and the Psalms.

The author of our book was concerned less with theology than with religion. So far as any theological or philosophical explanation of the mystery of suffering is concerned, he has none to offer.[7] The reader is told the explanation in Job's case,

---

[1] Cf. Davidson, *The Book of Job*, 1884, p. 41: "The speech of Eliphaz is one of the masterpieces of the book", marked by "great delicacy and consideration" (p. 31), "very wise and considerate as well as profoundly reverential" (p. 35). H. L. Ginsberg, *Leshonenu*, XXI, 1956–57, pp. 262 f., holds that the vision attributed to Eliphaz in 4: 12–20 should really be ascribed to Job, since in 33: 6 Elihu refers to 4: 19 in addressing Job.

[2] Cf. *The O.T. Wisdom Books*, 1930, p. 139.

[3] *Ibid.* p. 140.

[4] W. A. Irwin, *Z.A.W.* LI (N.F. x, 1933), pp. 205 ff., holds that Bildad does not espouse this shallow philosophy that misfortune is the proof of ungodliness.

[5] *Op. cit.* p. 67.

[6] *Op. cit.* p. 125.

[7] Cf. S. L. Terrien, *Job: Poet of existence*, 1957, p. 21: "The poet of Job did not attempt to solve the problem of evil, nor did he propose a vindication

but that was necessary in order to establish that Job was really an innocent sufferer. Neither Job nor his friends can deduce the reason, and when God speaks from the whirlwind to Job He does not disclose it. Had He done so the book would immediately have lost its meaning for those who suffer. For men must suffer in the dark, and a Job who was not left in the dark would have no message for others. It is true that God spoke to Job from heaven, whereas no such voice comes to us. But the voice brought no new revelation of truth, but merely reminded Job of what he could have perceived for himself. It merely reminded him of the unfathomable wonders of creation, and made him realize that there are mysteries beyond human penetration. To say this is not to suggest that theology and philosophy are futile disciplines. There are secrets of Nature that man cannot penetrate; but this does not mean that scientists ought not to investigate Nature. There are mysteries of experience that neither theology nor philosophy can fully elucidate; but this does not mean that the human spirit should not wrestle with the problems. But what the book of Job says is that there is something more fundamental than the intellectual solution of life's mysteries. The author has a message for the spirit rather than for the intellect. He is no academic writer[1] addressing himself to the select few profound thinkers. He knows that intellectual giants are few, but that all men have a spirit, and that all may suffer. When one is suffering it may be good to understand the cause; but it is better to be sustained to endure.

We may pause to note that the cause of Job's suffering was more than the Satan's insinuation against him. He was suffering to vindicate more than himself. He was vindicating

of God's justice. For him, any attempt of man to justify God would have been an act of arrogance. But he knew and promoted in the immediacy of God's confrontation *a mode of life*."

[1] Several writers have suggested that the author was personally involved in the problem, and that the book was born of his own experience. Cf. Buttenwieser, *op. cit.* p. 3: O. J. Baab, *Interpretation*, v, 1951, p. 336. Some have thought that it was the national experience of his people which inspired the work. Cf. Zöckler, *op. cit.* pp. 238 f.; Strahan, *op. cit.* pp. 15 ff.; Davidson-Lanchester, *op. cit.* p. xxix; H. Ranston, *op. cit.* p. 167. Of this, however, there seems little evidence.

God's trust in him. He was not so much abandoned by God as supremely honoured by God. The author does not, of course, suggest that this is always the reason for undeserved suffering. He is not so foolish as to imply that a single cause covers all cases, and so far from wishing the reader to deduce that this is always the case, he wishes to make it plain that the actual cause in any given case cannot be deduced by man. The cause or reason for the suffering is hidden in the heart of God. In the case of Job it was not unworthy of God—or of Job. It was the expression of God's confidence in him, and by his very suffering he was serving God. Yet Job could never know this. To the reader, then, the author is saying that when suffering comes undeserved, while he can never guess its explanation he may face it with trust that, if he could know the cause, he too might find that he was serving God and was honoured in his very agony.

I have said that there is an inner conflict in the mind of Job. While he repudiates the view of the friends that his suffering proves his sin, he yet has the ever lurking feeling that this ought to be so. He cannot wholly extricate himself from their ideas, and therefore he cannot extricate himself from the consequence of those ideas. Where suffering is believed to be the effect of sin, it is the evidence of a man's isolation from God, since sin is isolation from God. At the beginning of the Bible we find that when Adam sinned he was thrust out from the Garden of Eden.[1] But before he was thrust out and the angel set to guard the gate, Adam had hidden himself from God.[2] He was conscious that his sin had come between him and God and had erected a barrier. Here in this early story, which we so easily characterize as primitive and childish, there is a profound perception of the nature of sin. It separates man from God. If then suffering is thought to be the evidence of sin, it is by the same token the evidence that the sufferer is cut off from God. And this is what Job feels, despite all his protests. He still tries to cling to God and appeals to the God he has known; but he feels he cannot get at God, and all his appeals are but carried away on the wind.

[1] Gen. 3: 23 f.
[2] Gen. 3: 8.

By insisting that there is such a thing as innocent suffering the author of Job is bringing a message of the first importance to the sufferer. The hardest part of his suffering need not be the feeling that he is deserted by God, or the fear that all men will regard him as cast out from God's presence. If his suffering may be innocent it may not spell isolation from God, and when he most needs the sustaining presence of God he may still have it. Here is a religious message of great significance, and it is by his religious message, which matches the magnificence of his literary gift, that the author of our book created his masterpiece.

It is this which is brought out in the closing verses of the poetical portion of the book, in which Job bows himself in submission before God. "I had heard of thee with the hearing of the ear" he cries, "but now mine eye seeth thee; wherefore I repent and abhor myself in dust and ashes."[1] He does not repent of any sin which had brought his trial upon him. On that issue he is vindicated as against the friends. He repents of the charges he has brought against God, and of the doubts he has entertained. More significant is his recognition that with all the loss and the pain he had suffered, he had gained something even from his agony. In his prosperity he thought he had known God. Now he realizes that compared with his former knowledge his present knowledge is as the joy of seeing compared with a mere rumour. All his past experience of God was as nothing compared with the experience he had now found. He therefore no longer cries out to God to be delivered from his suffering. He rests in God even in his pain.[2]

This is not to explain the meaning of suffering. It is to declare to the reader that even such bitter agony as Job endured may

---

[1] Job 42: 5 f. B. Kennicott, *Remarks on Select Passages in the O.T.*, 1787, p. 60, strangely renders this verse: "Wherefore am I become thus loathsome and am scorched up, upon dust and ashes?" He also transferred 40: 1–14 to follow 42: 6 (pp. 161 ff.).

[2] Cf. G. A. Barton, *J.B.L.* xxx, 1911, p. 67: "He has pictured Job as finding the solution of his problem, not in a reasoned explanation or a theology, but in a religious experience . . . His hero, Job, finds his satisfaction in a first-hand experience of God"; J. Pedersen, *Israel I-II*, 1926, p. 372: "Only now, when he sees God himself, does he get a real impression of his might, and in this instinctive transport he abandons all claims."

be turned to spiritual profit if he finds God in it. This is to be distinguished from the thought of the Elihu speeches. Elihu supposed that the suffering itself was disciplinary. Here is no thought that the suffering is itself enriching. Rather is it that the fellowship of God is enriching, and that that fellowship may be found in adversity no less than in prosperity.

Many writers have suggested that the failure of the book to solve the problem of suffering is to be set in contrast to the Christian message.[1] It is supposed that for a fuller answer to the problem it was necessary to wait until a better doctrine of the Afterlife had been attained than Job knew. There are many passages in which the book of Job shows no advance on the thought of the Afterlife which the author's contemporaries cherished. Sheol is thought of as a place where good and bad alike go, where man is shut off from God and in ignorance of the fortunes of his family, and where he is conscious only of his misery.[2] It is true that Job longs for death, and speaks of Sheol as something to be desired, in comparison with his present misery.[3] But that is only his eloquent way of indicating the depth of his misery, and not his way of suggesting that after death any existence that was desirable in itself was to be hoped for. In one familiar passage he has been supposed to attain a faith in a more worthwhile Afterlife. As translated in the Authorized Version the passage runs: "I know that my redeemer liveth, and that he shall stand at the latter day upon the earth: And though after my skin worms destroy this body, yet in my flesh shall I see God: Whom I shall see for myself, and mine eyes shall behold, and not another."[4] In fact this is one of

---

[1] Cf. G. F. Oehler, *Theology of the O.T.*, Eng. trans. by G. E. Day, Zondervan Press reprint edition, p. 565: "The hope which here (*sc.* in Job 19: 25–27) flashes for a moment like lightning through the darkness of temptation, is as yet no mature faith in a happy and eternal life after death, and consequently does not furnish a solution to the enigmas with which the book is occupied." Cf. also J. E. McFadyen, *op. cit.* p. 306; H. Wheeler Robinson, *The Cross in the O.T.*, 1955, p. 48; T. H. Robinson, *Job and His Friends*, 1954, p. 124.

[2] Cf. Job 3: 17, 10: 21 f., 14: 21 f.

[3] Cf. Job 3: 13.

[4] Job 19: 25–27.

the most cryptic passages in the book, and both text and interpretation are far from sure.[1] Some scholars emend the text to

[1] For the history of the interpretation of these verses cf. J. Speer, *Z.A.W.*
xxv, 1905, pp. 47 ff. A brief selection of recent translations will sufficiently
indicate the difficulties of the text and the caution that is necessary in
building upon it. Kraeling (*op. cit.* pp. 87 f.) renders: "But I myself know
that my redeemer liveth, And as the last one on the dust (i.e. the ground)
he will arise. And after (the loss of) my skin that they have thus torn, and
bereft of my flesh I shall see God, Whom I shall see on my side, and mine
eyes shall behold, And not as an adversary. (My reins are consumed
within me)"; W. Vischer (*Hiob*, 6th edn., 1947, pp. 19 f.: "Und ich, ich
weiss, mein Löser lebt. Zu allerletzt wird er sich über dem Staub erheben.
Und nachdem meine Haut geschunden ist, werde ich, ohne mein Fleisch, Gott
schauen, ich—ihn—mir—schauen, meine Augen sehen, nicht ein Fremder!
Hiob verliert das Bewusstsein"; G. Hölscher (*op. cit.* p. 46): "Ich weiss, es
lebt mir ein Verteid'ger, und nachmals tritt er auf Erden auf; Dann, ob
meine Haut auch so zerschlagen, werd' ich doch ohne mein Fleisch Gott
schau'n; Ihn, den ich selber schauen werde, den meine Augen, kein
Fremder sehn; Meine Nieren schmachten in meinem Innern"; Oesterley
and Robinson (*Hebrew Religion*, 2nd edn., 1937, pp. 355 ff.): "But I know
that my vindicator so liveth, And as the last one upon the earth will he
stand up. And after my skin hath been thus destroyed, Away from my body
shall I see God, Whom I shall see on my side, and not another. And mine
eyes shall behold, and not as a stranger. My reins are consumed within me";
Kissane, *The Book of Job*, pp. 114 ff.: "And I know that my Defender
liveth, And the Eternal will stand forth on the dust; And after my skin is
stripped off, did I but see Him, Without my flesh were I to behold God,
He whom I should see would be on my side, And whom my eyes should
behold would not be estranged. My reins are consumed within me."
Larcher (*Le livre de Job*, 1950, pp. 95 f.: cf. pp. 27 ff.): "Je sais, moi, que
mon défenseur est vivant, que Lui, le dernier, se dressera sur terre. Une
fois ma peau détruite, je l'apercevrai, hors de ma chair, je verrai Dieu.
Celui que je verrai sera pour moi, à mes yeux, il n'apparaîtra plus indif-
férent. Et mes reins en moi se consument"; E. F. Sutcliffe (*Providence and
Suffering in the O. and N.T.*, 1955, p. 115; cf. also *Biblica*, xxxi, 1950, p. 377):
"I know that my redeemer liveth, And that my warrant will stand upon the
earth. Should my skin be torn from my flesh, Even after this I shall see God,
Whom I shall see and mine eyes behold" (19: 25 f. only): T. J. Meek (*V.T.*
vi, 1956, p. 101): "But I know myself that my vindicator lives, And coming
later, he will stand up on the dust; And even after this skin of mine has
been striken (sic ? struck) off, In my own flesh I shall see God, Whom I
myself shall see, And my own eyes shall behold, and not some stranger; My
emotions are spent within me"; A. Weiser, *Das Buch Hiob*, 2nd edn., 1956,
p. 141: "Doch ich, ich weiss: Es lebt mein Löser; zuletzt erscheint er auf
dem Staub: und ohne mein Haut, die so zerfetzt, ohne mein Fleisch werd'
ich Gott schauen. Ihn werd' ich schauen mir (zum Heil); mein eigen Aug',

take out all suggestion of an Afterlife,[1] while others emend it to make the suggestion much clearer.[2] Neither course seems to me to be justified. Professor Snaith says these verses "can be made to refer to life after death only by a most liberal latitude in translation, a strong attachment to the Latin version, and reminiscences of Handel's Messiah. The Hebrew text is difficult, but it is unlikely that the vindicator is God, and Job almost certainly means that he will be vindicated before he is dead."[3] Peake observes: "The hope of immortality is not expressed here, but only of a momentary vision of God, assuring him of vindication."[4]

While it must be agreed that the words are ambiguous, I think it is possible that the author is here reaching out after something more satisfying than the dreary doctrine of Sheol

kein Anderer, wird ihn sehen. Mein Herz schmachtet (danach) in meiner Brust"; F. Stier, *Das Buch Ijjob*, 1954, p. 97: "Ich aber weiss: Mein Löser lebt, steht auf als Letzter überm Staub. Und dann mein Helfer sich aufrichtet, meinen Zeugen schau ich: Gott. Ich gewahr, ich selber schaue, meine Augen sehn ihn, nimmer fremd—die Nieren mir vergehn im Leib"; N. H. Tur-Sinai (*The Book of Job*, 1957, pp. 304 ff.): "Yet I, I want to know my redeemer while alive—but he who cometh later will stand at my dust. After my body let them break it up! Out of my flesh I want to see (my) God, Whom I shall see for myself, mine eyes shall behold and not another. For this my reins go out within me." With these renderings it is instructive to compare that of B. Kennicott, *Remarks on Select Passages in the O.T.*, 1787: "For I know that my Vindicator liveth; And He, at the last, shall arise over this dust. And after that mine adversaries have mangled me thus, even in my flesh shall I see God; Whom I shall see on my side; and mine eyes shall behold, but not estranged from me: all this I have made up in mine own bosom." On these verses, cf. also A. B. Davidson, *The Book of Job*, 1884, pp. 291 ff.; J. Royer, *Die Eschatologie des Buches Job*, 1892, pp. 86 ff.; Driver-Gray, *Job*, pp. 171 ff., 127 ff.; S. Mowinckel in *Vom A.T.* (Marti Festschrift), 1925, pp. 207 ff.; H. Rongy, *Revue Ecclésiastique de Liége*, xxv, 1933, pp. 25 ff.; G. Hölscher, *Z.A.W.* LIII (N.F. XII, 1935), pp. 277 ff. (where the passage is studied in connection with Jubilees 23: 30 f.); J. Lindblom, *Studia Theologica* II (Riga), 1940, pp. 65 ff.; W. B. Stevenson, *The Poem of Job*, 1947, pp. 93 ff.; L. Waterman, *J.B.L.* LXIX, 1950, pp. 379 ff.; W. B. Stevenson, *Critical Notes on the Hebrew Text of the Poem of Job*, 1951, pp. 87 ff. M. Vernes (*R.H.R.* I, 1880, p. 232) dismissed 19: 25–29 as an interpolation.

[1] So Ball, *op. cit.* pp. 276 ff.
[2] So Dhorme, *op. cit.* pp. 256 ff. Cf. Larcher, *op. cit.* p. 96.
[3] Cf. *The Distinctive Ideas of the O.T.*, 1944, p. 90 n.
[4] *Op. cit.* p. 192.

reflected elsewhere in his book. But he has not securely grasped it.[1] Here is no clear faith in a worthwhile Afterlife, but at the best the belief that God will one day vindicate him and that he will be conscious of that vindication. Yet, having said this, I would return to say that no faith in an Afterlife can touch the problem with which the book of Job is concerned. The problem of suffering is as real a problem today as it was in the days of our author, and Christian theology is as impotent as Jewish to solve it.[2] It is sometimes thought that the faith that beyond this life there is another where the injustices and inequalities of this life may be rectified offers an answer to the problem. In truth it offers none. When the wicked is seen to prosper, it may be possible to find some comfort in the thought of what lies before him in the next world—though this is not a very exalted comfort. When the pious is seen to suffer, it may be possible to find some comfort in the thought of the bliss that awaits him hereafter. But this can offer no possible explanation of his present sufferings. The book of Job is far more profound in its message that here and now the pious sufferer has no reason to envy the prosperous wicked. The wicked may have his prosperity, but the pious may have God; and in God he has far more than the other. The inequalities of life belong to man's outer lot; but this is immaterial to his spiritual life.

This is already apparent in the story of Joseph, told in the most ancient document of the Pentateuch. "The Lord was with Joseph",[3] and therefore he could face alternate adversity and prosperity in serenity of spirit. And when we come to the New Testament we find that it cannot advance upon this. St. Paul was a Pharisee before he became a Christian, and as a Pharisee he already believed in the resurrection.[4] He continued to hold that belief after he became a Christian. But it brought him no

[1] Cf. the present writer's *Faith of Israel*, 1956, p. 165; cf. also Ranston *op. cit.* p. 160, and Davidson, *op. cit.* p. 293: "This principle, grasped with convulsive earnestness in the prospect of death, became the Hebrew doctrine of Immortality."

[2] Cf. Rabbi Yannai (third cent. A.D.): "It is not in our power to explain the well-being of the wicked or the sorrow of the righteous" (Pirqe Aboth IV, 15, translation of H. Danby, *The Mishnah*, 1933, p. 454).

[3] Gen. 39: 2, 21.

[4] Ac. 22: 3, 24: 21.

relevant message in suffering. He suffered from some acute malady that brought him agonizing pain—so agonizing that at times he cried out to be delivered from it. He does not appear to have found any consolation in thinking of the next world. He says: "Concerning this thing I cried unto the Lord thrice, that it might depart from me. And he hath said unto me, My grace is sufficient for thee: for my power is made perfect in weakness. Most gladly therefore" cries Paul, "will I rather glory in my weaknesses, that the power of Christ may rest upon me."[1] Here we see that Paul ceases to cry out for deliverance from his suffering, but finds enrichment in his suffering, so that he comes to rejoice in the suffering itself because it has brought him a new experience of the grace of God. This is fundamentally the same as we have found in the book of Job. It falls far short of an intellectual solution of the problem of suffering. But it achieves the spiritual miracle of the wresting of profit from the suffering through the enrichment of the fellowship of God. It was in this that the author of the book of Job was interested and to this that he leads the reader.

[1] 2 Cor. 12: 8 ff.

6

*The Prophet Jeremiah
and the Book of Deuteronomy*

6

THE PROPHET JEREMIAH
AND THE BOOK OF DEUTERONOMY[1]

ONE of the most debated questions in the field of Old Testament scholarship during the last forty years has been the date of Deuteronomy, and a whole crop of new theories has sprung up. Of these some have carried the composition of the book back to the time of the foundation of the monarchy,[2] or to the early monarchical period,[3] while others have held it to date from a time after the fall of Jerusalem in 586 B.C.[4] To examine in detail all the arguments that have

[1] First published in *Studies in Old Testament Prophecy* (T. H. Robinson Festschrift), 1950, pp. 157–74.

[2] Cf. E. Robertson, "Temple and Torah", in *B.J.R.L.* xxvi, 1941–42, pp. 183–205. Cf. also R. Brinker, *The Influence of Sanctuaries in Early Israel*, 1946, pp. 205 ff.

[3] Cf. T. Oestreicher, *Das deuteronomische Grundgesetz*, 1923, and "Dtn. 12¹³ f. im Licht von Dtn. 23¹⁶ f.", in *Z.A.W.* xliii, 1925, pp. 246–49 (cf. H. Gressmann, *ibid.* xlii, 1924, pp. 313–37); A. C. Welch, *The Code of Deuteronomy*, 1924, and *Deuteronomy: The Framework to the Code*, 1932; W. Staerk, *Das Problem des Deuteronomiums*, 1924, and "Noch einmal das Problem des Deuteronomiums", in *Sellin-Festschrift*, 1927, pp. 139–50. On this view cf. S. A. Cook, "Some Tendencies in O.T. Criticism", in *J.T.S.* xxvi, 1925, pp. 156–73, esp. pp. 162 ff.; and J. A. Bewer, "The Case for the Early Date of Deuteronomy", in *J.B.L.* xlvii, 1928, pp. 305–21. On this and the following view, cf. J. Battersby Harford, "Since Wellhausen: 4. Deuteronomy", in *Expositor*, Ninth Series, iv, 1925, pp. 323–49; R. Kittel, *G.V.I.* ii, 7th edn., 1925, pp. 439–45; W. C. Graham, "The Modern Controversy about Deuteronomy", in *J.R.* vii, 1927, pp. 396–418; and W. Baumgartner, "Der Kampf um das Deuteronomium", in *Th.R.*, N.F. i, 1929, pp. 7–25.

[4] Cf. R. H. Kennett, "The Origin of the Book of Deuteronomy", in *Deuteronomy and the Decalogue*, 1920, pp. 1–34 (reprinted in *The Church of Israel*, 1933, pp. 73–98), "The Origin of the Aaronite Priesthood", in *J.T.S.* vi, 1905, pp. 161–86, and "The Date of Deuteronomy", *ibid.* vii, 1906, pp. 481–500 (cf. F. C. Burkitt, in *J.T.S.* xxii, 1921, pp. 61–65); G. Hölscher, "Komposition und Ursprung des Deuteronomiums", in *Z.A.W.* xl, 1922, pp. 161–255; G. R. Berry, "The Code found in the Temple", in *J.B.L.* xxxix, 1920, pp. 44–51, and "The Date of Deuteronomy", *ibid.* lix, 1940, pp. 133–39; F. Horst, "Die Anfänge des Propheten Jeremia", in *Z.A.W.*

been advanced on either side would be far beyond the scope of this essay, though it will become necessary briefly to examine some of those advanced by the school that brings the book down to a late date. For to the present writer it seems necessary to fix the date of the Book of Deuteronomy before the prophet Jeremiah's relation to it can be profitably discussed.[1]

Most writers recognize many links of thought and language between Jeremiah's prophecies and Deuteronomy,[2] but whereas

XLI, 1923, pp. 94–153, and "Die Kultusreform des Königs Josia (II Rg. 22–3)", in *Z.D.M.G.* LXXVII, 1923, pp. 220–38 (cf. O. Eissfeldt's review in *Th.L.Z.* XLIX, 1924, cols. 224 f.); S. A. Cook, in *C.A.H.* III, 1925, pp. 406 f., 481–86; A. Loisy, *Religion d'Israël*, 3rd edn., 1933, pp. 200–5; Johs. Pedersen, *Israel: Its Life and Culture, III-IV*, 1940, pp. 569–92. Earlier advocates of a post-exilic date for Deuteronomy included C. W. P. Gramberg, *Kritische Geschichte der Religionsideen des A.Ts*, I, 1829, pp. xxvi, 153-55, 308–12; W. Vatke, *Die Religion des A. Tes nach den kanonischen Büchern*, 1835, pp. 504–9 n.; G. d'Eichtal, *Mélanges de critique biblique*, 1886, pp. 81 ff. (cf. M. Vernes, *M. Gustave d'Eichtal et ses travaux sur l'A.T.*, 1887, pp. 33–58); M. Vernes, *Précis d'histoire juive*, 1889, pp. 468–71, 795 n.; L. Horst, "Études sur le Deutéronome", in *R.H.R.* XVI, 1887, pp. 28–65; XVII, 1888, pp. 1–22; XVIII, 1888, pp. 320–34; XXIII, 1891, pp. 184–200; XXVII, 1893, pp. 119–76. Cf., too, J. Cullen, *The Book of the Covenant in Moab*, 1903, where it is argued that the original Deuteronomy was published in 621 B.C., but that it consisted of a few chapters only, the Code of Laws having been added subsequently. On the whole late date view, cf. H. Gressmann, "Josia und das Deuteronomium", in *Z.A.W.* XLII, 1924, pp. 313–37; W. Nowack, "Deuteronomium und Regum", in *Vom Alten Testament* (Marti Festschrift), 1925, pp. 221–31; K. Budde, "Das Deuteronomium und die Reform König Josias", *ibid.* XLIV, 1926, pp. 177–224; L. B. Paton, "The Case for the Post-exilic Origin of Deuteronomy", in *J.B.L.* XLVII, 1928, pp. 322–58. H. Hahn (*Old Testament in Modern Research*, 1954, p. 35) observes that Hölscher's theory crowded the entire legal development from Deuteronomy to the Priestly Code into a brief period of about fifty years, and weakened the connection between the literary and the religious history of Israel.

[1] W. A. Irwin, "An Objective Criterion for the dating of Deuteronomy", in *A.J.S.L.* LVI, 1939, pp. 337–49, claims that Dt. 28: 45–57 is an appendix to the chapter to which it belongs, by the same hand as the preceding verses, but reflecting the actual conditions of the siege of Jerusalem, and that therefore Deuteronomy was written before the Fall of Jerusalem by one who was still living at that time.

[2] Cf. W. Gesenius, *De pentateuchi Samaritani origine, indole et auctoritate*, 1815, p. 7, where he speaks of *Deuteronomii liber, cuius integra capita . . . prophetarum ingenium spirant;* cf. p. 7 n.: *In sermone et usu loquendi Deuteronomium ad Jeremiae sermonem inter omnes, qui hodie extant, V.T. libros proxime forsan accedit.*

those who believe that Deuteronomy, in whole or in part, formed the law-book of Josiah think its style and thought influenced Jeremiah, those who bring Deuteronomy down to a later date must perforce reverse the process. In an essay in the Wheeler Robinson *Festschrift* J. N. Schofield has attempted to establish that Jeremiah influenced the composition of Deuteronomy, and that therefore Deuteronomy cannot have been written until the sixth century B.C.[1] To make literary influence a criterion in this way is unduly hazardous, for its direction is always difficult to establish on merely literary grounds, and within that field judgments are likely to be subjective and speculative. It would seem wiser to fix the dates of the two works first, and then to seek to understand such influence as is apparent.

For the purpose of this essay the date of Jeremiah may be assumed without argument to be, broadly speaking, the last forty years before the Fall of Jerusalem.[2] This is not to claim that the Book of Jeremiah was compiled in that period. Its compilation can hardly have been made until the post-exilic period.[3] But there is no reason to doubt that many of the oracles contained in the book were uttered by Jeremiah during the last forty years of the kingdom of Judah, or that many of the narratives about him are authentic.[4] What does need to be

[1] "The Significance of the Prophets for dating Deuteronomy", in *Studies in History and Religion* (ed. E. A. Payne), 1942, pp. 44–60.

[2] J. P. Hyatt argued that Jeremiah began his ministry in 614–612 B.C., and therefore gave no approval to Josiah's reforms (cf. "The Peril from the North in Jeremiah", *J.B.L.* LIX, 1940, pp. 499–513; "Jeremiah and Deuteronomy", in *J.N.E.S.* I, 1942, pp. 156–73), but the evidence for this is unconvincing. Cf. T. C. Gordon (*E.T.* XLIV, 1932–33, pp. 562–65), who places the start of Jeremiah's ministry in 616 B.C. More recently Hyatt assigns the beginning of Jeremiah's ministry to the reign of Jehoiakim; see *I.B.* v, 1956, pp. 779, 797. So also H. G. May, *J.N.E.S.* IV, 1945, pp. 226 ff.

[3] Cf. Oesterley and Robinson, *Introduction to the Books of the O.T.*, 1934, pp. 290–307; Eissfeldt, *Einleitung in das A.T.*, 2nd edn., 1956, pp. 420–43; R. H. Pfeiffer, *Introduction to the O.T.*, 1941, pp. 500–11; A. Weiser, *Introduction to the Old Testament*, Eng. trans. by D. M. Barton, 1961, pp. 209–21.

[4] Hölscher (*Z.A.W.* XL, 1922, pp. 233–39) denied the authenticity of all the passages in Jeremiah that appeared to show dependence on Deuteronomy, and so Horst in the articles cited. While others have recognized later hands in Jeremiah, these radical excisions would seem to involve

fixed, however, is the date of the composition or of the issue of the Book of Deuteronomy. These two things do not hang necessarily together, since those who hold the Book of Deuteronomy to have been written long before could agree that it provided the law-book of Josiah.[1] Its influence on Jeremiah in that age could then be understood, and equally its lack of influence on earlier writers during the period when it had been lost.[2]

Sellin at one time held that Deuteronomy formed the basis of Hezekiah's reform.[3] This could not easily be accepted, for we have no hint in the Bible that Hezekiah based his reform on a written law, and it is quite gratuitous to assume one. Moreover, if Deuteronomy had been known a century before the time of Jeremiah, it would be surprising for its influence first to be felt in the time of that prophet. A work that had been lost for a much longer time might have ceased to exercise any influence, and have been completely forgotten, but a work that had been the basis of a reform less than a century earlier, and a reform associated with memorable events in the national history, might have been expected to leave some traces. Sellin later abandoned this view—though for one that is to the present writer scarcely less unsatisfactory. For he substituted the view that Deuteronomy was composed shortly before its

arguing in a circle. If everything that savours of Deuteronomy is removed, it is easy to conclude that what is left shows no trace of that Code. But this is rather a tribute to the ruthless surgery that has been applied than to the facts.

[1] Cf. Welch, "When was the worship of Israel centralized at the Temple?", in *Z.A.W.* XLIII, 1926, pp. 250–55.

[2] There are, however, serious difficulties in the way of supposing that Deuteronomy antedated Josiah's reform by centuries. Cf. Schofield, *op. cit.* pp. 49 f.

[3] *Introduction to the O.T.*, 1923 (Eng. trans., based on 3rd German edn., by W. Montgomery), pp. 73–81. For this view, cf. also J. G. Vaihinger, *P.R.E.*, 1st edn., XI, 1859, p. 328; Westphal, *The Law and the Prophets*, Eng. trans. by C. du Pontet, 1910, 304; Steuernagel, *Lehrbuch der Einleitung in das A.T.*, 1912, pp. 191–93; E. König, *Das Deuteronomium* (K.A.T.), 1917, pp. 48–51; G. A. Smith, *The Book of Deuteronomy* (Camb. B.), 1918, p. CII; H. Junker, *Biblica* XXXIV, 1953, pp. 493 f. A. Lods (*Histoire de la littérature hébraïque et juive*, 1950, p. 369) criticizes this view, which is rejected also by J. Hempel (*Die Schichten des Deuteronomiums*, 1914, p. 258).

discovery, and that its composition was a part of the plan of the reform of that time.[1]

The first question that falls to be considered is the reliability of the account of Josiah's reform in 2 Kg. 22 f. Not unnaturally those who have brought Deuteronomy down to a later date have sought to discredit that account. It is said that the law of Deuteronomy was too unpractical to have been adopted in this way[2] or that the story is just a fictitious narrative composed by a writer who himself knew Deuteronomy and wished the reader to think it formed Josiah's law-book.[3]

The dominant school of Biblical criticism has long held that the original edition of Joshua, and the books of Judges, Samuel and Kings were prepared by a school of writers under the influence of Deuteronomy, and M. Noth has argued that Deuteronomy and these historical books originally formed a single corpus.[4] The Swedish scholar, I. Engnell,[5] who is thought by a fellow Swede to have given the *coup de grâce* to the Wellhausen school of literary criticism,[6] similarly recognizes the corpus Deuteronomy-2 Kings to form "the Deuteronomic history". The last event mentioned in this work is the release of Jehoiachin in 561 B.C., and there is no reason to bring the conclusion of the work below this date. Indeed there are some who think the end of the work is an appendix attached to a book which was completed some decades before this.[7] It would be very difficult indeed to bring the completion of 2 Kings down much below 561 B.C., since we should in that case have expected to read something of the new stirrings of the national

---

[1] *Einleitung in das A.T.*, 6th edn., 1933, pp. 47 ff., 7th edn., 1935, pp. 46 ff. Sellin assigned the date of composition to 630–622 B.C. In the 8th edn., 1950, ed. by L. Rost, this narrow limit is abandoned (pp. 61 f.).

[2] Cf. Hölscher, *Z.A.W.* XL, 1922, pp. 227–30; M. Vernes, *Précis*, p. 469.

[3] Cf. L. Horst, *R.H.R.* XVII, 1888, pp. 11–22; Vernes, *Précis*, p. 795 n.; E. Havet, *Le Christianisme et ses Origines*, III, 1878, pp. 32–37.

[4] Cf. M. Noth, *Überlieferungsgeschichtliche Studien*, I, 1943, pp. 3–110.

[5] *Gamla Testamentet*, I, 1945, pp. 231 ff.

[6] G. A. Danell, *Studies in the Name Israel in the O.T.*, 1946, p. 13. Danell says that Engnell has "tried definitely to settle accounts with the methods of literary criticism", where it would appear that he believes the effort to have been successful.

[7] Cf. S. R. Driver, *L.O.T.*, 9th edn., 1913, p. 198; R. H. Pfeiffer, *Introduction to the O.T.*, 1941, p. 410.

life at the close of the exilic period, while if the writer were put so late as the time of Haggai and Zechariah, his interest in the Temple might have been expected to lead him to give some account of its rebuilding. If he is placed at 561 B.C.[1] he would be but sixty years after the time of Josiah's reform, when it would not have been easy to put out a fictitious account. If he is placed some decades earlier, memories would have needed to be even less long to challenge him successfully. And in either case, the composition of Deuteronomy, which provided the point of view of the writers of all these historical books, would have to be carried back some time before the completion of 2 Kings.

That Josiah must have carried through some reform would seem to admit of no doubt.[2] Such a reform was the inevitable religious side of a revolt against Assyria. Ahaz submitted himself to Assyria, and symbolized his submission by installing a new altar in the Temple after the pattern of one he had seen in Damascus.[3] That this was an Assyrian pattern, and that it was used for the worship of Assyrian deities as the overlords of Israel's God, is generally accepted. The old altar was not abolished, but removed to a subordinate position.[4] Hence when Hezekiah rebelled against Assyria, he would necessarily reject the Assyrian gods, and would restore the altar of his own God to the central position in the worship. *Some* reform of religion was therefore necessary, and it would provide the occasion for something more than the return to the *status quo ante* in all particulars. There followed the reign of Manasseh who was in all things subservient to Assyria, and who restored the worship of the Assyrian deities. The political and the religious policies

[1] L. Gautier, *Introduction à l'A.T.*, 2nd edn., 1914, reprinted 1939, pp. 305 f., places it not before 561 B.C. So J. E. Steinmueller, *Companion to Scripture Studies*, II, 1942, p. 98.

[2] Even Hölscher allows this, and indeed grants a substantial measure of historical value to the account in 2 Kings 22 f. Cf. "Das Buch der Könige, seine Quellen und seine Redaktion" in *Eucharistērion* (Gunkel Festschrift), 1923, I, pp. 158–213, esp. pp. 206–13. Similarly Kennett grants that it is based upon sound tradition. Cf. *Deuteronomy and the Decalogue*, p. 4 = *The Church of Israel*, p. 75.

[3] 2 Kg. 16: 10–13.

[4] 2 Kg. 16: 14.

went hand in hand.[1] But early in the reign of Josiah it was clear that the Assyrian power was not what it had been, and the death of Ashurbanipal was the signal for the disintegration of the Assyrian empire. Nabopolassar raised the standard of revolt in Babylon, and there is every reason to suppose that his agents sought to rouse the west, just as Merodach-baladan had sought to do a century earlier when he had tried to anticipate what Nabopolassar did successfully.[2] And even without any incitement, the west was likely to seize the occasion and resume its independence. For no successor of Ashurbanipal on the Assyrian throne was able to spare any strength to reassert his authority in the west.

Nor are we left merely to surmise. For there is no reason whatever to doubt that Josiah was on the opposite side to Pharaoh Necho,[3] and it is now known beyond a peradventure that the latter was on the side of Assyria.[4] It is true that the Biblical reference was to a time after the end of the Assyrian kingdom, but it cannot be supposed that Josiah was first showing where he stood at this time. Presumably he had assumed his independence and withheld his support from Assyria, and Necho had not interfered with him hitherto because he could hardly take action against the subjects of his ally unless asked to do so by their overlord, and Assyria was more anxious to secure assistance at the vital part of the kingdom than to have Josiah dealt with, so long as he did not actively hinder help reaching Assyria. But when the Assyrian kingdom had come to an end, Necho was left to continue the struggle alone, and proposed to annex the western part of his late ally's domains. Moreover, he needed more than ever to consolidate his position here now that the battle was approaching his own borders. Hence probability strengthens all such evidence as we have to

---

[1] O. Eissfeldt (*Einleitung*, 2nd edn., p. 278) similarly emphasizes the political background as evidence of reform.

[2] 2 Kg. 20: 12–19=Isa. 39: 1–8.

[3] 2 Kg. 23: 29.

[4] Cf. C. J. Gadd, *The Fall of Nineveh*, 1923, pp. 36 f. (l. 10.), 40 f. (l. 66). Accordingly 2 Kings 23: 29 can no longer be translated "*against* the king of Assyria"—unless with Reuss we suppose that Assyria may stand here for the Chaldaeans (*Histoire des Israélites depuis la Conquète de la Palestine jusqu'à l'exil*, 1877, p. 571).

confirm the view that Josiah made a bid for independence when the Assyrian empire was tottering, and the inevitable corollary of this is that he carried through *some* religious reform, rejecting the Assyrian deities and reviving the national worship of Yahweh as the focus of the political revival.

If, then, it be allowed that Josiah did effect some reform, it is hard to see why the account of 2 Kg. 22 f. should be supposed to be fictitious. If the writer's purpose was to make the reader suppose that Josiah's reform rested on Deuteronomy, though he himself knew full well that it did not, he was not very skilful, and large numbers of careful students missed this until de Wette drew attention to it,[1] though some earlier writers had connected Josiah's law-book with Deuteronomy.[2] But surely if the compiler were merely writing fiction, he might have made his purpose clearer. Moreover, 2 Kg. 23: 9 is strange reading on this view. It says that "nevertheless the priests of the high places came not up to the altar of Yahweh in Jerusalem." Unless there were some expectation that they would come to the altar, this is a pointless observation, and it is usual to read it in connection with Dt. 18: 6–8.[3] But surely no writer of a fictitious account designed to lead the reader to the false supposition that Deuteronomy was the basis of Josiah's reform would have added this. If his honesty had surprisingly revolted against misleading the reader here, and only here, he might just have said nothing about the point. The fact that he does manifest honesty here ought rather to encourage us to believe that in the rest of the account he is a reliable authority—especially as he is probably recount-

---

[1] *Beiträge zur Einleitung in das A.T.*, I, 1806, pp. 285–99. While de Wette is usually given the credit for having been the first among moderns to identify Josiah's law-book with Deuteronomy, it should be noted that he was anticipated by Hobbes (*Leviathan*, 1651, p. 201). It may be observed that the earliest of the nineteenth-century writers to date Deuteronomy in the post-Josianic age held that Josiah's law-book was a part of Exodus (Gramberg, *op. cit.*, I, pp. 306 f.), while Berry ʳthinks it was the Holiness Code (*J.B.L.* xxxix, 1920, pp. 44–51, lix, 1940, p. 138).

[2] So some of the Fathers, e.g., Athanásius (cf. *P.G.* xxvii, 1887, col. 44), Chrysostom (cf. *P.G.* lvii, 1862, col. 181, and lxi, 1862, col. 58), Jerome (cf. *P.L.* xxiii, 1883, col. 227, and xxv, 1884, col. 17) and Procopius (cf. *P.G.* lxxxvii, part i, 1865, cols. 915 f.).

[3] The embarrassment of this verse is reflected in the efforts of Hölscher to get rid of it. Cf. H. Schmidt, *Th.L.Z.* xlviii, 1923, cols. 290 f.

ing events that happened within his own memory. And this means that in pointing us to the provision of Deuteronomy which was not given effect, he is giving us as valuable information as in the description of the positive character of the reform to enable us to identify the law-book with Deuteronomy.[1]

It may here be observed that 2 Kg. 23: 9 is strong evidence against the view that Deuteronomy was prepared by the Jerusalem priests immediately prior to the reform, and foisted on the king by Hilkiah and his fellow-priests, who knew full well that its ink was hardly dry.[2] For the Jerusalem priesthood would hardly have incorporated in the law-book a provision whose enforcement they immediately and successfully resisted. Their attitude is revealed in 2 Kg. 23: 9, and hence it cannot be revealed also in Dt. 18: 6–8. To the present writer it seems probable that Deuteronomy was written early in the reign of Manasseh, and emanated from a small group of reformers who wished to embody the lessons of Hezekiah's reform in a plan for the next occasion that should offer.[3] They could not know that half a century would pass before such an occasion would arise, and that probably all of them would have died and their work

---

[1] Cf. H. Cazelles, *Le Deutéronome* (Bible de Jérusalem), 2nd edn., p. 15: "Il y a trop de rapports entre la réforme de Josias et les exigences deutéronomiques, pour ne pas admettre un lien entre le *Deutéronome* et cette réforme." Cf. also G. E. Wright, *I.B.* II, 1953, p. 322; A. Lods, *Histoire de la littérature hébraïque et juive*, 1950, pp. 348 f.

[2] So Budde (*Z.A.W.* XLIV, 1926, p. 222) and C. F. Kent (*Growth and Contents of the O.T.*, 1926, p. 189) and many older writers. Cf. N. W. Gottwald, *A Light to the Nations*, 1959, p. 338: "The view that Deuteronomy was not a creation *de novo* in 621 is psychologically and historically more tenable than a spur of the moment composition."

[3] Cf. H. Ewald, *G.V.I.* I, 3rd edn., 1864, pp. 186 f., III, 2nd edn., 1853, pp. 682 ff.; S. Davidson, *Introduction to the Old Testament*, I, 1863, p. 383; H. E. Ryle, in *D. B.* I, 1898, p. 603a; S. R. Driver, *op. cit.* p. 87; J. A. Bewer, *The Literature of the O.T.*, 1922, p. 122 f.; Oesterley and Robinson, *op. cit.* p. 59 f.; Meinhold, *Einführung in das A.T.*, 3rd edn., 1932, p. 211; A. Lods, *Les prophètes d'Israël et les débuts du Judaïsme*, 1935, p. 168 (= *The Prophets of Israel*, Eng. trans. by S. H. Hooke, 1938, p. 148), and *Histoire de la littérature hébraïque et juive*, 1950, p. 371; C. Kuhl, *The Old Testament: its origins and composition*, Eng. trans. by C. T. M. Herriott, 1961, p. 84; M. Noth, *History of Israel*, Eng. trans. revised by P. R. Ackroyd, 1960, p. 275; and especially A. R. Siebens, *L'origine du Code Deutéronomique*, 1929, p. 96, where it is assigned to a time during the first twenty years of the seventh century B.C.

lie not so much forgotten as unknown in the dust until 621 B.C.[1] When it was found none knew where it had come from, or what was its age, but the priesthood of Jerusalem was prepared to resist the one point where they felt their interests to be adversely affected.

It is often noted that the Chronicler makes Josiah's reform begin in his twelfth year[2] and this is sometimes thought to be an unhistorical ante-dating of it. But there is no reason to doubt that the reform began before the law-book was found. According to the account in 2 Kg. 22 the law-book was found when the Temple was being repaired.[3] But the repair of the Temple could well have been associated with its cleansing of Assyrian and other worship, which had thus begun already. The finding of the law-book gave direction to a reform which had its origin in the political situation with which it was associated. Without the law-book there was bound to be reform, as there was in the time of Hezekiah, and it might well have already taken a centralizing turn, following the precedent of the reform of Hezekiah. The opportune finding of the law-book brought new authority for what might else have been less systematically done on precedent. Hence the present writer finds no reason to deny substantial historicity to the Chronicler here, since he supplements rather than contradicts the compiler of Kings. When the assumption of independence was made and the consequent reform began we have no external means of knowing. That it was before 621 is probable, and not inconsistent with 2 Kings 22, but that it was so early as the twelfth year of Josiah is less probable. For while it may well have been that the closing years of Ashurbanipal revealed the weakness of his empire, it is not very probable that the west revolted before Nabopolassar led Babylon in independence.

In the Chronicler's account Josiah is credited with carrying his reform as far north as Naphtali.[4] The compiler of Kings says nothing of this, but does credit him with carrying it beyond the

---

[1] It should be remembered that it was dangerous to work for reform openly in the age of Manasseh (cf. 2 Kings 21: 16), and any plan would need to be kept secret.

[2] 2 Chr. 34: 3.

[3] 2 Kg. 22: 3–5.

[4] 2 Chr. 34: 6.

borders of Judah to Bethel.[1] Here again, there is no reason to doubt that Josiah went beyond the borders of Judah, at least so far as Bethel is concerned. For he could not have contemplated northern Israel remaining an Assyrian province while Judah became independent. The condition precedent to a successful revolt was the collapse of Assyrian power throughout the whole of Palestine and Syria. And since there was no longer any royal house in the northern kingdom to claim men's loyalty and to offer them leadership, nothing would be more natural than that Josiah should aspire to restore a united, independent kingdom.

Indeed, it is probable that this was already in the minds of the compilers of Deuteronomy. The northern connections of that code are often noted,[2] and are sometimes felt to be a difficulty on the Wellhausen view, since a code prepared in Jerusalem, left in the Temple and found there, might not have been expected to show such dependence on the E document, which is associated with the north. But if Deuteronomy was prepared after the collapse of the northern kingdom, it must have been plain to its compilers that any opportunity for the recovery of independence to Judah must carry with it the withdrawal of Assyrian power from northern Israel. That the people of northern Israel and of Judah regarded themselves as fundamentally one is indicated by the fact that while each had its own corpus of traditions, each was a corpus of traditions of all the tribes. Moreover, both groups worshipped Yahweh as their own national God. Hence it would be natural enough to think of renewed independence in terms of united independence. For no other could offer such hopes of success. This was merely plain commonsense. It was the Philistine menace which had

---

[1] 2 Kg. 23: 15 ff. Loisy (*op. cit.* p. 204) dismisses this as "de pure fantaisie."
[2] Cf. C. F. Burney, *The Book of Judges*, 1920, p. xlvi; A. Bentzen, *Die josianische Reform*, 1926, p. 86; F. Horst, *Das Privilegrecht Jahves*, 1930, p. 123; J. Hempel, *Die althebräische Literatur*, 1930–34, pp. 126, 139; Oesterley and Robinson, *op. cit.* pp. 57 ff.; L. Gautier, *Introduction à l'Ancien Testament*, I, p. 139; I. Engnell, *S.B.U.* II, 1952, col. 338; A. Alt, "Die Heimat des Deuteronomiums", *Kleine Schriften*, II, pp. 250–75; G. E. Wright, *I.B.* II, 1953, pp. 319, 326; H. Cazelles, in *Introduction à la Bible*, ed. by A. Robert and A. Feuillet, I, 1953, p. 371; N. W. Gottwald, *A Light to the Nations*, 1959, pp. 338, 340; F. Dumermuth, *Z.A.W.* LXX, 1958, p. 95. Cf. also below, p. 199, n. 1.

brought north and south together at the time of the foundation of the monarchy, and now again both stood in a like situation, since both were controlled by Assyria, though the north was reduced to the status of a province while the south retained its own king.[1] The combining of the two corpora of traditions after the end of the northern kingdom would be both a simple recognition that henceforth the fortunes of the sister kingdoms were bound more closely together than for a long time, and also a psychological preparation for united action when occasion offered.[2] And the compilers of Deuteronomy could hardly be blind to these things, so that whether J and E had been already combined in their day or not, it was the way of wisdom to link northern sentiment and sympathy as well as southern with the reform they contemplated.

It may indeed be that they contemplated Shechem as the central sanctuary. There is, of course, nothing in the Book of Deuteronomy to indicate that its central and sole legitimate sanctuary was to be Jerusalem. In the nature of the case it could not be named, since the book was written in the form of a Mosaic address.[3] Yet there is evidence of interest in the Shechem

---

[1] Deuteronomy's insistence that no foreigner may be made king (17: 15) is greatly stressed by those who date Deuteronomy late (cf. Kennett, *Deut. and the Decalogue*, p. 6 f. =*Church of Israel*, p. 77; Hölscher, *Z.A.W.* XL, 1922, p. 200; Burkitt, *J.T.S.* XXII, 1921, p. 62, and *J.B.L.* XXXIX, 1921, p. 167; Schofield, *op. cit.* p. 56 f.). It is surprisingly suggested that this may be a Palestinian protest against Deutero-Isaiah's hailing of Cyrus as the Lord's Anointed. But surely Deutero-Isaiah does not propose that Cyrus should be elected king of Israel! A work prepared early in the seventh century B.C. with strong northern connections might be much more likely to contain this provision. For in the latter part of the eighth century B.C. northern Israel had united with Damascus in a plan to dethrone the Davidic dynasty and to set up the son of Tabeel as king in Jerusalem (Isa. 7: 5 f.). The fact that this person's father had an Aramaic name would suggest that he was a foreigner. On other grounds, too, this passage can best be regarded as pre-exilic. Cf. Nyström, *Beduinentum und Jahwismus*, 1946, p. 164.

[2] Cf. A. Alt, "Die Heimat des Deuteronomiums", *Kleine Schriften* II, 1953, pp. 250–75.

[3] G. T. Manley (*The New Bible Dictionary*, ed. by J. D. Douglas, 1962, p. 608) asks "If the author's aim is to abolish the high places, why does he never mention them? If he wanted to centralise worship in Jerusalem, why not make it clear? Jerusalem is neither mentioned nor hinted at." The answer is simple. It is just that the author did not forget that his work was

district,[1] which had played a part in the ancient life of the nation, and with which patriarchal traditions were connected, and it may have seemed to the compilers that it would provide

composed as an address of Moses, before the Israelites had begun to worship at the high places or had occupied Jerusalem—which they did not occupy until at least two centuries after the time of Moses. The demand for a single sanctuary implied the condemnation of the high places to the author's readers, without anachronistically expressing it. As to the non-mention of Jerusalem, I am not persuaded that Jerusalem was the place originally intended in Deuteronomy. But if it were, by its very form Deuteronomy could not have named it without implying that for at least two centuries after the Conquest Israel should have had no sanctuary at all.

[1] Both Kennett (*J.T.S.* vii, 1906, pp. 493–99, and *Deut. and the Decalogue*, pp. 24 f. = *Church of Israel*, pp. 91 f.) and Welch (*Code of Deut.*, pp. 178–85, and *Deuteronomy: The Framework to the Code*, p. 54) draw attention to this. Both adduce Dt. 27: 1–8, which is not normally regarded as a part of the original Deuteronomy. But Welch thinks it reads as though it were written to form the conclusion of the Code. There is evidence of an interest in Shechem elsewhere in works edited by the Deuteronomic school, notably in Joshua and Judges, and Albright (*F.S.A.C.*, 1940, p. 241) holds that the nucleus of Deuteronomy was material from Shechem. Cf. also B. Luther, in E. Meyer, *Die Israeliten und ihre Nachbarstämme*, 1906, pp. 542–61; G. A. Danell, *op. cit.* p. 56; I. Engnell, *Symbolae Biblicae Upsalienses*, vii, 1946, pp. 21 f.; R. Brinker, *The Influence of Sanctuaries in Early Israel*, 1946, pp. 211 f.; E. Nielsen, *Shechem*, 1955, pp. 45, 85. N. Walker (*V.T.* iii, 1953, pp. 413 f.) thinks Deuteronomy was of Shechemite origin and was salvaged from Samaria after its fall and taken to Jerusalem at that time. This seems very improbable, since if a book purporting to be Mosaic were known at the time of Hezekiah's reform we should expect it to be used in connection with that reform, whereas no law book is referred to. More tenable is the view of J. Bright (*History of Israel*, 1960, pp. 299 f.), that a homiletical collection of ancient laws deriving ultimately from the tradition of the amphictyony was brought to Jerusalem after the fall of Samaria, and there reformulated in the seventh century. Oesterley and Robinson, following A. C. Welch (*The Code of Deuteronomy*, 1924, pp. 38 f., 191), think that Bethel was the sanctuary in the mind of the compiler (*loc. cit.*). J. N. Schofield (*Essays and Studies presented to S. A. Cook*, 1950, p. 27) thinks the first editor of the Code of Deuteronomy was attempting to rally "all Israel" to Bethel. It is to be noted that if Deuteronomy was compiled in the north in the period following the fall of Samaria, the legend of the mixed origin of the half-heathen Samaritans is seen to be without foundation. See my "The Samaritan Schism in Legend and History", in *Israel's Prophetic Heritage* (Muilenburg Festschrift), 1962, pp. 208–22. The northern links of Deuteronomy seem to be against the view of J. Hempel (*Die Schichten des Deuteronomiums*, 1914, p. 259) that the work might have been compiled in the last years of Hezekiah.

a better focus for the life of the nation than Jerusalem, and moreover it would be easier to choose a sanctuary with such ancient associations than to attempt to attach northern sentiment to Jerusalem, or southern to Bethel, despite its ancient associations, since Bethel had been the royal shrine of the northern tribes. Whether this was so or not, the northern associations of Deuteronomy would be both natural and wise in the age to which it is ascribed, and for the purpose for which it is believed to have been written.[1] But if the bid for independence had already been made by Josiah before the book was found, and if the cleansing and repair of the Jerusalem Temple had already begun, it was not surprising that Jerusalem stepped at once into the position of the unnamed location of the one legitimate sanctuary.[2] Nor would this result be other than helped by the fact that the law-book was found in the Jerusalem Temple itself.[3]

We may now turn to some passages in the Book of Jeremiah which confirm the view that Josiah carried through a reform which consisted of more than the abolition of Assyrian gods, and

[1] It is not, of course, to be supposed that the compilers of Deuteronomy wrote it all out of their heads. Its dependence on J and E, and especially on E, has long been recognized by critical scholars, and it may well have used an ancient tradition of a farewell address by Moses. Many recent writers have underlined the long growth which lay behind the work, and have justified its claim to be regarded as a Mosaic book on the ground that it ultimately derives from him. Cf. C. Epping, *Dictionnaire encyclopédique de la Bible*, 1960, col. 445; H. Cazelles, *Le Deutéronome* (Bible de Jérusalem), 2nd edn., 1958, p. 14; K. F. Krämer, *Numeri und Deuteronomium* (Herders Bibel-kommentar), 1955, p. 228. The full Mosaic authorship is maintained by J. Reider (*Deuteronomy*, 1937, p. XXVII), E. J. Young (*Introduction to the Old Testament*, 1949, p. 152), G. T. Manley (*The New Bible Dictionary*, ed. by J. D. Douglas, 1962, p. 308).

[2] It is to be remembered that at the time when Deuteronomy was compiled, on the view here taken, Jerusalem had a reactionary king who must have filled prophetic circles and all who were loyal to the purer Yahwism with despair. On the other hand, when the law was discovered, Judah had a pious king, who had already begun the reform of religion. In these circumstances it is not surprising that whatever sanctuary was in the mind of the compilers of Deuteronomy, Jerusalem should replace it.

[3] A. Bentzen (*Die josianische Reform*, 1926) argued that Deuteronomy originated with the country Levites; cf. also G. von Rad, *Studies in Deuteronomy*, Eng. trans. by D. Stalker, 1953, p. 66.

that the Book of Deuteronomy was known to the prophet. In the first place we may note that Jer. 44 provides evidence that at some time within living memory there had been a cessation of the worship of the queen of heaven. This is commonly held to be a reference to the old fertility cult that had its roots far back, before the Israelite entry into Canaan. Clearly some reform had temporarily stopped this worship. There is little reason to suppose that any other king than Josiah would have done this within living memory, and since it is in full accord with the reform that is ascribed to him, there seems no reason to doubt it.

To this it may be replied that those who deny the historicity of Josiah's reform claim support from Ezekiel, whose work shows unmistakably that all of the evils that Josiah is alleged to have uprooted still flourished at the beginning of the sixth century B.C.[1] It is unnecessary here to examine the problem of the date of Ezekiel's ministry, which has called forth such a variety of views in recent years.[2] For the present writer has no desire to evade or belittle the evidence of Ezekiel.[3] Indeed it may be supplemented from the Book of Jeremiah. For Jer. 7: 8 ff., 22: 20 ff. give evidence that practices contrary to the teaching of Deuteronomy were again current in Judah and Jerusalem in the reign of Jehoiakim.[4] But this is in no way surprising. For if Josiah's reform was the religious side of a bid for freedom which ended in the death of the king and the establishment of Egyptian rule, until the latter gave place to Babylonian, it could hardly hope to maintain itself. It would be discredited by failure, precisely as the women say to Jeremiah in 44: 18. Whether Egypt or Babylon imposed a religious policy on Judah as Assyria had done or not would matter little. All heart would have gone out of the reform movement, and there would be a steady drift back to the old ways which none would stay. When

[1] Cf. W. Nowack, "Deuteronomium und Regum", in *Vom A.T.* (Marti Festschrift), 1925, pp. 221–31.

[2] I have examined this problem in *B.J.R.L.* xxxvi, 1953–54, pp. 146–90.

[3] Hölscher dealt as drastically with the text of Ezekiel as he did with that of Jeremiah, but J. N. Schofield treats it with more respect and adduces its evidence against the reform, as some earlier writers had done.

[4] Jer. 7: 1–15 is generally held to be a parallel account of what is recorded in Jer. 26, and it is there dated in the beginning of the reign of Jehoiakim.

Manasseh succeeded Hezekiah and determined on a policy of complete loyalty to Assyria he would necessarily bring back actively the things that Hezekiah had suppressed. Jehoiakim may not have been reactionary in that sense, but he would hardly give the reform movement his active support, and a religious policy of *laissez faire* would inevitably bring back the deeply rooted popular ways. All that we read in Jeremiah and Ezekiel, therefore, is consistent with the account of a short-lived reform that collapsed with the death of Josiah. It may also have been hastened at its end by the failure to provide, as Deuteronomy had contemplated, for the country Levites. At the same time there would still be reforming circles who would lament the failure and who would await a new opportunity of reform. By these the history of the nation was collected, and set forth as a lesson for the instruction of men's hearts.

In Jer. 34 we read that during the siege of Jerusalem by Nebuchadrezzar the people in the city released their slaves, and then later reduced them to slavery again. For this they are rebuked most sternly by Jeremiah. It is stated explicitly that the release applied to both menservants and maidservants, and Jeremiah appeals to a covenant which God had made, which demanded the release of slaves after six years, which they had now violated. The Book of the Covenant had demanded the release of male slaves after six years, but had stated explicitly that this did not apply to female slaves. In his reference to the law Jeremiah only mentions males, but his comment implies that in his thought females were also included, and it is clear that the action of release was based on a law which included females. The Deuteronomic Code modified the older law by extending it to female slaves, and it is almost certainly to be found behind this incident. As has been said above, the provisions of Deuteronomy had long since sunk into neglect, and probably it was many years since any slaves had been set free. And now they were set free according to the provisions of Deuteronomy, and not according to the provisions of the older Code. It is impossible to suppose that Deuteronomy is here influenced by Jeremiah, and is later than Jeremiah's work, for Jeremiah appeals to an already known law, and the only relevant law on this subject of which we have knowledge is that of Deuteronomy. Schofield here stresses the agreement of the contents of Jer. 34: 14a with the provisions of the older law of Exod. 21: 2, and then expunges the rest of the verse as a post-Deuteronomic addition.[1] But this will hardly do. For, as has been said, in the rest of the narrative the content of the Deuteronomic law, as distinct from that of Exod. 21, is presupposed. And if it be supposed that the post-Deuteronomic editor re-edited the whole narrative to produce this impression, it still remains to ask why he should have refrained from altering v. 14a. If he was altering a narrative *in order to produce this impression*, he might have been expected to alter the verse which from his standpoint was vital. That this verse was not altered is the strongest evidence for the originality of the narrative, with its implicit reference to Deuteronomy, rather than the explicit reference that would otherwise have been expected.[2]

Since, then, there is reason to credit the account of Josiah's reform and to connect it with Deuteronomy, and also to suppose that Jeremiah was acquainted with some of the provisions of Deuteronomy, when we find literary affinities that might be explained in either direction, we are justified in finding the dependence to be by Jeremiah. This is not to make such dependence the basis of a theory as to the date of Deuteronomy, but rather its corollary.

It is sometimes claimed that Jeremiah was so original a person that it is antecedently improbable that he was a copier from Deuteronomy.[3] This purely *a priori* argument is of little

[1] *Op. cit.* p. 56. Cf. the more elaborate surgery of F. Horst, *Z.A.W.* xli, 1923, pp. 123 ff. Kennett (*Church of Israel*, p. 44, n.) dismisses chapter 34 as no evidence that there was any law relating to the freeing of slaves and ascribed to the period of the Exodus in the age of Jeremiah.

[2] Kennett points out that Jeremiah does not use the Deuteronomic word שְׁמִטָּה, but the word דְּרוֹר, which stands in the Holiness Code (cf. *J.T.S.* vii, 1906, p. 485). It becomes rather a Morton's fork, when every verbal agreement between Jeremiah and Deuteronomy is held to be evidence that Deuteronomy was influenced by Jeremiah and therefore of later origin, while every verbal disagreement is evidence that Jeremiah was ignorant of Deuteronomy, and therefore the latter was later. On such principles, if Jeremiah were contemporary with the finding of Deuteronomy, he would be allowed no possible means of indicating it.

[3] Cf. Kennett, *J.T.S.* vi, 1905, p. 182 f., vii, 1906, pp. 481–86; Berry, *J.B.L.* xxxix, 1920, p. 46, lix, 1940, pp. 133–39; Schofield, *op. cit.* p. 50 f.

weight. The most original English writer might be forgiven for referring to *Habeas Corpus*, and Jeremiah's originality is not called in question if he shows some knowledge of the provisions of the newly found law-book. Nor is his originality called in question by his use of some of the phrases of Deuteronomy, any more than a modern author's would be if he used such current terms as "existential" and "atom bomb". The vocabulary and style of Jeremiah were, like every author's, in large measure those of his age, and a book which was believed to be a divinely given law might be expected to exercise a profound influence on the style of writers in the age when it became known. But why Jeremiah's style should be taken up by legislators more than a generation after his death, and should then influence a whole range of historical writings, is more obscure. For, after all, Jeremiah's real originality was in his thought rather than in his style, and he delivered a message which cannot be found in its entirety in Deuteronomy.

It may here be observed that whereas Kennett claimed that Deuteronomy was influenced by Jeremiah, and is followed by Schofield, the German exponent of the same view of the date of Deuteronomy is in complete disagreement with them. For Hölscher is so sure that the Book of Jeremiah is influenced by Deuteronomy that he resorts to the surgery already noted to eliminate from it as secondary every passage which is reminiscent of Deuteronomy. Hence the exponents of the late date theory are in fundamental opposition on this important aspect of their case.

That Jer. 3: 1 is to be connected with Dt. 24: 1–4 is almost certain. It is improbable that Jer. 3: 1 is a post-Deuteronomic insertion in the text of Jeremiah,[1] and equally improbable that Jeremiah was enunciating a principle which was afterwards accepted by the compilers of Deuteronomy and embodied in their Code. For apart from the fact that Jeremiah's originality was not as a lawgiver, he here appeals to a principle which was already known and accepted. It is therefore simplest to suppose that the text of Deuteronomy, where the principle is laid down, was already known.

Schofield further cites the case of Jer. 11: 5, where there is

[1] Cf. Hyatt, *J.N.E.S.* I, 1942, p. 164.

verbal agreement with Dt. 8: 18, 6: 3, but notes that whereas in Deuteronomy the oath referred to is declared to have been made to the fathers in the pre-Exodic age, in Jer. 11: 5 it is said to have been made in the Exodic age.[1] This is held to indicate Jeremiah's ignorance of Deuteronomy. It can hardly be supposed that if Deuteronomy became known in 621 B.C., Jeremiah must thereafter have known it by heart, or have carried a copy on his person to consult in the midst of the utterance of his oracles. Allusions to it in spoken oracles would certainly be from memory, and it is improbable that Jeremiah ever possessed a copy. Hence it would be easily understandable if he made an allusion to some words that stood in an address purporting to have been made by Moses in the Exodic age, and placed them in the setting of that age. The conditions of modern authorship and research scarcely held in Jeremiah's day.

To the question of whether Jeremiah gave temporary support to the Deuteronomic reform we must now briefly turn.[2] That he was not consulted about the book by Josiah is often noted as significant.[3] Yet there is surely nothing surprising about it. Jeremiah was still quite young, and at no time was he regarded by his contemporaries with the respect with which we regard him. But especially was this so in 621 B.C., when he had no record of vindicated prophecy that would set his stock high with king or people. Moreover, it may possibly have been that Huldah was one of the official prophets, comparable with those retained by other kings, though of this we have no direct evidence.[4]

At some stage in his career, Jeremiah is said to have advocated the acceptance of some covenant, and the terms in which the account is cast are strongly reminiscent of Deuteronomy.[5] Editors of various schools differ widely in their attitude to the

[1] *Op. cit.* p. 53 f.

[2] I deal with this subject more fully in *B.J.R.L.* XLV, 1962–63, pp. 225 ff.

[3] Cf. Berry, *J.B.L.* LIX, 1940, p. 136; Hyatt, *loc. cit.* p. 166.

[4] Cf. A. R. Johnson, *The Cultic Prophet in Ancient Israel*, 2nd edn., 1962, p. 66 n.

[5] Jer. 11: 1–14. J. G. S. S. Thomson (*The New Bible Dictionary*, ed. by J. D. Douglas, 1962, p. 606 b) thinks this passage may contain hints of Jeremiah's enthusiasm for Josiah's reforms.

originality of this account.[1] Unless it is a purely gratuitous invention, it is evidence that Jeremiah advocated obedience to some covenant, and the only one we have any knowledge of in the period is the one found in the reign of Josiah. If it was that, and that was Deuteronomy, we could understand why the account is reminiscent of Deuteronomy. If it was Josiah's law-book, but yet not Deuteronomy, we are in worse case.[2] For there is even less reason to suppose that Jeremiah advocated the adoption of the Holiness Code, or any other suggested substitute for Deuteronomy, than there is for believing it was Deuteronomy. And if it was not Josiah's law-book at all, our case is even worse.

Nor are we encouraged when we turn to the reasons alleged against the identification with Deuteronomy. We are told that it is unthinkable that Jeremiah should have advocated the Deuteronomic reform because he was a man totally opposed to sacrifices,[3] and indeed to all forms of recognized worship, whose conception of religion was wholly inner and individual.[4]

[1] B. Duhm (*Das Buch Jeremia*, 1901, pp. 106–8) and C. Cornill (*Das Buch Jeremia*, 1905, pp. 143–45) regard the text as editorial, while F. Giesebrecht (*Das Buch Jeremia*, 1894, p. 67), S. R. Driver (*op. cit.* p. 255), A. S. Peake (*Jeremiah* [Cent. B.], I, pp. 11–14), W. Rothstein (in Kautzsch-Bertholet, *H.S.A.T.* I, 1922, pp. 755 f.), J. Skinner (*Prophecy and Religion*, 1922, pp. 89–107), G. A. Smith (*Jeremiah*, 3rd edn., 1924, pp. 143–46) and A. Condamin (*Le Livre de Jérémie*, 3rd edn., 1936, pp. 103–6) regard it as original. A. F. Puukko (*Kittel Festschrift*, 1913, pp. 142–46) holds it to be the free composition of a later writer, who based it on Baruch's book and on Deuteronomy, while P. Volz (*Der Prophet Jeremia*, 1928, p. 130) holds the passage to be composite, part referring to the events of 621 B.C., and part to 607 B.C., in the reign of Jehoiakim. Cf. also F. Nötscher, *Das Buch Jeremia*, 1934, pp. 105–7.
[2] So E. König, *Geschichte der alttestamentlichen Religion*, 1912, pp. 376–79; 2nd edn., 1915, pp. 441–45.
[3] Cf. Kennett, *Deuteronomy and the Decalogue*, pp. 12–16 = *Church of Israel*, pp. 81–85 (cf. also p. 35); and Schofield, *op. cit.* pp. 58 f. F. C. Burkitt, despite his general support of Kennett's view of the date of Deuteronomy, expresses his disagreement with him here (cf. *J.T.S.* xxii, 1921, p. 63).
[4] Cf. Skinner (*op. cit.* p. 105): "The disinclination to admit even a temporary co-operation of Jeremiah with the Deuteronomists rests less on the exegesis of particular texts than on the broad ground that his insight into the nature of religion makes it inconceivable that he could ever have had any sympathy with an attempt to convert the nation by a forcible change in its forms of worship."

It is improbable that this is a true picture of him,[1] and if it were he would have been an unpractical dreamer, who completely failed to see that if religion were purely inner and individual, it would not long survive at all. We are not justified in taking a selection either of the actual ideas that Jeremiah enunciated at different times, or of those into which we distort his ideas, and in excluding everything that will not fit into the resulting picture. While the seeds of many of his richest ideas can be found in early prophecies, Jeremiah could grow.[2] And there is nothing inherently improbable in his first hope that Josiah's reform would lead to purity in religion and in life being followed by disillusionment, and turning to opposition when he found men putting their trust in the written law and in obedience to the letter, rather than the acceptance of its spirit.[3] Moreover, we have to remember that the members of Jeremiah's own family at one time were bitterly opposed to him and plotted against his life.[4] If he advocated the reform of Josiah, this could well be understood. For he came of a priestly family of Anathoth,[5] probably attached to the local shrine there. And since the country priests did not secure rights in the central sanctuary, despite the provision of the Deuteronomic Code, they might well resent his advocacy of the reform, because its effect in practice did damage to their interests, whatever the purpose of the reform had been. If, on the other hand, Jeremiah did not advocate the reform, we are left without any clue for the understanding of this episode.

We may observe further that it is passing strange to be told that Jeremiah could not have advocated a reform based on

[1] Cf. the present writer's "The Unity of the O.T." in *B.J.R.L.* xxix, 1945–46, pp. 326–58.

[2] Schofield appears to think that only a completely static Jeremiah could be a great man, and that if he changed his attitude through the disappointment of his hopes he would forfeit our esteem (*op. cit.* p. 58). That Jeremiah's expectations were often not precisely realized is well known, and the fact troubled the prophet himself. But he can most be forgiven for not gauging men's response to his word, and for an apparent change of attitude which sprang out of his unchanging loyalty to his principles.

[3] Skinner (*op. cit.* p. 103) so interprets Jer. 8: 8.

[4] Jer. 11: 18 ff.

[5] But cf. T. J. Meek, *Expositor*, 8th series, xxv, 1923, pp. 215–22, where it is argued that Jeremiah was not of a priestly family of Anathoth.

Deuteronomy because he was in such fundamental opposition to its whole essence, while in the same breath we are asked to believe that Deuteronomy is a mere reflection of the ideas and style of Jeremiah.[1] It is more reasonable to believe that the creators of Deuteronomy were imbued with the prophetic idea that the forms of religion should not alone be pure in themselves, but should be made the organ of the spirit's approach to God, and that Jeremiah advocated its adoption because he believed that the purification of the ritual would be accompanied by the renewal of the spirit; but that when he found the old externalism being carried into the purified forms, he recognized that the spiritual disease had not been cured. In this there is a far more real consistency than inconsistency. It means that there was an inner failure of the Deuteronomic reform even before the death of Josiah dealt it its final blow, and it is the less surprising that it had no vitality to survive that event.

All probability therefore favours the view that Josiah's lawbook was Deuteronomy, and that Jeremiah had some knowledge of its contents and style, though not the sort of access that possession of a copy might have given, and that he at first advocated the Deuteronomic reform, but later perceived its spiritual failure and therefore condemned its insufficiency.

---

[1] It is interesting to note that some older writers even credited Jeremiah with the authorship of Deuteronomy (cf. Puukko, "Jeremias Stellung zum Deuteronomium", in *Alttestamentliche Studien* (Kittel Festschrift), 1913, pp. 126–53), while many modern writers, including Colenso (cf. *The Pentateuch and Book of Joshua critically examined*, VII, 1879, pp. 225–27), have accepted the Talmudic tradition that Jeremiah was the author of Kings, and therefore of the account of Josiah's reform (cf. R. Cornely, *Introductionis in S.S. libros compendium*, 10th edn., rev. by A. Merk, I, 1929, pp. 391 f.).

7

Jewish Proselyte Baptism and the Baptism of John

7

JEWISH PROSELYTE BAPTISM AND
THE BAPTISM OF JOHN[1]

THE question of the relation of the baptism of John the Baptist to the baptism of proselytes into Judaism has been not infrequently discussed, and it was formerly widely held that the practice of Judaism was dependent on the practice of John and of the Christian Church.[2] While there is no very clear evidence for the practice of baptizing proselytes at a date prior to the ministry of John, it is in the highest degree improbable that Judaism adopted a practice which had already become an essential practice of Christianity,[3] and the opinion is today generally held that, despite the paucity of the evidence, it is

---

[1] First published in *H.U.C.A.* xv, 1940, pp. 313–34.

[2] So, especially, by M. Schneckenburger, *Über das Alter der jüdischen Proselyten-Taufe und deren Zusammenhang mit dem johanneischen und christlichen Ritus*, 1828. For other authors who followed this view cf. G. B. Winer, *Biblisches Realwörterbuch*, 2nd edn., II, 1838, pp. 338 ff.; E. Leyrer, in *P.R.E.*, 1st edn., XII, 1860, p. 245; A. Plummer, *D.B.* I, 1898, p. 239 b; and further titles may be found in E. Schürer, *H.J.P.*, Eng. trans. by S. Taylor and P. Christie, II, II, 1890, p. 321 n. T. M. Taylor (*N.T.S.* II, 1955–56, pp. 193 ff.) maintains that there was no proselyte baptism before the destruction of the Temple, but that prior to this a proselyte took a purificatory bath after his circumcision and sacrifice (i.e. after his initiation was complete), and that after the destruction of the Temple the bath was continued but given a new significance. This is not only completely conjectural, but in the highest degree improbable. In the first place, purification was needed before sacrifice and not after; and in the second place, the passage to which Taylor appeals for the reversing of the order does not require the meaning he puts upon it, whereas the Talmud elsewhere (see the passage cited below on pp. 215 f) specifically states the order: immersion, Passover-offering.

[3] Cf. A. Calmet, *Commentaire littéral sur tous les livres de l'Ancien et du Nouveau Testament*, VII, 1726, p. 288: "Quelques-uns ont crû que les Juifs avoient imité cette cérémonie des Païens, qui baignoient dans l'eau ceux qu'ils initioient aux mystères; ou des Chrétiens, chez qui le Baptême étoit d'une nécessité indispensable pour tous ceux qui vouloient faire profession de la Religion de Jésus-Christ. Mais et les Païens, et les Chrétiens étoient trop odieux aux Juifs, pour croire que ceux-ci ayent voulu les imiter en cela."

P

scarcely to be doubted that the Jewish practice antedates the ministry of John the Baptist. Not seldom, however, questionable distinctions are drawn between the baptism of John and the baptism of proselytes. Thus A. Plummer[1] distinguishes the latter from John's baptism by connecting it with the ritual lustrations prescribed in the Old Testament to cleanse from ceremonial impurity, as against the ethical basis of repentance in the baptism of John, and by contrasting John's baptism as a rite administered by another with Jewish baptism as self-administered. That John's baptism had some features which distinguished it from the baptism of proselytes is indeed manifest, since otherwise it could hardly have been known—and we learn from the New Testament that it was known—as John's baptism; but how far the above differentiation is sound or adequate is more than doubtful.

Four issues are therefore raised: (1) What early evidence is there for the practice of baptizing proselytes in Judaism? (2) What was the nature of this baptism? (3) What was its relation to the ritual lustrations of the law? (4) How is it to be distinguished from the baptism of John?

I

That the Jewish baptism of proselytes is probably older than the beginning of the Christian era is the view of W. Brandt,[2] W. Heitmüller,[3] and J. Coppens,[4] and while this cannot be certainly established, it may reasonably be held to be probable. Marcus Dods,[5] indeed, believed that greater certainty could be

[1] Cf. *D.B.* I, 1898, p. 240 b.
[2] Cf. *Die jüdischen Baptismen*, 1910, pp. 58 f.
[3] Cf. *R.G.G.*, 1st edn., v, 1913, col. 1088; similarly E. Stauffer, *ibid.*, 2nd edn., v, 1931, col. 1003.
[4] Cf. *S.D.B.* I, 1928, col. 893.
[5] Cf. *D.C.G.* I, 1906, p. 169 a. So, too, Strack-Billerbeck, *Kommentar zum Neuen Testament aus Talmud und Midrasch*, I, 1922, p. 103, where it is said that the beginnings of proselyte baptism are certainly to be assigned to pre-Christian times. Amongst many other writers who have held that proselyte baptism antedates the Christian era we may note J. Jeremias, *Z.N.W.* XXVIII, 1929, pp. 312 ff. (cf. *Th. Z.* v, 1949, pp. 418 ff.); A. Oepke, *Th.W.B.* I, 1933, p. 533; T. F. Torrance, *N.T.S.* I, 1954–55, pp. 150 ff.; and J. Warns, *Baptism*, 1957, p. 18. Cf. also G. F. Moore, *Judaism*, III, 1930, pp. 109 f.;

attained, and declared Edersheim's and Schürer's treatment of this subject definitive, but this is as little justified as H. A. W. Meyer's[1] unqualified declaration on the other side, that "the baptism of proselytes did not arise until after the destruction of Jerusalem." With more caution than either, I. Abrahams[2] recognizes that "it can hardly be said that the evidence so far adduced *proves* the case."

Schürer, indeed, cumbers his discussion of the subject[3] with some confusion of the issues. For he argues on *a priori* grounds that "even apart from any explicit testimony, we should have had to assume that they (i.e. the rites of admission for proselytes, including baptism) were already currently practised in the time of Christ. For as no Jew could be admitted into fellowship with Israel except through circumcision, so it was quite as

---

W. F. Flemington, *The New Testament Doctrine of Baptism*, 1948, p. 4; T. W. Manson, *S.J.Th.* II, 1949, p. 392. J. Heron (*S.J.Th.* VIII, 1955, p. 45) makes the remarkable assertion: "It hardly seems necessary to go over this debate, since the new evidence of the Dead Sea Scrolls appears to settle the matter decisively in Jeremias' favour." As there is no evidence at all in the Scrolls for any water rite of initiation (see below, p. 230, n. 1), this is a large inference from silence.

[1] Cf. *Critical and Exegetical Handbook to the Gospel of Matthew*, Eng. trans. by P. Christie and F. Crombie, 1877, p. 109. J. Thomas (*Le Mouvement Baptiste en Palestine et Syrie*, 1935, p. 364) also thinks it improbable that any rite of proselyte baptism was generally recognized among the Jews before the end of the first century A.D.

[2] Cf. *Studies in Pharisaism and the Gospels*, I, 1917, p. 36. Cf. also R. Bultmann, *Theology of the New Testament*, Eng. trans. by K. Grobel, I, 1952, p. 40. S. Zeitlin (*H.U.C.A.* I, 1924, pp. 357 ff.; *J.B.L.* LII, 1933, pp. 78 f.; cf. *J.Q.R.*, N.S. XIV, 1923–24, p. 131, and *Historical Study of the Canonization of the Hebrew Scriptures*, 1933, p. 33 n.) holds that Jewish proselyte baptism is not older than A.D. 65, and that it was taken over into the Christian Church later than this. He ignores John the Baptist, and is doubtful if Jesus ever lived. L. Finkelstein (*J.B.L.* LII, 1933, pp. 203 ff.) has sufficiently exposed the weakness of the grounds on which these views are based. A. Büchler, too, has pronounced against them (*J.Q.R.*, N.S. XVII, 1926–27, p. 15 n.). F. Gavin (*The Jewish Antecedents of the Christian Sacraments*, 2nd edn., 1933, p. 85) says: "The usage grew up naturally and inevitably, beginning possibly earlier, but certainly by the second century." J. Thomas (*op. cit.* pp. 365 f.) says that proselyte baptism is attested at the end of the first century, and possibly existed from its beginning, but thinks it improbable that it was widely accepted.

[3] *Op. cit.* II, II, pp. 319 ff.

much a matter of course that a Gentile, who as such was unclean, . . . should be required, on entering into such fellowship, to take the bath of Levitical purification . . . Surely every one in the least acquainted with Pharisaic Judaism must know how frequently a native Jew was compelled . . . to take a bath with a view to Levitical purification . . . But a Gentile, not being in the habit of observing those regulations with regard to Levitical purity, would as such be unclean and that as a simple matter of course. In that case, how was it possible that he could be admitted into Jewish communion without his having first of all subjected himself to a Levitical 'bath of purification'? This general consideration is of itself so conclusive that there is no need to lay any very great stress upon individual testimonies."

Both Plummer[1] and Abrahams[2] endorse this judgment, without noting that it completely begs the question. It tacitly identifies the baptism of the proselyte with ordinary ritual lustration, and implies that it in no way differed from the ablutions which the proselyte would be required frequently to undergo, save that it was his first Jewish lustration. If this tacit assumption is correct, then this baptism differed *toto coelo*, both in character and significance, from the baptism of John and from Christian baptism. These are questions which are to be considered below. Here it is only necessary to raise a *caveat* against such *a priori* reasoning, and to express a preference for the more patient examination of evidence, even though it leads to less confident results.

To this, indeed, Schürer turns after thus discounting its importance, and it will be found excellently presented in Abrahams' valuable essay on "Pharisaic Baptism",[3] and in Coppens' long and learned article on "Baptism" in the Supplement to Vigouroux' *Dictionnaire de la Bible*.[4]

---

[1] *Loc. cit.* p. 240 a: "What may be regarded as conclusive is that the baptizing of proselytes would follow of necessity from the regulations which required a Jew to bathe in order to recover Levitical purity."

[2] *Op. cit.* p. 36: "Schürer . . . rightly insists that . . . a priori . . . proselytes must have been baptised in the time of Jesus. The heathen was in a state of uncleanness and must, at least as emphatically as the Jew in a similar state, have undergone the ritual of bathing."

[3] *Op. cit.* pp. 36–46.

[4] *S.D.B.* I, 1928, cols. 852–924; see especially cols. 892 ff.

It is recorded in the Mishnah[1] that "the School of Shammai say: If a man became a proselyte on the day before Passover, he may immerse himself and consume his Passover-offering in the evening. And the School of Hillel say: He that separates himself from his uncircumcision is as one that separates himself from a grave." This statement, which is repeated elsewhere in the Mishnah[2] as one of the six points on which the School of Hillel took a severer view than the School of Shammai, since in their view uncleanness would continue for seven days (Num. 19: 16), offers evidence that before the destruction of the Temple the immersion of proselytes was already practised,[3] since it was a matter of controversy. The Gemara on the passage[4] states that, in the time of Rabbi Simeon ben Eleazar (second century A.D.), it was held that the difference between the schools of Shammai and of Hillel concerned only the proselyte who was non-Israelite, and not an uncircumcised Israelite.

Abrahams, like Moore, recognizes that these passages do not provide any conclusive evidence for so early a time as the ministry of John the Baptist, but merely carry us back to a time prior to the fall of Jerusalem, since they do not necessarily record the views of Shammai and Hillel themselves, but may record a scholastic discussion.[5] He cites other evidence,[6] however, which establishes on the authority of Rabbi Eleazar ben Jacob, whose reliability is beyond question and who was recording what was within the range of his own experience, that the baptism of some Roman soldiers immediately followed their

---

[1] Pes. VIII, 8 (Vienna *Mishnah*, II, 1793, p. 75 b). The translation is that of H. Danby (*The Mishnah*, 1933, p. 148).

[2] 'Eduy. v, 2 (Vienna *Mishnah*, IV, 1793, p. 145 a; Eng. trans. by Danby, p. 431).

[3] Cf. Moore, *Judaism*, III, 1930, p. 110, where it is said that this "would take us back to a time before the fall of Jerusalem. There is, so far as I know, no earlier evidence; but there is nothing to indicate that proselyte baptism was of recent introduction."

[4] Pes. 92 a (ed. by L. Goldschmidt, *Der Babylonische Talmud*, II, 1901, p. 659; Eng. trans. by H. Freedman in Soncino *Talmud*, Seder Mo'ed IV, 1938, p. 492).

[5] *Op. cit.* p. 37.

[6] Jer. Pes. VIII (Krotoschin edn., 1866, p. 36 a; trans. by M. Schwab, v, 1882, p. 134) and Tosephta Pes. VII, 13 (ed. by M. S. Zuckermandel, 1880, p. 167, lines 21 f.).

conversion on the same day. This again only carries us to a time prior to A.D. 70, and is further less conclusive than would appear, since, owing to the ambiguity of the Hebrew language, it cannot be established whether this passage refers to a mere ritual lustration,[1] or whether it refers to a witnessed ceremony that is in any way comparable with what we understand by baptism. For there is no distinction in Hebrew between "bath" and "baptism". The probability, however, is that the reference here is to the latter, since the fact that there is testimony to the immersion would suggest that it was witnessed.

Another Talmudic passage is also adduced, where we read[2] of a difference of opinion between Rabbi Joshua ben Hananiah and Rabbi Eliezer ben Hyrcanus, who lived towards the end of the first century A.D., as to whether circumcision without baptism sufficed to make one a proselyte—an opinion sustained by Eliezer—or whether baptism without circumcision sufficed— an opinion sustained by Joshua. The former judgment is based on the consideration that "this is what we find in our fathers, that they were circumcised but not baptized", while the latter is based on the argument that "this is what we find in our mothers, that they were baptized but not circumcised." It is added that the recognized view is that both circumcision and baptism are requisite to become a proselyte, and this latter view is found elsewhere in the Talmud. Thus we read[3] that Rabbi Johanan (end of the second century A.D.) expressed the opinion that no one became a proselyte until he had been circumcised and baptized and, to make it still more explicit, added that one who has not been baptized is still a pagan.

In the Talmud the account of the differing opinions of Joshua and Eliezer is followed by a discussion of its meaning, in the

[1] Schneckenburger (op. cit. p. 117) neutralized the evidence of the above quoted passage from the Mishnah by holding that it referred to a ritual lustration merely, and not to an initiation ceremony. This is quite as unjustified as to assume uncritically that it was an initiation ceremony. Where language is ambiguous, its evidence cannot be pressed either way.

[2] Yeb. 46 a (Goldschmidt's edn., IV, 1922, p. 156; Eng. trans. by I. W. Slotki in Soncino Talmud, Seder Nashim I, 1936, pp. 302 f.).

[3] 'Ab. Zar. 59 a (Goldschmidt's edn., VII, 1903, p. 998; Eng. trans. by A. Cohen in Soncino Talmud, Seder Nezikin VII, 1935, p. 293); Yeb. 46 a b (Goldschmidt's edn., IV, 1922, pp. 156 f.; Eng. trans. by I. W. Slotki in Soncino Talmud, Seder Nashim I, 1936, pp. 302, 304).

course of which Exod. 19: 10 is quoted against Rabbi Eliezer as evidence that the fathers were baptized, and it is acknowledged that Rabbi Joshua had nothing more than conjecture for his assertion that the mothers were baptized, and Slotki[1] states that Rabbi Eliezer's meaning is that "those who departed from Egypt as heathens and received the Torah on Mount Sinai . . . were, so to speak, converted to Judaism." I find no justification for this view, however. Moore[2] records that Rabbi Judah the Prince inferred from Jos. 5: 2 that the fathers had been circumcised before leaving Egypt. Maimonides[3] drew the same inference from Exod. 12: 48, while both Rabbi Judah and Maimonides based on Exod. 19: 10 the assumption that the fathers were baptized at Sinai. But whatever psychological arguments might be based on these texts, no logical arguments relevant to the baptism of proselytes can be founded on them. For this supposed baptism could have had no relation to the circumcision, and if the fathers had been circumcised and had eaten the Passover prior to this baptism, it is hard to see how Rabbi Joshua could base on this fact his case for the necessity of baptism for the admission of the proselyte, since none could partake of the Passover until he had been fully admitted. The case would clearly be given away to Rabbi Eliezer. Nor could Rabbi Eliezer have implied, as Slotki asserts, that the fathers were heathens when they departed from Egypt, and were converted to Judaism at Sinai. For this would involve the assumption that the fathers had not legitimately partaken of the Passover in Egypt, and also that they had been circumcised at Sinai, since conversion at Sinai could not have taken place on the basis of any circumcision save one that took place there. I know of no warrant for either of these assumptions in the fancies of the Rabbis.

It is surely more natural to give the arguments by which the opinions of Joshua and Eliezer were sustained a wider reference, Rabbi Eliezer stressing the fundamental significance of circumcision, since it and not baptism was the door by which a male Jew was admitted to the covenant, and Rabbi Joshua stressing

[1] *Ibid.* p. 302, n. 6.
[2] Cf. *Judaism*, I, 1927, p. 334 n.
[3] *Issure Biah* XIII, 2 f. (*De jure pauperis et peregrini*, ed. by H. Prideaux, 1679, p. 113).

the fundamental significance of baptism, since it alone was open to women. The already noted ambiguity of the word rendered "baptize" then again appears. For in the reference to the mothers it has the meaning of ordinary ritual lustration, whereas in the reference to the fathers it does not have that meaning, but that of an initiation rite. For the fathers were no more exempt than the mothers from ordinary ritual lustration. In the Talmudic discussion of the story, the double use of the word is again apparent, though the senses are changed. For there it is assumed that the women must have been baptized as a rite of initiation, though it is acknowledged that there is no record of this, whereas in the case of the men only a ritual lustration is implied, since it is deduced from the washing of the garments. Where only a single word covered private ablution and initiation rite, it was inevitable that there should be this confusion in the kind of word-play that formed the stock of so much of the Rabbinic discussion, and it occasions no surprise that, however the *mots* be interpreted, strict logical validity is unsatisfied.

In so far as the proselyte is concerned in this story, however, it is almost certain that the reference is to a witnessed ceremony, and not to an ordinary ritual lustration, since an unwitnessed lustration could scarcely be held by Rabbi Joshua or anyone else to be an adequate basis of admission into Judaism, in lieu of circumcision.

We seem, then, here at last to be on firm ground, and if the immersion of the proselyte at the end of the first century A.D. was different from ordinary lustration, then the probability is that the earlier references are also to this different ceremony, since Judaism is not likely in this period to have assimilated its rite in any way to what had by now become the Christian rite of baptism.

We may conclude, therefore, that while it cannot be definitely established by specific evidence, it is probable that a baptismal rite was practised in the case of proselytes to Judaism in the period preceding the destruction of the Temple, and in the absence of any special reason for its creation between the ministry of John the Baptist and the fall of Jerusalem, when, on the contrary, there were strong reasons against its adoption, it may reasonably be presumed to be of older origin. The difference between the schools of Hillel and Shammai may well go back to the founders of those schools, and the rite itself therefore antedate their time.[1]

It is, however, quite impossible to date the beginnings of the ceremony. That so far back as proselytes were admitted into Judaism that admission was associated with lustration may be accepted as certain, but precisely when it ceased to be merely lustration and became the ceremony which will be examined in the following section cannot be established by any evidence whatever. There is no adequate reason to doubt, however, that it was already the practice by the beginning of the Christian era.

II

The fuller testimony to the character of the rite[2] administered to these converts is found in the Talmud in contexts where it cannot be dated. The evidence itself is therefore late, but if it is allowed that it is probable that there was a baptismal rite in Judaism at the beginning of the Christian era, this late Jewish testimony as to its character may be accepted, in the absence of any other, since Judaism is likely to have clung tenaciously to its own practice in this matter.

There is general agreement that the tradition that the male proselyte was required to undergo circumcision and baptism and to offer a sacrifice[3] is trustworthy.[4] This tradition clearly

---

[1] Edersheim assumed that it did go back to the founders and then argued that this *proved* that the baptism of proselytes was customary before the time of Christ (*Life and Times of Jesus the Messiah*, II, 1887, p. 747). This is as completely unjustified as Schneckenburger's argument on the other side.

[2] On Jewish proselyte baptism cf. now the finely documented study of G. R. Beasley-Murray, *Baptism in the New Testament*, 1962, pp. 18 ff.

[3] Ker. 9 a (Goldschmidt's edn., IX, 1935, p. 497; Eng. trans. by I. Porusch in Soncino *Talmud*, 1948, p. 66); Sifre on Num. § 108—on Nu. 15: 14 (ed. by H. S. Horovitz in *Corpus Tannaiticum*, I, III, I, *Siphre ad Numeros*, 1917, § 108, p. 112; Eng. trans. by P. P. Levertoff, 1926, p. 92); Mekilta de R. Simeon ben Yohai on Ex. 12: 48 (ed. by D. Hoffmann, 1905, pp. 29 f.); Gerim II, 4 (ed. by R. Kirchheim, *Septem libri Talmudici parvi Hierosolymitani*, 1851, p. 38, or ed. by M. Higger, *Seven Minor Treatises*, 1930, p. 72; Eng. trans. by Higger, *ibid.* p. 47); Maimonides, *Issure Biah* XIII, I (Prideaux' edn., p. 113).

[4] So Schürer (*op. cit.* II, II, pp. 319 f.), Moore (*op. cit.* I, pp. 331 f., 334), J. Bonsirven (*Le Judaïsme palestinien*, I, 1934, pp. 29 f.).

refers to the time prior to the destruction of the Temple, after which sacrifice ceased to be offered. Hence, in the above-mentioned controversy between Joshua ben Hananiah and Eliezer ben Hyrcanus, which took place after the destruction of the Temple, there is no mention of sacrifice.[1] For women there was no circumcision, though the translators of Schürer incorrectly made him say that Maimonides expressly states that circumcision and sacrifice are binding on women.[2] In the case of children born before their parents became proselytes, they were circumcised and baptized at the same time as their father, but they retained the right to renounce the engagements entered into in their name on attaining maturity.[3] Children already in embryo at the time of the conversion of their mother, but born later, were exempt from the necessity of the ceremonial immersion.[4]

Abrahams objects to any distinction between the baptism of John and the baptism of proselytes based on the argument that the one was administered and the other was not. He maintains that the baptism of proselytes was administered, or at least witnessed, and notes the reading of the Western text of Lk. 3: 7, according to which the people went out to be baptized "before" John.[5] It can hardly be doubted that John's baptism was not merely witnessed, but administered, in the sense that the person undergoing the rite was plunged beneath the water by the person administering it.[6] That the baptism of proselytes was

---

[1] The statement of R. Eliezer ben Jacob (*circa* A.D. 135), recorded in the Mishnah (Ker. II, 1, Vienna *Mishnah*, v, 1793, p. 116 b; Eng. trans. by Danby, p. 564), that "a proselyte's atonement is yet incomplete until the blood (of his offering) has been tossed for him (against the base of the altar)", is clearly a scholastic judgment as to what was formerly the case.

[2] *Op. cit.* II, II, p. 320 n. What Maimonides actually says is that baptism and sacrifice are binding on women (*Issure Biah* XIII, 4, Prideaux' edn., p. 114), and this was correctly stated in the German edition of Schürer from which the English edition was translated (*G.J.V.*, 2nd edn., II, 1886, p. 560).

[3] Ket. 11 a (Goldschmidt's edn., IV, 1922, p. 488; Eng. trans. by S. Daiches in Soncino *Talmud*, Seder Nashim III, 1936, pp. 35 f.).

[4] Yeb. 78 a (Goldschmidt's edn., IV, 1922, p. 280; Eng. trans. by I. W. Slotki in Soncino *Talmud*, Seder Nashim II, 1936, p. 530).

[5] *Op. cit.* p. 38.

[6] Cf. Jn. 1: 25 f., where we are told that John baptized, and Mk. 1: 9, Mt. 3: 13, where it is said that Jesus was "baptized by John". M.-J.

witnessed is beyond dispute, since we have explicit testimony on the point, but it is more difficult to establish whether the proselyte immersed himself, or was immersed. Abrahams[1] says that "in the case of the male proselytes there seems to have been no act on the part of the witnesses", and in agreement with this Brandt[2] says "the convert made a complete immersion", while Coppens[3] says "they were plunged into the pool". The point can hardly be settled on linguistic grounds. Abrahams rightly notes that sometimes the *ḳal* is used and sometimes the causative of the verb, but little weight can be attached to this. For the causative may just as easily mean "cause a person to immerse himself" as "immerse a person", while the *ḳal* does not exclude the possibility of an administered rite. For in Syriac the corresponding word, though not phonetically cognate, means either "to plunge" or "to be plunged". To the Jewish mind it was more important to insist that the immersion should be complete than to define how it should be achieved.

In all ritual immersion it was regarded as essential that every part of the body should be reached by the water,[4] and we find in the Talmud discussions as to how far even a knot in the hair invalidates a lustration.[5] It is specifically laid down that the immersion of a proselyte must conform to the same standard of completeness as the immersion of a woman after menstruation,

Lagrange (*L'Évangile de Jésus-Christ*, 1936, p. 58) says: "On s'immergeait dans l'eau en sa présence, de façon qu'on ait été comme lavé par lui." Cf. J. Gnilka, *R.Q.* III, 1961–2, p. 198, where the activity of John in baptism is stressed.

[1] *Op. cit.* p. 38.

[2] In *E.R.E.* II, 1909, p. 408 b. Cf. C. Taylor, *The Teaching of the Twelve Apostles*, 1886, p. 51: "In Jewish baptism the proselyte, if not an infant, performed the act of immersion himself."

[3] *Loc. cit.* col. 893.

[4] Cf. Pes. 107 a (Goldschmidt's edn., II, 1901, p. 703; Eng. trans. by H. Freedman in Soncino *Talmud*, Seder Mo'ed IV, 1938, p. 564); "Nothing must interpose between his flesh and the water." Cf. Mishnah, Miḳ. IX, 1–4 (Vienna *Mishnah*, VI, 1793, p. 171 a b; Eng. trans. by Danby, pp. 742 f.).

[5] 'Erub. 4 b (Goldschmidt's edn., II, 1901, pp. 11 f.; Eng. trans. by I. W. Slotki in Soncino *Talmud*, Seder Mo'ed III, 1938, pp. 20 f.). Cf. C. Taylor, *op. cit.*, p. 52: "A ring on the finger, a band covering the hair, or anything that in the least degree broke the continuity of contact with the water, was held to invalidate the act."

and that whatever is considered as an interception between the body and the water in ritual bathing is equally to be considered an interception in the immersion of proselytes.[1] Complete nudity and complete immersion were therefore essential.

While, therefore, it is impossible to establish with certainty whether the immersion was, or was not, the unaided act of the proselyte, the probability that it was may be reasonably allowed. Indeed, on the principle that every part of the body must be touched by the water, it is difficult to see how it could be otherwise. A heathen bought by a Jew as a slave had to be circumcised and to submit to the ritual ablution of his body, but here the master was required to hold him firmly while he was in the water, in order to distinguish this ceremony clearly from the immersion of a true proselyte.[2] This would seem to imply that no hand touched the proselyte in the actual ceremony of the immersion.

That witnesses were essential to the ceremony is clearly stated. There is some disagreement, however, as to the number required. In one passage[3] we read that "two learned men must stand beside" the proselyte, but it is stated below in the name of Rabbi Johanan that this should be corrected to three,[4] in agreement with what is found earlier in the same tractate, where we read that "the initiation of a proselyte requires the presence of three men."[5] Elsewhere it is also stated that the presence of three witnesses is necessary,[6] and this is deduced from the principle that they form a court, and that three is the minimum constitution of a court.[7]

The witnesses do not appear to have been merely passive spectators, however. They were required to question the

---

[1] Yeb. 47 b (Goldschmidt's edn., IV, 1922, p. 161; Eng. trans. by Slotki, p. 312).

[2] Yeb. 46 a (Goldschmidt's edn., p. 155; Eng. trans. by Slotki, p. 300).

[3] Yeb. 47 b (Goldschmidt's edn., p. 161; Eng. trans. by Slotki, p. 311).

[4] Yeb. 47 b (Goldschmidt's edn., p. 162; Eng. trans. by Slotki, p. 314).

[5] Yeb. 46 b (Goldschmidt's edn., p. 158; Eng. trans. by Slotki, pp. 306 f.).

[6] Ḳid. 62 b (Goldschmidt's edn., v, 1912, p. 915; Eng. trans. by H. Freedman in Soncino *Talmud*, Seder Nashim VIII, 1936, p. 313). Cf. Maimonides, *Issure Biah* XIII, 6 (Prideaux' edn., p. 114).

[7] Yeb. 46 b (Goldschmidt's edn., p. 158; Eng. trans. by Slotki, p. 307). This is based on Num. 15: 16, where it is said "one law and one ordinance shall be for you and for the *ger*." See Strack-Billerbeck, *op. cit.* I, 1922, p. 111.

proselyte beforehand, and to warn him of the full meaning of the step he was taking, and to make sure that his motives in seeking admission to the Jewish faith were worthy,[1] and during the actual ceremony, when he stood partly immersed in the water, they were charged with the task of reciting to him some of the laws, both major and minor, of the faith he was embracing,[2] before his complete immersion took place. It is therefore clear that, whether the actual immersion was his own unaided act or not, the ceremony was fundamentally an administered one.

It was further laid down that baptism could only take place during the daytime,[3] and that it was not permitted on the Sabbath or on any holy day.[4]

In the case of a woman proselyte, while it was essential that the ceremony should be administered by men, it was carefully ensured that there should be no immodesty. The men remained out of sight, while women accompanied the proselyte to the place of immersion. After she was seated in water up to her neck they exhorted her in the principles of the Jewish faith,[5] but they were not eye-witnesses of the ceremony. They administered it from a position where the proselyte was not visible to them.[6]

---

[1] Yeb. 47 a (Goldschmidt's edn., pp. 160 f.; Eng. trans. by Slotki, pp. 310 f.) Cf. Gerim 1, 3: "He who embraces Judaism through the desire to marry a Jewish woman, through personal love of the Jews, or through fear of the Jews, is not a genuine proselyte . . . He who embraces Judaism not for the sake of God is no genuine proselyte" (ed. by Kirchheim, p. 38, ed. by Higger, p. 69; Eng. trans. by Higger, p. 48). E. G. Hirsch (*J. E.* x, 1909, p. 223 a) thinks the measures to test the sincerity of the proselyte reflect the bitter experience of the Hadrianic persecution.

[2] Yeb. 47 b (Goldschmidt's edn., p. 161; Eng. trans. by Slotki, p. 311).

[3] Yeb. 46 b (Goldschmidt's edn., p. 158; Eng. trans. by Slotki, p. 306). Cf. Jer. Yeb. viii (Krotoschin edn., 1866, p. 8 b; trans. by M. Schwab, vii, 1865, p. 111); Mishnah, Meg. ii, 4 (Vienna *Mishnah*, ii, 1793, p. 154 b; Eng. trans. by Danby, p. 204) and Gemara 20 a (Goldschmidt's edn., iii, 1899, p. 620; Eng. trans. by M. Simon in Soncino *Talmud*, Seder Mo'ed viii. 1938, p. 122).

[4] Cf. Maimonides, *Issure Biah* xiii, 6 (Prideaux' edn., p. 114). For a discussion of the point so far as the Sabbath is concerned, cf. Yeb. 46 b (Goldschmidt's edn., pp. 157 f.; Eng. trans. by Slotki, pp. 305 f.).

[5] Yeb. 47 b (Goldschmidt's edn., p. 161; Eng. trans. by Slotki, p. 311).

[6] Cf. Gerim 1, 4: "A man is present at the immersion of a man; a woman is present at the immersion of a woman" (ed. by Kirchheim, p. 38, ed. by Higger, p. 69; Eng. trans. by Higger, p. 48).

Brandt says[1] that after the exhortation of the men representatives, "she thereafter drew her head under water, and at the moment it was necessary for the witnesses to look on; then, as she came out of the bath, the men retired with averted faces", and states that this is set forth in Yeb. 45–47. I have failed to find any reference to this in the specified folios, however.

It may be noted that in the Early Church complete nudity was essential in baptism, as in the Synagogue.[2] For Cyril of Jerusalem[3] refers to the nakedness of the candidates in baptism as imitating the nakedness of Christ on the Cross, and Chrysostom[4] compares it with the nakedness of Adam in the Garden of Eden. That this nudity was required equally in the case of women is apparent from Chrysostom's Epistle to Innocent, Bishop of Rome,[5] in which he gives an account of the incursion of a body of soldiers into a church, where women were already stripped in preparation for baptism, and tells how they ejected the clergy by force, and filled the women with such terror that they fled without waiting to cover themselves.

Careful directions are given in the Jewish sources as to the amount of water that was requisite for baptism, and the kind of water that was to be preferred. For all ritual lustrations the quantity required was forty seahs, or a cubit square and three cubits deep.[6] Of the kinds of water suitable for ritual ablutions, including the immersion of proselytes, living water was most to be preferred, failing which "smitten" waters, i.e. salty or warm waters[7], were permissible, after which came well water, and

[1] Cf. *E.R.E.* II, 1909, p. 408 b. Similarly in *Die jüdischen Baptismen*, 1910, p. 60.
[2] Cf. W. B. Marriott, in *D.C.A.* I, 1875, p. 160 b: "A comparison of all the evidence leads to the conclusion that the catechumen entered the font in a state of absolute nakedness."
[3] *Catechesis* XX, Mystagogia II, 2 (*P.G.* XXXIII, 1857, col. 1077).
[4] *Homilies on Epistle to Colossians* VI, 4 (*P.G.* LXII, 1862, col. 342).
[5] *P.G.* LII, 1862, col. 533.
[6] Cf. Pes. 109 a (Goldschmidt's edn., II, 1901, p. 703; Eng. trans. by H. Freedman in Soncino *Talmud,* Seder Mo'ed IV, 1938, p. 564); 'Erub. 4 b (Goldschmidt's edn., II, 1901, p. 11; Eng. trans. by I. W. Slotki in Soncino *Talmud,* Seder Mo'ed III, 1938, p. 20); Midrash Num. Rab. XVIII, 21 (Eng. trans. by J. J. Slotki in Soncino *Midrash,* VI, 1939, p. 738); Mishnah, Miḳ. I, 7 (Vienna *Mishnah,* VI, 1793, p. 160 a; Eng. trans. by Danby, p. 733).
[7] Cf. Mishnah, Parah VIII, 9 (Vienna *Mishnah,* VI, 1793, p. 136 b; Eng. trans. by Danby, p. 707).

finally any quantity of water not less than forty seahs.[1] With this may be compared the provisions for Christian baptism given in the *Didache*, or *Teaching of the Twelve Apostles* VII, 1-4,[2] where it is laid down that baptism should be in living water, if possible, but otherwise in other water, and that cold water is to be preferred to warm.

III

That this baptism of proselytes is different from the ritual lustrations prescribed in the law is already quite clear, and while it might be antecedently assumed that lustration would be required of every proselyte by a people that required the frequent lustration of its members, and readily agreed that the baptism of proselytes is a special development from the general ritual lustration, it must be recognized that it is something that goes fundamentally beyond mere lustration.[3]

Like ordinary ritual lustration, it involved the total immersion of the body in water, to ensure the physical purification of the body. But it was clearly directed to something deeper than physical purification. Bousset[4] says there was nothing sacramental about the baptism of proselytes, but Abrahams[5] and Bonsirven[6], rightly in my judgment, deny this. It was an initiation ceremony equally with the circumcision of the male proselyte, and for the female proselyte the only initiation ceremony after the destruction of the Temple. Prior to that destruction both male and female proselytes were required to offer a sacrifice, but there was less of an initiatory character about that than about the baptism. For sacrifices were a part of the normal

---

[1] Mishnah, Miḳ. I, 7 f. (Vienna *Mishnah*, VI, 1793, p. 160 a; Eng. trans. by Danby, p. 733). Cf. also Coppens, *loc. cit.* col. 894.

[2] Cf. Lightfoot, *The Apostolic Fathers*, 1891, p. 220; Eng. trans. p. 232.

[3] B. J. Bamberger (*Proselytism in the Talmudic Period*, 1939, p. 44) insists, rightly in my view, that proselyte baptism was both purificatory and initiatory. Cf. also N. A. Dahl, who maintains (*Interpretationes ad Vetus Testamentum pertinentes* [Mowinckel Festschrift], 1955, p. 41) that the baptism of proselytes was a special variety of ritual lustration.

[4] Cf. *Die Religion des Judentums im späthellenistischen Zeitalter*, 3rd edn., ed. by H. Gressmann, 1926, p. 199.

[5] *Op. cit.* p. 42.

[6] *Op. cit.* I, p. 30.

life into which the proselyte entered, if he lived in Palestine, prior to the destruction of the Temple, whereas this was a ceremony to be observed once for all.[1]

If to this it is replied that lustrations were also a part of the normal life into which the proselyte entered, whether within Palestine or without, and whether before the destruction of the Temple or afterwards, the answer is that whereas other lustrations were purely private rites, requiring the presence of no witnesses, the presence of witnesses was of the essence of this rite.[2] Moreover, the other lustrations were wholly the work of the individual concerned, whereas here catechism and solemn exhortation formed an integral part of the rite. It was therefore not an act of ritual purification alone, but an act of self-dedication to the God of Israel, involving spiritual factors as well as physical, with a fundamentally sacramental character.

It must be recognized, however, that differences of opinion here are partly due to the different connotation of the word "sacramental" as employed by different writers. Oesterley and Box[3] say: "Baptism among the Jews did not partake of a sacramental character; but it *ought* to have done so logically, because, as we conceive, the prototype of baptism among the Israelites did partake of a sacramental character." They indicate what they mean by a sacrament by asking[4]: "Did the Jews believe that through material means spiritual grace was conferred?" If it is meant to ask whether the Jews believed that the mere act of immersion mediated grace to the proselyte, independently of the spiritual state of the person immersed, the answer is clearly in the negative. Such an idea has not been unknown in the Christian Church, indeed, as witness the forcible baptisms of Muslims and Jews by the order of Christian kings, but it can scarcely be maintained that such an idea would alone legitimate the use of the word "sacrament" for the rite of baptism, and it is improbable that Oesterley and Box would so maintain. But if it is meant to ask whether the Jews believed that the act of

[1] Cf. Abrahams, *op. cit.* p. 42.

[2] Cf. Moore, *op. cit.* I, p. 333: "The rite itself differs fundamentally from such baths of purification in that the presence of official witnesses is required." Cf. T. F. Torrance, *N.T.S.* I, 1954–55, p. 151.

[3] *The Religion and Worship of the Synagogue,* 1911, p. 286.

[4] *Ibid.* p. 283.

immersion mediated grace to the true proselyte, the answer is quite definitely in the affirmative. And it is a legitimate use of language to speak of it as sacramental.[1]

It has been already shown that Jewish writers urged the importance of ensuring that the proselyte was acting from pure motives, and was a sincere believer in the faith of Judaism. The spiritual state of the proselyte was therefore essential to the valid performance of the baptismal rite. But given that desired spiritual state, it was believed that the baptismal rite made one a member of the Jewish community, and an heir of the promises. After the immersion the representatives who had first exhorted the proselyte cried to him: "Whom hast thou joined, thou blessed one? Thou hast joined Him who created the world by the utterance of words, blessed be He. For the world was created solely for Israel's sake, and none are called the children of God, save Israel. None are beloved of God, save Israel."[2] The baptism that had completed the work of faith and mediated admission into the elect community was clearly regarded as a channel of grace. Moreover, the Rabbis discussed whether conversion, which was not reckoned conversion until it was completed in baptism, cancelled all previous sins. Rabbi Jose maintained that it did not, and that proselytes are called to account for their pre-baptismal sins, but Rabbi Judah held that because the proselyte was regarded as a new-born child, his previous sins were cancelled.[3] While, therefore, Judaism

[1] Cf. *O.E.D.* VIII, II, 1914, p. 13, s.v. *sacrament:* "Those who accept the number seven, and many of those who admit only two sacraments, say that the sacraments differ from other rites in being channels by which supernatural grace is imparted. By those Protestants who deny that baptism and the Lord's Supper in themselves convey supernatural grace, the specific difference of the sacraments from other observances is regarded as consisting in their paramount obligation as having been expressly commanded by Christ Himself, and in the special spiritual benefits obtained by their faithful use."

[2] Gerim I, I (ed. by Kirchheim, p. 38, ed. by Higger, p. 68; Eng. trans. by Higger, p. 47).

[3] Gerim II, 5 (ed. by Kirchheim, p. 41, ed. by Higger, p. 72; Eng. trans. by Higger, p. 50). In contrast to this O. Cullmann states (*Theology of the New Testament,* Eng. trans. by K. Grobel, 1952, p. 39) that "proselyte baptism was considered to free a man from ritual defilement, whereas Christian baptism, like that of John . . . , evidently promised purity from sin."

was far from believing that baptism was a ceremony which merely *ex opere operato* conferred supernatural grace, neither did it regard baptism as an empty form, which was merely required to conform to a regulation. It regarded it as the channel of supernatural grace to him whose spiritual condition made him the fit recipient of that grace.

Abrahams,[1] quoting the Midrash Rabba[2]: "He who makes a proselyte is as though he created him", observes that conversion was regarded as a rebirth, and the observation that the proselyte is as a new-born child occurs more than once in the Talmud.[3] Hence Calmet suggested[4] that this idea was already current in the time of Jesus, and that this may explain His surprised question to Nicodemus (Jn. 3: 10): "Art thou a teacher in Israel and understandest not these things?" when the latter was puzzled by His talk of a new birth. Be that as it may, there can be little doubt that proselytism was regarded as the entrance upon a wholly new life, and that the rite of baptism, or complete immersion in water, was a singularly fitting rite to symbolize this change. This symbolic meaning differentiated the baptism of proselytes from ordinary lustrations, which implied no change of heart, but merely the cleansing of the body from pollution—often from pollution in itself quite innocent, or even inevitable.[5]

That, quite apart from the baptism of proselytes, lustration

[1] *Op. cit.* p. 41.

[2] Gen. Rab. xxxix, 14, on Gen. 12: 5 (Eng. trans. by H. Freedman in Soncino *Midrash*, I, 1939, p. 324).

[3] Yeb. 22 a, 48 b, 62 a, 97 b (Goldschmidt's edn., pp. 69, 166, 216, 353; Eng. trans. by Slotki, I, pp. 131, 320, 414, II, p. 668); Bek. 47 a (Goldschmidt's edn., IX, 1935, p. 161; Eng. trans. by L. Miller and M. Simon in Soncino *Talmud*, 1948, p. 322).

[4] *Loc. cit.* p. 286.

[5] Marcel Simon (*Verus Israel*, 1948, p. 333) says: "Il (i.e. proselyte baptism) est identique aux ablutions lévitiques dans sa forme, rite d'immersion, et aussi dans ses effets; il élimine cette impureté rituelle qui, accidentelle chez Juif, est chez un *goy* congénitale. La pureté qu'il confère aux prosélytes ne leur est pas acquise une fois pour toutes. Il ne les dispense pas de recourir par la suite aux ablutions usuelles." This does not seem to me sufficiently to bring out the difference between proselyte baptism and ordinary lustrations. That proselyte baptism would be followed by ordinary lustrations is undeniable, but these would not require to be witnessed, and would have no initiatory significance.

had acquired a more than physical association and had come to symbolize inner purity and repentance, may be established by more than one reference.[1] Thus Josephus tells[2] how he became a disciple of Banus, who, *inter alia*, performed frequent ablutions in cold water for purity's sake, and the *Books of Adam and Eve* narrate how Adam and Eve expressed their penitence, after their banishment from Eden, by standing in the Tigris, with the water up to their necks, for some forty days.[3] Again, we read in one of the Jewish books of the *Sibylline Oracles:* "O ill-starred mortals, let not these things be, and drive not the great God to divers deeds of wrath; but have done with swords and moanings and killing of men, and deeds of violence, and wash your whole bodies in ever-running rivers, and, stretching your hands to heaven, seek forgiveness for your former deeds, and with praises ask pardon for your bitter ungodliness."[4]

Probably all of these passages come from the first century A.D., and they serve to show that even private lustration was then thought of as fittingly expressing repentance, and therefore as fundamentally a moral, even more than a physical, act. It can occasion no surprise, therefore, that the witnessed ablu-

---

[1] Among the Qumran sectaries it was seen that no waters could purify the man whose heart was evil and that no one could be cleansed without repentance (*Manual of Discipline*, col. V, lines 13 f.). On this passage cf. N. A. Dahl, *Interpretationes* (Mowinckel Festschrift), 1955, p. 43. In the light of this passage the statement of J. Starr, made before the Scrolls were discovered (*J.B.L.* LI, 1932, p. 233), that it is by no means evident that the practices of the Essenes were motivated by a desire to be free of sin rather than of levitical impurities, falls.

[2] *Life* 2 (11). For an account of various groups which practised ablutions on a scale surpassing that required by the Law, cf. J. Thomas, *Le Mouvement Baptiste en Palestine et Syrie*, 1935. It is unfortunate that these groups are now commonly called "Baptist" groups, since this name confuses the issues, and does not distinguish rites of initiation from customary rites.

[3] Cf. R. H. Charles, *Apocrypha and Pseudepigrapha*, II, 1913, p. 135; E. Kautzsch, *Apokryphen und Pseudepigraphen*, II, 1900, p. 512. There is some difference between the Greek and the Slavonic texts as to the number of days spent in the water by Eve, the one making it thirty-seven days and the other forty-four, but both agree in assigning forty days to Adam. The Slavonic text says that Adam "plunged himself altogether into the flood, even to the hairs of his head."

[4] Cf. Charles, *op. cit.* II, p. 396; Kautzsch, *op. cit.* II, p. 204. The translation quoted above is Lanchester's, in Charles.

tion of the proselyte, associated with catechism and exhortation, should have acquired a deeper significance than the purely ceremonial washing, whose form it had in part adopted.

IV

We may now turn to our final question, and consider the relation of this baptism of proselytes to John's baptism.[1] That this Jewish baptism had some features in common with John's

[1] Nothing has been said so far about the Qumran sectaries or the Essenes. When the present article was written the Dead Sea Scrolls had not been discovered, and the Essene question had not come to the fore anew as it has now. That the Qumran sect is to be identified with the Essenes at some stage in their history is so generally (though not universally) accepted that it may be taken for granted here (cf. *B.J.R.L.* XLIV, 1961–62, p. 121 [below p. 241]). Facile assumptions that John the Baptist had associations with the Essenes have been made by many writers (cf. W. H. Brownlee, in *The Scrolls and the New Testament*, ed. by K. Stendahl, 1957, p. 52; J. M. Allegro, *The Dead Sea Scrolls*, 1956, p. 164; C. T. Fritsch, *The Qumrân Community*, 1956, p. 112; A. Powell Davies, *The Meaning of the Dead Sea Scrolls*, 1957, p. 142; J. Daniélou, *Les Manuscrits de la Mer Morte et les Origines du Christianisme*, 1957, p. 15; A. S. Geyser, *N.T.* I, 1956, p. 71; O. Betz, *R.Q.* I, 1958–59, p. 222). These assumptions rest on no tangible evidence whatsoever (cf. *New Testament Essays* [T. W. Manson Memorial Volume], 1959, pp. 218 f.). On the basis of these assumptions it is concluded that John's baptism was derived from Qumran. In the Scrolls there is no reference anywhere to a water rite of initiation. Cf. J. Gnilka, *R.Q.* III, 1961–62, pp. 189 ff. Nor does Josephus mention such a rite in his account of the Essenes. He does, however, tell us that the Essenes daily bathed before eating (*War* II, VIII, 5 [129]). This is clearly more closely related to the ritual lustrations of the Old Testament, or to those of the sects in which these were multiplied (cf. above, p. 229 n.2), than to an initiatory rite of baptism. It is frequently assumed that the first of these lustrations would have a special character. This is doubtless true, since all who wished to join the sect had to wait for a period before being allowed to share in these lustrations on an equal footing with the members. The first lustration may therefore have had something of the character of a first communion among Christians. But this assumption is not the slightest evidence for an initiatory rite comparable with John's baptism or with Jewish proselyte baptism. For, as has been said above, Jewish proselyte baptism was a witnessed and administered rite. Nowhere in our sources on the Qumran sect or the Essenes is there any reference to such a rite. And lest we hasten to assume that Jewish proselyte baptism must have provided a model for the sect, let us note (a) that Jewish proselyte baptism was reserved for Gentiles who became Jews, whereas those who joined the sect were already Jews, and (b) that we are specifically told by Josephus (*War* II,

baptism, and also with Christian baptism, may be readily allowed.[1] All involved the complete immersion of the body in

viii, 5 [129]), that the Essenes girded their loins with linen cloths before bathing, and it is impossible to infer from this that the first lustration was administered to one who was completely nude, whereas we have seen above that complete nudity was essential to proselyte baptism, as it was to early Christian baptism.

For these reasons neither the Scrolls nor the accounts of the Essenes seem to me to be of any relevance to the subject of this paper. Cf. *New Testament Essays*, pp. 218 ff., and *B.J.R.L.* XLIV, 1961–62, pp. 141 ff. (below, pp. 263 ff.). N. A. Dahl (*Interpretationes* [Mowinckel Festschrift], 1955, p. 44) observes that we should be cautious not to make John into a member of the Essene sect and regards the two movements as independent and parallel to one another. J. Steinmann (*St. John the Baptist and the Desert Tradition*, Eng. trans. by M. Boyes, 1958, p. 59) makes the surprising statement: "The baptism which John was to give obviously recalls the Essene baptism." The choice of the word "obviously" is remarkable, since we nowhere have any record of an Essene baptismal rite of initiation at all. R. North (*The Bible in Current Catholic Thought* [Gruenthaner Memorial Volume], 1962, p. 130) holds "that it is impossible to conceive the Baptist preaching steadily a message so similar to that of Qumran in a desert area so adjacent, without being fully conscious of the kinship his message bore to theirs; nay more, without actually *dissociating* himself from them unless he was willing that this kinship should be acknowledged." That John knew of the Qumran sect is doubtless true, but since we nowhere have any record of an initiatory water rite of the Qumran sect or of the Essenes, and if there was such a rite it took place after a long probation and was a private rite for the admission of Jews to a kind of monastic life and was followed by daily lustrations, whereas John's baptism was administered without a long probation and in public to Jews and Gentiles, but did not lead to a monastic life and was not followed by daily lustrations, it is hard to see why he should have dissociated himself from them or why this should be needed.

[1] Cf. T. W. Manson, *The Mission and Message of Jesus*, 1937, p. 333: "The baptism of John can perhaps be most readily understood by reference to the Jewish baptism of proselytes." Similarly A. Gilmore, *Christian Baptism*, 1959, p. 74; cf. also E. Lohmeyer, *Johannes der Täufer*, 1932, p. 151. On the other hand, G. R. Beasley-Murray (*Baptism in the New Testament*, 1962, p. 42) declares that there is no point at which contact can be found between John's baptism and proselyte baptism. Similarly N. A. Dahl (*Interpretationes* [Mowinckel Festschrift], 1955, pp. 36 ff.) links John's baptism with ritual purifications as fitting a person to participate in worship. That this is an important aspect of its meaning may be allowed, but since Dahl agrees (p. 41) that proselyte baptism was a special variety of ritual ablution, it must have had some further meaning, or there would have been nothing special about it.

water, and probably in their original administration all were performed on completely nude persons. All were rites that were performed once for all, and all symbolized a change of heart and expressed a self-dedication to a new way of life.

It is not seldom stated that John's baptism and Christian baptism were moral purifications, and the baptism of proselytes a merely physical purification. Thus Plummer[1] says: "The legal washings merely cleansed from levitical uncleanness; his (i.e. John's) was a symbol and seal of moral purification"; Schürer[2] similarly says: "It is correct to say that the baptism of John and Christian baptism are essentially different from that of the Jewish proselytes, and that because the two former were not intended to impart *Levitical* purity, but merely to serve as a symbol of *moral* cleansing"; and Armitage Robinson[3]: "The Jewish baptisms were the outcome of the Jewish distinction between clean and unclean—a distinction which was done away by Christianity. Christian baptism is a purification, not from ceremonial, but from moral impurity"; while Lagrange[4] says of Jewish baptism, in contrast to John's baptism of repentance: "The bath was at most a preparation of the proselytes for circumcision;[5] it was not, within Judaism, a visible sign of repentance and renewal of life"; while finally Coppens[6] says: "With John the confession of sins was associated with the baptismal ablution. For the meaning and efficacy there was an even greater distinction between the two baptisms. John the Baptist did not secure for his disciples levitical purification, or bring new members into the religious community of Israel, but by the penitence of which baptism was the symbol, he prepared Israelites for the imminence of the messianic kingdom."

While it may be at once recognized that the observation of Coppens penetrates more closely to the essence of the matter than any short statement I have found elsewhere, in so far as it shares with the others the suggestion that the baptism of proselytes was merely ritual, it lies open with them to the

[1] *D.B.* I, p. 240 b.
[2] *Op. cit.* II, II, p. 324 n.
[3] *E. Bib.* I, 1899, col. 472.
[4] *L'Évangile de Jésus-Christ*, 1936, p. 59.
[5] This is a curious reversal of the order of circumcision and baptism.
[6] *Loc. cit.* cols. 893 f.

charge of unfairness. Abrahams[1] rightly took exception to such an idea, and the argument of the preceding section sufficiently answers it. Repentance belonged as intimately to the conditions of Jewish baptism as to John's, or to Christian baptism. For conversion was itself repentance, if it were sincere, and Judaism was as concerned that it should be sincere and pure in its motives as Christianity. Moore[2] well says: "For the Gentile to participate in this promise, as in all others, the indispensable condition is repentance, or conversion, in which he abandons his false religion for the true, the heathenish freedom of his way of life for obedience to the revealed will of God in his Law; in a word, becomes a proselyte to Judaism." Oesterley, too, recognizes that Judaism and Christianity are not to be contrasted in this respect, and observes[3] that "the renunciation of Satan at Christian baptism coincided precisely with the insistence on leading a moral life henceforth, which was a condition for Gentile proselytes to Judaism"; similarly, again, Harnack,[4] who said: "The Jewish synagogue had already drawn up a catechism for proselytes and made morality the condition of religion; it had already instituted a training for religion. Christianity took this up and deepened it."

In denying that the baptism of proselytes is to be characterized as ceremonial and not moral, and in stressing its ethical basis in repentance, however, I have no desire to minimize the real differences between the two baptisms. That there were fundamental differences I have already recognized, and it but remains to indicate their character. These differences would seem to have been threefold:

[1] Cf. Yeb. 47 a b (Goldschmidt's edn., pp. 160 f.; Eng. trans. by Slotki, pp. 310 f.). This passage is translated in Moore, *op. cit.* I, p. 333, and in Strack-Billerbeck, *op. cit.* I, pp. 110 f.

[2] *Op. cit.* I, p. 529. J. Starr (*J.B.L.* LI, 1932, p. 232) denies that any element of repentance is discernible anywhere in the rite of the proselyte bath, and claims the support of Moore for this view. What Moore emphasizes in the pages Starr refers to (pp. 332–34) is that proselyte baptism is not merely an ordinary ritual of purification, but an initiatory rite. In the passage I have cited Moore makes it clear that he recognized that repentance was the condition precedent.

[3] *The Jewish Background of the Christian Liturgy*, 1925, p. 142.

[4] *Mission and Expansion of Christianity*, Eng. trans. by J. Moffatt, I, 1908, pp. 391 f.

(a) The baptism of John was administered in public. The baptism of proselytes took place in the presence of witnesses, at least two or three in number, but there is nothing to suggest that it was a public ceremony. The Jewish leaders required adequate evidence that the novice had undergone the ceremony, but it was not in itself of the nature of a public confession of faith. In the case of the baptism of John, there is no evidence that the presence of any witness beside John himself was necessary to the validity of the baptism. It was a sacrament that in its essence concerned only a man and his Maker, and that did not need to be witnessed by others to achieve its fundamental purpose; yet, at the same time, it was a sacrament which did not seek to conceal itself from the eye of any man, but which became a public profession of his repentance and faith.

(b) It symbolized a change of life rather than a change of creed, and could be administered equally to Jews and non-Jews. It was not, so far as our records go, associated with any demand for circumcision, in the case of non-Jews, nor had it any relation to the sacrificial system of the Temple, as had the baptism of proselytes in the age of John. It was the sole rite in which John was interested, and it symbolized his sole interest in the bringing of men's conduct into accord with the will of God in all human relationships. The baptism of proselytes involved, as has been said, moral factors; but they were not the sole factors. The convert was reminded not alone of the major ethical demands of the law he was taking upon himself, but also of the minor regulations, to which he must henceforth conform. He entered both into a life of fellowship and high demands, and into a cultus. There is no evidence that John was interested in a cultus, or made cultic demands upon his disciples.

(c) The baptism of John, as Coppens rightly notes, differed most of all from the baptism of proselytes in its eschatological association.[1] It was the initiation ceremony, not alone into a new life, but into a new age, which John believed to be on the

---

[1] Starr (*loc. cit.*) also emphasizes the eschatological colouring in John's baptism, in contrast to Jewish proselyte baptism. Cf. also J. Gnilka, *R.Q.* III, 1961–62, pp. 204 f.

point of being established.[1] The old age was about to pass away in a divine judgment. The axe was already laid at the root of the tree of the existing world order. In its place a new world order would be established, and only children of the new age could have any place in it. The baptism of proselytes admitted strangers into an existing society, while the baptism of John aimed to prepare them for admission into a wholly new society —a society which did not yet exist, and which would not be created by them, but by divine intervention in the world, but for which they might, by response to the Baptist's message, be prepared.[2]

Just as Judaism had adopted the ordinary ritual lustration for the rite of the initiation of proselytes, and had filled it with a new meaning in baptism, so John adopted this rite of baptism and gave it a fresh meaning for his disciples.[3] It is neither necessary to deny his debt to Judaism, as it was so stoutly denied by a long succession of Christian theologians, particularly during the nineteenth century, nor to minimize the real difference between his baptism and Jewish baptism. On the other hand, it is unnecessary to depreciate Jewish baptism as unspiritual, in order to throw the baptism of John into greater relief.

---

[1] Cf. A. Schweitzer, *The Mysticism of Paul the Apostle*, Eng. trans. by W. Montgomery, 1931, pp. 230 ff.; E. Lohmeyer, *Johannes der Täufer*, 1932, pp. 153 ff.; H. G. Marsh, *The Origin and Significance of New Testament Baptism*, 1941, pp. 23 ff.; W. F. Flemington, *The New Testament Doctrine of Baptism*, 1948, p. 17; J. Schneider, *Die Taufe im Neuen Testament*, 1952, p. 23; A. Gilmore, *Christian Baptism*, 1959, p. 73; G. R. Beasley-Murray, *Baptism in the New Testament*, 1962, p. 32.

[2] On the meaning of John's baptism cf. J. Gnilka, *loc. cit.* pp. 202 ff.

[3] J. Gnilka (*loc. cit.* p. 206) is cautious about finding the source of John's baptism in proselyte baptism, and suggests that it may be a completely independent development on the part of John.

8

The Qumran sect and Christian Origins

8

THE QUMRAN SECT AND
CHRISTIAN ORIGINS[1]

O F ALL the questions raised by the study of the Dead Sea
Scrolls the most controversial is that of the influence of
the Qumran community on the Early Church, and the
significance of the Scrolls for the understanding of Christian
origins. That they are not without such significance most
scholars would agree, but the nature of the significance can be
established only by careful study of the evidence. Sometimes
the evidence of the New Testament has been conjecturally read
into the Scrolls to exaggerate the links, or the New Testament
has been "qumranized" to eliminate patent differences. Already in 1951 one writer in a French journal suffered himself
to be so far carried away as to write: "Henceforth . . . we *know*
that the Messiah of Galilee has contributed nothing, absolutely
nothing, which was not long familiar to those who believed in
the New Covenant",[2] i.e. to the members of the Qumran sect,
who are referred to in one of the works which they treasured as
those who entered into the New Covenant in the land of
Damascus.[3] How true or false this sweeping judgment is we
shall perhaps see better after we have looked at the evidence.

For our present purpose the pre-Christian origin of the
Qumran sect will be accepted without discussion. While there
are still a few writers who maintain that the Scrolls are of post-
Christian origin,[4] the overwhelming majority hold them to be

[1] First published in *B.J.R.L.* XLIV, 1961–62, pp. 119–56.

[2] Étiemble, in *Les Temps Modernes*, VI, no. 63 (January 1951), pp. 1291 f.
Cf. also P. Guth, *Le Figaro Littéraire*, February 24, 1951: "Entre 67 et 63
avant Jésus-Christ aurait été executé un premier Christ, presque semblable
au second."

[3] *Zadokite Work* IX. 28 (p. VIII, line 21, p. XIX, lines 33 f.); cf. VIII. 15 (p. VI,
line 19). E. Lohmeyer (*Diatheke*, 1913, p. 116) records that the word
"covenant" occurs thirty-five times in the *Zadokite Work*, and that this is
greater than the number of occurrences in any book of the Old Testament.

[4] S. Zeitlin continues to maintain that the Scrolls are mediaeval texts
written by illiterate authors. His articles will be found in many issues of the

pre-Christian. They do not agree as to the precise period in which the work of the Teacher of Righteousness and the founding of the sect lay, and various dates in the second or first century B.C. are favoured.[1] The disagreements here are of little significance for the subject of the present lecture. If the Qumran sectaries already belonged to the Jewish world in which Jesus and His disciples lived, the precise date of the origin of the sect is not material to the study of the influence they may have exercised on the younger faith. Professor Barthélemy observes that through the Scrolls we can for the first time make ourselves contemporary with our Lord.[2] In the Gospels we see the

Jewish Quarterly Review. J. L. Teicher, in a series of articles in the *Journal of Jewish Studies,* has argued that the Scrolls come from Ebionite Christians, for whom Paul was the Wicked Priest. H. E. del Medico, in *The Riddle of the Scrolls,* Eng. trans. by H. Garner, 1958, has assigned the Scrolls to a succession of post-Christian dates. Cecil Roth, in *The Historical Background of the Dead Sea Scrolls,* 1958, and in various articles, has maintained that the Scrolls were composed by Zealots, and that the Teacher of Righteousness was Menahem ben Judah, who died in A.D. 66, or his kinsman, Eleazar ben Jair. This view has been characterized by S. Sandmel (*J.B.L.* LXXXI, 1962, p. 12) as the one that "wins by a length in my opinion the race for the most preposterous of the theories about the Scrolls." G. R. Driver, who earlier favoured a later dating of the Scrolls (cf. *The Hebrew Scrolls from the Neighbourhood of Jericho and the Dead Sea,* 1951) has pushed back the date to the first century of our era, and now shares Dr. Roth's view of the Zealot origin of the sect (cf. *E.Th.L.* XXXIII, 1957, pp. 798 f.).

[1] For a discussion of this question by the present writer, cf. *B.J.R.L.* XL, 1957–58, pp. 114 f. Dates in the second century B.C., somewhat later than those proposed by the present writer, have been advanced by J. T. Milik (*Ten Years of Discovery in the Wilderness of Judaea,* Eng. trans. by J. Strugnell, 1959), F. M. Cross (*The Ancient Library of Qumrân,* 1958), and E. F. Sutcliffe (*The Monks of Qumran,* 1960). R. de Vaux (*L'Archéologie et les manuscrits de la Mer Morte,* 1961, p. 90) says that the identification of the Wicked Priest who was contemporary with the Teacher of Righteousness with Alexander Jannaeus or his successor would seem to be archaeologically excluded, and he favours the view that the Teacher of Righteousness was contemporary with Simon or Jonathan, and more probably the former. M. Black (*The Scrolls and Christian Origins,* 1961, p. 20) favours the identification of the Teacher with Onias III, for which the present writer has argued, and observes that "to all other theories it may be objected that the Founder of a movement so famous and influential as that of the Hasidim must have left some trace in our known historical records, and in no single case except that of Onias can this be reasonably claimed."

[2] *Scripture,* XII, No. 20 (October 1960), p. 119.

Pharisees and the Sadducees through the eyes of Jesus and the Evangelists, but in the Scrolls we are able to enter into the life and thought of a third group of Jews through their own writings. This third group is identified with the Essenes by most of the scholars who have discussed the Scrolls,[1] though there are a few who dispute the identification.[2]

The Essenes are described to us from the outside by writers of the first century of our era,[3] by Philo,[4] Pliny[5] and Josephus;[6] but if the Qumran sectaries were really the same as the Essenes,

[1] This identification has been advocated by none more vigorously than by A. Dupont-Sommer. For his latest statement of the case for this view, cf. *Les Écrits esséniens découverts près de la Mer Morte*, 1959, pp. 51 ff. Cf. also G. Vermes, "Essenes-Therapeutai-Qumran", *Durham University Journal*, June 1960, pp. 97 ff.

[2] Cf. M. H. Gottstein, *V.T.* iv, 1954, pp. 141 ff., where anti-Essene traits are found in the Scrolls. Cf. also B. Otzen, *S.Th.* vii, 1953, pp. 156 f. C. Rabin has argued for the identification of the sect with a Pharisaic group (*Qumran Studies*, 1957, pp. 53 ff.); J. L. Teicher for the identification with the Ebionites (see above, p. 239, n. 4; A. M. Habermann for the identification with the Sadducees (*Megilloth Midbar Yehuda*, 1959, pp. xv, 25 ff.; cf. *Ha-aretz*, March 5, 1956, and the criticism of J. M. Grintz, *ibid.* May 11, 1956; cf. also R. North, *C.B.Q.* xvii, 1955, pp. 164 ff.); C. Roth and G. R. Driver for the identification with Zealots (see above, p. 239, n.4). Before the discovery of the Scrolls some of these identifications of the sect had been proposed on the basis of the *Zadokite Work*. Thus L. Ginzberg (*M.G.W.J.* lvii, 1913, pp. 289 ff.), W. Staerk (*Die jüdische Gemeinde des Neuen Bundes in Damaskus*, 1922, p. 97), J. Jeremias (*Jerusalem zur Zeit Jesu*, 2nd edn., 1958, ii B, p. 131) and H. W. Beyer (in *Th.W.B.* ii, 1935, p. 614) had argued for the identification with the Pharisees; N. A. Dahl (*Das Volk Gottes*, 1941, p. 129) for the identification with an offshoot from the Pharisees; R. Leszynsky (*Die Sadduzäer*, 1912, pp. 142 ff.) for identification with the Sadducees; M.-J. Lagrange (*R.B.* xxi, 1912, p. 335, and *Le Judaisme avant Jésus-Christ*, 1931, pp. 332 f.) for identification with the Zealots. H. E. del Medico maintains that there never was a sect of Essenes (*Le Mythe des Esséniens*, 1958). K. H. Rengstorf argues that the Scrolls were a part of the Temple library, and that Qumran belonged to the Temple authorities (*Hirbet Qumran und die Bibliothek vom Toten Meer*, 1960).

[3] For other ancient references to the Essenes, cf. H. Mosbech, *Essæismen*, 1916, pp. 29 ff. Cf. also M. Black, *The Scrolls and Christian Origins*, 1961.

[4] *Quod omnis probus liber sit*, xii f. (79–91); cf. Eusebius, *Praeparatio Evangelica*, VIII, 11.

[5] *Hist. Nat.* V, xv (73). On Pliny's account of the Essenes cf. J.-P. Audet, *R.B.* lxviii, 1961, pp. 346 ff.

[6] *Antiq.* XIII, v, 9 (171–3), XVIII, i, 5 (18–22), *B.J.* II, viii, 2–13 (119–64).

we see them here from the inside. There are, indeed, some differences between the Essenes as described to us by these first century writers and the sect of the Scrolls as they are reflected in the texts we now have. It is on this ground that some deny that the sect is to be identified with the Essenes. Yet the similarities are so great that it is more probable that they should be identified, and the identification is often stated categorically.[1] The Essenes were a secret sect, whose teachings were not to be divulged outside the circle of its own members.[2] Some knowledge of its way of life and thought must have been known outside, or it could scarcely have attracted new members. That knowledge may not have been in all respects accurate, and this could account for some of the differences between what we read in the Scrolls and the accounts of the first century writers. More of the differences can probably be accounted for by the fact that in the Scrolls we see the sect at an earlier point in its life than that reflected in the first century writers.

The members of the sect cherished messianic expectations.[3] We know from the New Testament that such expectations were widespread, and in the second and first centuries B.C. a number of works were written in which such expectations are expressed. They are not always of a single pattern. In the New Testament we have no reference to any Messiah but the descendant of David. It is frequently stated that in the Scrolls we find the expectation of two Messiahs,[4] a Davidic and an Aaronic, and

[1] Cf. J. T. Milik, *R.B.* LXII, 1955, p. 497, where it is said to be "absolument certaine".

[2] Josephus, *B.J.* II, VIII, 7 (141); cf. *Manual of Discipline*, col. IX, line 17.

[3] Cf. A. S. van der Woude, *Die messianischen Vorstellungen der Gemeinde von Qumrân*, 1957; K. Schubert, *Biblische Zeitschrift*, N.F. II, 1957, pp. 177 ff. Cf. also E. L. Ehrlich, *Z.A.W.* LXVII, 1956, pp. 234 ff.

[4] Cf. M. Burrows, *A.Th.R.* XXXIV, 1952, pp. 202 ff., and *The Dead Sea Scrolls*, 1955, pp. 264 f.; G. Vermes, *Discovery in the Judean Desert*, 1956, p. 116; A. S. van der Woude, in *La Secte de Qumrân et les origines de Christianisme* (Recherches Bibliques IV), 1959, pp. 121 ff.; J. Liver, *H.T.R.* LII, 1959, pp. 149 ff. N. Walker (*J.B.L.* LXXVI, 1957, p. 58) suggests that the sectaries at first looked for two Messiahs, and that the fusing of the civil and priestly offices into one by John Hyrcanus led them to look for only one Messiah. It is very doubtful if the Qumran sect approved of the Hasmonaean assumption of the high priesthood, or would be influenced in this way (cf. M. Burrows, *More Light on the Dead Sea Scrolls*, 1958, p. 298).

in the *Manual of Discipline* we find the expression "the messiahs of Aaron and Israel".[1] We must, however, beware of reading

[1] *Manual of Discipline*, col. IX, line 11. In *Deux Manuscrits hébreux de la Mer Morte*, 1951, p. 33, del Medico rendered by the singular without comment, but in *The Riddle of the Scrolls*, p. 227, he has the plural. G. Lambert (*Le Manuel de Discipline du Désert de Juda*, 1951, p. 83) thought the plural strange, and so K. Schubert (*Z.K.Th.* LXXIV, 1952, p. 53). M. Black (*S.J.Th.* VI, 1953, p. 6 n., and *S.E.Å.* XVIII–XIX, 1955, pp. 87 ff.) renders by the singular, taking the final letter of the first word as *yodh compaginis* instead of the plural ending. As normally understood the passage speaks of the coming of the Prophet and the Messiahs of Aaron and Israel. W. H. Brownlee (*The Dead Sea Manual of Discipline*, 1951, pp. 35 f.) thought the Prophet was the Messiah, and his priestly and lay followers were referred to as "the anointed ones of Aaron and Israel" (this is rejected by P. Wernberg-Møller, *The Manual of Discipline*, 1957, p. 135). In the *Zadokite Work* there are several references to "the Messiah of Aaron and Israel" (IX. 10 [p. XIX, lines 10 f.], 21 [p. XX, line 1], XV. 4 [p. XII, lines 23 f.]). It has been supposed that the *Zadokite Work* originally had the plural in these cases, and that a late scribe changed it to the singular (so J. T. Milik, *Verbum Domini*, XXX, 1952, pp. 39 f.; cf. K. G. Kuhn, *S.N.T.*, p. 59), and J. Liver (*H.T.R.* LII, 1959, p. 152) so far outruns the evidence as to say that it is now proved conclusively that the singular is either a scribal error or an emendation. L. H. Silberman (*V.T.* V, 1955, pp. 77 ff.) questions the view that two Messiahs were expected, and thinks the sect simply looked forward to the time when the legitimate line of Aaronic priests and Davidic kings would be restored, and thinks the function of the prophet was to indicate the right persons to anoint them. Before the discovery of the *Manual of Discipline* M.-J. Lagrange (*R.B.* XXIII, 1914, p. 135) and F. F. Hvidberg (*Menigheden af den Nye Pagt i Damascus*, 1928, p. 281) had argued that the phrase in the *Zadokite Work* indicated that the Messiah would arise from the sect, and after the discovery of the *Manual* the present writer adopted this view and pointed out that the sect is described in its text as a "house of holiness for Israel . . . and a house of unity for Aaron" (col. IX, line 6), observing that "the sect itself therefore represents Israel and Aaron, and the title of the Messiah has reference to the character of the sect, and not his personal descent" (*The Zadokite Fragments and The Dead Sea Scrolls*, 1952, p. 41). This view is now adopted by W. S. LaSor (*V.T.* VI, 1956, pp. 425 ff.), who thinks that the proposed emendation of the text of the *Zadokite Work* is unnecessary. Cf. *Studies and Essays in honor of A. A. Neuman*, 1962, pp. 364 f., where LaSor maintains that the theory that the text of the *Zadokite Work* had been emended now falls to the ground, since a Qumran fragment of the *Zadokite Work* has the singular. W. H. Brownlee (*S.N.T.*, p. 45) regards the emendation as very risky, and so M. Delcor (*Revue Thomiste*, LVIII, 1958, pp. 762, 773). N. Wieder (*J.J.S.* VI, 1955, pp. 14 ff.) has argued that the Karaites believed in two Messiahs, and Delcor (*loc. cit.* p. 773) thinks it improbable that Karaite scribes would have altered the text to a singular.

into the term Messiah all that the term means for us. It simply means "an anointed one",[1] and in the Old Testament it is never used for the expected Davidic leader. It is used of kings and priests, and even of Cyrus.[2] But by the beginning of the Christian era it had become a technical term for the deliverer whose advent was awaited. It was not unnatural that an anointed High Priest, alongside the kingly Messiah, should be thought of, and especially in such a sect as that of Qumran, in which the priests had the highest place. They could therefore speak of "the anointed ones of Aaron and Israel". One of the texts, to which we shall return, makes it plain that the Aaronic anointed one should have precedence over the Davidic.[3] Such a conception appears to be found also in the *Testaments of the Twelve Patriarchs*.[4] The *Zadokite Work*, which has been known since the beginning of this century and which is now generally recognized to have emanated from the Qumran sect, shows that there was an expectation that the Messiah would come within forty years of the death of the Teacher of Righteousness.[5] There

[1] Silberman (*loc. cit.*) objected to the use of the term "Messiah" here, because of its misleading associations, and so LaSor (*V.T., loc. cit.*). On the messianism of the Qumran sect, cf. LaSor, *Studies and Essays in honor of A. A. Neuman*, pp. 343 ff.

[2] Isa. 45: 1.

[3] See below, pp. 266 ff. Cf. J. Gnilka, "Die Erwartung des messianischen Hohenpriesters in den Schriften von Qumran und im Neuen Testament", *R.Q.* II, 1960, pp. 395 ff.

[4] Cf. G. R. Beasley-Murray, *J.T.S.* XLVIII, 1949, pp. 5 ff. This view is accepted by B. Otzen (*S.Th.* VII, 1954, pp. 151 ff.) and A. S. van der Woude (*Die messianischen Vorstellungen*, pp. 194 ff.). Cf. also J. Liver, *H.T.R.* LII, 1959, pp. 163 ff. It is rejected by A. J. B. Higgins (*V.T.* III, 1953, p. 330), who maintains that all the passages indicate is the superiority of the priesthood to the kingship. E. J. Bickerman (*J.B.L.* LXIX, 1950, p. 252) declares "the doctrine of the Messiah from the tribe of Levi allegedly professed by the author" to be "a figment, created by modern readers of the work".

[5] In IX. 21 (p. xx, line 1) there is a reference to the period from the day when the Unique Teacher was gathered in to the coming of the Messiah, while in IX. 39 (p. xx, lines 13 ff.) we are told that from the day when the Unique Teacher was gathered in until the consuming of all the men of war who returned with the Man of Falsehood would be about forty years. The Unique Teacher, or possibly the Teacher of the Community (cf. S. M. Stern, *J.B.L.* LXIX, 1950, p. 24; L. Rost, *Th.L.Z.* LXXVIII, 1953, col. 144; G. Molin, *Die Söhne des Lichtes*, 1954, p. 57), is generally identified with the Teacher of Righteousness (so R. H. Charles, *Apocrypha and Pseudepigrapha*,

are some who think that the Teacher of Righteousness was expected himself to rise from the dead and to be the Messiah,[1] though there is little clear evidence for this[2] and some evidence, to which we shall come, against it. Since the Teacher of

II, 1913, p. 800; G. Hölscher, *Z.N.W.* XXIX, 1929, p. 39; A. Dupont-Sommer, *The Dead Sea Scrolls*, Eng. trans. by E. Margaret Rowley, 1952, p. 63), and it is probable that the destruction of the men of war was associated with the coming of the Messiah (cf. the present writer's *The Relevance of Apocalyptic*, 2nd edn., 1947, p. 76). It should be noted that L. Rost (*loc. cit.* cols. 143 ff.) and T. H. Gaster (*The Scriptures of the Dead Sea Sect*, 1957, pp. 35 f.) differentiate the Unique Teacher from the Teacher of Righteousness, while C. Rabin (*The Zadokite Documents*, 2nd edn., 1958, p. 37 n.) does not commit himself.

[1] So A. Dupont-Sommer, *op. cit.* pp. 34 f., 44, *Les Écrits esséniens découverts près de la Mer Morte*, 1959, p. 123 n.; cf. C. T. Fritsch, *The Qumrān Community*, 1956, p. 82. This view is rejected by J. van der Ploeg (*Bi. Or.* VIII, 1951, pp. 12 f.), J. Bonsirven (*Études*, CCLXVIII, 1951, p. 216), R. de Vaux (*La Vie Intellectuelle*, April, 1951, p. 67), M. Delcor (*R.B.* LVIII, 1951, pp. 521 ff.), R. Tamisier (*Scripture*, V, 1952, pp. 37 f.), M. Black (*S.E.Å.* XVIII, 1955, pp. 85 f., and *The Scrolls and Christian Origins*, 1961, p. 160 n.), G. Molin (*Die Söhne des Lichtes*, 1954, p. 148), and F. F. Bruce (*The Modern Churchman*, N.S. IV, 1960–61, p. 51). Before the discovery of the Scrolls, in discussing the *Zadokite Work*, the view that the Teacher was expected to rise and be the Messiah had been advanced by S. Schechter (*Fragments of a Zadokite Work*, 1910, p. XIII; cf. G. Margoliouth [*Expositor*, 8th ser., II, 1911, p. 517]), and rejected by G. F. Moore (*H.T.R.* IV, 1911, p. 342), J. A. Montgomery (*B.W.*, N.S. XXXVIII, 1911, p. 376), and J. B. Frey (*S.D.B.* I, 1928, p. 397). J. D. Amusin (*The Manuscripts of the Dead Sea*, 1960, p. 251) thinks the Teacher was expected to return, and that this expectation later gave rise to the myth of the risen and returning Christ. This is surely rather much to hang on a single obscure and doubtful passage! (Amusin's book is in Russian, and therefore inaccessible to me. I am indebted to the author for a copy, and to Mr. Arie Rubinstein for access to its contents.)

[2] Cf. J. van der Ploeg, *The Excavations at Qumran*, Eng. trans. by K. Smyth, 1958, p. 203: "There is no mention in the Qumran writings of any resurrection of the Teacher or of his second coming as Judge. That he 'appeared' after his death to Jerusalem when Pompey took it in 63 B.C. is something that Dupont-Sommer invented." Cf. K. Smyth, *The Furrow*, April 1957, p. 222: "Dupont-Sommer reached this result by remoulding a few lines of the Habacuc Commentary nearer to his heart's desire, with the help of mis-translations, mis-readings of text, and the insertion of his own matter into lacunae." Cf. also J. Carmignac, *R.Q.* I, 1958–59, pp. 235 ff. On the rendering of the word "appeared" in *Habakkuk Commentary*, col. XI, line 7, cf. Carmignac, *Le Docteur de Justice et Jésus-Christ*, 1957, pp. 38 ff.

Righteousness was a priest,[1] if such an expectation were held he would be thought of as an Aaronic Messiah. Already, before the discovery of the Qumran Scrolls, George Foot Moore, in discussing the *Zadokite Work*, had said that if the author had intended to identify the Teacher of Righteousness with the coming Messiah, he would have expressed so singular and significant a belief unmistakably.[2]

It is already clear that the messianism of the Qumran sect was very different from that of the New Testament. For the Church Jesus was the Messiah, and it had no place for a second. The thought of His Messiahship was drawn from the Old Testament and not from Qumran. He was believed to be the Davidic Messiah, and it is hard to suppose that for Jesus or His followers any priestly Messiah was contemplated as having precedence over Him. No such idea appears anywhere in the New Testament.

It is true that in the Epistle to the Hebrews the work of Christ is interpreted in priestly terms. But the priest is not a second figure who stands beside and above Jesus. He is identified with Jesus. Nor is the priesthood of Jesus, as it is set forth in this Epistle, an Aaronic priesthood.[3] It is specifically dissociated from such a priesthood, and described as a priesthood after the order of Melchizedek. The Qumran sectaries called their priestly members Sons of Zadok,[4] and it is probable that by this

---

[1] Cf. *P.E.Q.* LXXXVI, 1954, pp. 69 ff., where in a fragment of a commentary on Ps. XXXVII (col. II, line 15) published by J. M. Allegro, we find a reference to "the Priest, the Teacher of Ri[ghteousness]". Cf. also *Habakkuk Commentary*, col. II, line 8.

[2] *H.T.R.* IV, 1911, p. 342.

[3] Cf. F. F. Bruce, *N.T.S.* II, 1955–56, pp. 180 ff.

[4] *Zadokite Work* VI. 2 (p. IV, line 3), *Manual of Discipline* col. V, line 2, *The Rule of the Congregation*, col. I, lines 2, 24, col. II, line 3 (Barthélemy and Milik, *Qumran Cave I*, 1955, p. 110), *Benedictions*, col. III, line 22 (*ibid.* p. 124). In the *Manual of Discipline*, col. IX, line 14, we find *bny hṣdwḳ* (P. Wernberg-Møller, in *The Manual of Discipline*, 1957, p. 42, proposed to read here *hṣdyḳ*, but in *R.Q.* II, 1960, p. 233, he withdraws this reading; cf. M. Martin, *The Scribal Character of the Dead Sea Scrolls*, II, 1958, p. 443) where the use of the article is strange if the meaning is "sons of Zadok" (so rendered by W. H. Brownlee, *The Dead Sea Manual of Discipline*, 1951, p. 36; K. Schubert, *Z.K.Th.* LXXIV, 1952; H. Bardtke, *Die Handschriftenfunde am Toten Meer*, 2nd edn., 1953, p. 102; P. Wernberg-Møller, *op. cit.* p. 27; E. F. Sutcliffe, *The Monks of Qumran*, 1960, p. 154). It has

name they indicated their rejection of any other High Priest than one of the family of Zadok, who was the Jerusalem priest of the time of David and Solomon. They did not offer sacrifices in the Temple,[1] and it is probable that this was because they did not recognize the priesthood there as in the true line of succession from Zadok, and not because they rejected the Temple cultus in itself.[2] They looked for a rightful priest, and in their organization the priests were accorded the place of honour.[3] Jesus was not a priest, and did not function as such in the company of His disciples. When the Epistle to the Hebrews presents His work in priestly terms, His priesthood is exercised in a single act, and it takes place not in the Temple but on Calvary, where He offered Himself.

We know very little of the life of the Teacher of Righteousness. The references to him in the Scrolls indicate that he lived in stormy times and was opposed by one who is called the Wicked Priest, who persecuted him. The *Zadokite Work* speaks

frequently been said, by the present writer among others, that the members of the sect called themselves the "sons of Zadok", but Wernberg-Møller shows (*V.T.* III, 1953, pp. 311 ff.; cf. *The Manual of Discipline*, p. 90) that the "sons of Zadok" are conceived as the priestly members of the sect as opposed to the lay members (so also J. M. Grintz, *Ha-aretz*, May 11, 1956).

[1] There are references to sacrifices in *Zadokite Work* XIII, 27, XIV. 1 (p. XI, lines 17–21), which probably dates from the time before the breach with the Temple was complete. But the later texts do not speak of such sacrifices being offered. On Josephus's statement about the Essenes and sacrifice see below, p. 252, n. 4. On the significance of the bones of animals found at Qumran, cf. R. de Vaux, *R.B.* LXIII, 1956, pp. 549 f., and J. van der Ploeg, *J.S.S.* II, 1957, pp. 172 f.

[2] Cf. J. M. Baumgarten, *H.T.R.* XLVI, 1953, pp. 153 f.; J. Carmignac, *R.B.* LXIII, 1956, pp. 524 ff.; M. Burrows, *More Light on the Dead Sea Scrolls*, p. 258; K. Schubert, *The Dead Sea Community*, Eng. trans. by J. W. Doberstein, 1959, p. 56; E. F. Sutcliffe, *op. cit.* pp. 82 f.; also cf. H. Mosbech, *Essæismen*, 1916, pp. 263 ff. M. O. Cullmann (*E.T.* LXXI, 1959–60, p. 39) thinks it likely that the sectaries considered their separation from Jerusalem was only temporary, but says (pp. 39 f.): "Although in principle the specific rites of Qumran were not at all considered to be *opposed* to the bloody sacrifices, the long exclusive practice of their particular rites, baptism and the sacred meal, and the long abstention from sacrifices must sooner or later have given birth to the idea that sacrifices were not at all pleasing to God."

[3] Cf. *Manual of Discipline*, cols. V, lines 2 f., IX, line 7.

of his being "gathered in",[1] and this expression is used in the Old Testament for natural death.[2] There is an obscure passage in the *Habakkuk Commentary* which is believed by many scholars to mean that he suffered martyrdom.[3] In another text there is a reference to an enemy of the sect, called the Lion of Wrath, who hung men alive.[4] It is probable that this refers to crucifixion, and it has therefore been held that the Teacher of Righteousness was crucified,[5] and thus suffered the same death as Jesus. If this were established beyond any doubt, it would have no special significance. Many others had been crucified before Jesus, and not a few had suffered this death as martyrs for their faith. In fact, the text that mentions the crucifixions does not mention the Teacher of Righteousness. How he died we have no means of knowing.

More important than the manner of his death is the significance attached to it by his followers. In the New Testament the death and resurrection of Jesus do not figure each in a single,

---

[1] *Zadokite Work* IX. 21 (p. xx, line 1), IX. 39 (p. xx, line 14).

[2] For a careful study of the use of this expression, cf. B. Alfrink, *O.T.S.* v, 1948, pp. 118 ff. Cf. also G. R. Driver in *Studies and Essays in honor of A. A. Neuman*, 1962, pp. 137 ff. K. Schubert (*Z.K.Th.* LXXIV, 1952, p. 25) holds that the language in the *Zadokite Work* implies the natural death of the Teacher, and so J. Carmignac (*Le Docteur de Justice et Jésus-Christ*, 1957, p. 55), J. Bourke (*Blackfriars*, XL, 1959, p. 165), and M. Delcor (*Revue Thomiste*, LIX, 1959, p. 145). J. van der Ploeg (*The Excavations at Qumran*, p. 202) says: "That the Teacher was put to death is an assumption that still lacks confirmation from the texts."

[3] *Habakkuk Commentary*, col. XI, line 5. Several writers have denied Dupont-Sommer's interpretation of this passage. Cf. E. Cavaignac, *R.H.R.* CXXXVIII, 1950, pp. 156 f.; M. Delcor, *Essai sur le Midrash d'Habacuc*, 1951, p. 44; M. H. Segal, *J.B.L.* LXX, 1951, p. 142; R. Tamisier, *Scripture*, V, 1952–53, p. 38; K. Elliger, *Studien zum Habakuk-Kommentar vom Toten Meer*, 1953, pp. 281 ff. For Dupont-Sommer's defence of his view, cf. *V.T.* I, 1951, pp. 200 f. C. T. Fritsch (*op. cit.* p. 81) accepts the view that the Teacher of Righteousness came to a violent end at the hands of the Wicked Priest.

[4] Cf. J. M. Allegro, *J.B.L.* LXXV, 1956, pp. 89 ff.

[5] Cf. Allegro, Letter to *The Times*, March 20, 1956 (cf. also *Time Magazine*, February 6, 1956) and *The Dead Sea Scrolls*, 1956, pp. 99 f. Allegro believes the Teacher of Righteousness was crucified by Alexander Jannaeus. E. Stauffer, on the other hand, identifies the Teacher with Jose ben Joezer, who was crucified in Maccabaean times (*Z.R.G.G.* VIII, 1956, pp. 250 ff.).

obscure passage, but throughout the whole, and they are fundamental for the understanding of the entire theology of the Church from its earliest days. Whatever the Church derived from Qumran it did not derive this. Even if the Teacher of Righteousness was in fact crucified and was expected to rise from the dead, his death and resurrection did not dominate the thought and faith of the Qumran sect,[1] and no one could read the Scrolls and the New Testament without being at once aware that they move in two different theological worlds.[2] By its Christology the New Testament stands in the sharpest contrast with the Scrolls.[3]

[1] There is a reference in the *Habakkuk Commentary* (col. VIII, lines 2 f.) to those who have faith in the Teacher of Righteousness, and this has been interpreted to mean that the Teacher was the object of saving faith (cf. Dupont-Sommer, *The Dead Sea Scrolls*, p. 44; C. T. Fritsch, *op. cit.* p. 82). Again, it will be observed, much is being based on a single passage, which does not naturally bear the meaning placed on it. Cf. O. Cullmann, *S.N.T.*, p. 23: "this faith in the Teacher of Righteousness is not, as for Paul, faith in an *act of atonement* accomplished in the *death* of Christ for the forgiveness of sins. In fact, the concept of faith itself is different, containing nothing of the sense of opposition to the works of the law." The meaning here is nothing more than *fidelity* to the Teacher of Righteousness, and it is so rendered by K. Elliger, *Studien zum Habakuk-Kommentar vom Toten Meer*, 1953, p. 196: "ihrer Treue zu dem Lehrer der Gerechtigkeit" (cf. H. Bardtke, *op. cit.* p. 128). Cf. also J. van der Ploeg, *The Excavations at Qumran*, p. 202; E. F. Sutcliffe, *The Monks of Qumran*, p. 118. M. Burrows (*More Light on the Dead Sea Scrolls*, p. 121) says: "Faith in the teacher means confidence in his teaching, not in a work of atonement accomplished by his death"; K. G. Kuhn (*S.N.T.*, p. 78) observes: "In the Qumran texts we find no trace of such an ultimately redemptive significance of a historical person." Cf. also H. Kosmala, *Hebräer-Essener-Christen*, 1959, pp. 390 f.

[2] Cf. Burrows, *op. cit.* pp. 66 f.: "No objective historian, whatever may be his personal belief about the resurrection of Jesus, can fail to see the decisive difference here in the beliefs of the two groups. What for the community of Qumran was at most a hope was for the Christian an accomplished fact, the guarantee of their hopes."

[3] Fritsch (*op. cit.* p. 82) says the Teacher of Righteousness must have been regarded as more than human. In this he is following Dupont-Sommer, who goes so far as to suppose that the Teacher was held to have been pre-existent as a divine being, and became incarnate (*The Dead Sea Scrolls*, p. 34). This assumption is based on nothing more substantial than a reference to the Teacher's "body of flesh". Had the Teacher really been thought of as an incarnate divine being, we should have expected some clearer indication of this belief in the writings of the sect. Yet nowhere does it figure in any of

It has been conjectured, though without the slightest evidence, that Jesus lived for some years amongst the Qumran sectaries.[1] Professor F. C. Grant characterizes this as fantastic nonsense.[2] The idea that Jesus derived His teaching from the sect is one that cannot survive the most superficial examination.[3] Professor Stauffer has argued that many of the teachings of Jesus were directed expressly against the sectaries,[4] and that their influence on the later writers of the New Testament was greater than on Jesus Himself.[5] For instance, in the New Testament we read: "Ye have heard that it was said 'You shall love your neighbour and hate your enemy'. But I say unto you 'Love your enemies and pray for those who persecute you'."[6] It has often been pointed out by commentators that in the Old Testament we do not find the command to hate enemies.[7] In

their texts, or in any of the first century accounts of the Essenes. It is derived not from the literature of the sect, but from the New Testament, and then attributed to them. Cf. J. Carmignac, *Le Docteur de Justice et Jésus-Christ*, pp. 37 ff.

[1] See F. C. Grant, *Ancient Judaism and the New Testament*, 1960, p. 18, where an unnamed source for the suggestion is referred to. Cf. B. Hjerl-Hansen, *R.Q.* 1, 1958–59, pp. 495 ff. The suggestion had already been rejected long ago by J. B. Lightfoot, *Saint Paul's Epistle to the Colossians and to Philemon*, 1900, pp. 395 ff.

[2] *Op. cit.* p. 19; cf. p. 133, where he speaks of "the preposterous inferences and hypotheses which many persons have advocated since the Dead Sea Scrolls were discovered—inferences which sometimes openly betray their propounders' unfamiliarity with ancient Judaism as well as with New Testament history and exegesis." Cf. also Cullmann, *S.N.T.*, p. 18: "That Jesus was . . . a member of the Essene Community is pure and groundless speculation."

[3] Cf. M. Burrows, *More Light on the Dead Sea Scrolls*, pp. 88 f.; G. Graystone, *The Dead Sea Scrolls and the Originality of Christ*, 1956, p. 89. D. Flusser (*Aspects of the Dead Sea Scrolls* [Scripta Hierosolymitana, IV], 1958, pp. 215 f.) says: "The synoptic Gospels show few and comparatively unimportant parallels to the Sectarian writings. This seems to indicate that the Scrolls will not contribute much to the understanding of the personality of Jesus and of the religious world of his disciples."

[4] Cf. *Die Botschaft Jesu damals und heute*, 1959, pp. 13 ff.

[5] *Ibid.* p. 16.

[6] Mt. 5: 43 f.

[7] Cf. Strack-Billerbeck, *Kommentar zum Neuen Testament*, I, 1922, p. 353; E. Percy, *Die Botschaft Jesu*, 1953, p. 153; K. Schubert, *S.N.T.*, p. 120.

the Scrolls, however, we do find such a command.[1] Whether Jesus had the Qumran community in mind or not when He uttered such sayings,[2] it is certain that His attitude on many questions was quite other than that of the sectaries.[3] The contrast between His attitude to Sabbath observance and theirs is particularly notable. Jesus was criticized by the Pharisees for what they regarded as His laxity. But the Scrolls teach a sabbatarianism that was much more strict than that of the Pharisees, and the members of the sect would have been shocked by the saying of Jesus: "The sabbath was made for man, not man for the sabbath."[4] When Jesus was watched to see if He would heal the man with a withered hand on the Sabbath, He said "What man of you, if he has one sheep and it falls into a pit on the sabbath, will not lay hold of it and lift it out? Of how much more value is a man than a sheep!"[5] According to the teaching of the Qumran sect neither animal nor man should be so helped on the Sabbath. In the *Zadokite Work* we read: "No one should help an animal to foal on the sabbath day. And if it should drop (its foal)[6] into a well or a pit, let not one raise it on the sabbath day . . . And if a man falls

---

[1] *Manual of Discipline,* cols. I, line 10, IX, lines 21 f.; cf. col. X, lines 19 f. Cf. P. Guilbert, *Les Textes de Qumran,* I, 1961, p. 23: "L'expression non biblique de Matthieu 5, 43 peut avoir vu le jour dans une atmosphère semblable à celle de la secte, où la haine des ennemis, c'est-à-dire des infidèles, est exprimée en propres termes." Cf. also Morton Smith, *H.T.R.* XLV, 1952, pp. 71 ff. But cf. E. F. Sutcliffe, *R.Q.* II, 1960, pp. 345 ff., where it is observed that there was to be no private hatred or revenge, and that the hatred enjoined in the Qumran texts was the hatred of wicked men, as in the Old Testament. There can be little doubt, however, that the enemies of the sect were regarded as wicked men.

[2] K. Schubert (*S.N.T.,* p. 121) says Mt. 5: 43 f. is to be understood within the framework of Jesus's encounter with Essene concepts. J. D. Amusin (*op. cit.* pp. 253 f.) thinks this passage from Matthew and also 1 Jn. 2: 9 ff. may have been directed against the Qumran sect.

[3] Cf. Cullmann, *S.N.T.,* pp. 30 f.

[4] Mk. 2: 27.

[5] Mt. 12: 11 f.; cf. Lk. 14: 5. Amusin (*op. cit.* pp. 255 f.) thinks these passages were polemically directed against the Qumran sectaries.

[6] This follows the rendering of C. Rabin (*The Zadokite Documents,* p. 56) and Gaster (*op. cit.* p. 87), since the verb appears to be Hiph'il. R. H. Charles (*Apocrypha and Pseudepigrapha,* II, p. 827) renders "if it falls", and so Sutcliffe (*op. cit.* p. 144; cf. p. 120).

into a place of water or into some other place, let not one raise
him[1] with a ladder or rope or instrument."[2]

In the *Zadokite Work* there are references to offerings on the
altar,[3] but Philo tells us the Essenes did not offer sacrifices in
the Temple,[4] and in the sectarian texts found at Qumran there

[1] This follows the rendering of Charles (*loc. cit.* p. 828) and Sutcliffe (*op. cit.* p. 144). Rabin (*op. cit.* p. 56) for "let not one raise him" renders "from which one cannot come up, let any man bring him up", and thus conjecturally supplies וֹהַלֵי after יֵעֲלֶה .Cf. Vermes, *The Dead Sea Scrolls in English*, 1962, p. 113: "Should any man fall into water or fire, let him be pulled out with the aid of a ladder". Gaster (*op. cit.* p. 87) does not render the negative, but emends it to yield the noun "darkness", i.e. "a place of darkness". But the context, which in a series of sayings has the negative with a verb, stating a prohibition, favours a similar construction here. J. Maier (*Die Texte vom Toten Meer*, I, 1960, p. 61) renders: "Ein lebendiger Mensch, der ins Wasser oder sonst wo hineinfällt, den darf man nicht mit einer Leiter, einem Strick oder einem (anderen) Gerät herausholen."

[2] *Zadokite Work*, XIII. 22–6 (p. XI, lines 13–17).

[3] *Zadokite Work*, XIII. 27, XIV. 1 (p. XI, lines 17–21).

[4] *Quod omnis probus liber sit*, XII (75). In Whiston's translation of Josephus, *Antiq.* XVIII, I, 5 (19) we find a similar statement that the Essenes did not offer sacrifices, but the text is here uncertain. The Greek manuscripts, all of which are late, do not contain the negative, and say that they sent offerings to the Temple and offered sacrifices with superiority of purificatory rites, for which reason they were excluded from the common court of the Temple and offered their sacrifices by themselves. The Greek *Epitoma*, which is attested at a date earlier than surviving manuscripts of the *Antiquities*, and the Latin rendering of the *Antiquities*, which was made in the sixth century, have the negative (cf. J. Thomas, *Le Mouvement baptiste en Palestine et Syrie*, 1935, pp. 12 f.n.; also Sutcliffe, *op. cit.* pp. 230 f.). The rendering of Whiston is accepted by Lightfoot (*op. cit.* pp. 369 f.), H. Mosbech (*Essæismen*, 1916, pp. 263 ff.), J. M. Baumgarten (*H.T.R.* XLVI, 1953, p. 155), Burrows (*The Dead Sea Scrolls*, 1955, p. 285), and D. H. Wallace (*Th.Z.* XII, 1957, pp. 334 ff.), and it is generally believed that the Essenes did not offer sacrifices. Cf. D. Flusser, *Aspects of the Dead Sea Scrolls*, 1958, p. 235: "As the Qumran covenanters thought that the Temple was polluted, they could not take part in the Temple service of their time. This inability to offer real sacrifices engendered an ambivalent attitude to the sacrificial rites." Fritsch (*op. cit.* p. 108) says the Qumran community evidently believed that sacrifices were useless. This goes too far. Cf. J. Carmignac, *R.B.* LXIII, 1956, pp. 530 f., where it is argued that the sect did not repudiate sacrifices on principle. It is hard to see how a sect which set so high a value on the Law could reject them on principle. Mlle. A. Jaubert, *N.T.S.* VII, 1960–61, p. 17, thinks the sectaries frequented the Temple, and notes that one of the gates of the Temple bore their name. (Cf. M.-J.

are no references to animal sacrifices. [1] This was probably, as has been already said, due to the fact that the Jerusalem priesthood was not recognized by the sectaries as legitimate, [2] and on this account they had nothing to do with the Temple or its sacrifices. Jesus and His disciples did not boycott the Temple, but visited it and He taught there. When He cleansed a leper He told him to go to the Temple and offer the prescribed sacrifice. [3] The Early Church did not keep away from the Temple, [4] and when Paul made a vow he fulfilled it by sacrificing in the Temple. [5]

The members of the sect of the Scrolls had each his place in the meetings of the sect, [6] and every year there was a review of the conduct of all the members, leading to advancement to a

Lagrange, *Le Judaïsme avant Jésus-Christ*, 1931, pp. 318 f.) This does not necessarily mean that they offered sacrifices, and while the uncertain statement of Josephus cannot be pressed, the unambiguous statement of Philo should not be set aside. J. M. Allegro (*The Dead Sea Scrolls*, p. 100) thinks the sect had its own altar at Qumran and there offered sacrifice, and that the Teacher of Righteousness was in the act of sacrificing when the Wicked Priest came to Qumran. But, as Burrows (*More Light on the Dead Sea Scrolls*, p. 366) says, this is quite incredible, since it would be a violation of the Law which the sect was pledged to obey. F. C. Conybeare (in *D.B.* i, p. 769 b) suggests that the passage in Josephus does not necessarily mean that they sent animal sacrifices to the Temple, even if the negative is omitted, but argues that the sacrifices they offered by themselves were the sacrifices of a devout and reverent mind, which Philo says they offered (*Quod omnis probus liber sit*, xii [75]). Cf. also Lucetta Mowry, *The Dead Sea Scrolls and the Early Church*, 1962, pp. 219 ff.

[1] Cf. Burrows, *The Dead Sea Scrolls*, p. 237: "The Manual of Discipline makes no reference at all to the temple or to sacrifice except in obviously figurative expressions." S. E. Johnson goes beyond the evidence when he roundly says that in the *Manual* the existing Temple cultus was repudiated (*S.N.T.*, p. 136). Cf. M. Delcor, *Revue Thomiste*, LVIII, 1958, p. 759. In the *War Scroll* there is a reference to the future offering of sacrifice (col. II, lines 5 f.). S. Holm-Nielsen points out that in the *Hymns Scroll* there is a complete absence of references to the Temple and Temple worship (*Hodayot: Psalms from Qumran*, 1960, p. 309).

[2] To this it should be added that the objection of the Qumran sectaries to the official calendar (see below pp. 270 ff.) meant that in their eyes the Jerusalem sacrifices at all the festivals were offered on the wrong days, and were therefore invalid.

[3] Mt. 8: 4, Mk. 1: 44, Lk. 5: 14.
[4] Ac. 2: 46, 3: 1 ff., 5: 20 ff., 42.
[5] Ac. 21: 26 ff.
[6] *Manual of Discipline*, cols. V, lines 20 ff., VI, lines 4 f., 8 ff.

higher place or relegation to a lower.[1] The disciples of Jesus were similarly interested in questions of precedence, and we read that as they walked in the way they argued with one another about their claims to the highest place.[2] That Jesus had nothing of the Qumran attitude to such a question is beyond doubt. He rebuked His disciples for even discussing it, and said: "If anyone would be first, he must be last of all and servant of all."[3]

On the subject of ritual ablutions, the attitude of Jesus stands in complete contrast to that of the sect. There are references in the Scrolls to purificatory waters, though it is recognized that no waters can purify the man who does not obey the laws of God and submit himself to the discipline of the sect.[4] From Josephus we learn that the Essenes bathed the whole body daily before partaking of food.[5] While this is not stated explicitly in the Scrolls, it is probable that the members of the sect followed this practice if the sect is to be identified with the Essenes, and likely that the statement in the *Manual of Discipline* that those who sought to enter the sect could not touch "the purity of the many" before the last year of their probation[6] is an allusion to it. The "purity of the many" is believed by many scholars to allude to the waters of purification in which the members daily bathed.[7] That Jesus and His disciples did not follow such a practice is clear from the fact that when the disciples were criticized for not even washing their hands before eating, Jesus defended them.[8] Moreover, in the Johannine account of the Last Supper we read only of the washing of the disciples' feet by Jesus,[9] and not of the bathing of their body.

[1] *Manual of Discipline*, col. II, lines 19 ff.

[2] Mk. 9: 33 ff.; cf. Lk. 9: 46 ff.

[3] Mk. 9: 35.

[4] *Manual of Discipline*, col. V, lines 13 f.

[5] *B.J.* II, viii, 5 (129).

[6] *Manual of Discipline*, col. VII, lines 18 ff.

[7] Gaster (*op. cit.* p. 60) renders: "the formal state of purity enjoyed by the general membership of the community", and on p. 107, n. 58, brings this into association with the passage in Josephus. S. Lieberman thinks the meaning is the solid food of the community as opposed to liquids (*J.B.L.* LXXI, 1952, p. 203). Cf. Vermes, *The Dead Sea Scrolls in English*, 1962, p. 27.

[8] Mt. 15: 1 ff., Mk. 7: 1 ff.; cf. Lk. 11: 37 ff.

[9] Jn. 13: 3 ff.

It has been argued that the Church owed much to the Qumran sectaries for its organization.[1] It would not be surprising for the infant Church to learn from the experience of others in this matter. The services of the Early Church were modelled on those of the Synagogue, and since in the first days the Church was regarded by its Jerusalem members as a Jewish sect it would not be remarkable if its organization was modelled on that of another contemporary Jewish sect. It is possible that the community of goods in the Jerusalem church[2] was influenced by the community of goods at Qumran.[3] It does not seem to have lasted long in Jerusalem, or to have been practised in the churches established elsewhere, and it cannot be said to have belonged to the essential pattern of the Church.

While the sect of the Scrolls had its headquarters at Qumran, all its members were not concentrated there. There were smaller groups scattered throughout the land.[4] But wherever there was a company of sectaries they had at their head an officer, who presided at their meetings and without whose permission none was allowed to speak.[5] His title[6] may be rendered

[1] Cf. J. Schmitt, in *La Secte de Qumran* (Recherches Bibliques IV), 1959, pp. 216 ff. (p. 230: "Le judaïsme communautaire est, à n'en pas douter, le milieu d'où l'Église de Jérusalem tient les formes les plus marquantes de son organisation naissante"). The similarities between the Essenes and the Church had long been noted. F. C. Conybeare (*loc. cit.* p. 770 b) gives an account of them, and concludes that "the most we can say is that the Christians copied many features of their organization and propagandist activity from the Essenes". Cf. also J. B. Lightfoot (*op. cit.* pp. 395 ff.), who recognizes Essene influence in the Church before the close of the Apostolic age.

[2] Ac. 4: 32 ff.

[3] Cf. S. Segert, "Die Gütergemeinschaft der Essäer", in *Studia Antiqua Antonio Salač septuagenario oblata*, 1955, pp. 66 ff.

[4] *Manual of Discipline*, col. VI, lines 3, 6; cf. Josephus, *B.J.* II, VIII, 4 (124–26). R. de Vaux (*Les "petites grottes" de Qumran*, 1962, pp. 35 f.) suggests that some of these groups may have occupied the various Qumran caves, in some cases living in tents or huts and only using the caves for storage purposes. In *Zadokite Work* XVII. 1 (p. XIV, line 3) we find reference to "camps" of the sect.

[5] *Manual of Discipline*, col. VI, lines 8 ff.

[6] *meḇhakkēr*. Cf. *Zadokite Work* X. 10 f., 13 (p. IX, lines 18 f., 22), XV. 7, XVI. 1 (p. XIII, lines 6 f.), XVI. 7 f. (p. XIII, lines 13, 16), XVIII. 2 (p. XIV, line 13), XIX. 8, 10, 12 (p. XV, lines 8, 11, 14), *Manual of Discipline*, col. VI, lines 12, 20.

by the word Inspector.[1] There is a reference to an "Inspector who is over all the camps",[2] who would seem to have been the head of the whole sect. For the admission of new members an Overseer[3] acted in the first instance.[4] Whether he is the same as the Inspector is not clear,[5] or, if they were different persons, what the relation of the one to the other was. It has been held that the office of bishop in the Early Church corresponded to that of Inspector in the Qumran sect.[6] This has been disputed,[7] and the single use of the term *episkopoi*, or bishops, in the book

---

[1] Vermes (*The Dead Sea Scrolls in English*, 1962, p. 19) prefers the rendering "Guardian", as Overseer "smacks more of a gang of labourers than of a religious community".

[2] *Zadokite Work*, xvii. 6 (p. xiv, line 9.)

[3] *pakîdh.*

[4] *Manual of Discipline*, col. VI, line 14.

[5] F. M. Cross (*Ancient Library of Qumrân*, p. 176 n.) identifies them, and so J. van der Ploeg (*The Excavations of Qumran*, p. 135; cf. *Bi.Or.* ix, 1952, p. 131b), W. H. Brownlee (*The Dead Sea Manual of Discipline*, 1951, p. 25), P. Wernberg-Møller (*The Manual of Discipline*, 1957, p. 107), and G. Vermes (*op. cit.* p. 19), while J. T. Milik holds the identification to be probable (*Ten Years of Discovery*, p. 100). On the other hand, G. Lambert (*N.R.Th.* lxxiii, 1951, p. 944) appears to differentiate them. Cf. also J. F. Priest, *J.B.L.* lxxxi, 1962, pp. 55 ff. P. Guilbert (*Les Textes de Qumran*, i, 1961, p. 47) also differentiates them.

[6] Cf. I. Lévi, *R.E.J.* lxi, 1911, p. 195; K. Kohler, *A.J.Th.* xv, 1911, p. 416; A. Büchler, *J.Q.R.*, N.S. iii, 1912–13, p. 464; W. Staerk, *Die ⁺üdische Gemeinde des Neuen Bundes in Damaskus*, 1922, p. 68; G. Hölscher, *Z.N.W.* xxviii, 1929, p. 39; J. Jeremias, *Jerusalem zur Zeit Jesu*, 2nd edn., 1958, ii B., pp. 132 ff.; J. Daniélou, *R.H.P.R.* xxxv, 1955, p. 111, and *Les Manuscrits de la Mer Morte et les origines du Christianisme*, 1957, pp. 36 f.

[7] Cf. K. G. Goetz, *Z.N.W.* xxx, 1931, pp. 89 ff.; H. W. Beyer, in *Th.W.B.* ii, 1935, pp. 614 f.; P. Guilbert, *loc. cit.* Bo Reicke (*S.N.T.*, p. 154) says: "There is little reason to assume that the church got its episcopal office from the Essenes and their *mebaqqer*" (cf. *Symbolae Biblicae Upsalienses*, No. 6, 1946, p. 16 n.); cf. F. F. Bruce, *The Modern Churchman*, N.S. iv, 1960–61, p. 53: "The *mebaqqer* or superintendent of one of the branches of the Qumran community has little in common with the Christian *episkopos* but the meaning of the title." M. Delcor (*Revue Thomiste*, lix, 1959, p. 136) distinguishes the *mᵉbhakkēr* from the *episkopos* on the ground that the former was accompanied by a priest, and was therefore himself a layman. It is very doubtful if this is correct, since it is unlikely that a sect which gave its leadership into the hands of priests would have put the examination of converts in lay hands (but note that G. Vermes [*The Dead Sea Scrolls in English*, p. 25] thinks he was a Levite). Moreover, the *episkopos* was not a

of Acts would suggest that the office was not quite the same as that of Inspector amongst the Qumran sectaries. For Paul called the elders of the church at Ephesus to meet him at Miletus,[1] and in addressing them he called them bishops.[2] This would suggest that in the church at Ephesus there were several bishops, and not a single person with the authority of the Qumran Inspector. Similarly, Paul's letter to the Philippians is addressed to the members of the church with its bishops and deacons.[3] That the office of bishop later developed into something more comparable with the inspectorship of the Qumran sect[4] is not evidence that the Church took this over from the sect, but would suggest that it developed in the life and experience of the Church. The term *episkopos* closely corresponds in meaning with the Qumran term Overseer, and it may well be that the Church owed something to Qumran for the adoption of the term, though the total organization of the Church was very different from that of the sect.

The affairs of the sect were managed by a council of twelve members and three priests.[5] It has been held that this means twelve men of whom three should be priests,[6] in accordance with the sect's conceding of special influence and authority to the priests. We should more naturally understand the reference

priest in the sense in which the priestly members of the sect were, i.e. a descendant of Aaron. Cf. R. P. C. Hanson (*A Guide to the Scrolls*, 1958, p. 67): "There is no evidence that the early Christians divided their members into 'laymen' and 'clergy or ministers' at all." Cf. also F. Nötscher, in *Die Kirche und ihre Ämter und Stände* (Festgabe für Cardinal Frings), 1960, pp. 315 ff. (reprinted in *Vom Alten zum Neuen Testament*, 1962, pp. 188 ff.).

[1] Ac. 20: 17.
[2] Ac. 20: 28. R.S.V. conceals the use of the word *episkopoi* here by rendering "guardians".
[3] Phil. 1: 1. The references to bishops in 1 Tim. 3: 2, Tit. 1: 7, do not give any indication how many bishops there were in a single church.
[4] Cf. Beyer (*loc. cit.* p. 615): The *mᵉbhakkēr* "hat seine Entsprechung tatsächlich mehr im Bischof des 3. Jhdts als in dem, was wir von den ἐπίσκοποι des Urchchristentums wissen."
[5] *Manual of Discipline*, col. VIII, line 1.
[6] C. T. Fritsch (*op. cit.* p. 120) states this as if it were not open to question (cf. p. 63). Bo Reicke (*S.N.T.* p. 151) says that "perhaps the inclusion of the three priests is to be preferred."

STUDIES IN THE OLD TESTAMENT

to mean that the three priests were in addition to the twelve,[1] but we need not press that. On the view that they were within the twelve, this has been thought to have provided the model for Jesus,[2] who chose twelve disciples, of whom three seem to have formed an inner circle. For the choice of twelve disciples there is no need to look to Qumran for inspiration. The Old Testament is a sure source for the ideas of Jesus, while the sect of Qumran is at best less sure. The twelve tribes of Israel almost certainly supplied the inspiration for both. Indeed, we find Jesus in the Gospels promising the disciples that they should sit on twelve thrones judging the twelve tribes of Israel.[3] Moreover, the special position of Peter, James and John[4] cannot well be traced to Qumran. For in the organization of the sect the three, whether within or without the twelve, were priests, and this was fundamental to the whole spirit of the sect. Peter, James and John were not priests. The members of the sect were divided into three categories, according to the *Manual of Discipline*.[5] These were priests, Levites, and lay members. According to the *Zadokite Work* there were four categories: priests, Levites, children of Israel, and proselytes.[6]

[1] Cf. J. T. Milik (*Ten Years of Discovery*, p. 100), who thinks the twelve laymen represented the twelve tribes of Israel, and the three priests the families of Levi's three sons, Gershon, Kohath and Merari. Dupont-Sommer (*Les Écrits esséniens découverts près de la Mer Morte*, 1959, p. 105 n.) inclines to follow this view, and holds that the interpretation of fifteen men is more natural (cf. *The Jewish Sect of Qumran and the Essenes*, Eng. trans. by R. D. Barnett, 1954, pp. 81 f., where the inclusion of the three within the twelve was favoured). So R. P. C. Hanson, *A Guide to the Scrolls*, 1958, p. 66 ("not even the arithmetic corresponds in this alleged resemblance"); E. F. Sutcliffe, *J.S.S.* IV, 1959, p. 134; and P. Guilbert, *op. cit.* p. 55.

[2] Cf. C. T. Fritsch, *op. cit.* p. 120. Bo Reicke (*S.N.T.*, pp. 151 f.) notes a parallel, but adds that "we cannot say that Jesus is directly dependent on the Qumran sect in this matter." Cf. J. van der Ploeg, *The Excavations at Qumran*, p. 135.

[3] Mt. 19: 28, Lk. 22: 30.

[4] O. Cullmann (*S.N.T.*, p. 21) thinks the three priests may have had their parallel in the three pillars of Gal. 2: 9 f.: James, Cephas and John. Cf. S. E. Johnson, *ibid.* p. 134; Bo Reicke, *ibid.* p. 151; J. van der Ploeg, *loc. cit.*

[5] *Manual of Discipline*, col. II, lines 19 ff.

[6] *Zadokite Work*, XVII. 1 ff. (p. XIV, lines 3 ff.).

258

Here there is no necessary contradiction,[1] since the *Manual of Discipline* tells us of the long probation of those who joined the sect, who stood outside the full membership of the sect.[2] It is probable that these correspond to the proselytes of the other text.[3] In the Early Church we find nothing of this, and there is no evidence that priests or Levites had any special status within the Church.[4] In estimating the relations between the Church and the sect, similarities and differences must alike be taken into account.

Again, in the organization of the sect the twelve men and three priests would seem to have a permanent place as the supreme council of the community.[5] In the Church the twelve disciples did not form part of the enduring pattern of the organization. When Judas was replaced by Matthias,[6] it was not with the idea of maintaining a constant council of twelve living members. As Professor Manson has pointed out, when James was martyred by Herod Agrippa,[7] his place was not filled. This, as Professor Manson says, was because his place was not vacant.[8] Judas had forfeited his place by his misconduct and not by his death. The twelve disciples had been promised that they should judge the twelve tribes of Israel[9] and the Early Church took this literally, and believed that James would be raised from the dead to take his place. But this could not apply

---

[1] M. Burrows (*O.T.S.* VIII, 1950, p. 184) says the *Zadokite Work* adds a fourth class to the threefold classification of the Manual.

[2] *Manual of Discipline*, col. VI, lines 13 ff.

[3] Nowhere does the Qumran community show any interest in the making of converts from the Gentiles, and the proselytes of the *Zadokite Work* were almost certainly Jewish converts to the sect, just like the postulants of the *Manual*.

[4] We are told in Ac. 6: 7 that many priests accepted the Christian faith, but there is no evidence that they had any special status.

[5] E. F. Sutcliffe (*J.S.S.* IV, 1959, pp. 134 ff.) disputes this, and holds that they were the first fifteen men of the Qumran community, and F. F. Bruce (*J.S.S.* VII, 1962, p. 120) thinks there is much to be said in favour of this interpretation.

[6] Ac. 1: 23 ff.

[7] Ac. 12: 2.

[8] Cf. *Ethics and the Gospel*, 1960, p. 74. Cf. S. E. Johnson (*S.N.T.*, p. 134): "A more likely supposition is that the Twelve are the community's council for the coming Messianic Age, when they will sit on thrones judging the twelve tribes of Israel."

[9] Mt. 19: 28, Lk. 22: 30.

to Judas, and therefore his place was filled. It was filled by one who had companied with the disciples throughout the ministry of Jesus, from the time of John the Baptist's baptism. That this was regarded as an essential qualification would imply that no permanent body of twelve living men was in mind.

The admission of new members to the sect is provided for in the *Zadokite Work* and in the *Manual of Discipline,* and is described by Josephus in his account of the Essenes. The *Zadokite Work* probably comes from a time early in the history of the sect, and the *Manual of Discipline* from a later time.[1] The procedure was simpler as described in the *Zadokite Work,* while that in the *Manual of Discipline* is closer to that described by Josephus. The *Zadokite Work* tells us that the candidate for membership was examined by the Inspector as to his works, his understanding, his might, his strength, and his wealth, and if the Inspector was satisfied he was enrolled in the membership.[2] According to the *Manual of Discipline,* a candidate was examined by the Overseer, and if he was satisfied, the candidate was admitted to the covenant, but was not yet admitted to the fellowship.[3] He underwent an unspecified period of probation, after which he was considered by "the many"—which may mean by a general meeting of the members—and a decision was taken as to whether he should be allowed to enter on a further year of probation. During this year he was still not permitted to touch "the purity of the many".[4] It is probably meant that he was not allowed to perform daily ablutions in the water used by the members of the sect.[5]

[1] Cf. the present writer's paper "Some Traces of the History of the Qumran Sect", *Th.Z.* xiii, 1957, pp. 530 ff. (cf. *B.J.R.L.* xxxv, 1952–53, pp. 144 f.); cf. too P. Wernberg-Møller, *D.T.T.* xvi, 1953, p. 115; B. Otzen, *S.Th.* vii, 1953, p. 141; J. O. Teglbjerg, *D.T.T.* xviii, 1955, pp. 246 f.; J. van der Ploeg, *J.E.O.L.* xiv, 1955–56, p. 104; K. Smyth, *The Dead Sea Scrolls,* 1956, p. 7; R. P. C. Hanson, *A Guide to the Scrolls,* 1958, pp. 63 f., and H. A. Butler, *R.Q.* ii, 1960, pp. 532 ff.

[2] *Zadokite Work,* xvi. 4 f. (p. xiii, lines 11 f.).

[3] *Manual of Discipline,* col. VI, lines 14 ff.

[4] *Manual of Discipline,* col. VI, line 16.

[5] W. H. Brownlee (*The Dead Sea Manual of Discipline,* 1951, p. 25) brings this into connection with Josephus's phrase "the purer kind of holy water" (*B.J.* II, viii, 7 [138]), but allows that here it might include, in addition to the lustrations, the sectarian meals. Cf. *supra* p. 254, n. 7.

At the end of this year, he was again considered by "the many" as to his understanding of the Law and his way of life.[1] If he was still regarded as satisfactory, his property was turned over to the sect, but was kept separate from the treasury of the sect during a final probationary period of a year.[2] During this year he was not allowed to touch the food of the members.[3] This may mean that he was not allowed to sit at the same table as the full members, though it has been argued that it means that he was not allowed to prepare the food for the members.[4] At the end of this year, his case was again considered, and if he won the approval of the members he became a full member of the sect and his property was incorporated in that of the sect.[5] According to Josephus in his account of the Essenes, the preliminary period, which is undefined in the *Manual of Discipline*, lasted for a year, like the others.[6] During this year the candidate was subjected to the same mode of life as the members, though he was not admitted to the sect.[7] If he was found satisfactory at the end of this time he was allowed to share the waters of purification used by the sect, but had two more years of probation before he was admitted to full membership.[8]

It is hard to suppose that Jesus or the first disciples copied any of this. For it would have taken three years for anyone to be fully enrolled amongst the disciples or in the Church—assuming that the initial period of probation was a year, as Josephus says. This means that none of the twelve disciples would have completed his probation during the ministry of

[1] *Manual of Discipline*, col. VI, line 18.
[2] *Manual of Discipline*, col. VI, lines 19 ff.
[3] *Manual of Discipline*, col. VI, line 20. S. Lieberman (*J.B.L.* LXXI, 1952, p. 203) thinks the word *mashkeh*, which is here used, referred to drink only. Cf. also E. F. Sutcliffe, *Heythrop Journal*, I, 1960, pp. 53 f. Others think the word, like *mishteh*, stood for the whole meal. So M. Burrows, *O.T.S.* VIII, 1950, pp. 163 f.; T. H. Gaster, *op. cit.* p. 61; A. Dupont-Sommer, *Les Écrits esséniens*, p. 102. Cf. P. Guilbert, *Les Textes de Qumran*, I, 1961, p. 48.
[4] Cf. E. F. Sutcliffe, *loc. cit.*, pp. 62 f.
[5] *Manual of Discipline*, col. VI, line 22.
[6] *B.J.* II, VIII, 7 (137).
[7] *Ibid.*
[8] *B.J.* II, VIII, 7 (138).

Jesus,[1] and so none would have been eligible for membership of the supposed council corresponding to the council of the Qumran sectaries. Nor is there any evidence that the Early Church required a period of three years of probation before admission to its membership.

This very important difference between the Church and Qumran becomes even clearer when we turn to the question of baptism. It has been maintained that Christian baptism was derived from the Qumran sect through the baptism of John, who is sometimes thought to have been a member of the sect.[2] Of none of this is there any evidence, and the whole character and significance of John's baptism were so different from anything that is known from Qumran that it is in the highest degree improbable.[3] All that we are concerned with here, how-

---

[1] The ministry of Jesus is usually thought to have lasted three years, but a one-year ministry (a common view held in the 2nd and 3rd centuries) or a two-year ministry (cf. E. F. Sutcliffe, *A Two-Year Public Ministry*, 1938) has been proposed; on this question, cf. G. Ogg, *The Chronology of the Public Ministry of Jesus*, 1940.

[2] Cf. G. L. Harding, *I.L.N.*, September 3, 1955, p. 379 ("John the Baptist was almost certainly an Essene, and must have studied and worked in this building"); J. M. Allegro, *The Dead Sea Scrolls*, 1956, pp. 163 ff.; C. T. Fritsch, *op. cit.* pp. 112 ff.; A. Powell Davies, *The Meaning of the Dead Sea Scrolls*, 1957, pp. 142 f.; W. H. Brownlee, *S.N.T.*, pp. 33 ff. (cf. p. 57: "It was John the Essene who proclaimed the coming Messianic Age in the wilderness"). J. Daniélou (*op. cit.* p. 15) says: "les découvertes des manuscrits ont confirmé de façon qui semble indubitable les contacts de Jean avec les moines de Qumrân." Cf. K. Schubert, *The Dead Sea Community*, Eng. trans. by J. W. Doberstein, 1959, p. 126, and A. S. Geyser, *N.T.* 1, 1956, pp. 70 ff. (p. 71: "we can now assume with comparative certainty that John was brought up by Essenes"). M. Delcor (*Revue Thomiste*, LVIII, 1958, p. 766) thinks it probable that as a child John came under their influence, and so J. A. T. Robinson, *H.T.R.* L, 1957, pp. 175 ff.; D. Howlett, *The Essenes and Christianity*, 1957, pp. 141 f.; and O. Betz, *R.Q.* 1, 1957–58, p. 222. On the other hand G. Molin (*Die Söhne des Lichtes*, 1954, p. 170) thinks this is questionable, and W. Eiss (*Qumran und die Anfänge der christlichen Gemeinde*, 1959, p. 14) thinks it very improbable. G. Graystone (*The Dead Sea Scrolls and the Originality of Christ*, 1956, p. 113; cf. pp. 93 ff.) thinks it is improbable that the Baptist ever visited Qumran. The suggestion that John may have been an Essene is no new one. It was already rejected by J. B. Lightfoot (*op. cit.* pp. 398 ff.).

[3] On this question, cf. the present writer's essay on "The Baptism of John and the Qumran Sect" in *New Testament Essays: Studies in Memory of T. W. Manson*, 1959, pp. 218 ff. Lucetta Mowry, who thinks the eschatology

ever, is to see how far Christian baptism reflects anything of which we have knowledge in the faith and practice of the Qumran sect.[1]

Josephus tells us that the Essenes bathed the whole body daily before eating.[2] This is not what we mean by baptism, and there is no evidence that this practice was taken over by Jesus or the Church. In the Qumran texts it is probable that the references to "the purity of the many" are to these daily ablutions.[3] By baptism we mean a water rite of initiation, and only a rite of initiation. There is no reference either in the Scrolls or in Josephus to a special water rite of initiation amongst the Qumran sectaries or the Essenes.[4] It is likely that the first of the daily ablutions after admission to the appropriate stage of probation would have a special character for the candidate for membership of the sect, just as the first Communion has a special character for Christians. But there is a fundamental difference between baptism and the first Communion. The one is an unrepeatable act of initiation, while the other is the first of a repeatable series of experiences. The daily ablutions of the sect were not administered rites, but washings of the body which each performed for himself. We have no evidence that

of the sect may have influenced John, observes (*The Dead Sea Scrolls and the Early Church*, 1962, pp. 133 f.) that the similarities between John and the sect "do not necessarily imply that John had at any time become a member of the Qumran community, for John worked independently, as had the great prophets of ancient times, and was concerned to bring his message to the entire nation."

[1] Cf. O. Betz, *R.Q.* I, 1958–59, pp. 213 ff.
[2] *B.J.* II, VIII, 5 (129).
[3] See above, page 254.
[4] Cf. E. F. Sutcliffe, *Heythrop Journal*, I, 1960, pp. 179 ff. (p. 188: "There is no mention of any rite performed by one for another nor of any ablution forming part of a ceremony of initiation. Such a meaning cannot legitimately be read into the statement that admission to the two years of probation after the year of postulantship carried with it the right to share the purer waters of purification, as this implies continual use and not a single act"). Similarly J. Gnilka (*R.Q.* III, 1961–62, pp. 189 ff.) notes that we have no record of any initiation ceremony of baptism at Qumran. Cf. also P. Benoit, *N.T.S.* VII, 1960–61, p. 280. In view of this silence in our sources it is surprising to be told that John the Baptist took over his baptism from the Essene rite of initiation. Cf. W. H. Brownlee, *S.N.T.*, 1958, pp. 36 f.; O. Betz, *R.Q.* I, 1958–59, p. 222.

the first of these ablutions was different in this respect from the rest. Christian baptism was an administered rite, as also was the baptism of John,[1] and we have no evidence that either was followed by similar daily rites. Both were rites of initiation and only of initiation.[2]

A further notable difference that is relevant to our discussion of the organization of the sect and of the Church is in the timing of the experience. If it were established that the form of the first Essene ablution coincided with the form of Christian baptism, we should still have to note that the former did not take place until the end of the second period of probation, according to the *Manual of Discipline,* or the end of the first, according to Josephus—i.e. until after at least a year, and perhaps two years. In the New Testament we read that on the day of Pentecost three thousand people were converted by the preaching of Peter, and they were baptized the same day.[3] When Philip fell in with the Ethiopian eunuch and joined him in his chariot, they stopped when they came to water, and the eunuch was immediately baptized.[4] Again, when Paul converted the Philippian gaoler, he baptized him the same night.[5]

Yet even if the first Essene ablution could rightly be regarded as identical with Christian baptism in its form and its timing,

[1] Cf. Jn. 1: 25 f., where we are told that John baptized, or Mk. 1: 9, Mt. 3: 13, where we are told that Jesus was baptized by John. Whether John plunged a man under the water, or whether the person baptized plunged himself, we do not know; but in either case it was an administered rite, and in this respect comparable with Jewish proselyte baptism (cf. T.B. *Yebamoth*, 47 a b), as distinct from ordinary Jewish lustrations or the daily ablutions of the sect. Cf. J. Gnilka, *R.Q.* III, 1961–62, p. 198. Nowhere in the Scrolls or in the first century accounts of the Essenes is there any reference to an administered rite of baptism. Cf. J. Daniélou, *R.H.P.R.* XXXV, 1955, p. 106: "En effet, dans l'essénisme, il s' agit de participation aux bains rituels de la communauté et non d'un rite spécial d'initiation."

[2] O. Betz (*R.Q.* I, 1957–58, p. 218) thinks it probable that the first Essene bath had the character of proselyte baptism and had nothing to do with the daily lustrations. This is a large inference to make from silence, since we are nowhere told anything at all about the first Essene bath. It is a necessary assumption that there must have been a first bath; it is gratuitous to ascribe to it a different character from those of which it was the first.

[3] Ac. 2: 41.

[4] Ac. 8: 36 ff.

[5] Ac. 16: 33.

we should still have to ask how far the two accorded in significance. Christian baptism betokens a relation to Christ, whereas
we have no knowledge of anything comparable with this in the
sect of the Scrolls. The Teacher of Righteousness is unmen-
tioned in any reference to Essene ablutions, and there is no
reason to suppose that the first ablution, or any ablution, be-
tokened any relation to him. While there is little reason to
trace the form of Christian baptism to the Qumran sect, there
is even less to look there for the origin of its significance.[1]

In his account of the Essenes Josephus has given us a picture
of their daily meals,[2] of which the members partook in solemn
silence, and this has been held to be the source of the Christian
Eucharist.[3] The *Manual of Discipline* tells us that only when one
had been admitted to full membership of the Qumran sect
could he be allowed to touch the "drink" of the members.[4]
This is probably an allusion to the daily meals of the Qumran
community.[5] It may be allowed that during the period when
the members of the Jerusalem church had all things in common
its members shared a daily table. But this is not to be identified
with the Eucharist without more ado; nor if it were could the
Eucharist then be traced back to Qumran. During the ministry
of Jesus, our Lord and His disciples doubtless ate together. But
the Last Supper is not merely one of such meals. It had a
special character, and the Eucharist of the Church does not
commemorate the daily meals of Jesus and His disciples, or
even the last of a series. It commemorates the character of that
meal in itself, without reference to any that had preceded it,
and its character derived from its association with the imminent
death of Jesus. We have no knowledge of any such commemora-

---

[1] Cf. W. D. Davies, *Christian Origins and Judaism*, 1962, p. 113: "There is
no real parallel in the Scrolls to Christian baptism, because they lack any
real counterpart to the dying and rising with Christ which Paul and other
early Christians took to be the essence of baptism."

[2] *B.J.* II, viii, 5 f. (129–33).

[3] Cf. A. Powell Davies, *The Meaning of the Dead Sea Scrolls*, 1957, p. 130:
"The early Christian sacrament *was* the Essenic sacrament with, *perhaps*,
some Christian adaptations." Cf. also D. Howlett, *The Essenes and
Christianity*, 1957, p. 147.

[4] *Manual of Discipline*, col. VI, line 20.

[5] See above, p. 261, n. 3.

tive character of the meals of the sect. Nowhere in Josephus or in the Scrolls is the Teacher of Righteousness mentioned in connection with the meals. So far as we know, they did not betoken any relationship between the members and him, or commemorate any incident of his life or the moment of his death. In this they differ *toto coelo* from the Christian sacrament.

One writer on the Scrolls has observed that the presiding priest at the sacred meals of the sect may have said: "This is my body", and that the wine that was drunk may have been thought of as the blood of the Messiah. He then concludes that the sacred meal of the sect was almost identical with the Christian sacrament.[1] Such nonsense is an insult to the intelligence of his readers. If the account of the meals of the sect is imaginatively reconstructed from the New Testament, it is not surprising that similarities are found, since they are first unwarrantably imposed without a shred of evidence. It should be clear to any ordinary intelligence that we can only discuss the relation of the Scrolls to the New Testament if we let each literature speak for itself, and refrain from tampering with the evidence to make it say what we wish to find.[2]

The daily meals of the sect are more naturally understood in terms of the communal meals of monastic orders,[3] which no members of such orders would confuse with the sacrament. They are sacred meals in the sense that the members are conscious that they belong to a religious order, and they are eaten with a solemnity and a quiet which is appropriate to the presence of the God whose blessing is invoked.

Reference has already been made to a passage which indicates that in the messianic expectation of the sect the Aaronic

[1] Cf. A. Powell Davies, *op. cit.* p. 130.

[2] It is curious that Powell Davies should say: "there is no certainty that the accounts of the Lord's Supper in the New Testament have not been edited to accord with the practice of a later time" (*ibid.*). There is complete certainty that he has edited his account of the meal of the Qumran sect to accord with his own theory.

[3] Cf. J. van der Ploeg, *J.S.S.* II, 1957, pp. 163 ff., and *The Excavations at Qumran*, p. 213; E. F. Sutcliffe, *Heythrop Journal*, I, 1960, pp. 48 ff. Cf. also F. Nötscher, in *Lex tua veritas* (Junker Festschrift), 1961, pp. 145–74 (reprinted in *Vom Alten zum Neuen Testament*, 1962, pp. 83–111), where the Qumran meals are considered in a wider setting.

anointed one should have precedence over the Davidic. This passage[1] describes what is often called the messianic banquet. It says that in the days of the Messiah, he should come with the priests and members of the sect, and they should sit down in the order of their dignity. No one should eat until the priest had first blessed the food, and then the priest should eat first, and after him the Messiah of Israel, followed by the rest of the company, each in the order of his dignity. The text continues by saying that in accordance with this rule the members of the sect should act at every meal, when at least ten are assembled.[2] It is clear, therefore, that this is not really a description of any special messianic banquet.[3] It is a description of the regular meals of the sect, and the Messiah takes no special part in it. If he should be present, he should occupy the second place, but beyond that the meal is conceived as an ordinary meal, and no sacramental significance is given to it.

This passage is important in another connection, to which reference has also been made. It says: "If God should cause the Messiah to be born[4] in their time", his place should be as

---

[1] *The Rule of the Congregation*, col. II, lines 11 ff.

[2] *The Rule of the Congregation*, col. II, lines 21 f.

[3] Cf. M. Burrows, *More Light on the Dead Sea Scrolls*, p. 101; T. H. Gaster, *op. cit.* p. 29; also J. van der Ploeg, *The Excavations at Qumran*, p. 213: "The text of the Two Column Document as a whole does not give the impression that it means to describe a sacred or 'Messianic' banquet." J. D. Amusin (*op. cit.* pp. 241 f.), while finding a messianic colouring in this text, is cautious about any possible connection with the significance of the Last Supper.

[4] D. Barthélemy (*Qumran Cave I*, 1955, p. 117), adopting a suggestion of J. T. Milik's, emends the text to read "brings" instead of "causes to be born", and this is adopted by F. M. Cross (*The Ancient Library of Qumrân*, p. 64); cf. Vermes (*The Dead Sea Scrolls in English*, p. 121): "when [the Priest-] Messiah shall summon them." R. Gordis (*V.T.* vii, 1957, pp. 191 ff.) argues against Milik's emendation. T. H. Gaster (*op. cit.* p. 260) similarly rejects this "daring but unfortunate conjecture", and proposes a different emendation to yield the sense "when the Messiah is present". Cross (*loc. cit.*) says this is to be rejected categorically. Y. Yadin (*J.B.L.* LXXVIII, 1959, pp. 240 f.) proposes yet another emendation, to yield the sense "on the occasion of their meeting". The reading of the MS. is beyond question, and it should probably be understood, with Burrows (*op. cit.* p. 303) in the same way as Ps. 2: 7, where it refers to the adoption and establishment of the King as God's son. Similarly A. Dupont-Sommer, *Les Écrits esséniens*, p. 123 n. Cf. also E. F. Sutcliffe, *R.Q.* ii, 1960, pp. 541 ff.

defined.[1] It is clear that he is the lay Messiah, since he is called the Messiah of Israel and yields precedence to the priest. The one who presides at the meal is simply called the priest. It has been said already that this passage is often held to contemplate two Messiahs,[2] a lay and a priestly, and it well illustrates the danger of the use of the word Messiah, instead of "anointed one". For while it is clear that the lay Messiah is here the coming expected one who should restore the kingdom,[3] it is equally clear that the priest is just the person who happens to be the head of the community at that time. Though he was an anointed one, no reference is made to that here, and we have no business to import the term Messiah, with all that it signifies to us, into this passage.[4] If the priestly Messiah, who should take precedence of the Davidic Messiah in the messianic age, had really been thought of as the risen Teacher of Righteousness, it would be nothing short of astonishing for him to be introduced without the slightest reference to this remarkable expectation. What those who suppose the sect cherished this hope need to do is not merely to press a doubtful interpretation of a passage in another text, but to explain the complete absence of any allusion to it here.

Philo tells us that the Essenes were a pacific sect.[5] But there is no reason to suppose that they conceived the Davidic Messiah in any other than the conquering terms that characterized the popular expectation in the time of Jesus. They cherished the text described as the *War of the Sons of Light against the Sons of Darkness*, which kept alive dreams of the day when the nations of the world should be successively destroyed in battle. Jesus discouraged any reference to Himself as the Messiah, because He conceived His messiahship in quite other terms. It was not

---

[1] *The Rule of the Congregation*, col. II, lines 11 f.

[2] See above, p. 124.

[3] Cf. the text published by J. M. Allegro in *B.J.L.* LXXV, 1956, pp. 174 f., where there is a reference to the rightful Messiah of the house of David.

[4] Cf. M. Black, in *Studia Patristica*, ed. by K. Aland and F. L. Cross, I, 1957, p. 447: "The fact that the High Priest takes precedence of the Messiah of Israel may mean very little; presumably he would do so in any Temple rite or priestly function, but this does not mean that we are to regard the High Priest as in the strict sense a 'Messianic' figure."

[5] *Quod omnis probus liber sit*, XII (78).

by killing but by dying that He purposed to save His people.[1] The Qumran sect seem to have abandoned their pacific way of life in the war with Rome, and to have joined the rebels[2] in the belief that the long-dreamed-of time for the establishment of the kingdom had come. It was during the war with Rome that the Qumran centre was destroyed, and Josephus tells us that the Romans persecuted the Essenes with the utmost cruelty,[3] while they bore themselves with superhuman fortitude. One of the Essenes became a commander in the rebel forces.[4] All this stands in the strongest contrast to our Lord's conception of the way the kingdom would be established.

The Copper Scroll, which records the places where vast quantities of treasure were hidden, is probably an inventory of Temple treasure, as Dr. Rabin first suggested.[5] By some it has

---

[1] S. G. F. Brandon has argued (*Annual of Leeds University Oriental Society* II, 1961, pp. 11 ff.; cf. *The Fall of Jerusalem and the Christian Church*, 1951, pp. 101 ff.) that the Gospels give a distorted picture of Jesus, and that He was really a political revolutionary, like the Zealots. He argues that it was after A.D. 70 when the Gospels were written, and that they portrayed Him in the present character so as to free the Church from any odium associated with the Jewish War. But the Epistles of Paul were certainly written before A.D. 70, and they betray no Zealot character. Professor Brandon holds that it was only after the Fall of Jerusalem that the Pauline influence triumphed over the older and more original stream of Christianity (*The Fall of Jerusalem*, pp. 54 ff., 185 ff., 206 ff.). The Epistles of Paul are the oldest Christian writings we possess, and they show unmistakably that the portrayal of Jesus as One who came to save men by dying, and not by killing, was completely independent of the Jewish War. The conjectural reconstruction of the Gospels cannot displace the Pauline Christ for a Zealot Christ.

[2] Mlle. A. Jaubert thinks the Zealots were an offshoot from the Essenes (*N.T.S.* VII, 1960–61, p. 12). Hippolytus (*Ref. omn. haer.* IX. 26) reckoned the Zealots among the Essenes.

[3] *B.J.* II, VIII, 10 (152 f.).

[4] *B.J.* II, xx, 4 (567).

[5] *The Jewish Chronicle*, June 15, 1956, p. 19. So also K. G. Kuhn, *Th.L.Z.* LXXXI, 1956, pp. 541 ff. Y. Yadin (*The Message of the Scrolls*, 1957, p. 159) says it is not excluded that the Copper Scroll is a list of the treasures of the sect, and this is the view of Dupont-Sommer (*Les Écrits esséniens*, pp. 400 ff.). The text of the Copper Scroll, accompanied by facsimiles and with a full introduction and commentary by J. T. Milik, has now been published in *Les "petites grottes" de Qumran*, 1962, pp. 201 ff.

been thought to record mere folklore,[1] but it seems improbable that copper would be used for such a purpose. If it is an inventory of Temple treasure, it is likely that it was prepared by the rebels who had charge of the Temple. There were two copies of this inventory,[2] one deposited in one of the Qumran caves and one deposited elsewhere. Doubtless both were prepared in the same place, and there is no reason to think that was at Qumran,[3] where texts on quite different materials were copied. Jerusalem would be the most natural place, since it was from there that the treasure was distributed. But the deposit of one of the copies in one of the Qumran caves would strengthen the suggestion that in the time of the war against Rome the Zealots regarded the Essenes as their trusted allies. Their conception of the messianic age was thus very different from that of Jesus, and He can scarcely be supposed to have derived His from them.

The Qumran sect did not use the current official calendar, but used one which ensured that the festivals should fall on the same day of the week every year.[4] It was a fifty-two week calendar, and not a luni-solar calendar like the official Jewish calendar. It had no place for intercalary months every few years, giving years of variable length. This calendar was the calendar of the book of *Jubilees*, to which there is a reference in the *Zadokite Work*,[5] and fragments of which have been found amongst the Scrolls. Mlle. Jaubert has very acutely argued that

---

[1] So J. T. Milik, *B.A.* xix, 1956, p. 63, *R.B.* lxvi, 1959, p. 322, and *Ten Years of Discovery*, pp. 42 f.; J. Jeremias, *E.T.* lxxi, 1959–60, p. 228. This view is rejected by A. Dupont-Sommer, *Les Écrits esséniens*, pp. 397 ff.

[2] Cf. J. M. Allegro, *The Treasure of the Copper Scroll*, 1960, p. 55 (col. XII, line 11).

[3] So Allegro, *op. cit.* p. 125.

[4] Cf. D. Barthélemy, *R.B.* lix, 1952, pp. 199 ff.; A. Jaubert, *V.T.* iii, 1953, pp. 250 ff., vii, 1957, pp. 35 ff., *R.H.R.* cxlvi, 1954, pp. 140 ff., *La Date de la Cène*, 1957, and *La Secte de Qumran* (Recherches Bibliques, IV), 1959, pp. 113 ff. Cf. also J. Morgenstern, *V.T.* v, 1955, pp. 34 ff.; J. Obermann, *J.B.L.* lxxv, 1956, pp. 285 ff.; J. B. Segal, *V.T.* vii, 1957, pp. 250 ff.; E. R. Leach, *V.T.* vii, 1957, pp. 392 ff.; J.-P. Audet, *Sciences Ecclésiastiques*, x, 1958, pp. 361 ff.; S. Talmon, *Aspects of the Dead Sea Scrolls* (Scripta Hierosolymitana, IV), 1958, pp. 162 ff.; E. Vogt, *Biblica*, xl, 1959, pp. 102 ff.; E. Kutsch, *V.T.* xi, 1961, pp. 39 ff.

[5] *Zadokite Work*, xx. 1 (p. xvi, lines 2 ff.).

Jesus and His disciples followed this calendar, and has attempted by this means to resolve the vexed question of the relation of the Synoptic dating of the Last Supper and the Johannine dating.[1] According to the Synoptics the Last Supper was a Passover meal, while according to the Fourth Gospel it took place before the Passover. Mlle. Jaubert holds that Jesus celebrated the Passover on the sectarian date, and that it took place on Tuesday, when the Qumran Passover would fall, and she adduces some patristic evidence for this date.[2] This would allow more time for all the events that have to be fitted in between the Supper and the Crucifixion, which then took place before the official Passover day, to which the Fourth Gospel refers. It would also explain why there is no reference to a Passover lamb in any of the accounts of the Last Supper.

While this is a very attractive view, it is not wholly without difficulties.[3] Nowhere does Jesus show the slightest interest in calendar questions,[4] and since He is reported to have visited the Temple at some of the festivals, He would appear to have observed them on the official dates.[5] Probably the reasons which have already been suggested for the Qumran sect's avoidance

---

[1] Cf. *R.H.R.* CXLVI, 1954, pp. 140 ff., *La Date de la Cène*, 1957, and *N.T.S.* VII, 1960–61, pp. 1 ff.

[2] E. Vogt has shown that both calendar dates of Passover could fall in the same week (*Biblica*, XXXIX, 1958, pp. 72 ff.).

[3] It has been rejected by Blinzler (*Z.N.W.* XLIX, 1958, pp. 238 ff.), P. Benoit (*R.B.* LXV, 1958, pp. 590 ff.), and J. Jeremias (*J.T.S.* N.S. X, 1959, pp. 131 ff.). On the other hand it has been accepted by many writers, including E. Vogt (*Biblica*, XXXVI, 1955, pp. 408 ff.), P. W. Skehan (*C.B.Q.* XX, 1958, pp. 192 ff.), H. Haag (*S.D.B.* VI [Fasc. 34, 1960], 1146 f.), and, with some reservations, by R. F. McDonald (*American Ecclesiastical Review,* CXL, 1959, pp. 79 ff.) and J. A. Walther (*J.B.L.* LXXVII, pp. 116 ff.). M. Black (*New Testament Essays: Studies in Memory of T. W. Manson,* 1959, pp. 19 ff.) also somewhat cautiously accepts it. Cf. also C. U. Wolf, *The Christian Century*, March 18, 1959, pp. 325 ff. Mlle. Jaubert has replied to Blinzler's arguments in *N.T.S.* VII, 1960–61, pp. 1 ff. M. Delcor (*Revue Thomiste,* LVIII, 1958, pp. 778 f.) expresses grave objections to Mlle. Jaubert's view, but the objections expressed are fully answered by her in the article cited. Further criticisms of her view are offered by M. Zerwick (*Biblica,* XXXIX, 1958, pp. 508 ff.) and E. Kutsch (*V.T.* XI, 1961, pp. 39 ff.).

[4] Cf. K. Schubert, *The Dead Sea Community*, 1959, p. 142.

[5] Cf. J. T. Milik, *Ten Years of Discovery*, 1959, pp. 112 f.

of the Temple were reinforced by the non-use of the calendar to which they attached such great importance. Mlle. Jaubert has shown that this calendar was not invented by the author of *Jubilees*, but that there is evidence in the Old Testament that it was accepted by some of the sacred authors.[1] It is therefore possible that others, besides the Qumran sect, clung to this calendar, though if Jesus and His disciples did in fact follow it, they could well have been influenced by the Qumran sect in so doing. It would be curious, however, for them to be so influenced in a matter which plays no part in the teaching of Jesus, when in so many ways the teaching and practice of Jesus and the Early Church show such striking differences from those of the sect.

Similarities of phrase and idea between the Scrolls and the New Testament have been noted by many writers.[2] Professor Stauffer finds that they are closer in the case of the Evangelists and other New Testament writers than they are in the case of the teaching of Jesus Himself.[3] Wherever they are found they can be examined dispassionately. It has always been recognized that the uniqueness of the New Testament does not lie in the

---

[1] Cf. A. Jaubert, *La Date de la Cène*, pp. 31 ff.

[2] Before the discovery of the Scrolls Bo Reicke had collected a large number of parallels between the *Zadokite Work* and the New Testament. Cf. "The Jewish 'Damascus Documents' and the New Testament" (*Symbolae Biblicae Upsalienses*, No. 6), 1946.

[3] Cf. *Die Botschaft Jesu damals und heute*, 1959, p. 16: "Die Qumranisierung der Jesustradition wächst mit dem zeitlichen Abstand der Traditionsträger von Jesus." M. Burrows (*More Light on the Dead Sea Scrolls*, p. 103) observes that "few parallels have been found for sayings of Jesus outside of the Sermon on the Mount", while K. Schubert (*S.N.T.*, p. 273) notes that even in the Sermon on the Mount "it is remarkable that the Essene parallels are found almost exclusively in Mt. 5". J. Coppens (*Les Documents de Juda et les Origines du Christianisme*, 1953, p. 26) observes that the contacts of the Scrolls with Apostolic preaching are greater than with the teaching of Jesus. Cf. also G. Graystone, *The Dead Sea Scrolls and the Originality of Christ*, 1956, p. 28. J. B. Lightfoot (*op. cit.* p. 407) had already recognized that Essene influences came into Christianity before the close of the Apostolic age, and detected them in the Roman Christian community to which Paul wrote. O. Cullmann (*Neutestamentliche Studien für Rudolf Bultmann* [B.Z.N.W. XXI], 1954, pp. 35 ff.) has argued that Essenes joined the Jewish Christians after the fall of Jerusalem in A.D. 70 (cf. H. J. Schoeps, *Z.R.G.G.* VI, 1954, pp. 1 ff.).

originality of the individual sayings of Jesus. Innumerable parallels to the Golden Rule have been found, not only in Jewish literature but in the literature of the world, without our being in any way troubled. The uniqueness of Jesus lies rather in the example which He Himself set, and in the spring of power He offers His followers to enable them to follow His example.[1] His own eager love for men and readiness to sacrifice His life for them are set before the eyes of the Christian, who by the transmuting touch of His personality on them and by the power of His redeeming death are lifted into His spirit and given power to follow Him. And however many parallels of phrase are found in the Scrolls and the New Testament, they do not touch this profound and fundamental aspect of the uniqueness of Christ.

We must always remember that Jesus and His disciples lived in the Jewish world of a particular time, and moved in the realm of ideas of their age. The Qumran community belonged to that age, and doubtless influenced that realm of ideas, and if there are links of word and thought it was because Jesus and His followers were alive to the world in which they lived.[2] As one writer has said, they show the contemporary character of the language of the New Testament;[3] or, as another puts it, "in any given age new ideas and new modes of expression pass into currency and become common property."[4] Nor must we forget that the Old Testament was precious to both the Qumran

---

[1] Cf. the present writer's "The Chinese Sages and the Golden Rule" (*B.J.R.L.* xxiv, 1940, pp. 321 ff.), p. 350.

[2] Cf. R. E. Brown (*S.N.T.*, p. 206): "The ideas of Qumran must have been fairly widespread in certain Jewish circles in the early first century A.D."; M. Burrows (*More Light on the Dead Sea Scrolls*, p. 54): "If the Dead Sea Scrolls are at all typical of the language and thinking of Palestine at the time when Christianity came into being, the disciples of Jesus and Jesus himself would naturally use these forms of expression and ways of thinking whenever they could, as a means of communication." Cf. also C. G. Howie (*The Dead Sea Scrolls and the Living Church*, 1958, p. 99): "The Church and Essenism developed in the same age and came out of the same general background. Facing similar problems in like circumstances the two movements could not have been absolutely dissimilar in doctrine." Cf. also P. Benoit, *N.T.S.* vii, 1960–61, pp. 278 ff.

[3] Cf. R. E. Murphy, *The Dead Sea Scrolls and the Bible*, 1956, pp. 77 f.

[4] E. F. Sutcliffe, *The Monks of Qumran*, p. 118.

community and Jesus and His disciples. It formed "a common reservoir of terminology and ideas", to use the words of Professor Albright, for Jews of every sect and for Christians.[1] Light and darkness are figures for the good and the bad in the *War Scroll,* and in the Fourth Gospel we find the same figures.[2] But before we trace the one directly to the other, we should recognize that the Old Testament is the source of these figures.[3] There the wicked are spoken of as walking in darkness and the righteous in light.[4] Moreover, as has been said, there is difference as well as similarity here between the Scrolls and the New Testament.[5] In the thought of the Qumran sect the battle between light and darkness was to be waged with carnal weapons, whereas to Jesus and His followers it was to be waged with spiritual weapons.

In the Scrolls we find teaching about the two ways, the way of the righteous directed by the spirit of truth, and the way of the wicked directed by the spirit of perversity.[6] In the early Christian writings, the *Epistle of Barnabas* and the *Didache,* we find a similar thought of the two ways.[7] While these early Christian writings may owe much, directly or indirectly, to the Qumran sect,[8] we should remember that the same thought is already found in Ps. 1.

[1] *The Background of the New Testament and its Eschatology* (C. H. Dodd Festschrift), ed. by W. D. Davies and D. Daube, 1956, p. 169.

[2] Cf. F. Nötscher, *Zur theologischen Terminologie der Qumrantexte,* 1956, pp. 92 ff.

[3] Cf. H. M. Teeple, *N.T.* IV, 1960-61, p. 18; Nötscher, *op. cit.* p. 129. C. G. Howie (*op. cit.* p. 89) says: "Since therefore the light-darkness motif is found both in the Qumran literature and in the New Testament, it is safe to assume that it began in its present form with the Essenes." This is to ignore the common source of both in the Old Testament.

[4] Prov. 4: 19; Ps. 97: 11. Cf. also Isa. 2: 5, 50: 10, 59: 9; Ps. 56: 13 (Heb. 14).

[5] H. Bardtke (*Die Handschriftenfunde am Toten Meer: Die Sekte von Qumrān,* 1958, p. 210) says: "Der Dualismus zwischen Licht und Finsternis begegnet uns im Johannesevangelium in einer ganz anderen Form."

[6] *Manual of Discipline,* col. III, lines 13 ff.

[7] *Ep. Barnabas,* XVIII-XX, *Didache,* I-V.

[8] On the Scrolls and the Epistle of Barnabas, cf. L. W. Barnard, *S.J.Th.* XIII, 1960, pp. 45 ff.; on the Scrolls and the Didache and the Shepherd of Hermas, cf. J.-P. Audet, *R.B.* LIX, 1952, pp. 219 ff., LX, 1953, pp. 41 ff. Cf. also J. D. Amusin, *op. cit.* p. 248.

We have already noted the Gospel passage in which the twelve disciples are promised that they shall sit on twelve thrones to judge the twelve tribes of Israel. In the Habakkuk Commentary we read that "in the hands of his elect God will put the judgment of all the nations."[1] Here again, it is probable that both are based on the thought of Dan. 7, which promised the everlasting dominion to the saints of the Most High,[2] though we should not forget that the Qumran sectaries looked for physical triumph over their foes, while the New Testament passage does not.

Reference has already been made to the fact that the Qumran community referred to themselves as those who had entered into the new covenant.[3] This immediately recalls our Lord's reference at the Last Supper to the new covenant.[4] Here again it is unnecessary to derive the one from the other, since both derive from Jer. 31: 31. Moreover, there is a great difference between the Scrolls and the New Testament here. Sutcliffe says: "The Christian covenant was in reality new and brought with it the abrogation of the levitical, but not the moral, precepts of the Old Law. The covenant of the brotherhood was not a new one, but a renewal of the obligation to observe the old and indeed in its strictest interpretation."[5]

A more interesting link between the Scrolls and the New Testament is to be found in the injunction in the *Zadokite Work* that none may bring a charge against a fellow-member unless he has previously reproved him before witnesses.[6] In Mt. 18: 15 ff. Jesus gave similar teaching, saying that one who is wronged should first speak in private to the one who wronged him, and then before witnesses, and only finally bring the matter to the church.

It is impossible for us here to examine all the links of this kind

---

[1] *Habakkuk Commentary*, col. V, line 4.

[2] Dan. 7: 27.

[3] *Zadokite Work*, VIII. 15 (p. VI, line 19), IX. 28 (pp. VIII, line 21, XIX, lines 33 f.), VIII. 37 (p. XX, line 12).

[4] Mt. 26: 28, Mk. 14: 24 (in both the best manuscripts omit "new"); Lk. 22: 20 (the whole verse is omitted by some manuscripts); 1 Cor. 11: 25.

[5] *The Monks of Qumran*, p. 120. Cf. D. Flusser, *Aspects of the Dead Sea Scrolls* (Scripta Hierosolymitana, IV), 1958, pp. 236 ff.

[6] *Zadokite Work*, X. 2 (p. IX, line 3).

that have been found. Some writers have directed attention to the special closeness of those links between the Fourth Gospel and the Scrolls,[1] while others have examined the Pauline links,[2]

[1] Cf. W. Grossouw, *Studia Catholica*, xxvi, 1951, pp. 295 ff.; Lucetta Mowry, *B.A.* xvii, 1954, pp. 78 ff.; F. M. Braun, *R.B.* lxii, 1955, pp. 5 ff.; W. F. Albright, *loc. cit.* pp. 153 ff.; R. E. Brown, *S.N.T.*, pp. 183 ff. (cf. p. 195: "in no other literature do we have so close a terminological and ideological parallel to Johannine usage"; p. 205: "there remains a tremendous chasm of thought between Qumran and Christianity"); A. R. C. Leaney, *A Guide to the Scrolls*, 1958, pp. 95 ff.; G. Baumbach, *Qumrān und das Johannes-Evangelium*, 1958. W. H. Brownlee (*S.N.T.*, p. 46) goes so far as to say: "one may *almost* say that in John's portrayal of Jesus we have the Essene Christ", while O. Cullmann (*ibid.* p. 22) says the Fourth Gospel "belongs to an ideological atmosphere most clearly related to that of the new texts", and K. G. Kuhn (*Z.K.Th.* xlvii, 1950, p. 210) says: "wir bekommen in diesen neuen Texten *den Mutterboden des Johannes-evangeliums* zu fassen." See also Kuhn, in *Neotestamentica et Patristica* (Cullmann Festschrift), 1962, pp. 111 ff. Cf. however, the more cautious assessment of H. M. Teeple, *N.T.* iv, 1960–61, pp. 6 ff. (esp. p. 25, where he says almost all the parallels between the Scrolls and the Fourth Gospel could have been suggested by the Septuagint). On the attitude to the Temple in the Fourth Gospel and the Scrolls, cf. O. Cullmann, *N.T.S.* v, 1958–59, pp. 157 ff. On the influence of the Qumran sect in the Gospel of Matthew, cf. K. Stendahl, *The School of St. Matthew*, 1954; S. E. Johnson, *Z.A.W.* lxvi, 1954, pp. 115 ff.; B. Gärtner, *S.Th.* viii, 1955, pp. 1 ff.; S. Lassalle, *Bulletin du Cercle Ernest Renan*, No. 71, April 1960, pp. 1 ff. Cf. also W. D. Davies (*H.T.R.* xlvi, 1953, pp. 113 ff.) on Mt. 11: 25–30 and the Scrolls. On the Scrolls and the Gospel of Luke, cf. W. Grossouw, *Studia Catholica*, xxvii, 1952, pp. 5 ff. On the Scrolls and Acts cf. S. E. Johnson, *Z.A.W.* lxvi, 1954, pp. 106 ff. On the Scrolls and the Gospel of Matthew and the Epistle of James, cf. Leaney, *op. cit.* pp. 91 ff., and on the links with the Gospel of Luke and Acts, *ibid.* pp. 109 ff. On the general question of Qumran exegesis and New Testament exegesis of the Old Testament, cf. G. Vermes, *Cahiers Sioniens*, v, 1951, pp. 337 ff.; cf. also F. F. Bruce, *Biblical Exegesis in the Qumran Texts*, 1960, and J. van der Ploeg, *Bijbelverklaring te Qumrân*, 1960.

[2] Cf. W. D. Davies, *S.N.T.*, pp. 157 ff., where the author argues that "the Scrolls and the Pauline Epistles share these terms (i.e. flesh and spirit), but it is not their sectarian connotation that is determinative of Pauline usage" (p. 182). On flesh and spirit, cf. further D. Flusser, *Aspects of the Dead Sea Scrolls* (Scripta Hierosolymitana, IV), 1958, pp. 252 ff. Cf. also W. Grossouw, *Studia Catholica*, xxvii, 1952, pp. 1 ff.; S. E. Johnson, *H.T.R.* xlviii, 1955, pp. 157 ff.; J. Daniélou, *op. cit.* pp. 94 ff.; K. Schubert, *The Dead Sea Community*, pp. 155 ff.; A. R. C. Leaney, *op. cit.* pp. 104 ff.; R. E. Murphy, *Sacra Pagina*, ii, 1959, pp. 60 ff.; and W. Grundmann, *R.Q.* ii, 1960, pp. 237 ff. On Ephesians and Qumran cf. K. G. Kuhn, *N.T.S.* vii, 1960–61, pp. 334 ff.

or the links to be found in the Epistle to the Hebrews.[1] Professor F. C. Grant declares that the contacts and parallels between the New Testament and the Scrolls are comparatively insignificant when set against the innumerable contacts and parallels between the New Testament and other literature of the Hellenistic age.[2] This does not mean that the parallels with the Scrolls are to be ignored or depreciated. Quite the reverse. Christ is not to be exalted by the depreciation of others, and it is as wrong to use the Scrolls simply as a foil for the teaching of the New Testament as it is to use them simply as a quarry for passages to attack the originality of the New Testament. We may gladly recognize all that is fine and good in the thought of the Qumran sectaries, with their deep religious interest and the purity of their lives. Their devotion to the Old Testament and their austere life of obedience to the will of God as they understood it is worthy of all admiration.[3]

The Scrolls are therefore to be recognized as of importance for the understanding of the background of Christianity, and for the light they shed on currents of Judaism in the period in which Christianity came into being.[4] It should be clear that

[1] Cf. Y. Yadin, *Aspects of the Dead Sea Scrolls* (Scripta Hierosolymitana, IV), 1958, pp. 36 ff. Cf. also J. Daniélou, *op. cit.* pp. 106 ff.; C. Spicq, *R.Q.* I, 1958–59, pp. 365 ff.; J. Coppens, *Les affinités qumrâniennes de l'Épître aux Hébreux*, 1962.

[2] Cf. *Ancient Judaism and the New Testament*, p. 20; cf. also p. 21: "the few and superficial resemblances between the New Testament and the Dead Sea Scrolls do not prove the dependence of Christianity upon the Essenes." See also F. C. Grant, *The Gospels: their Origin and Growth*, 1957, p. 75.

[3] W. D. Davies (*Christian Origins and Judaism*, 1962, p. 98) says: "It is not enough to claim that all the parallels between the Scrolls and the New Testament can be explained in terms of their common dependence on the Old Testament and on Judaism; the parallels cannot be so easily dismissed. We have, therefore, to guard against an excess of enthusiasm and an excess of caution; against claiming too much and claiming too little. I shall suggest that the Scrolls are more important than some scholars have grudgingly admitted and less revolutionary than has been claimed by others."

[4] Cf. L. Cerfaux, *La Secte de Qumrân* (Recherches Bibliques, IV), 1959, pp. 238 f.: "Les documents de la Mer Morte nous rendront d'immenses services . . . Nous aidant à préciser le vocabulaire chrétien, ils exerceront une influence bienfaisante sur notre exégèse." Cf. also J. D. Barthélemy, *Freiburger Zeitschrift für Philosophie und Theologie*, VI, 1959, pp. 249 ff.

they do not justify the extreme statement of the French writer which was quoted at the beginning of this lecture,[1] and anyone who reads the Fourth Gospel, or indeed any part of the New Testament, and who then reads the Scrolls in any of the translations that have been published, will be quickly aware that there is a world of difference between them.[2] One of the translators, Professor T. H. Gaster, has said with the fullest justification that in the Scrolls "there is no trace of any of the cardinal theological concepts . . . which make Christianity a distinctive faith."[3] They do not offer the single and sufficient explanation of Christian origins. They do bring their contribution to the understanding of the soil in which Christianity was planted.[4]

[1] The views of some Russian authors, recorded by Amusin (*op. cit.* pp. 234 ff.) but not otherwise available to the present writer, may be noted. R. Y. Vipper (*Rome and Christianity,* 1954) thinks the Essenes were the precursors of Christianity, and the Essenes and the Christians were but as grandparents and grandchildren. A. P. Kazhdan (*Religion and Atheism in the Ancient World,* 1957) is more cautious, and says we cannot derive Christianity from Essenism, but thinks the latter exerted a considerable influence on the formation of Christianity and on the growth of the Christian myth, while S. I. Kovalev (in the *Annual of the Museum of the History of Religion and Atheism,* 1958) is yet more cautious, and says we have no reason to regard the Essenes as direct precursors of Christianity either in matters of ideology or organization. Y. A. Lenzman (*The Rise of Christianity,* 1958) says the *Manual of Discipline* has nothing in common with early Christianity, but thinks the figure of the Teacher of Righteousness provided the most important element of the legend of Jesus. K. B. Starkova (in the Preface to her translation of the *Manual of Discipline,* 1959) says that in the light of the Qumran texts we can understand more clearly the birth of Christianity and the rise of Christian literature. (I am again indebted to Mr. Arie Rubinstein for access to these views.)

[2] O. Cullmann (*S.N.T.*, pp. 31 f.) says: "Is it not significant that Josephus and Philo can both describe the Essenes in detail without once mentioning the Teacher of Righteousness? . . . Would it be possible to describe primitive Christianity without naming Christ? To ask the question is to have answered it." Cf. also K. Schubert, *The Dead Sea Community*, p. 144: "The milieu of Jesus and the milieu of the Qumran texts do belong in the same broad framework of the messianic movement, but Jesus himself clearly dissociated himself in many things from his Qumrân Essene predecessors and contemporaries."

[3] *The Scriptures of the Dead Sea Sect*, p. 22.

[4] Cf. K. G. Kuhn, *S.N.T.*, p. 87: "The abiding significance of the Qumran texts for the New Testament is that they show to what extent the primitive church, however conscious of its integrity and newness, drew

Scholars have long recognized that Judaism was not a decadent and moribund faith in the time of Jesus, and that Pharisaism is not truly reflected in the New Testament. There we see Pharisaism at its worst, and as it is sometimes condemned in Jewish sources.[1] But Pharisaism at its best was deeply religious, and the Christian debt to it is one which should never be forgotten. Now, through the Scrolls we have knowledge of another contemporary group, which in its different way preserved amongst the Jews a deep religious devotion, and helped to create the climate in which the Christian faith could be born. In many ways God prepared for the coming of His Son.

upon the Essenes in matters of practice and cult, organisation and constitution." It may be added that the study of the limit of such borrowing is no less important than the study of its extent. Cf. W. Eiss, *Qumran und die Anfänge der christlichen Gemeinde,* 1959, p. 22, and Lucetta Mowry, *The Dead Sea Scrolls and the Early Church,* 1962, pp. 246 f. Cf. also W. D. Davies, *op. cit.* p. 117: "The Scrolls make much more clear to us the world into which Jesus came; and the patterns which the early Christian movement assumed, both ecclesiastically and theologically, are thereby illumined in a most enriching manner. But the Scrolls also make more luminously clear the *new* thing which emerged with the coming of Christ, so that they emphasize even while they clarify the mystery of the gospel." J. Gray (*Archaeology and the Old Testament World,* 1962, p. 229) says: "Many of the beliefs of early Christianity which strike us as strange and bizarre, especially in the realm of angelology and apocalyptic, are seen more clearly than ever in the light of the Qumran Texts to be signs of the local and temporal limitations of the Gospel. What most impresses us from a study of the Qumran Texts is the extent to which the Spirit of God transcends these limitations. All that was best in Judaism, all that the saints of Qumran legitimately valued, was brought to fulfilment in the Christian faith, but in such a manner that all things were made new."

[1] Cf. J. Klausner, *Jesus of Nazareth,* Eng. trans. by H. Danby, 1925, pp. 213 ff., 227, 321.

INDEX

(a) Subjects

Aaron, and Egyptian magicians, 60n.; and priesthood, 53; Messiah from, 242f.; 244n.

Abel, murder of, 171; sacrifice of, 79, 171

Abraham, had no priest, 90n.; God of, 46; sacrifices of, 89n.

Absalom, 97

Abū Bakr, 19n.

Adam, in Books of Adam and Eve, 229; nakedness of, 224; sin of, 177

Adultery, not atoned by sacrifice, 94

Aeschylus, and Job, 142

Afterlife, Job and, 179ff.

Ahab, 125; and Elijah, 127, 171; and Naboth, 97; repentance of, 97

Ahaz, altar of, 192

Akhenaten, 46ff.; his religion pantheism, 47n.; not source of Mosaic monotheism, 46ff.; worshipped as god, 47n.

Alexander Jannaeus, 240n., 248n.

Altar, of Ahaz, 192; does not imply sacrifice?, 89n.

Amarna religion, 47n.

Amenophis IV, see Akhenaten

Ammon, henotheistic, 43; left no enduring influence, 43f.

Amos, and Bethel, 128; and monotheism, 35f.; and sacrifices, 73f., 86n., 87; cultic official?, 85n., 122n.; hepatoscoper?, 85n., 123

Animism, 36; patriarchs and, 45n.

Apocrypha, 15; Anglicanism and, 15n.; Luther and, 15n.; Westminster Confession and, 15n.

Ark, and Philistines, 80n.

Articles, Thirty-nine, 15n.

ārum, 49n.

'āshām, 77n., 80n., 101

Ashurbanipal, 193, 196

Assyrians, and Israelite unity, 198; boastfulness of, 61n.; religious policy of, 192, 200f.

Atn-prln, 122n.

Aton, 48n.

Atonement, Day of, 81, 91, 99, 103

Authority of Bible, 3ff.; derived from Christ, 17n.; derived from Church, 4ff.; derived from God, 7; derived from Gospel, 7n.; inner, 8ff., 30; not derived from Church, 7; objective tests of, 8, 11, 17ff.

Authority of Church, 4ff.

Baal, 49n., 54; Abraham and, 89n.; and Yahweh, 60f.; prophets and, 127

Babylon, monotheistic tendencies of, 45n., 48n.; not source of Israelite monotheism, 48n.; polytheistic, 45; religious policy of, 201; terror of, 36n.

Babylonian Job, 157ff., 170

Banquet, messianic, 267n.

Baptism, not recorded at Qumran, 230n., 231n., 263f.

Baptism (Christian), 211n.; and John's, 232ff.; and Qumran rites, 262ff.; forcible, 226; in Didache, 225; nudity in, 224; relation to Christ, 265; timing of, 264

Baptism (Jewish proselyte), a sacrament?, 225ff.; administration of, 227f.; and John's, 211ff.; and Passover, 215; antiquity of, 211ff.; character of, 219ff.; circumcision and, 216, 219, 232; must be complete, 223; not on Sabbath, 223; nudity in, 222, 232; quantity of water required, 224; relation to lustrations, 214, 216, 221f. 225; witnessed, 220f., 222f., 226, 230

Baptism (John's), 262ff.; administered, 234, 264; and Christian, 232; and Jewish proselyte baptism, 211ff., 230ff.; character of, 234f.; eschatological meaning of, 234f.; not derived from Qumran, 263n.

Barak, 19n.

bārū, 122

Barnabas, Epistle of, 274; Scrolls and, 274n.

Baruch, 10n.

Bathsheba, 96, 127

Behemoth, 145, 166n.

Behistun inscription, 156n.

Ben Sira, and sacrifice, 99

Bethel, 127f., 197, 199n.

Bible, Authority of, see Authority of Bible; Canon of, 5n., 6n., 7, 14, 15; fallible elements in, 12; inspiration of, 3ff.; Jewish attitude to, 4n., 21n.; literary criticism of, 3; Protestants and, 3ff.; Roman Catholics and, 3ff.; sublimity of, 29; textual criticism of, 3, 13n.; unity and diversity of, 20f., 24n.

Biblical Commission, 5n.

Bibliolatry, 10

Bildad, 146, 162ff., 175

Bishops, and Qumran officers, 255ff.

bôķēr, 123n.

Books of Adam and Eve, 229

Cain, 53, 57n., 171

Calebites, and Judah, 54

Calvary, 247

Canaanite religion, and Israel, 68f., 72f., 76ff., 89n.

Canon of Scripture, 5n., 6n., 7, 14f.; Alexandrian?, 15n.; Job and, 146

Chemosh, 43, 48

Childbirth, and sacrifice, 93n.

Christ, and messianic prophecy, 20ff.; and Old Testament hopes, 28; and Servant songs, 23n.; and Suffering Servant, 22, 25f.; Cross of, 23f., 25, 29; resurrection of, 23n., 30, 249n.; test of inspiration, 16f.

Christian origins, Qumran sect and, 239ff.

Chronicler, and Josiah's reform, 196, 198f.

Church, a remnant of Jews, 27; and Bible, 4ff.

Circumcision, 211n., 213, 225; and baptism, 216, 219, 232

Community of goods, at Qumran and in Church, 255

Confession, and forgiveness, 82, 91, 96

Copper Scroll, 269f.; treasure from Temple?, 269; treasure legendary?, 270

Corporate personality, 106

Covenant, Book of, 202; New, of Damascus, 239, 275; New, of Gospels, 275; New, of Jeremiah, 10f., 275; of Sinai, 42n., 55; occurrences of word in Zadokite Work, 239n.; response to deliverance, 58f.

Cross, of Christ, 23ff., 25, 29, 172f.

Cult, prophets and, 111ff.; see also Prophets

Cyrus, 198n.; called Messiah, 244

D document, 37n.; see also Deuteronomy

Damascus, and Syro-Ephraimitic war, 198n.; New Covenant of, 239, 275

Darius I, 156n.

David, and Bathsheba, 96, 127; and Gibeonites, 13n.; and monotheism, 37n., 43; and Uriah, 96, 171; and Zadok, 247; Messiah the son of, 242f.; rebuked by Nathan,

(b) Authors

INDEX

(c) Texts